# The Princes of the Mughal Empire, 1504–1719

For roughly two hundred years, the Mughal emperors ruled supreme in northern India. How was it possible that a Muslim, ethnically Turkish, Persian-speaking dynasty established itself in the Indian subcontinent to become one of the largest and most dynamic empires on earth? In this rigorous new interpretation of the period, Munis D. Faruqui explores Mughal state formation through the pivotal role of the Mughal princes. In a challenge to previous scholarship, the book suggests that far from undermining the foundations of empire, the court intrigues and political backbiting that were features of Mughal political life – and that frequently resulted in rebellions and wars of succession – actually helped spread, deepen, and mobilize Mughal power through an empire-wide network of friends and allies. This engaging book, which trawls a diverse archive of European and Persian sources, takes the reader from the founding of the empire under Babur to its decline in the 1700s. When the princely institution atrophied, so too did the Mughal Empire.

**Munis D. Faruqui** is an associate professor in the Department of South and Southeast Asian Studies at the University of California, Berkeley. He is a co-editor of two forthcoming volumes: *Religious Interactions in Mughal India* (forthcoming), and *Expanding Frontiers in South Asian and World History: Essays in Honor of John F. Richards* (Cambridge University Press, forthcoming).

# The Princes of the Mughal Empire, 1504–1719

MUNIS D. FARUQUI

*Department of South and Southeast Asian Studies,*
*University of California, Berkeley*

CAMBRIDGE
UNIVERSITY PRESS

# CAMBRIDGE
## UNIVERSITY PRESS

University Printing House, Cambridge CB2 8BS, United Kingdom

Cambridge University Press is part of the University of Cambridge.

It furthers the University's mission by disseminating knowledge in the pursuit of education, learning and research at the highest international levels of excellence.

www.cambridge.org
Information on this title: www.cambridge.org/9781107547865

© Munis D. Faruqui 2012

First published 2012
First paperback edition 2015

*A catalogue record for this publication is available from the British Library*

*Library of Congress Cataloguing in Publication data*
Faruqui, Munis Daniyal, 1967–
Princes of the Mughal Empire, 1504–1719 / Munis D. Faruqui.
p.  cm.
Includes bibliographical references and index.
ISBN 978-1-107-02217-1
1. Mogul Empire – History.   2. Mogul Empire – Court and courtiers.
3. Princes – Mogul Empire.   I. Title.
DS461.F37   2012
954.02′50922–dc23
2012007342

ISBN 978-1-107-02217-1 Hardback
ISBN 978-1-107-54786-5 Paperback

*For Clare*

# Contents

# Maps and Illustrations

## MAPS

## ILLUSTRATIONS

# Acknowledgments

This book has been a long time in the making. It is the outcome of not only my own research and teaching, but the scholarship of others as well. Among the many specialists cited in the bibliography, I am particularly indebted to the prior work of Muzaffar Alam, M. Athar Ali, Karen Barkey, Jos Gommans, Irfan Habib, Farhat Hasan, Iqtidar Alam Khan, Leslie Peirce, James Scott, and Sanjay Subrahmanyam. My greatest intellectual debt, however, is to my late supervisor and friend John F. Richards. I wish he had lived to see this book.

At various stages of this project – while trying to come up with a viable dissertation topic, learning languages, working on grant applications, toiling in the archives in Iran and India, writing my dissertation, thinking about converting my dissertation into a book, and finally writing it and bringing it to publication – I have been the recipient of immeasurable friendship, kindness, and support. Among others, I'd like to thank Marigold Acland, Shabbir Ahmed, Muzaffar and Rizwana Alam, Soheila Amirsoleimani, Hannah Archambault, Natalia Barbera, Richard Barnett, Monika Biradavolu, Craig Borowiak, Ali Boutouta, Una Cadegan, Marybeth Carlson, Kavita Datla, Dick Davis, Penny Edwards, Carl Ernst, Ellen Fleischmann, Teri Fisher, Will Glover, Sally and Bob Goldman, Shireen Habibi, Jonathan Haddad, Shagufta and Imtiaz Hasnain, Brad Hume, the late Mazhar Husain, Nasreen Husain and her family, Ruquia Hussain, Vasant Kaiwar, Emma Kalb, Ayesha Karim, the late Iqbal Ghani Khan and the entire Saman Zaar clan, Matthew Klingle, Brendan LaRocque, Bruce Lawrence, Laura Leming, Martin Lewis, Linda and Theo Majka, Karuna Mantena, Rama Mantena, Monica Mehta, Caroline Merithew, Barbara and Tom Metcalf, Shireen Moosvi,

Pinaki Mukherjee, Parviz Nayyeri, James Penney, Fran and Fred Pestello, Patrick Rael, B. Nageswara Rao, Raka Ray, John Remick, Ann Richards, Alex von Rospatt, Milan and Sanjay Shahani, Sarah Shields, Rob Sikorski, Malini Sood, Matthew Specter, Susan Tananbaum, Prakash Upadhyaya, Nilgun Uygun, Rahul Vatsyayan, Kären Wigen, Muhammad Qasim Zaman, the anonymous reviewers of this book, and the students in my Mughal graduate seminars in 2010 and 2011. In a sea of names, there nonetheless are a few people who have done more than anyone else to offer enduring encouragement – Stephen Dale, David Gilmartin, Sunil Kumar, and Cynthia Talbot – and unquestioned friendship – Vasudha Dalmia, Jeff Hadler, and Farina Mir. It will take many, many lives to repay the goodwill of so many people.

This book would have either never been written or taken much longer to complete without generous financial support from many quarters. They include the History Department at Duke University, the Center of International Studies at Duke University, the Oceans Connect Program at Duke University, the American Institute of Indian Studies, the Summer Research Fellowship Program at the University of Dayton, the Center for Asian Studies at the University of Texas–Austin, the American Historical Association, the Committee on Research at the University of California–Berkeley, and the Sidney and Margaret Ancker Distinguished Professorship Research Fund at the University of California–Berkeley. I would like to especially thank Berkeley's "Family Friendly Edge Policy" for helping me juggle the responsibilities of being a new dad and an assistant professor.

If the ability to undertake historical work depends on access to different archives, I'd like to acknowledge the ease and comfort of working in the National Library (Kolkata), Maulana Azad Library (Aligarh), the Center for Advanced Study Library (Aligarh), the Asiatic Society of Bengal (Kolkata), the National Archives (Delhi), Teen Murti Library (Delhi), and the British Library (London).

Ultimately, this book would not have been possible without the love and support of my sister and parents – Mariam, Erna, and Faseeh Faruqui – and my extended family – Saira and Rohit Shahani and Jennifer, Vasant, and Mark Talwalker. They have waited a long time for this book to be published, yet their enthusiasm, interest, and encouragement never faltered. My greatest gratitude, however, goes to my wife, Clare Talwalker, and our children Aynaz and Sivan. Although they sacrificed many a foursome family activity for years, they barely complained. I promise to make it up to them.

# Mughal Family Tree

MUGHAL EMPERORS & SELECT PRINCES

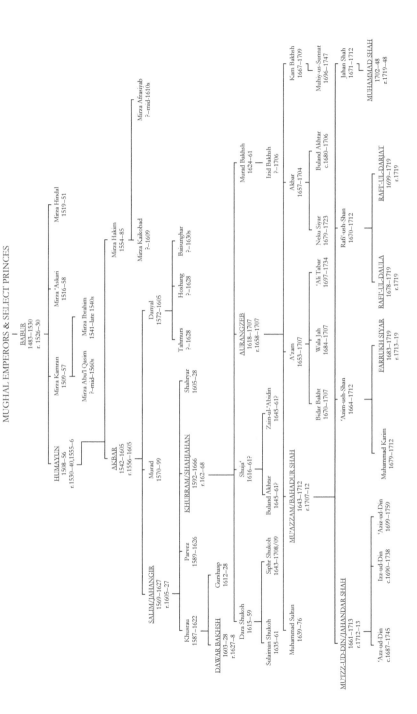

# Chronology

| | |
|---|---|
| 1483 | Birth of Babur in Ferghana (contemporary Uzbekistan) |
| 1494 | Babur becomes ruler of Ferghana upon death of his father |
| 1501 | Uzbeks defeat Babur; he is forced to vacate Samarqand |
| 1504 | Babur captures Kabul |
| 1507 | Uzbeks take Herat; Babur last Timurid prince to still rule a kingdom |
| 1508 | Babur assumes the title of *padshah*; birth of oldest son Humayun |
| 1519 | Badakhshan given to Humayun as his princely appanage |
| 1526 | Babur invades India; the Lodis defeated; the Mughal Empire established |
| 1527 | Babur defeats Rajput coalition under Rana Sangha at Khanua; Humayun sent back to Badakhshan, sacks Delhi treasury on way out |
| 1529 | Humayun returns to Mughal court without Babur's permission |
| 1530 | Death of Babur; Humayun ascends throne |
| 1531 | Mirza Kamran annexes the Punjab |
| 1540 | Humayun defeated by Sher Khan Suri, flees India; Mughal rule collapses |
| 1540–52 | Humayun and Mirza Kamran battle for supremacy |
| 1542 | Birth of Akbar |
| 1551 | Akbar given Ghazni as his princely appanage |

| | |
|---|---|
| 1553 | Mirza Kamran captured by Humayun, blinded, and exiled to Mecca |
| 1555 | Humayun invades India, reestablishes the Mughal Empire |
| 1556 | Death of Humayun; Akbar ascends the throne |
| 1564–6 | Revolts of the Uzbeks and Mirzas |
| 1566 | Mirza Hakim invades India, defeated by Akbar |
| 1569 | Birth of Salim/Jahangir |
| 1570s | Akbar introduces the *mansabdari* and *jagirdari* systems |
| 1581–2 | Mirza Hakim re-invades India, defeated by Akbar |
| 1583 | Akbar offers his sons first experience of running the Mughal Empire |
| 1585 | Death of Mirza Hakim; Kabul annexed by Akbar; end of princely appanages; Akbar's three sons accorded adult status |
| 1591 | Murad sent to govern Malwa in face of rising tensions with Salim |
| 1592 | Birth of Khurram/Shah Jahan |
| 1594 | Akbar gives seven-year-old Khusrau imperial rank |
| 1599 | Akbar moves to the Deccan following Murad's death |
| 1599–1604 | Salim's rebellion |
| 1605 | Death of Danyal and Akbar; Salim/Jahangir ascends the throne |
| 1606 | Khusrau's rebellion; imprisoned following capture |
| 1607 | Khusrau blinded; Khurram accorded adult status |
| 1611 | Jahangir marries Mehr-un-Nisa/Nur Jahan |
| 1612 | Khurram marries Arjomand Banu Begum (later Mumtaz Mahal) |
| 1614 | Khurram defeats Rajput kingdom of Mewar |
| 1615 | Birth of Dara Shukoh |
| 1616–17 | Khurram enjoys military success in the Deccan |
| 1618 | Birth of Aurangzeb |
| 1618 | Raja Bikramajit, retainer of Khurram, conquers Kangra |
| 1620 | Shahryar married to Ladli Begum, daughter of Nur Jahan |
| 1621–2 | Khurram undertakes second successful campaign in the Deccan |
| 1622–7 | Khurram's rebellion |
| 1624 | Khurram defeated by Parvez and Mahabat Khan at Tons |
| 1626 | Rebellion of Mahabat Khan; death of Parvez |
| 1627 | Death of Jahangir; war of succession follows |

| 1628 | Khurram/Shah Jahan ascends the throne |
| 1634 | Aurangzeb accorded adult status |
| 1636–44 | Aurangzeb serves as governor of the Deccan |
| 1643 | Birth of Mu'azzam |
| 1644 | Aurangzeb returns to imperial court without permission, stripped of rank |
| 1646–7 | Failed Mughal campaign against Balkh and Badakhshan |
| 1649–53 | Failed Mughal campaigns against Qandahar |
| 1652–7 | Aurangzeb serves as governor of the Deccan |
| 1653 | Birth of A'zam |
| 1656–7 | Aurangzeb wages war against kingdoms of Bijapur and Golkonda |
| 1657–9 | War of succession involving Shah Jahan's four adult sons |
| 1658 | Shah Jahan forced to abdicate, imprisoned in Agra; Aurangzeb ascends the throne |
| 1659 | Muhammad Sultan's rebellion against Aurangzeb, imprisoned until death in 1676 |
| 1661 | Birth of Mu'izz-ud-Din/Jahandar Shah |
| 1666 | Death of Shah Jahan |
| 1676 | Asad Khan appointed chief minister, serves until 1707 |
| 1681 | Akbar rebels against Aurangzeb |
| 1683 | Birth of Farrukh Siyar |
| 1685–7 | Mughal campaigns against Bijapur and Golkonda |
| 1687–95 | Mu'azzam imprisoned by Aurangzeb |
| 1690s | Emergence of Ghazi-ud-Din Khan, Chin Qilich Khan, and Zulfiqar Khan as key imperial generals |
| 1693 | Kam Bakhsh briefly placed under house arrest |
| 1695 | Mu'azzam and his sons given administrative positions in northern India |
| 1700–2 | All major princes removed from command positions in the Deccan |
| 1701–5 | A'zam serves as governor of Gujarat |
| 1707 | Death of Aurangzeb; war of succession follows; Mu'azzam/Bahadur Shah I ascends the throne |
| 1712 | Death of Bahadur Shah; war of succession ensues; Jahandar Shah ascends the throne with the help of Zulfiqar Khan |

1713        Jahandar Shah overthrown; Farrukh Siyar ascends the
            throne; Sayyid brothers emerge as most powerful nobles in
            the empire

1719        Farrukh Siyar overthrown; Sayyid brothers successively
            appoint Rafiʻ-ul-Darjat and Rafiʻ-ul-Daula as emperors;
            end of the open-ended system of succession

# Note on Transliteration and Translation

All foreign words not commonly used in English have been italicized; a nonitalicized letter "s" indicates the plural form. I have chosen not to use diacritical marks for names of persons or places. But I do use (') and (') for the *'ain* and *hamza* respectively. Although I have generally relied on F. Steingass's *Comprehensive Persian English Dictionary* when transliterating Persian words and phrases, I have chosen to spell certain combined words differently. For example, instead of *u'l*, indicating the Arabic definite article *al*, I have generally chosen *ul* placed between two hyphens. Elsewhere, I have favored phonetic forms such as "Ghazi-ud-Din," "Rafi'-ush-Shan," and "Shukrullah" instead of "Ghaziu'd-Din," "Rafi'u'sh-Shan," and "Shukru'llah." I have also made certain exceptions for commonly accepted usages, such as "Mughal" in place of "Mughul," "Aurangzeb" instead of "Aurang-zib," and a few others. Finally, although I maintain the English spellings of the printed Persian language editions in my footnotes – hence *Ma'asir-ul-Umara* is kept as *Maasir-ul-Umara* (for volume 1) and *Maasiru-l-Umara* (for volumes 2 and 3) and Mu'tamid Khan as Motamad Khan – I follow the previously mentioned conventions for in-text references. All translations are mine, unless otherwise noted.

# Introduction

On December 6, 1992, Hindu nationalists attacked and destroyed the sixteenth-century Babri Mosque. In the lead-up to this event and in its aftermath, India was wracked by terrible violence in which thousands of people were killed or injured. Most of the victims were Muslims. I watched my television screen in shock and horror as the violence unfolded. I recall being especially struck by one news story in which a reporter interviewed Hindu nationalist supporters outside a row of burning shacks while a mob danced around the camera crew shouting this slogan: *Babur ki santan, jao Pakistan ya Qabristan!* (Descendants of Babur, go to Pakistan or the graveyard!).

At the time, I was at a loss understanding the link between, on the one hand, the Emperor Babur, the early sixteenth-century founder of the Mughal Empire in whose name the Babri Mosque had been constructed in 1528, and, on the other hand, Indian Muslims of the late twentieth century. Although of Indian Muslim descent myself, I knew my family was not descended from Babur or any of his heirs. Indeed, if my family had any connection to the Mughal Empire, it was unknown. Separately, the suggestion that Indian Muslims were a cancer in the Indian body politic that had to be either expelled to Pakistan or killed prompted me to wonder what horrors the Mughals were thought to have visited upon India to generate such genocidal sentiments almost five centuries later. Indeed, nothing I had read pointed to Mughal policies deliberately aimed at the violent oppression or exploitation of their overwhelmingly Hindu subjects. To the contrary, the popular legacy of the Mughal period, as I understood it, suggested a standout example of Hindu–Muslim cooperation across political, social, and cultural realms. Such thoughts framed my interest in

I

the Mughals when I entered graduate school in the mid-1990s. In the years that have followed, I have long pondered exactly how a Muslim, ethnically Turkish, and Persian-speaking dynasty managed to rule 150 million people, themselves of many linguistic and ethnic backgrounds, and to constitute one of the largest empires in human history at its height in 1700.[1] Certainly brutal and unmitigated violence against the Mughals' majority Hindu subjects seemed a highly unlikely explanation.

As I discovered, violence (or at least its threat) did play a critical part in constituting Mughal imperial power, but not in ways that might be assumed by modern Hindu nationalists. Rather than religious conflict, one of the central engines driving Mughal state formation was the competition and occasional bursts of violence that framed political struggles occurring within the Mughal royal family itself. These struggles, which took place against the backdrop of imperial succession politics, not only pitted prince against prince, but also prince against even the emperor (who may have been a father, grandfather, brother, paternal uncle, or cousin). It has been widely suggested that this princely competition weakened the empire. I argue, on the contrary, that – with the attendant construction of independent households, forging of empire-wide networks of friends and allies, disobedience toward and rebellion against the emperor, and wars of succession – princely competition was a central mechanism in the mobilization of Mughal power. Understanding the dynamic and complicated story of political competition within the Mughal family and its impact on the empire offers fresh insight into the success as well as ultimate failure of the Mughal imperial enterprise. If intervening in popular partisan views of the Mughal Empire is one goal of this book, then a second is to complicate our understanding of the processes of Mughal state formation by telling the story of the princes of the Mughal Empire.

## PRINCES IN THE STORY OF MUGHAL STATE FORMATION

For more than two centuries, between 1504 (the year the founder of the Mughal Empire, Zahir-ud-Din Muhammad Babur, established himself in Kabul) and 1719 (the first time a prince attained the Mughal throne on the basis of an ordered succession system), the Mughals determinedly refused to institute clearly articulated rules of succession. The Mughals themselves and contemporary imperial historians almost never commented on this

---

[1] John F. Richards, "The Mughal Empire," in *The Magnificent Mughals*, ed. Zeenut Ziad (Karachi, 2002), p. 3.

fact, although the occasional European traveler noted it. The unspoken rule – deriving from Islamic law and from Turco-Mongol ideas – that every son had an equal share in his father's patrimony and all males within a ruling group had the right to succeed to the throne simply favored an open-ended system.

Following the collapse of the Mughal Empire and the onset of British rule, which had its own obsessions about dynastic continuity and longevity, historians and others began to pay closer attention to the Mughal "failure" to institute a system of primogeniture or some other form of ordered succession. This interest was mostly framed within the context of debates about collapses of Mughal rule, first briefly in the 1540s and then ultimately in the 1710s. In the nineteenth and early twentieth centuries, the prevailing wisdom had it that recurrent princely rebellions and wars of succession destabilized the empire and offered no long-term benefits. Against this backdrop, seeming Mughal insistence on an open-ended system of succession was treated as a sign of political conservatism or a trace of backward tribalism, and thus a failure of enlightened rule. The fact that members of the Mughal royal family were known to have maimed and killed one another, or tried to, only added to the emerging consensus that this was a pernicious and dysfunctional system. That consensus, as this book demonstrates, was as narrow and obfuscating as it was simple for its subscribers to embrace. In particular, by casting all intra-familial strife as negative, it masked the key role that princely competition and conflict played in Mughal state formation.

Historians as well as other observers of the Mughal Empire have been pondering the reasons for Mughal success and the nature of Mughal state formation for centuries now. As far back as the seventeenth century, European travelers variously highlighted the Mughals' "despotic" power, theatricality, and access to economic riches in their efforts to pinpoint the empire's political vitality. Up to the early nineteenth century, the European public treated the then-collapsed empire mostly with respectful deference. This was largely a consequence of early British colonialism's desire to fashion itself as a direct heir to what it viewed as a sophisticated and, on balance, successful exercise in imperial rule. By the late nineteenth century, however, such favorable readings had mostly vanished. The British now saw advantage in treating their own empire as not only standing outside Indian history but as representing a complete rupture from India's past.

This cleavage came to be symbolized as the stark difference between the civilized character of the British Empire as compared to the backwardness of its Indian and, especially, Mughal forerunners. There were two key lines of attack. The first was anchored in the British Raj's complex administrative machinery and the other in its post-Enlightenment capacity for religious tolerance. Against both markers, the Mughal Empire was judged deficient. Mughal success was dismissed as an outcome of its unrestrained despotism, and its failure attributed to rising "religious intolerance" toward its majority Hindu subjects.

Starting in the early 1900s, waves of Indian nationalist historians began to contest different elements within this colonial historiography. By far the most significant challenge came from successive generations of often Marxist-oriented historians based at Aligarh Muslim University (in the north Indian city of Aligarh). Between the 1940s and the 1980s, the "Aligarh School" developed a powerful counterview of the Mughal Empire. Largely focusing their attention on Mughal administrative institutions, these scholars asserted that the Mughal Empire was – not unlike a modern state – a highly centralized, systematized, and stable entity.[2] The force of this argument was such that the strength of Mughal administrative institutions now became the starting point for most discussions (and explanations) of imperial successes and failures. Religion was largely discounted as a factor in the Mughal collapse. By the early 1960s, the Aligarh view of the Mughal Empire was widely accepted within and outside India.

From the 1970s onward, however, debates about the nature of empire in India took on new life thanks to a fresh cluster of historians – many of them based in England. Especially interested in questioning long-held views of the British Empire as a European leviathan, these scholars pointed to the many ways in which the Raj had been built on Indian foundations, depended on active Indian collaboration, and was administratively less forceful than once imagined. These insights soon carried over into a fundamental reassessment of the Mughal Empire by non-Aligarh-based Mughal historians. They questioned the Aligarh School's exalted view of imperial institutions, arguing that the diffuse and fractured manner in which early modern societies functioned resisted the possibility of strong centralized institutions, not only in India but also in other parts of the early

---

[2] For representative examples, see M. Athar Ali, "Towards an Interpretation of the Mughal Empire," *Journal of the Asiatic Society of Great Britain and Ireland* 1 (1978): 40; Zahiruddin Malik, "The Core and the Periphery: A Contribution to the Debate on the Eighteenth Century," *Social Scientist* 18, no. 11–12 (1990): 3–35; Iqtidar Alam Khan, "State in Mughal India: Re-examining the Myths of a Counter-vision," *Social Scientist* 30, no. 1–2 (2001): 16–45; Shireen Moosvi, "The Pre-Colonial State," *Social Scientist* 33, no. 3–4 (2005): 40–53.

modern world. Furthermore, they questioned the evolutionary assumption that a centralized state is necessarily a modern or better state.

What emerged by the late 1990s was a new perspective, one that considered the Mughal Empire less as a "medieval road-roller," to quote Sanjay Subrahmanyam, and more as a spider's web in which strands were strong in some places and weak in others, shedding light on the need to account for regional phenomena caught between the various strands.[3] According to this interpretation, the empire hung loosely over Indian society, exerting only a fleeting impact on local societies, local landed elites (*zamindars*), and everyday life. Unfortunately, these debates (on the one hand, that the Mughals ran a tight administrative ship and, on the other, that their administration was largely ineffectual) had an irresolvable quality, and they took on an increasingly rancorous tone as well.[4] Thus one historian in the mid 1990s observed that the study of the state in early modern South Asia "has become one of the most controversial issues in contemporary Indian historiography."[5]

Against this backdrop, there has been a renewed push to comprehend the sources of Mughal power beyond its administrative, military, and fiscal institutions.[6] Farhat Hasan's *State and Locality in Mughal India* is of special note.[7] Even though expressing discontent with the fiscal or military prisms through which most studies of the Mughal state are conducted, Hasan is determined to not "de-privilege" the state. *State and Locality* offers four particularly valuable insights: (i) the Mughal state could not simply command obedience, but had to "manufacture" it by implanting itself within local political, social, and economic networks of power;

---

[3] Sanjay Subrahmanyam, "The Mughal State – Structure or Process? Reflections on Recent Western Historiography," *Indian Economic and Social History Review* 29, no. 3 (1992): 321. See also Muzaffar Alam and Sanjay Subrahmanyam, "Introduction," in *The Mughal State, 1526–1750*, ed. Muzaffar Alam and Sanjay Subrahmanyam (Delhi, 1998), 57; M. N. Pearson, "Premodern Muslim Political Systems," *Journal of the American Oriental Society* 102, no. 1 (1982): 47–58.

[4] M. Athar Ali, "The Mughal Polity: A Critique of 'Revisionist' Approaches," *Modern Asian Studies* 27, no. 4 (1993): 699–710. See also the Wink-Habib debates: Irfan Habib, "Review of *Land and Sovereignty in India*," *Indian Economic and Social History Review* 25, no. 4 (1988): 527–31; André Wink, "A Rejoinder to Irfan Habib," *Indian Economic and Social History Review* 26, no. 3 (1989): 363–7; and Irfan Habib, "A Reply to André Wink," *Indian Economic and Social History Review* 26, no. 3 (1989): 368–72.

[5] Hermann Kulke, *The State in India: 1000–1700* (Delhi, 1995), p. 1. This view is echoed by Alam and Subrahmanyam, "Introduction," p. 2.

[6] For a sense of the range of possibilities and approaches, see Alam and Subrahmanyam, "Introduction," pp. 1–71.

[7] Farhat Hasan, *State and Locality in Mughal India: Power Relations in Western India, c. 1572–1730* (Cambridge, 2004).

(ii) besides collecting taxes, the Mughal state also contributed and garnered support by offering security and playing a key role in redistributing monetary and social resources among the most powerful elements in Indian society; (iii) the Mughal state was continuously being molded and constrained by the society that it ostensibly governed; and (iv) the Mughal state was a dynamic and continuously evolving entity quite unlike the static and stable creation that emerges from Mughal imperial sources or most modern accounts of the empire.[8]

Whereas Hasan undertook a fine-grained study of the operations of the Mughal state in urban Gujarat, the present book explores his insights as they apply to the empire as a whole. In the 1990s, even before Hasan's book, early modern historians Muzaffar Alam and Sanjay Subrahmanyam put out a call for scholarship on state formation in South Asia that took on its "evolution over time" and "variation over space."[9] *Princes of the Mughal Empire* wrestles with precisely this challenge. It asks the following: given the empire's wobbly bases in the localities (to which a scholar such as Hasan aptly points), how did the empire successfully manage relations with so many communities, over so vast an area, for its just under two hundred years of effective rule? Of what was the imperial fabric (or spider's web) woven, over the many decades before the empire's collapse into a patchwork of regional successor states? This book demonstrates that such questions can be usefully explored by focusing on how the dynasty's princes built and sustained their power in the long years leading up to the inevitable succession struggles.

The past century has produced a large number of biographies and article-length treatments of Mughal princes. None of them consider the role that princes may have played in forging Mughal power.[10] As a result, such crucial princely activities as building a household or cultivating

---

[8] Ibid., pp. 1–8.

[9] Alam and Subrahmanyam, "Introduction," pp. 6, 17–18.

[10] Bikramajit Hasrat, *Dara Shikuh: Life and Works* (Delhi, repr. 1982); Muhammad Quamruddin, *Life and Times of Prince Murad Bakhsh 1624–1661* (Calcutta, 1974); Iqtidar Alam Khan, *Mirza Kamran* (Bombay, 1964); Iftikhar Ghauri, *War of Succession between the Sons of Shah Jahan, 1657–1658* (Lahore, 1964); S. Moinul Haq, *Prince Awrangzib: A Study* (Karachi, 1962). Other books that include significant treatments of princes include S. M. Burke, *Akbar the Greatest Mogul* (Delhi, 1989); Zahiruddin Faruki, *Aurangzeb and His Times* (Delhi, repr. 1972); B. P. Saxsena, *History of Shahjahan of Dihli* (Delhi, repr. 1962); Shibli Nomani, *Aurangzeb 'Alamgir par ek nazar* (Karachi, repr. 1960); Ishwari Prasad, *The Life and Times of Humayun* (Calcutta, 1956); Jadunath Sarkar, *History of Aurangzib*, vols. 1–5 (Calcutta, 1924–30); Beni Prasad, *History of Jahangir* (Oxford, 1922). Among articles, see M. Athar Ali, "The Religious Issues in the War of Succession, 1658–1659," in *Mughal India: Studies in Polity, Ideas, Society, and*

networks of support have been almost completely ignored, never mind considered within a broader framework of conversations about Mughal state formation. More generally, other scholars of the Mughal Empire have also overlooked the distinctive role of princes in the life of the empire.[11] And yet, as I will argue, from the day that princes were born, and for the duration of their lives as princes, they were critical actors on the Mughal stage. Their centrality ultimately derived from the competitive political energy that framed Mughal succession struggles over the course of the sixteenth and seventeenth centuries. Especially after the 1580s and Emperor Akbar's decision to no longer grant his sons semi-independent territories, the rules of this contest were simple and are best summed up by the terse Persian phrase: *ya takht, ya takhta* (either throne or funeral bier).[12] And it was indeed to the throne or until their deaths that generations of princes scrambled to establish loyal followings, accrue wealth and influence, and build their political power and military strength. They knew that failure to engage would not only mean loss of the Mughal throne but also certain death.

Against the backdrop of a hyper-competitive and open-ended system of succession, royal princes were celebrated and carefully cultivated from the very moment of their birth. Given that every prince was a potential

*Culture* (Delhi, 2006); S. M. Azizuddin Husain, "Aurangzeb ki takht nashini," *Islam aur asr-i jadid* (April 1994): 44–73; Arshad Karim, "Muslim Nationalism: Conflicting Ideologies of Dara Shikoh and Aurangzeb," *Journal of the Pakistan Historical Society* 33, no. 4 (1985): 288–96; Jalaluddin, "Sultan Salim (Jahangir) as a Rebel King," *Islamic Culture* 47 (1973): 121–5; R. Shyam, "Mirza Hindal," *Islamic Culture* 45 (1971): 115–36; Ram Sharma, "Aurangzib's Rebellion against Shah Jahan," *Journal of Indian History* 44, no. 1 (1966): 109–24; R. K. Das, "The End of Prince Shuja," *Procs. Ind. Hist. Cong.* 28 (1966): 165–8. B. B. L. Srivastava, "The Fate of Khusrau," *Journal of Indian History* 42, no. 2 (1964): 479–92; B. P. Ambashthya, "Rebellions of Prince Salim and Prince Khurram in Bihar," *Journal of the Bihar and Orissa Research Society* 45 (1959): 326–41; Yusuf Abbas Hashmi, "The War of Succession among the Sons of Shah Jahan and the Stand of Aurangzeb," *Procs. All Pak. Hist. Conf.* 1 (1951): 247–70; Henry Beveridge, "Sultan Khusrau," *Journal of the Royal Asiatic Society* 39 (1907): 599–601.

[11] Harbans Mukhia, *The Mughals of India* (London, 2004); John F. Richards, *The Mughal Empire* (Cambridge, 1993); Stephen Blake, *Shahjahanabad: The Sovereign City in Mughal India, 1639–1739* (Cambridge, 1991); Douglas Streusand, *Formation of the Mughal Empire* (Delhi, 1989); Muzaffar Alam, *The Crisis of Empire in Mughal North India: Awadh and the Punjab 1707–1748* (Delhi, 1986); M. Athar Ali, *The Mughal Nobility under Aurangzeb* (Delhi, repr. 1997); Satish Chandra, *Parties and Politics at the Mughal Court* (Aligarh, 1959).

[12] Khafi Khan, *Muntakhab al-Labab*, ed. Kabir-ud-Din Ahmad, vol. 2 (Calcutta, 1874), p. 596. Although the meaning is exactly the same, Niccolao Manucci, who lived in India for most of the latter half of the seventeenth century, offers us a slight variant on the phrase: *ya takht, ya tabut. Mogul India or Storio do Mogor*, trans. William Irvine, vol. 1 (New Delhi, repr. 1996), p. 232.

emperor, broad similarities marked their early education, their access to powerful noblemen, and their visibility at the imperial court. Most importantly, however, young princes received early and unrelenting exposure to the psychological uncertainty that accompanied an open-ended system of succession. Knowing that their lives ultimately depended on their own achievements, networks of support, and their ability to out-maneuver their male relatives, Mughal princes were trained from early on to be independent minded, tough, and ruthless. These traits would be especially important as they approached adulthood.

There were two signs of a prince's transition to adult status: the first was his marriage; the second was an official right to share in the empire's financial resources. Prior to 1585, this latter moment had been marked by the grant of a semi-independent princely territory (often referred to by modern scholars as an appanage[13]). After 1585, a prince's adult status was recognized by the grant of a formal rank (*mansab*) in the imperial hierarchy with concomitant access to income via landholdings (*jagirs*) that were reshuffled every few years. Adult status led to an explosion in the size of princely households. Some part of the growth was linked to the infusion of large numbers of women and eunuchs who were expected to take care of an emerging domestic establishment. The other key element was the individuals with administrative and military skills whose overriding responsibility was to enable the prince to collect the financial resources promised to him. The search for money consumed an increasing part of an adult prince's attention. After the 1580s, with the end of princely appanages, that task got much harder as princes and their *jagirs* were regularly transferred around the empire.

If princely households reinforced and extended the imperial bureaucracy's efforts to improve its administrative mechanisms, they also allowed the prince to act as a military leader in his own right. With his household's help and resources, a prince could organize imperial campaigns, storm well-guarded forts, and protect convoys carrying tribute or tax payments. Since intra-familial conflict (whether in the form of princely rebellions or wars of succession) was a permanent threat, a princely household was in perpetual readiness to fight other princely households or even the emperor's imperial establishment.

---

[13] The term is derived from a thirteenth-century French adaptation of the Latin term *appanare*, meaning to "equip with bread." From the sixteenth century onward – in both French and English – it is commonly used to refer to grants of land to younger sons of a ruler.

As might be expected, princes were always on the lookout for important or talented individuals and groups to recruit into their households. Preference was often accorded to men not already linked to competing princes or the emperor. Thus, over the course of the late sixteenth and seventeenth centuries, princely households provided a vital avenue for social mobility in the Mughal Empire. Through them, a wide range of political, ethnic, and class outsiders were first assimilated, acculturated, and socialized within the Mughal system. Following a successful accession, many in the victorious prince's circle would be inducted into the imperial nobility, a practice that simultaneously replenished the nobility's ranks and provided a counterweight to holdovers from the previous reign.

Princes never stopped building alliances with notable individuals and groups beyond their households. With the end of fixed territorial appanages in the 1580s, these efforts took on a more plainly imperial character. Rather than focusing on single or even contiguous territories, princes now had to compete and cultivate friends and allies across the entire expanse of the empire. From the very start of this era, Akbar urged his sons to venture forth and cultivate their influence. Akbar not only connected his young sons with powerful people in and beyond the Mughal court, he also experimented with sending them on temporary and varied assignments.

Under Akbar, too, the empire shifted from an Islam-imbued to a more pluralistic project. As such, after the 1580s, Mughal princes approached each and every group, regardless of religion, as potentially useful in their alliance building efforts. Relentless political competition within the imperial family ensured that princely efforts rarely lost momentum. They continued to break new ground in their attempts to woo and nurture individuals and groups that had either been frozen out of the Mughal system or disenfranchised by political shifts within it. Simultaneously, since political loyalty and support could never be assumed and was always being contested, princes were constantly renewing earlier claims to friendship. One crucial impact of such frenetic activity was this: imperial political, social, and monetary resources remained in constant circulation, which created powerful and widespread investment not only in individual princes but also in the dynasty as a whole.

Between Akbar's and Aurangzeb's reigns, imperial expansion into new regions was often accompanied or immediately followed by local recruitment drives by princes in their capacity as governors, generals or even rebels. Inasmuch as administrative and political consolidation in the northern heartlands was crucial to the construction of the empire, it was the almost unique ability of the Mughals to accommodate and harness the energies of formerly nonsubject and even oppositional groups along the edges of their growing realm that enabled and indicated the empire's vitality throughout much of the seventeenth century. By understanding these transactions, which often occurred in the context of princely initiatives aimed at winning friends and allies, we may begin to comprehend the empire's reach even in regions where its administrative institutions were weak or nonexistent. As might be expected, starting with Salim/Jahangir's accession in 1605 and continuing until Mu'azzam/Bahadur Shah in 1707, the best "networked" prince inevitably became the next Mughal emperor.

The decision by an emperor to grant a prince full adult status (sometime between the late teen years and the mid-twenties) led to an intensification of efforts to build a powerful household and gather allies around the prince's person. As one contemporary observer noted, "when these princes once leave the paternal house, they work and scheme to make themselves friends. They write secretly to the Hindu princes and the Mahomedan generals, promising them that when they become king they will raise their allowances ... if any of these princes mounts the throne, he fancies that they will have been faithful to him."[14] Adulthood also imposed important limits on the emperor's capacity to control the actions of his son. Inevitably, emperors found themselves on a collision course with their princes as the latter moved to assert their own political identities and/or sought to protect resources they considered vital to their political future. At this point, we begin to see instances of princely disobedience. An emperor's ability to respond effectively to these challenges was a sign of his continued political relevance. An inability or unwillingness to assert his authority was liable to be read as a mark of weakness, which could encourage more direct political challenges. Humayun faced precisely this predicament vis-à-vis his refractory brothers. Ultimately, emperors had to strike a fine balance between some oversight of male relatives and undue restraint of their activities. Allowing for some measure of princely dissent and disobedience was a crucial safety valve that prevented the Mughal Empire from being constantly wracked by destructive princely rebellions.

The decision by princes to rebel was always a difficult one. A rebellion taxed both the loyalty of supporters and household resources. Worse yet, a prince could lose his life in the course of a rebellion or suffer physical mutilation and permanent imprisonment as punishment. A prince who rebelled was thus a prince who believed he had no other choice. All princely rebellions point to the despair that fueled them. Prince Akbar's

---

[14] Manucci, *Mogul India*, p. 320.

letter to his father Aurangzeb following the onset of his rebellion in 1681 provides an excellent example of a grievance that might drive a prince over the edge. It also offers the clearest and most poignant reflection on Mughal succession in our available sources. After the requisite opening salutations, Akbar writes:

The duty of a father is to bring up, educate, and guard the health and life of his son. Praise be to God, [that] up till now I have left no stone unturned in service and obedience, but how can I enumerate the favors of your Majesty? ... it is brought to the notice [of Aurangzeb] that to help and side with the youngest son is the foremost duty of a revered father always and everywhere, but your Majesty, leaving aside the love of all the other sons, has bestowed the title of 'Shah' upon the eldest son [i.e., Mu'azzam] and declared him the heir-apparent. How can this action be justified? Every son has got an equal right in his father's property. Which religion permits preference of one over the others?[15]

Here, Prince Akbar suggests that all princes had equal rights to the empire, and that an emperor ought to honor those rights by not favoring any particular son. Or, if he did favor a son, it should be the youngest or weakest one, in the spirit of egalitarianism. In the post-1580 imagination of a single empire wherein rulership demanded that every royal prince must fight, the ethics of impartiality was of great importance. When this principle was viewed as repeatedly flouted, a prince was more than likely to rebel.

Princely rebellions were deeply unsettling affairs for the empire. Beyond highlighting the brittleness of the political order, they fundamentally questioned an emperor's right to rule. The system was unforgiving, and aging or ill emperors were especially vulnerable to challenges. As every emperor from Akbar to Aurangzeb could attest, there was no question of resting on past laurels. Turning back a princely challenge meant passing a crucial test of continuing imperial and political relevance. Success demanded that an embattled emperor unsheathe the full panoply of weapons at his disposal. Through active military operations, attempts to root out enemies within the Mughal establishment, initiatives aimed at winning over influential individuals and groups, and efforts to consolidate or strengthen the administrative machinery of the state, the emperor's counteroffensive benefited long-term Mughal dynastic authority. Given that these efforts usually followed similar initiatives undertaken by rebellious princes, these complementary processes inadvertently helped entrench Mughal power across

---

[15] B. N. Reu, "Letters exchanged between Emperor Aurangzeb and his son Prince Muhammad Akbar," *Procs. Ind. Hist. Cong.* 2 (1938): 356.

northern and central India. Besides drawing new groups into the ambit of Mughal politics, princely rebellions and the subsequent imperial response often tied formerly peripheral areas more closely to the imperial center. The intensification of Mughal control over Awadh and Bengal after the respective rebellions of Salim (in the early 1600s) and Khurram (a generation later) corroborates this assertion. No matter the outcome of a particular conflict between father and son, I argue, rebellions ultimately served to reinforce the foundations of dynastic power and authority.

If princely rebellions offered an important avenue for Mughal state formation, the wars of succession that followed the incapacitation or death of an emperor had similar effects as princes mobilized every conceivable political, military, and economic resource in their quest to be the next emperor. This book argues, however, that a competitive system of succession – especially when actual moments of struggle were well spaced and involved only a limited number of contenders – had other important consequences as well. These included forcing princes to articulate a vision of who they were and what they might bring to the empire as emperor. This proved especially true after the 1580s when princes were expected to compete against one another to rule a now indivisible empire. Invariably, the run-up to and the actual moment of a succession struggle was a fearful time for almost everyone, from the princes down to common individuals with no real stake in the outcome. But something concrete resulted from this period of apprehension, since it forged a bond that simultaneously refocused attention on the dynasty and confirmed its authority to rule.

Judging from the Mughal example, an open-ended system of succession required that certain broad conditions be in place. The first was the need to limit the number of princely contenders in any given generation. Toward this end, the Mughals moved over the course of the sixteenth century to curtail the right of males from collateral branches to lay claim to the imperial throne. As wars of succession became the primary mode for deciding the next emperor, the extermination of failed princely contenders also became a political necessity. There could be no second acts, lest these draw attention, energy, and resources away from the next and rising generation of princes. And yet, although defeated contenders for the throne were themselves destroyed, the Mughals generally refused to seek revenge against the myriad supporters and diverse networks that had fought for a defeated prince. Instead, new reigns were marked not only by the induction into the imperial hierarchy of large numbers of a victorious prince's supporters but also by efforts to forgive and sometimes accommodate the aspirations of the vanquished. In the end, even as a new emperor settled into his job, the next generation of princes was gearing up to renew the cycle of princely competition.

Although this book's main focus is the central role played by princes in Mughal state formation and Mughal imperial success, it also relates the story of the decline of the princely institution along with that of the dynasty's political effectiveness. Scholars of Mughal India agree that the empire began to show signs of weakness in the last decades of the seventeenth century. They disagree, however, about the reasons behind that weakness. Of the many explanations offered, we can list here the most significant: nonstop and essentially fruitless campaigning in the Deccan from the 1680s onward ground down the dynasty's military morale and administrative efficiency;[16] imperial attempts to extract additional revenues from previously lightly taxed frontier zones prompted tribal incursions that an overstretched empire could not crush;[17] growing regional prosperity encouraged regional and local elites to obstruct financial transfers to the Mughal state and to manipulate the central authorities for their own purposes;[18] intellectual malaise vis-à-vis important scientific and technological developments in the West discouraged self-strengthening efforts;[19] Mughal pecuniary rapaciousness prompted peasant rebellions that ultimately consumed the empire;[20] and Emperor Aurangzeb's religious intolerance toward the Hindu majority caused an anti-Mughal backlash.[21] Without discounting the likelihood that multiple factors combined to undermine the Mughals' capacity to rule, I propose that the gradual sclerosis of the princely institution also had a devastating impact.

Starting in the mid-1680s, the princely institution came under increasing stress. Some of this was due to Aurangzeb's willingness to sharpen political competition between different generations of princes as well as between princes and a small cluster of nonroyal nobles. Other factors

---

[16] Richards, *The Mughal Empire.*

[17] C. A. Bayly, *The Imperial Meridian: The British Empire and the World* (Cambridge, 1989).

[18] Hasan, *State and Locality*; Chetan Singh, *Region and Empire, Panjab in the Seventeenth Century* (Delhi, 1991); Alam, *The Crisis of Empire in North India*; André Wink, *Land and Sovereignty in India: Agrarian Society and Politics under the Eighteenth Century Maratha Svarajya* (Cambridge, 1986); Richard Barnett, *North India between Empires, Awadh, the Mughals, and the British, 1720–1801* (Berkeley, 1980); Karen Leonard, "The 'Great Firm' Theory of the Decline of the Mughal Empire," *Comparative Studies in Society and History* 21, no. 2 (1979): 151–67.

[19] M. Athar Ali, "The Passing of Empire: The Mughal Case," *Modern Asian Studies* 9 (1975): 185–96.

[20] Irfan Habib, *The Agrarian System of Mughal India* (Bombay, 1963).

[21] Sarkar, *History of Aurangzib.*

further exacerbated the downward slide of princely power, but they had less to do with Aurangzeb's machinations and more with the structural troubles of the empire as a whole. With access to promised financial resources becoming more difficult after the 1680s – largely because of a breakdown of law and order across the empire – princes increasingly found that they could not pay for their massive and complex households. As they tried to retrench, princes were forced to turn to Aurangzeb for help. He reacted sympathetically, perhaps seeing an opportunity to exert greater oversight over his growing number of heirs. Among his most consequential gestures of support was the transfer of large numbers of imperial officials into princely households, but this influx came at great cost to the cohesion and discipline of those households. As the capacity of princes to sustain large and independent households and alliances as well as to rebel against the emperor faded, so too did a crucial force in the dynasty's political control of the empire.

### SUCCESSION IN CONTEMPORANEOUS ISLAMIC EMPIRES

Although *Princes of the Mughal Empire* is not intended to be a comparative work, it is interesting to consider briefly the political trajectories of princes in two of the other great Islamic empires of the early modern period, namely the Ottoman and Safavid Empires, to see how distinct their experiences were from those of the Mughal Prince. Let us look at the Ottomans first.

As in the earliest period of the Mughal dynasty, princely brothers assisted the first Ottoman rulers as governors and military commanders. Following the reign of the third Ottoman ruler Murad I (r. 1362–89), however, and until the early 1600s, Ottoman succession was narrowed to the direct heirs of a reigning emperor. The throne also passed to whichever prince could defeat and kill his competitors inside the Ottoman royal family.[22] Codifying these practices was an imperial decree issued by the ruler Mehmed II (r. 1444–6, 1451–81) that simply stated: "For the welfare of the state, the one of my sons to whom God grants the sultanate may lawfully put his brothers to death. A majority of the *'ulama'* consider this permissible."[23] The Mughal system, as noted earlier, was never thus codified.

---

[22] Colin Imber, *The Ottoman Empire, 1300–1650* (New York, 2002), p. 98.
[23] Cited in Halil Inalcik, *The Ottoman Empire: The Classical Age 1300–1600* (New York, 1973), p. 59.

From the mid-seventeenth century onward, the Ottomans gradually moved to control princely competition. At first, this meant preventing all but the oldest son from taking up a provincial assignment during their father's reign.[24] After 1600, even the most senior prince was confined to the imperial court, thereby severely curtailing most opportunities to build independent political, economic, or social networks of power beyond the emperor's gaze.[25] This transition dovetailed with another key development: the Ottomans abandoned the concept of father-to-son succession in favor of a system based on agnatic seniority. With this, the Ottomans put an end to intra-princely competition and the need for dynastic fratricide since brothers automatically succeeded one another. Such a dramatic shift away from a competitive and open-ended system of succession was echoed in the Safavid Empire around the same time.

Isma'il I founded the Safavid dynasty in 1501. Like the Ottoman Empire, its early succession practices reflected Turco-Mongol–inspired ideas that vested imperial sovereignty in all male members of the royal clan or family. Succession-related struggles thus consumed the Safavid family, with princely revolts occurring, some princes being killed or murdered, and others exiled. Not until 'Abbas I (r. 1588–1629), thought of as the greatest Safavid ruler, do we see a revamping of the dynasty's succession practices. Starting in the 1590s, 'Abbas I moved to dramatically curtail the freedom of his heirs. Like his Ottoman counterparts, 'Abbas confined his sons to the imperial court. According to Roger Savory, he also "went to extraordinary lengths to segregate his sons from political and military leaders in the state and his morbid suspiciousness caused him to lend too ready an ear to informers."[26] He thus killed or blinded three of his five adult sons (in 1615, 1621, and 1627). When he died, in a remarkable sea change from previous handovers, his eighteen-year-old grandson Sam Mirza (Safi I, r. 1629–42) ascended to the Safavid throne without a fight. Over the rest of the seventeenth century, the empire not only settled into a system of designated succession, but also a pattern of keeping princes imprisoned for the duration of their lives.

In trying to explain shifting Ottoman and Safavid succession practices, earlier generations of historians often focused on the psychological

[24] Leslie Peirce, *The Imperial Harem: Women and Sovereignty in the Ottoman Empire* (New York, 1993), p. 96.

[25] Ibid., p. 98.

[26] Roger Savory, *Iran under the Safavids* (Cambridge, 1980), p. 94. See also Andrew Newman, *Safavid Iran: Rebirth of a Persian Empire* (London, 2006), pp. 50–1, 201.

makeup of individual emperors.[27] Although not entirely discounting the personal in their respective works, Leslie Peirce, Kathryn Babayan, and Stephen Dale remind us of the value of looking for broader answers.[28] By highlighting shifting claims to political legitimacy in the sixteenth century, they offer crucial insights into why both the Ottoman and the Safavid Empires discarded open-ended systems of succession that were characterized by free-roaming princes who fought one another to attain the throne.

The Ottomans and Safavids synthesized diverse political traditions to legitimize their rule, but one legitimizing principle that stands out in the early phases of both dynasties was the claim that their rulers were *ghazi*s, Islamic warriors who fought against religious enemies. As Peirce notes, *ghaza* (the pursuit of religiously sanctioned warfare) was "an ideology that fit a frontier state of nomadic origin; it was an Islamic calque that suited a tribal society given to raiding and seeking booty, yet it provided a moral code and Islamic legal justification that could rally other elements in what was rapidly becoming an increasingly complex society."[29] Yet ultimately, the imperatives driving *ghaza* became difficult to reconcile with the emerging desire for settled imperial rule and a balance of military power that, especially in the case of the Ottomans in the Balkans, was slowly shifting against them.

For both the Ottomans and the Safavids, moves away from the *ghaza* ideal led to a new focus on the personal piety of the monarchs along with their guardianship and patronage of Sunni (in the case of the Ottomans) or Shi'ite (for the Safavids) law, religious personnel, and institutions. With a different ideological sanction in place, it became possible for sixteenth-century polemicists such as the Ottoman Lutfi Pasha to argue that princes simply inherited the right to rule versus having to forge it through battle and conquest.[30] As the need for forceful and militaristic kings ebbed with military retrenchment, so too did Ottoman and Safavid willingness to afford princes the administrative or military experience necessary to maintain expansionist ambitions. Both the Ottomans and Safavids filled the political vacuum left by the removal of princes by empowering small constellations of nobles who were generally either ethnic or religious outsiders.[31]

---

[27] Savory, *Iran under the Safavids*; and Inalcik, *The Ottoman Empire*.

[28] Peirce, *The Imperial Harem*; Kathryn Babayan, *Mystics, Monarchs and Messiahs: Cultural Landscapes of Early Modern Iran* (Cambridge, MA, 2002); Stephen Dale, *The Muslim Empires of the Ottomans, Safavids, and Mughals* (Cambridge, 2010).

[29] Peirce, *The Imperial Harem*, p. 157.

[30] Ibid., p. 167.

[31] Ibid., pp. 153–85; Babayan, *Mystics, Monarchs and Messiahs*, pp. 356–60.

Like the Ottomans and the Safavids, the Mughals drew on multiple and sometimes overlapping traditions – Turco-Mongol, Islamic-Prophetic, Islamic-mystical, secular-Persian – to fashion an ideology of dynastic legitimacy.[32] In their absorption of Turco-Mongol ideals, special attention was paid to the notion of the empire as primarily legitimated through warfare and conquest.[33] Although the Mughals only sporadically concerned themselves with the notion of *ghaza* – and how could they when the vast majority of their subjects were non-Muslims and their enemies primarily Muslim? – they actively subscribed to the nonsectarian idea that they had a divine mandate for universal dominion.[34] This view was articulated in everything from the reign names of emperors Jahangir (World Conqueror), Shah Jahan (Ruler of the World), and Aurangzeb (whose regnal title was 'Alamgir or Universe Conqueror) to the occasional deployment of visual markers such as world globes in imperial portraits.[35]

Most significantly, this mandate manifested itself in a commitment to imperial expansion. Indeed, it was a rare year in the sixteenth and seventeenth centuries when the Mughals did not field an imperial army to chisel away at the internal or external frontiers of their empire. Until the early eighteenth century, the Mughal army was virtually invincible, and the dynasty faced no significant enemies either in South Asia or on its external frontiers. Against this backdrop of military strength and continued expansionism, no one questioned a system that nurtured active princes who could bring substantial political, military, and administrative experience to bear as emperors.

Arguably, Mughal tolerance for obstreperous princes, tumultuous rebellions, and succession struggles did not come only from the ideology and practical considerations of military expansion; rapidly rising wealth and economic expansion across seventeenth-century South Asia also accommodated it. In contrast to the seventeenth-century Ottoman and Safavid Empires, the Mughal Empire continued to experience rapid

---

[32] Muzaffar Alam, *The Languages of Political Islam in India, c. 1200–1800* (Chicago, 2004); John F. Richards, "The Formation of Imperial Authority under Akbar and Jahangir," in *Kingship and Authority in South Asia*, ed. John F. Richards (Madison, 1978); Sanjay Subrahmanyam, "The Mughal State – Structure or Process?" 321.

[33] M. N. Pearson, "Shivaji and the Decline of the Mughal Empire," *Journal of Asian Studies* 35 (1976): 221–35; John F. Richards, "The Imperial Crisis in the Mughal Deccan," *Journal of Asian Studies* 35 (1976): 237–56.

[34] For the place of *ghaza* in the empire, see Jos Gommans, *Mughal Warfare: Indian Frontiers and Highroads to Empire, 1500–1700* (London, 2002), pp. 44–51.

[35] Sumathi Ramaswamy, "Conceit of the Globe in Mughal Visual Practice," *Comparative Studies in Society and History* 49, no. 4 (2007): 751–82.

economic growth thanks to an ever-increasing influx of New World silver, India's centrality as the workshop of the early modern world economy, and a dramatic commercial revolution. Among other things, this economic expansion was expressed in the increasing availability of credit; rising importance of long-distance trade; increasing manufacture of such high-value products as cotton and linen textiles, refined sugar, and indigo; and the expansion of agriculture and urbanization.[36] These developments simultaneously presented opportunities and challenges for the Mughals.

In terms of opportunities, increasing wealth obviously held out the promise of constructing a larger and more complex state. On the downside, it also threatened to create new power nodes – represented, for example, by rising merchants and religious or landed elites – whose legitimacy did not necessarily rely on an already existing political order. The greatest challenge for the Mughals thus lay in either harnessing or crushing these potentially destabilizing forces in the fulfillment of their own imperial aspirations.

Inasmuch as the Mughal dynasty, like its Middle Eastern counterparts, depended on political and administrative mechanisms to realize its ambitions, India's sheer wealth, geographic size, and social diversity presented even greater challenges. This is another area in which the Mughal experience is distinct from that of the Ottomans or Safavids, and in which the efforts of generations of Mughal princes to build their own power come into play. As long as the princes' capacity to build alliances and tie rising

---

[36] Sanjay Subrahmanyam, *Explorations in Connected History*, vols. 1–2 (Delhi, 2005); André Wink, "India: Muslim Period and Mughal Empire," in *Oxford Encyclopedia of Economic History*, ed. Joel Mokyr (Oxford, 2003), pp. 25–9; Scott Levi, *The Indian Diaspora in Central Asia and Its Trade, 1550–1900* (Leiden, 2002); Claude Markovits, *The Global World of Indian Merchants 1750–1947* (Cambridge, 2000); R. J. Barendse, *The Arabian Seas, 1640–1700* (Leiden, 1998); Andre Gunder Frank, *ReOrient: Global Economy in the Asian Age* (Berkeley, 1998); John F. Richards, "Early Modern India and World History," *Journal of World History* 8, no. 2 (1997): 197–209; Kumkum Chatterjee, *Merchants, Politics and Society in Early Modern India* (Leiden, 1996); Stephen Dale, *Indian Merchants and Eurasian Trade, 1600–1750* (Cambridge, 1994); Richard Eaton, *Rise of Islam and the Bengal Frontier* (Berkeley, 1993); John F. Richards, "The Seventeenth Century Crisis in South Asia," *Modern Asian Studies* 24, no. 4 (1990): 625–38; S. Arasaratnam, *Merchants, Companies and Commerce on the Coromandel Coast 1650–1740* (Delhi, 1986); Om Prakash, *The Dutch East India Company and the Economy of Bengal 1630–1720* (Princeton, 1985); Tapan Raychaudhuri and Irfan Habib, ed., *The Cambridge Economic History of India, Vol. 1, c. 1200–1750* (Cambridge, 1982); John F. Richards, "Mughal State Finance and the Premodern World Economy," *Comparative Studies in Society and History* 23 (1981): 285–308; Ashin Das Gupta, *Indian Merchants and the Decline of Surat, c. 1700–1750* (Wiesbaden, 1979); Sushil Chaudhuri, *Trade and Commercial Organization in Bengal 1600–1720* (Calcutta, 1975).

groups to the dynasty exceeded the cost of challenges posed by their political ambitions, the Mughal system never had any reason to waver in its commitment to free-roaming princes or the notion that the empire belonged to whoever could wrest it for himself. Nowhere is this better expressed than in Emperor Jahangir's great bewilderment – "This was astonishing news!" – upon hearing that 'Abbas I of the Safavid dynasty had murdered his oldest son. The subject troubled Jahangir so much that he returned to it fifteen months later, in 1616, in a conversation with a visiting Safavid ambassador. Implicit in Jahangir's memoirs is the sense that 'Abbas had acted improperly in protecting his imperial authority so fiercely against what Jahangir saw as the acceptable and perhaps necessary give-and-take of intra-familial competition.[37] The Mughal "failure" to institute ordered rules of succession until the dynasty's collapse was imminent in the late 1710s seems to have been based on an unstated understanding that an open-ended mode of succession had served its imperial aspirations best in the vibrant political, economic, and social environment of sixteenth- and seventeenth-century South Asia. It follows that the moment princes failed to act as hinges between the dynasty and society, they lost their place in the political life of the empire.

## SOURCES AND STRUCTURE

In this book, I have combined a longitudinal with a chronological organization. With the former, I identify key themes in the story of the princely institution: the creation of princely households; the ceaseless efforts to cultivate networks of friends and allies; the inevitable princely disobedience and occasional rebellion; and, finally, wars of succession. With the latter, I identify three main periods in the history of the princely institution: the early period (1504–56), the high period (1556–1680s), and the late period (1680s–1707). Following this introductory chapter, a prologue traces the shifts in Mughal succession practices in each of these periods. Whereas two of the remaining six chapters focus on the early and late periods respectively, between them are four chapters that examine princely households, alliance building, rebellion, and succession during the high period of Mughal rule. I thus demonstrate that in the thriving middle years of the empire, the princely institution too was at its zenith.

[37] Nur-ud-Din Muhammad Jahangir, *Jahangirnama*, ed. Muhammad Hashim (Tehran, 1980), pp. 167, 192–3.

Chapter 1, the Prologue, undertakes a detailed discussion of Mughal succession practices between the early sixteenth century and the end of Emperor Aurangzeb's reign in 1707. Whereas Central Asian norms, such as allowing any male from the extended Mughal family to compete for political power, largely dominated before 1556, Emperor Akbar (r. 1556–1605) conclusively excluded all but those in his direct line from vying for the throne. Akbar also ended the practice of granting appanages to adult princes. Although subsequent rulers including Jahangir and Shah Jahan attempted moves toward a system of quasi-designated succession, their efforts failed. Aurangzeb's reign witnessed an increasingly crowded princely arena that created fundamental problems for an open-ended system of succession. Highlighting these and other subtleties of the Mughal system of succession, this chapter lays the foundation for the rest of the book.

The early period, from the time of Babur's conquest of Kabul in 1504 to the end of Humayun's reign in 1556 is the focus of Chapter 2. Here I show how the early Central Asian–inspired corporate-style clan dynasty invested power across the entire Mughal family. As the aspiration to empire emerged, and as clan gave way to more imperial conceits, the semi-independent princely appanages became an increasingly intolerable threat. As this chapter demonstrates, we see early traces of this shift under Emperor Humayun, who sought to articulate a language of obedience and showed diminishing tolerance for challenges from other royals, including his brothers. The conflict between Humayun and his brother Mirza Kamran sets up the transition to a reconstituted princely institution under Akbar.

Chapter 3 is focused on the theme of the princely household as it functioned at its zenith. It describes a Mughal prince's earliest relationships, his coming-of-age rituals, and his never-ending efforts (and their impact on the empire) to build and fund a powerful household. Most examples are drawn from the period between 1585 and the 1680s. I argue that households often became microcosms of the empire's diversity and a place in which generations of successful imperial officials and nobles were first exposed to imperial norms and to a Persian-based and Islamicate milieu. This chapter also discusses the invaluable administrative and political experience Mughal princes garnered through managing their households.

Chapter 4 moves beyond household relationships to consider wider ties cultivated by princes with the empire's powerful political, economic, and social actors. Although often less intimate and less reliable than household relationships, they nonetheless were crucial not only for a prince's ambition to succeed to the throne but also for the dynasty's ability to draw upwardly mobile regional leaders and groups under its authority. As a consequence of Akbar's decision to discontinue the institution of princely appanages after the 1580s, princes had to look to the entire expanse of the empire to build their networks of support. This chapter demonstrates that between the early seventeenth century and the first decade of the eighteenth century, the best-networked prince always won the throne.

Princely efforts to build strong households and alliances invariably led to tensions with one another and with the emperor. Chapter 5 explores nonviolent princely dissent and also violent princely rebellions. Every Mughal emperor, barring the founder Babur, had to contend with one or more rebellions over the course of his reign. Although historians have generally viewed rebellions as a scourge that distracted and weakened the empire, this chapter argues how they in fact extended a Mughal-centered political culture and deepened Mughal power.

Chapter 6 explores the succession struggle that marked every transition of Mughal power after Akbar's reign. It details a prince's preparations – gathering men, material, and intelligence and preemptively killing rivals – and then describes how newly crowned emperors labored ex post facto to assert the inevitability of their success. New emperors made grand gestures of forgiveness, displaying benevolence toward supporters of a defeated princely opponent, but their newly ennobled courtiers were largely drawn from the ranks of what used to be their own princely retainers. In this manner, the Mughal nobility was infused with fresh blood every few decades, evidencing an incorporative dynamism that, in good times, characterized the success of the empire as a whole.

The seventh chapter focuses on the last decades of Emperor Aurangzeb's reign (between the 1680s and 1707) and argues that the princely institution began to weaken during this period. One of the greatest difficulties for princes was a growing financial crisis that undermined their capacity to staff their households. The effect on discipline, cohesion, and strength was devastating. An unprecedented number of royal competitors together with the rise of a powerful cadre of nobles who no longer felt compelled to support one or another prince added to princely woes. These developments had disastrous consequences for the power of the Mughal Prince as well as for the dynasty as a whole.

The Conclusion focuses on what transpired between Aurangzeb's death in 1707 and the final move away from a competitive system of succession in 1719. The phenomena outlined in the previous chapter – weakened

princely households and the inability of princes to form alliances on profitable terms with the most powerful elements in the empire – made for a new
political environment. The book concludes by considering how post-
Mughal successor states and elites came to fill the vacuum left by the
eclipse of the Mughal prince.

*Princes of the Mughal Empire* encompasses eight generations of
Mughal royals, beginning with Humayun and his brothers and ending
with the great-grandsons of Aurangzeb. All counted, this book directly
refers to an often bewildering cast of forty-one princes. Most are brothers
or sons of an emperor; in a much smaller number of cases, they are
nephews or more distant relatives of an emperor. Far from telling the full
stories of each, however, the primary focus is on the lives of about a dozen
of the most critical (and often better documented) players. To aid the
reader and avoid confusion, I provide a genealogical tree indicating the
emperors and their regnal dates, pre- and post-accession names (if these
changed), and the death dates of all other princes. To further assist the
reader, I have compiled a timeline of key events between 1504 and 1719.

This study has drawn on an extensive archive. It includes European
traveler accounts as well as the records of the English East India Company.
However, the book is primarily based on Persian sources from the Mughal
period, both published and archival, including officially sanctioned court
chronicles, privately written historical accounts, imperial memoirs, administrative documents, biographical dictionaries written by imperial noblemen
and religious scholars, collections of imperial and noble correspondence,
Sufi hagiographies, and local and regional histories. By far the most valuable
archival resource, however, has been a massive and thus far underutilized
collection called the *Akhbarat-i Darbar-i Mu'alla* (News Bulletins of the
Exalted Court).[38] Without access to this collection – thousands of daily

---

[38] From the reign of Akbar to at least the middle of the eighteenth century, the most powerful
political actors in the Mughal system maintained teams of secretaries who provided daily
reports of events at the other major courts (imperial, princely, and noble) across the
empire. These secretaries in turn relied heavily, though not exclusively, on a diary of events
compiled by a court or household official and usually read aloud in court the next day. Of
the dozens, if not hundreds, of individual collections of bulletins that may have once
existed, only one has partially survived, that of the Raja of Amber in Rajasthan. The
bulk of the collection covers Aurangzeb's reign. Encompassing thousands of pages of text
and tens of thousands of individual entries, these *akhbarat* mostly offer us snapshots of
events, generally of a political nature, at Aurangzeb's imperial court. Included in this
collection is one particularly important volume for this book. Rather than a summary of
events at the Mughal court, this volume's bulletins were generated from the Gujarat-based
court of Aurangzeb's third son, A'zam. At the time, the prince was serving as governor of

reports of the Mughal court – I could have never come to grips with the breadth of difficulties buffeting the princely institution at the end of the seventeenth and the beginning of the eighteenth centuries. Nor could I have offered an intimate portrait of the social life of a prince and his household.

In September 2010, the Allahabad High Court in northern India ruled that both Hindus and Muslims would henceforward share the contested site on which the demolished Babri Mosque once stood. Hundreds of thousands of Indian troops and police were deployed in several towns and cities across the country in anticipation of violence from one side or the other. Thankfully, it did not occur. This is undoubtedly not the final judgment on who has a right to the site or what can be built on it. This episode nonetheless reminds us that across South Asia, history remains a lived experience. Nowhere is this more so than in people's various and tortured relationship to the region's Mughal past. If this book can offer new ways to appreciate Mughal imperial success beyond an impoverished boilerplate history of the Mughal/Muslim as "foreigner," "outsider," and "despoiler," it will have been well worth my efforts.

the region and military commandant (*faujdar*) of Jodhpur. These bulletins – covering roughly eleven months between 1702 and 1703 and encompassing around one thousand individual reports – offer our only sustained ground-level view of the life and responsibilities of a Mughal prince.

# I

# Prologue: Setting the Stage, 1504–1707

At the heart of the story of the Mughal Prince was the imperative to succeed to the Mughal throne. It is a story that necessarily begins with Babur (d. 1530), the founder of the Mughal Empire, and moves through changing succession approaches adopted in the subsequent reigns of Humayun (d. 1556), Akbar (d. 1605), Jahangir (d. 1627), Shah Jahan (d. 1666), and Aurangzeb (d. 1707). Over the course of these reigns, a period lasting 181 years, the imperial commitment to an open-ended system of succession never faltered. Broader norms characterizing Mughal succession practices were not static, however, and this prologue provides a broad overview of the shifts in the system and explains how they delineate in turn three main periods in the history of the princely institution.

## THE OPEN-ENDED AND EVOLVING SYSTEM OF MUGHAL SUCCESSION

Zahir-ud-Din Muhammad Babur succeeded his father to the throne of the small Central Asian principality of Ferghana at the age of eleven. The Central Asian steppe tradition of the time allowed all male members of the broader Chaghatai and Timurid families (from whom the Mughals claimed descent) to assert individual claims to political sovereignty. The custom was practiced by an imperial clan, each of whose members competed fiercely with one another in a world of aggressive and shifting loyalties. According to Mughal historian Stephen Dale, by the late fifteenth century, two or three generations of Chaghatais and Timurids (all of whom claimed nominal descent from the great Mongol leader Chingiz Khan) struggled for power in a broad arc of territory covering much of contemporary Central Asia.[1] Eventually despairing of his prospects after a series of betrayals and reverses, Babur decamped to Kabul, a small outpost on the fringes of the former Timurid Empire. He took the city in 1504 from his uncle, no less. In 1507–8, following the Uzbek capture of Herat, Babur assumed for himself the symbolically powerful title of *padshah* (emperor) in place of the more commonly used *mirza* (a ruler's son). In Babur's mind, his action was fully justified because he was the sole surviving Timurid to still rule a kingdom. Equal measures of melancholy and amazement tinge Babur's comment around that time: "Only I was left in Kabul."[2]

Jack Goody provides us with crucial terminology for explaining different succession systems. Thus a "royal descent group" refers to a ruling lineage that is but one of a number of similar groups, whereas a "stem dynasty," by contrast, maintains agnatic succession over time.[3] As Babur's personal authority grew, so did his efforts to mold the succession politics of his nascent realm closer toward a "stem dynasty." He did so in two ways. First, he made sure that his sons were the primary focus of his growing realm's political attention. Following Chaghatai and Timurid political traditions, Babur granted his sons semi-independent and semipermanent territorial holdings (*ulus*es) once they were old enough.[4] Thus Humayun got Badakhshan in 1519 and Mirza Kamran received Qandahar in the early 1520s. After Babur invaded India in 1525–6, he augmented Mirza Kamran's holdings by also giving him temporary charge of Kabul. Babur's third son, Mirza 'Askari, held Multan until the fall of 1528, and Mirza Hindal was briefly awarded Badakhshan in 1529. Although Babur continued to depend heavily on his extended family, especially men such as

[1] Stephen Dale, *The Garden of Eight Paradises: Babur and the Culture of Empire in Central Asia, Afghanistan and India (1483–1530)*(Leiden, 2004), 68–70, 200–7. For a deeper historical context, see Beatrice Manz, *The Rise and Rule of Tamerlane* (Cambridge, 1989), 41–3.

[2] Zahir-ud-Din Muhammad Babur, *The Baburnama: Memoirs of Babur, Prince and Emperor*, trans. W. M. Thackston (New York, 2002), 257.

[3] Jack Goody, *Succession to High Office* (Cambridge, 1966), 26.

[4] According to Stephen Dale, the term *ulus* has multiple meanings. As well as pointing to a territorial unit, it can also refer to a tribe, confederation of tribes, community, or "nation." *The Garden of Eight Paradises*, 101, 158.

Muhammad Zaman Mirza and Esan Temur Sultan, to command armies and represent him at the regional level, his focus on his sons is noteworthy and seems to point to an effort to limit the number of individuals within the Timurid extended family who might succeed him.

Also in line with Chaghatai and Timurid tradition, Babur expressed a preference for one son to succeed to the supreme title of emperor. However, in a milieu where nomadic warriors constantly shifted loyalties and territories, and in a world still populated with princely appanages, this meant that the heir apparent was nothing more than a "first-among-equals."

For almost a decade, between 1519 and 1528, Humayun appears to have been Babur's preferred candidate to follow him as *padshah*. Thus it was Humayun who received the lion's share of spoils after the city of Agra was conquered in 1526. Also in 1528, Babur wrote asking his son to honor a distribution of land and spoils that gave him six parts to five for the emperor's second son Mirza Kamran. In the last years of his life, however, Babur seems to have been plagued by growing doubts about Humayun's ability to keep the empire and his brothers united. Evidence of this discontent can be seen in his decision to ignore Humayun and instead recall Mirza 'Askari from Multan to help him in the 1528–9 campaign against Bihar and Bengal. Such favor for Mirza 'Askari may well have prompted Humayun's precipitous abandonment of Badakhshan in 1529 and unauthorized return to the imperial court. On his deathbed, Babur is said to have asked for his youngest son Hindal, not Humayun, hinting at the depth of the older prince's imperial disfavor.[5] Mughal sources are largely silent about the embarrassing episode wherein, just before Humayun's ascent to the throne, Babur's closest advisors sought to position the emperor's brother-in-law and Babur loyalist Mahdi Khwaja as a possible replacement.

That Humayun eventually ascended to the throne signaled Babur's success in focusing imperial attention on his sons as well as dominating the political ambitions of all other clan members – in other words, a shift for the Timurids from "royal descent group" to "stem dynasty." This succession practice was sustained through Humayun's reign and reached its full realization in Akbar's when it was made clear to all that the only legitimate contenders for the imperial throne were males in the emperor's direct line.

---

[5] Gulbadan Begum, *Ahwal-i Humayun Badshah*, British Library, Ms. Or. 166, f. 17b.

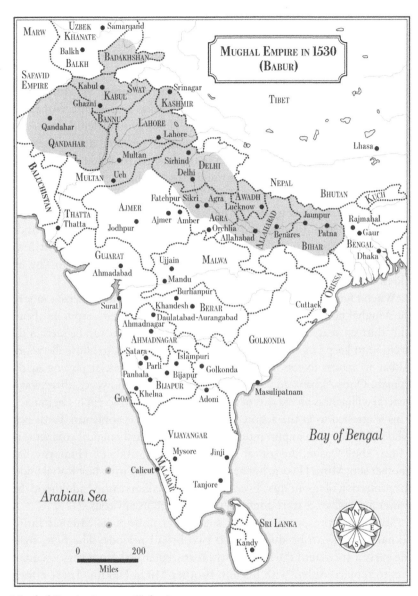

Mughal Empire in 1530 (Babur)

Between 1530 and 1555, however, the shift had not been so clearly established that it could not be challenged. Humayun was forced to face down multiple kinsmen who sought imperial authority. In the first decade of his rule, for instance, he fought long and hard against Muhammad

Zaman Mirza, grandson of the last great ruler of Herat (Sultan Husain Bayqara) and Babur's son-in-law. That struggle ranged across Malwa and the Punjab and even drew the Mughals into conflict with the ruler of Gujarat after he offered Muhammad Zaman Mirza his protection. Ultimately, Muhammad Zaman Mirza surrendered to Humayun's greater authority and was later killed fighting against the emperor's nemesis Sher Khan Suri in 1539. In 1546, Humayun ordered the execution of Yadgar Nasir Mirza, a first cousin, for repeated acts of treason. And after losing his empire in India (a topic to be discussed more fully in the next chapter), Humayun also fought his half brothers Mirza Kamran and Mirza 'Askari for many years. By the end of Humayun's reign, however, the surviving *mirza*s had been successfully reduced to the ranks of imperial nobility and were no longer considered viable candidates for the throne. By clearing away the competition around him, Humayun had paved the way for a relatively smooth succession by his oldest son and heir, Akbar.

When Humayun died unexpectedly in 1556, the broad consensus among the Mughal nobility was that Akbar was the rightful heir despite his being only thirteen years old. Dangers nonetheless lurked. This can be seen in the decision to keep Humayun's death a secret long enough to allow the young Akbar to return to the imperial court from his provincial posting in the Punjab. Once Akbar had assumed his father's place, however, there was a general willingness on the part of the Mughal nobility to accept his legitimacy. This is attested to in the action of Humayun's senior noblemen Tardi Beg, who surrendered an important prisoner (and potential political competitor), Mirza Abu'l Qasim, the son of Mirza Kamran, to Akbar.[6] Humayun had another son, Mirza Hakim, but he was an infant living in distant Kabul under the protection of his mother. Even after Mirza Hakim reached adulthood, his power and influence were confined to Kabul and its environs.

Seen from the perspective of succession politics in Mughal India, Akbar's reign can be divided into two broad periods. The first, from the early 1560s until the mid-1580s, featured efforts from various quarters to replace Akbar with his half brother Mirza Hakim. These efforts included the joint rebellion of Mirza Sharaf-ud-Din Husain Ahrari (married to Akbar's half sister) and Shah Abu'l Ma'ali between 1562 and 1564, a rebellion by the Mirzas in 1566, and the massive North India–based rebellion of 1580–1. In all these, Mirza Hakim played a key role as a symbol of opposition to Akbar. This testified, on the one hand,

---

[6] Shaikh Abu'l Fazl, *Akbarnamah*, ed. Abdul Rahim, vol. 1 (Calcutta, 1878), 365.

to the success of their father Humayun's efforts to contain claims to the Mughal throne to the emperor's direct heirs, but on the other hand, it indicated how imperial authority continued to be destabilized by the existence of princely appanages.

Against this backdrop, it must be noted that Akbar did not entirely abandon his vigilance against threats to his power offered by more distant kinsmen. Over the years, potential or real opponents were politically co-opted (such as Mirza Sulaiman of Badakhshan in 1575), imprisoned (such as Muzaffar Husain Mirza in 1577), or killed (such as Mirza Abu'l Qasim in the mid-1560s and Ibrahim Husain Mirza and Muhammad Husain Mirza in 1573. In addition, despite their fierce rivalry, Akbar worked to protect his half brother's hold over Kabul against other kinsmen. In 1564–65, for instance, he sent forces to help Mirza Hakim drive Mirza Sulaiman of Badakhshan out of the city he had successfully occupied. In the decades that followed, Mirza Hakim's hold on Kabul ironically relied on the threat of intervention by Akbar from India.

The rise of Akbar's sons, Salim, Murad, and Danyal, to political prominence, as well as the demise of Mirza Hakim and the Kabul appanage, mark the second phase of Akbar's reign. A key moment came in 1582 when Akbar attacked Kabul to punish Mirza Hakim for invading India the previous year. Rather than commanding the imperial forces himself, Akbar deputized his second son, the twelve-year-old Murad, to be their nominal commander. As the Mughal forces approached Kabul, Mirza Hakim was forced to engage them in battle. Murad's subsequent victory over his uncle not only signaled the emergence of a new imperial hierarchy, but also opened the way for Akbar to incorporate Kabul into the empire. This he finally did in 1585, after Mirza Hakim's death. With Kabul's seizure and the imprisonment of Mirza Hakim's young sons Kaikobad and Afrasiyab in India, Akbar signaled his determination to abandon the custom of granting princes individual appanages. Henceforward, succession politics would be focused exclusively on Akbar's direct heirs and played out on an imperial stage that spanned the entire Mughal Empire.

From the birth of his oldest son Salim in 1569, Akbar strove to make sure his sons became the most powerful centers of power in Mughal India (see Chapter 4). In 1585, these efforts intensified – along with granting his sons imperial ranks below only himself, Akbar also recused himself as a candidate for additional marriages. The significance of this move cannot be underestimated. As Ruby Lal has shown, not only were royal marriages crucial for producing heirs and building political partnerships, but they also helped highlight the dynasty's accommodation to and symbolic protection of the world around it.[7] By allowing his sons to contract dozens of marriages among themselves over the next twenty years, Akbar was demonstrably setting up each of them to take on the mantle of emperor in an empire that was now indivisible.

The move to favor only his sons had important repercussions for Akbar. This became evident in 1591 when Akbar fell seriously ill. Salim, Murad, and Danyal (who were twenty-two, twenty-one, and eighteen years old, respectively) began mobilizing their supporters in anticipation of a war of succession, and the imperial court teetered on the brink of civil war. Luckily, Akbar's health improved in time to prevent an outbreak of hostilities. But Akbar was now forced to concede the necessity of geographically separating his sons.[8] Over the next decade, each was in turn moved out of the imperial court and sent to either govern a province or lead a military expedition.

As relations among his sons worsened throughout the 1590s, Akbar himself felt increasingly threatened by the eldest, Salim. Let us consider the situation of Salim in the new post-appanage era of the Mughal Empire. Although being the oldest son did tend to come with certain favors and advantages, it did not in fact guarantee assumption of the Mughal throne. What was Salim to do about his brothers now that princely appanages had been done away with? A fight was inevitable. Instead of an advantage, then, the position of heir apparent was a burden. It came with added expectations of loyalty and service to the emperor that conflicted with maintaining an independent and powerful household and cultivating networks of support to ward off future rivals. Salim found this balance increasingly difficult to strike; starting in the early 1590s, he began to defy Akbar. In subsequent generations, favored sons – among them Khurram (who rebelled in 1622), Muhammad Sultan (who rebelled in 1659), and Mu'azzam (who was imprisoned between 1687 and 1695) – would face similar opposing incentives.

In 1594, Akbar made a fateful decision. It was fully intended to undercut Salim. He decided to grant Salim's oldest son, Khusrau, a high imperial rank (*mansab*), even though Khusrau was only seven years old at the time. Along with the *mansab*, Akbar allowed the young prince to draw on the financial resources of the newly conquered province of Orissa. The emperor also appointed the prince's maternal uncle, Salim's brother-in-law Raja Man Singh, as his guardian/protector (*ataliq*). The

---

[7] Ruby Lal, *Domesticity and Power in the Early Mughal World* (Cambridge, 2005), 166–73.

[8] 'Abd al-Qadir Badauni, *Muntakhab al-Tawarikh*, ed. W. N. Lees and Ahmad Ali, vol. 2 (Calcutta, 1865), 378.

Raja was simultaneously made the governor of the neighboring province of Bengal. To add political and military muscle to the minor prince's military establishment, Akbar also assigned seasoned Rajput and Afghan troops to his command.

Through his elevation of Khusrau, Akbar appears to have sought to impress on all concerned parties, but especially on Salim, that he was willing to supersede their claims to the throne if they questioned his authority. In an effort to deepen the wedge between Salim and Khusrau, Akbar insisted that the young prince remain under his exclusive charge. The emperor went so far as to openly declare that he "loved grandchildren more than sons."[9] Remarkably, Khusrau began to be treated, or thought of, as Salim's younger brother. Khusrau even took to referring to his father as Shah Bhai (Imperial Brother).[10] Inevitably, relations between princely father and son began to mirror the deterioration in the ties between Akbar and Salim.

Adding to these pressures, Akbar decided sometime in 1597 to remove Salim from the imperial court. The emperor faced stiff resistance, however. The prince argued that he should remain at court in light of the emperor's advancing age (Akbar was in his late fifties), and this drew support from Salim's own influential circle. Still, in mid-1599, Akbar forced Salim to accept command of an expedition against the recalcitrant Rajput state of Mewar. In addition to being unceremoniously removed from his central perch at the Mughal court, Salim learned that Akbar had permitted his younger brother Danyal to use red tents at his camp – an imperial prerogative that until then was exclusively reserved for the emperor himself. There can be no doubt that Akbar was working to make the next succession a more competitive one. Sometime in 1599, Salim reached the end of his tether and in the fall of that year began his rebellion against Akbar.

As I argue in Chapter 5, Salim's five-year rebellion was part of a long-term effort to force the emperor to make political concessions. In the end, it failed. For Akbar, however, who was determinedly reshaping how succession worked in the Mughal Empire, Salim's rebellion uncovered important fault lines in this emerging dispensation. To what extent was a favored prince to be elevated over his competitors? What happened when a chosen or favored prince turned hostile or was deemed no longer a favorite, for whatever reason? What degree of consent and control might an emperor exert over the succession process? What would be the fate of the remaining royal brothers?

[9] Shaikh Abu'l Fazl, *Akbarnamah*, ed. Abdul Rahim, vol. 3 (Calcutta, 1886), 735.
[10] Kamgar Husaini, *Ma'asir-i-Jahangiri*, ed. Azra Alavi (Bombay, 1978), 53.

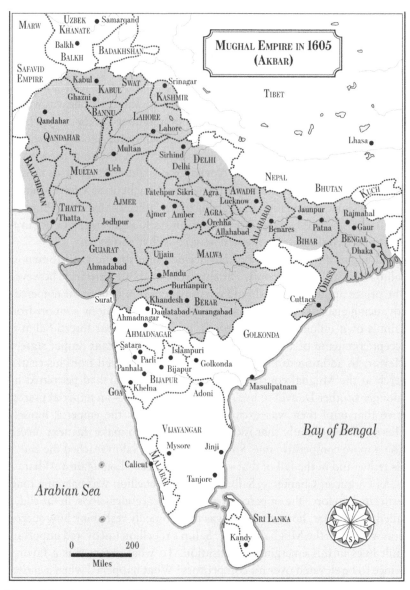

Mughal Empire in 1605 (Akbar)

Almost to the end of his reign in October 1605, Akbar seems to have held out hope that Salim's imperial claims might somehow be thwarted. In the end, it was the premature deaths of both Murad and Danyal (in 1599 and 1605, both from alcohol poisoning) that spared the Mughal Empire its first war of succession in the post-appanage period. Only Akbar's grandson Khusrau remained as an alternative to Salim, and Mughal dynastic history contains the remarkable episode wherein, just days before Akbar's death, a gathering of powerful imperial nobles met to override Khusrau's candidacy. In the end, they ruled (out of political expedience rather than conviction) that the customs and laws of the Chaghatai did not permit a son to trump the imperial claims of a still-living father.[11] Akbar, in one of his final acts as emperor, acquiesced to the wishes of his nobles.

After having won the throne through a show of obedience to Chaghatai ideals, Salim (now Emperor Jahangir) proceeded to immediately break faith with those same ideals by not honoring his earlier pledge to grant Khusrau the governorship of Bengal. The presumption, at least on Khusrau's part, was that Bengal would become his appanage. When Jahangir reneged on the promise by not allowing Khusrau to depart from the imperial court, the inevitable result, in April 1606, was a princely rebellion. This Jahangir quickly crushed, confirming his commitment to the indivisibility of the empire. There was another crucial way in which Jahangir reaffirmed Akbar's determination to move away from Central Asian, Timurid-based succession practices. Like his father, he vigorously quashed the political pretensions of collateral branches of the imperial family. An example was his extraordinary treatment of his deceased brother Danyal's three minor sons: he ordered their conversion to Christianity. Francisco Pelsaert, a Dutch traveler in Mughal India, writes:

He did so not because he thought well of or was attached to that religion, but in order to turn away the affections of everyone from them. He did not wish that they should enjoy the support of the great nobles for their father's sake, who was much loved by everyone.[12]

---

[11] Asad Beg Qazwini, *Waqa'i' Asad Beg*, Center for Advanced Study Library (Aligarh Muslim University), Rotograph 94, f. 29b. Amir Timur's decision in 1405 to designate his grandson Pir Muhammad bin Jahangir as his heir offers proof that the dynastic claims of living sons were sometimes ignored. Beatrice Manz, *The Rise and Rule of Tamerlane* (Cambridge, 1989), 128.

[12] Francisco Pelsaert, *A Dutch Chronicle of Mughal India*, ed. and trans. B. Narain and S. R. Sharma (Lahore, repr. 1978), 74.

In addition, Jahangir repeatedly imprisoned, banished, and publicly degraded his uncle Mirza Hakim's sons and grandsons.[13] Outraged by his own son Khusrau's rebellion and disloyalty, he wrote: "If such treatment is received from a son of my loins, what can be expected of nephews and cousins?"[14]

In 1607, Jahangir decided to blind the imprisoned Khusrau. This action followed the discovery of another plot to overthrow him by Khusrau's supporters. By blinding his son, Jahangir effectively disqualified Khusrau from ever ascending to the Mughal throne. But the emperor still had two adult sons – Parvez and Khurram, eighteen and fifteen years old, respectively – who could potentially succeed him. Jahangir elected to groom his third son, Khurram. Although Parvez continued to receive military and administrative assignments over the next decade, he was effectively sidelined.

We can view the rise of Khurram as a mark of Jahangir's efforts to shift the Mughals toward a system of quasi-designated succession. Between 1607 and 1621, Khurram received every conceivable honor. None perhaps was more important than the open acknowledgment that he was the emperor's preferred choice to succeed to the throne. Enabling Khurram's rise were his high-profile military appointments and military successes throughout the 1610s. Jahangir himself never led military campaigns as emperor, preferring that Khurram and others do so in his stead. Khurram also enjoyed a close alliance with his influential stepmother Nur Jahan, who had married Jahangir in 1611. Khurram took Nur Jahan's niece Arjomand Banu Begum (better known as Mumtaz Mahal) in marriage in 1612, and from that point on (with one notable exception in 1619), she was the only woman to have children with Khurram. Indeed, history tends to remember their relationship, monumentalized as it eventually was in the building of the Taj Mahal, while forgetting Khurram's far less appealing handling of his older brother Khusrau (as will be shown next). Through

---

[13] It is recounted that Mirza Afrasiyab was once ordered to serve as an attendant behind Jahangir's throne during a public audience with a visiting envoy from Shah 'Abbas of Iran. The humiliation was too much for the proud prince, however, and he refused to do as told. Jahangir ordered his imprisonment thereafter. Shaikh Farid Bhakkari, *Dhakhirat al-Khawanin*, ed. S. Moinul Haq, vol. 2 (Karachi, 1970), 204–5. Sir Thomas Roe, the visiting English ambassador to Jahangir's court, recounted how one of the princes begged to be gifted a feather, three or four pictures, and an old pair of spurs, highlighting the relative penury of the Mirza's sons. Sir Thomas Roe, *The Embassy of Sir Thomas Roe to India, 1615–1619* (Delhi, repr. 1990), 143.

[14] Nur-ud-Din Muhammad Jahangir, *Jahangirnama*, ed. Muhammad Hashim (Tehran, 1980), 34.

most of the 1610s, Jahangir appears to have left the empire's workings to the combined charge of Nur Jahan and Khurram.

Meanwhile, after being blinded in 1607, Khusrau was placed under the control of Ja'far Beg/Asaf Khan (a Parvez loyalist). Three years later, responsibility for overseeing Khusrau was shifted to Ani Singh Ra'i Dalan, a loyal servitor to the emperor. Another six years on, in 1616, in an ominous move for Khusrau, he was transferred to a sworn enemy, Abu'l Hasan/Asaf Khan – Khurram's father-in-law and Nur Jahan's brother. Even Jahangir's own mother, Maryam-uz-Zamani, strongly opposed this move out of concern that allowing physical harm to befall a prince of the royal blood would set a terrible precedent.[15] Unfortunately for Khusrau, Nur Jahan managed to calm her mother-in-law's fears. Despite repeated petitions by other high-ranking imperial supporters to give Khusrau more freedom within the confines of the court, the emperor remained steadfast in his commitment to punish his son, a commitment that Nur Jahan and Khurram undoubtedly encouraged. Finally, in what amounted to Khusrau's death warrant, he was handed over to Khurram as part of an imperial quid pro quo designed to get Khurram to lead the Mughal forces in the Deccan in 1620. Within two years, Khusrau was dead, murdered on Khurram's orders. Then, within a matter of months, Khurram himself was in rebellion against both Jahangir and Nur Jahan.

The roots of Khurram's rebellion ran deep. Nur Jahan's status as both imperial wife and his stepmother was complicated; her loyalties were often divided between serving her husband while he still lived, positioning herself for a post-Jahangir political dispensation, and working with Khurram's political ambition. For Khurram, questions must have arisen regarding her continued influence once he had replaced Jahangir as emperor. By 1619–20, Nur Jahan had reached the conclusion that Khurram would undermine her power in a post-Jahangir dispensation, and, in a provocative move, she arranged for the marriage of her only biological child, her daughter Ladli Begum, to Jahangir's youngest son and Khurram's half brother, Shahryar (he was fifteen at the time). Over the next few years, she actively helped Shahryar build his princely household and raise his political profile at the Mughal court. Nur Jahan also encouraged a reconciliation of sorts between Jahangir and his other son, the estranged Parvez. Having favored Khurram for more than a decade and groomed him as his heir, Jahangir's actions offered a clear reversal. As with Akbar and Salim, so also with Jahangir and Khurram: as Jahangir had a change of heart regarding the once-favored

---

[15]  Roe, *The Embassy of Sir Thomas Roe to India*, 256, 262.

older son, he allowed the always present pressures of princely competition to rise to the surface of dynastic politics.

By the mid-1620s, Jahangir was simultaneously working with three major princely contenders: Parvez; Shahryar; and, most surprisingly, Dawar Bakhsh, son of the murdered Khusrau, whose prominence grew out of sympathy and support for his deceased father. Jahangir had special plans for Dawar Bakhsh, stating in a 1626 imperial communication that the prince had been ordered "to take vengeance for his father's murder by putting that wretched one [i.e., Khurram] to the sword."[16]

So many princely contenders created turmoil. Nur Jahan favored Shahryar, whereas the nobility was split in its support for Parvez, Dawar Bakhsh, and – secretly – Khurram. These fractures came to the surface in a 1626 rebellion by one of Jahangir's powerful nobles, Mahabat Khan, a Parvez loyalist. Over the course of six months, the Khan managed to place Jahangir and much of the imperial court under arrest. Although Mahabat Khan's final political goals are unclear, he likely intended to keep Jahangir under his control until the emperor (who was in bad health) died, allowing him to place Parvez on the throne. During the course of Mahabat Khan's rebellion, Parvez quietly supported the nobleman from his princely base in the Deccan. The collapse of Mahabat Khan's revolt and Parvez's sudden death in October 1626 (like his uncles Murad and Danyal from alcohol poisoning) reconfirmed Nur Jahan's power, however.

Parvez's demise meant that officially only Shahryar and Dawar Bakhsh remained as potential heirs. Although Shahryar was the stronger of the two, thanks to the ongoing support of Nur Jahan, neither prince had wide-reaching and independent webs of political support, nor did either have large enough contingents of troops or deep enough financial resources to pose a real threat to Khurram. All eyes were now trained on Khurram, who, after considering flight to Iran in early 1626, returned to the Deccan upon hearing of Parvez's death. In October 1627, Jahangir finally died and fighting broke out at the imperial court. The first round of conflict pitted the resident princes and their supporters against each other. Khurram watched from the sidelines.

On one side were Nur Jahan and Shahryar; on the other were Dawar Bakhsh and Asaf Khan – Nur Jahan's brother and Jahangir's chief advisor (*vakil*). It was clear to most contemporary onlookers that although on Dawar Bakhsh's side, Asaf Khan was acting as a proxy for his son-in-law

---

[16] *A Descriptive List of Farmans, Manshurs and Nishans: Addressed by the Imperial Mughals to the princes of Rajasthan*, ed. N. R. Khadgawat (Bikaner, 1962), 62.

Khurram. In the battle that followed, Shahryar was defeated and, shortly thereafter, blinded on Dawar Bakhsh's orders. When news of Shahryar's defeat reached Khurram, he began marching northward out of the Deccan. As Khurram approached Agra, he sent a message to Asaf Khan to imprison Dawar Bakhsh (who had been acting emperor for the past two months); Dawar Bakhsh's younger brother Gurshasp; the blind Shahryar; and his uncle Danyal's surviving sons, Tahmurs and Hoshang. A few days later, in the third week of January 1628, Khurram conveyed a fresh set of orders through a trusted household retainer that all five princes be put to death.

With this gruesome order, Khurram asserted his exclusive right to the throne. His execution of five princes also set a bloody precedent for future princely rivalry. No longer would princes escape with their lives in lieu of their eyes. Henceforth, and until the end of competitive successions in 1719, Mughal princely wars of succession were expected to be bloody and brutal affairs that would result in the death of all claimants to the imperial throne, barring the one who rose to the top.[17]

Khurram attained the throne and reigned for thirty years, from 1628 to 1658, as Emperor Shah Jahan. The central feature of his long reign was his attempt to frame, in the words of historian John F. Richards, "a more formal, more forbidding, and grand monarchy and empire."[18] Shah Jahan's ambition unfolded on multiple fronts, including massive building projects (two noteworthy examples being a new capital called Shahjahanabad and the Taj Mahal as a mausoleum for his wife Mumtaz Mahal); extensive patronage of the arts and literature; administrative consolidation; and, most significant, a renewed push to expand the Mughal Empire's frontiers. Of course, shaping the future succession practices of the dynasty figured importantly in his overall schemes.

Following the bloodletting of 1628, the historical record for Shah Jahan's reign is almost completely silent regarding the activities of princes from collateral lines of the Mughal royal family. What happened to the grandsons

---

[17] Shah Jahan's responsibility in rendering fratricide an integral part of future imperial succession struggles did not escape contemporary comment. As François Bernier, a mid-seventeenth-century French traveler to Mughal India noted: "not only was the crown to be gained by victory alone, but in case of defeat life was certain to be forfeited. There was now no choice between a kingdom and death; as Chah-Jehan [i.e., Shah Jahan] had ascended the throne by imbruing his hands in the blood of his own brothers, so the unsuccessful candidates on the present occasion [i.e., the 1657–9 war of succession between Shah Jahan's sons] were sure to be sacrificed to the jealousy of the conqueror." François Bernier, *Travels in the Mogul Empire, AD 1656–1668*, trans. A. Constable (Delhi, repr. 1997), 25–6.

[18] John F. Richards, *The Mughal Empire* (Cambridge, 1993), 119.

of Khusrau, the sons of Parvez, or the heirs of Danyal, Murad, and Mirza Hakim? We know that they were alive during Shah Jahan's reign, but there is barely any mention of them and their activities in the imperial sources, which seem deliberately silent on the affairs of non-lineally related royals. Nor do other sources provide any commentary. The concerted focus on the direct sons of the emperor is striking. Such a movement may be understood as a strategy for tackling what Jack Goody has described as the "dangerous proliferation of the royal personality"[19] or growth in the number of mutually hostile heirs. Shah Jahan's determination to restrict the number of princely competitors even extended to withholding daughters from marriage and sexual contact to control their bearing of royal children. Although unusual in the South Asian context, this strategy occasionally occurred in other imperial contexts.[20] Thus Shah Jahan denied his three adult daughters – Jahan Ara, Roshan Ara, and Gauhar Ara – the right to marry, though he happily encouraged their political participation in concert with one of their four brothers. In this way, Jahan Ara emerged as a firm supporter of Dara Shukoh, whereas Roshan Ara and Gauhar Ara became partisans of Aurangzeb and Murad, respectively.

The surviving sons of Shah Jahan – Dara Shukoh, Shuja', Aurangzeb, and Murad – were full brothers, all sons of Mumtaz Mahal, which was unusual for Mughal princely competitors. Although we know little of Shah Jahan's relations with them prior to his accession in 1628, we do know that from the early 1630s onward, he favored the oldest, Dara Shukoh. And in contrast to both Akbar and Jahangir, who eventually revisited their original choice, Shah Jahan never shifted in his support of Dara Shukoh.

Evidence of Dara Shukoh's favored status is manifold. An example is his imperial rank. By 1657, the last full year of Shah Jahan's reign, Dara Shukoh had been elevated to the extraordinary standing of 50000/40000. The first figure represented his rank in the imperial hierarchy (*zat*); the second indicated the number of horsemen (*sawar*) he was expected to maintain from his income.[21] Compare this to the combined rank of 55000/42000 for Shuja', Aurangzeb, and Murad. Unlike his three younger brothers who were either frequently rotated through assignments or kept far removed from the imperial court, Dara Shukoh was more-or-less permanently based at the court,

[19] Goody, *Succession to High Office*, 27.

[20] Nancy Kollmann, *Kinship and Politics: The Making of the Muscovite Political System, 1345–1547* (Palo Alto, 1987); Jane Bestor, "Bastardy and Legitimacy in the Formation of a Regional State in Italy: The Estense Succession," *Comparative Studies in Society and History* 38 (1996): 549–85.

[21] For further discussion about the *mansabdari* system, see Chapter 3.

giving him a powerful voice in the day-to-day administration of the empire. Unlike his brothers, he was also given the right to share in certain imperial prerogatives such as the use of red-colored tents. Perhaps the strongest proof of Dara Shukoh's higher status, however, was his 1633 marriage to Nadira Begum, the daughter of Shah Jahan's deceased brother Parvez and a granddaughter of Akbar's younger son Murad. Theirs was the most expensive wedding ever staged in Mughal history, and the bride's trousseau of Rs. 800,000 (more than $12 million in 2009 dollars) was the largest ever. Since Babur's reign, the Mughals had avoided contracting marriages between male heirs of an emperor and first cousins from collateral branches. By this marriage, therefore, Shah Jahan sought to consolidate already forged imperial networks within which his oldest son would become the main pivot. The marriage might also have signified that Dara Shukoh was too exalted to marry outside the royal family (unlike his brothers who did). The consequent progeny, purportedly, would be doubly favored on account of their unusual dual Mughal lineage. Indeed, Shah Jahan extended extraordinary privileges to Dara Shukoh's two sons – Sulaiman Shukoh and Siphir Shukoh – as well. Sulaiman Shukoh was granted the right to use red imperial tents in 1653 and four years later was granted a status rank (*zat*) in the imperial hierarchy that placed him just under his uncles Shuja' and Aurangzeb, and on par with Murad.

Such favoritism bred enormous resentment among Shah Jahan's other sons. Especially as Shah Jahan aged through the 1650s, Dara Shukoh's influence grew ever stronger, to the great alarm of his brothers. In a 1657 letter to his older sister Jahan Ara, Aurangzeb angrily demanded why "despite twenty years of service and loyalty, he is not considered worthy of the same level of confidence as his brother's son [i.e., Sulaiman Shukoh]."[22] Far from forestalling a destructive war of succession, Shah Jahan's actions, in fact, intensified the conflict between Dara Shukoh and the rest of his sons. Despite Shah Jahan's efforts, his other sons were not content to accept either their father's plans for his succession or their older brother's presumption to be next in line.

In the early 1650s, Shuja', Aurangzeb, and Murad agreed to a secret alliance against Dara Shukoh. Its details are explicitly captured in Aurangzeb's surviving princely correspondence.[23] No amount of

[22] Aurangzeb, *Adab-i 'Alamgiri*, ed. Abdul Ghafur Chaudhuri, vol. 2 (Lahore, 1971), 829.
[23] Aurangzeb, *Adab-i 'Alamgiri*, 790–7. In one of his letters to Murad, Aurangzeb urges his younger brother to send all communications in a secret script called *khat-i mukhtara*. See page 791.

engineering by Shah Jahan, short of the execution or permanent incarceration of his younger sons, could have prevented the conflagration that followed his temporary illness and inability to rule in 1657. In their capacity as imperial generals and provincial governors, Shuja', Aurangzeb, and Murad represented Shah Jahan's authority in regions where the emperor did not or could not go. And in this sense as well as in their position as direct lineal competitors, the princes played a crucial role in the political life of the empire.

The incapacitation of Shah Jahan in the last months of 1657 led to a full-blown war of succession among his four adult sons. The emperor, of course, threw his support behind Dara Shukoh; nonetheless, Aurangzeb methodically bested the heir apparent as well as his other brothers. Shah Jahan's efforts to promote Dara Shukoh and initiate a new model of Mughal dynastic succession – in which the emperor's favored son would either ascend the Mughal throne unopposed or easily vanquish challenges from his brothers – simply did not come to pass.

Among the most interesting features of the 1657–9 war of succession are recurring conversations about partitioning the empire among the contestants. In the fall of 1657, for example, Aurangzeb and Murad signed a contract (*qaulnama*).[24] The two brothers agreed that following Dara Shukoh's defeat, Murad would get the north and northwest areas including Punjab, Kabul, Kashmir, Multan, and Thatta, whereas Aurangzeb would get the rest of the empire. When Aurangzeb and Murad together prevailed over the imperial forces in the battles of Dharmat (April 1658) and Samugarh (May 1658), their sister Jahan Ara offered another proposal. Working on behalf of Shah Jahan, she broached the possibility of dividing the empire five ways among Dara Shukoh (the Punjab and neighboring regions), Shuja' (Bengal), Murad (Gujarat), Aurangzeb (much of northern and central India), and Aurangzeb's oldest son Muhammad Sultan (the Deccan). Around the same time, Shah Jahan engaged in secret negotiations with Muhammad Sultan to try to persuade him to abandon his father and accept the Deccan as his patrimony. Meanwhile another agreement to partition the empire was signed in early May 1658 by Dara Shukoh and Shuja'. Under its terms, Shuja' would get Bengal, Orissa, and parts of Bihar, leaving the rest of the empire to Dara Shukoh. In July 1658, Aurangzeb improved on that offer. He extended the same terms with the additional carrot of all of Bihar.

---

[24] 'Inayat Khan, *'Inayatnama*, British Library, Ethe 411, ff. 38b-40b.

Ultimately, Aurangzeb's victory over his brothers (Dara Shukoh and Murad were executed in 1659 and 1661 respectively; Shuja' disappeared in Burma in the early 1660s) meant that the empire was never divided. Whereas the schemes to partition the empire might be offered as evidence of the continued echo of Chaghatai-Timurid ideals into the seventeenth century, in fact, the notion of an indivisible empire prevailed.

During Aurangzeb's long reign, from 1658 to 1707, he actively reaffirmed Mughal succession practices as they had evolved since Akbar's reign. For instance, he rotated most of his sons (and later grandsons) between provincial and military assignments. The one exception was his youngest son, Kam Bakhsh, in whose leadership skills Aurangzeb had little confidence. Unlike the favor shown Dara Shukoh, however, Kam Bakhsh's permanent presence at the imperial court appears to have generated little anxiety on the part of his brothers because this prince did not receive all the honors and privileges that had been bestowed upon his uncle. Like previous emperors, Aurangzeb tried to keep his sons geographically separated, mostly to prevent conflicts. Especially toward the end of his life, Aurangzeb even went so far as to carve out areas of influence for each of his sons. After his son Mu'azzam's release from prison in 1695 (following a treasonous attempt to undermine Mughal war goals in the Deccan), he and his sons largely dominated the empire's northwestern provinces and Bengal: A'zam and his sons were dominant in Gujarat, Malwa, Rajasthan, and northern parts of the Deccan. Kam Bakhsh was given nominal authority over parts of Bijapur and Golkonda.

Aurangzeb gave his own stamp to the unfolding succession practices of the Mughals. Like Babur, Humayun, Akbar, and Shah Jahan before him, he accorded his oldest available son the honor of being considered the most important among the empire's princes.[25] Unlike earlier generations of rulers, however, he moved toward making it a more clearly honorific position. Thus, after renaming Mu'azzam his nominal heir following his release from prison in 1695, Aurangzeb permanently removed him from the imperial court. Between 1695 and Aurangzeb's death in 1707,

---

[25] At the beginning of Aurangzeb's reign, his oldest son Muhammad Sultan was his acknowledged heir. He was disqualified, however, when he switched sides to support his uncle Shuja' during the last phase of the war of succession. Subsequently, Aurangzeb anointed his second son Mu'azzam. Mu'azzam would hold this position until his own removal in 1687, after it was revealed that he had plotted to undermine the Mughal conquest of Golkonda. During the years of Mu'azzam's imprisonment between 1687 and 1695, Aurangzeb's third son A'zam was his father's nominal heir apparent. But the position reverted back to Mu'azzam upon his release.

Mu'azzam served in northern India and was never allowed to return to the imperial court, despite a number of requests to do so in the early 1700s. Aurangzeb thus undercut any advantage Mu'azzam may have accrued vis-à-vis his princely rivals. In fact, when Aurangzeb died in 1707, Mu'azzam's status offered him no edge over his primary rival A'zam. To the contrary, the smart money was on A'zam to succeed to the Mughal throne. Although remaining true to the tradition of maintaining a nominal heir, Aurangzeb appears to have sought to avoid unduly favoring one son over another. Such caution likely had its roots in what Aurangzeb judged to be the mistakes of his father. Indeed, Aurangzeb often blamed his father's overt favoritism of Dara Shukoh for Shah Jahan's downfall.[26] Despite his precautions, Aurangzeb was not entirely successful in circumventing accusations of favoring one son over another as witnessed by his rebellious fourth son Akbar's stinging rebuke (see Introduction).

Aurangzeb faced a unique challenge among Mughal emperors. His long life meant that besides having three politically competing sons in 1700 (Mu'azzam, A'zam, and Kam Bakhsh) and a fourth, Akbar, living in exile in Iran but always threatening to renew his claim to the throne in the event of Aurangzeb's death, he also had nine adult grandsons to consider. By the time of his death in 1707, his adult great-grandsons would begin supplementing the princely ranks as well. Aurangzeb offered them all an active stake in the Mughal system. Whether inadvertently or by design, this stoked intergenerational tensions (see Chapter 7). It also ensured an exceptionally crowded political stage for the Mughal succession.

Returning to an earlier point about Aurangzeb's willingness to work with, but also modulate, imperial succession practices, we see evidence of the same approach in his dealings with collateral branches of the royal family. Thus, although he did order the murder of Dara Shukoh's oldest son, Sulaiman Shukoh, who had commanded armies in his own right during the 1657–9 war of succession, other nephews or more distant relations did not suffer so harsh a fate. Although he did keep the surviving sons of Dara Shukoh and Murad under close supervision for the duration of their lives, he also offered them annual stipends and, on special occasions, gifts. More significantly, Aurangzeb contracted marriages between those princes and his own daughters. For instance, Dara Shukoh's sole surviving son, Siphr Shukoh, was married to Aurangzeb's daughter

---

[26] Aurangzeb, *Anecdotes of Aurangzib*, trans. Jadunath Sarkar (Calcutta, repr. 1988), 37, 44, 45, 48–9.

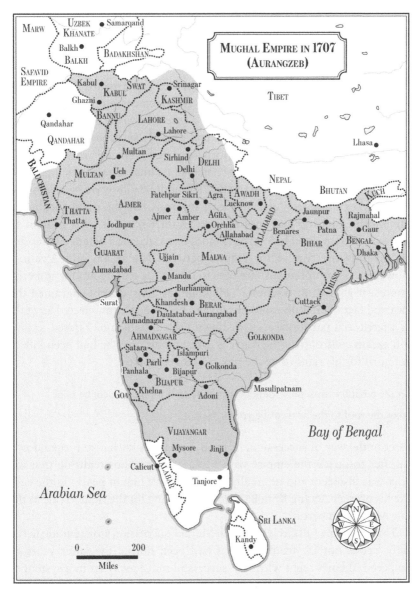

Mughal Empire in 1707 (Aurangzeb)

Zubdat-un-Nisa. Another daughter, Mehr-un-Nisa, was married to Murad's son Izid Bakhsh. The latter had at least two sons – Dawar Bakhsh and Dadar Bakhsh – who occasionally appear in the historical record as having received imperial favors in the early 1700s.

Aurangzeb's generally benevolent treatment toward the extended Mughal family, his willingness to allow those daughters who had no political ambitions to marry, and his refusal to mutilate sons who rebelled against him highlight his attempt to step back from the worst excesses of the previous few generations of Mughal succession. Toward the end of his life, Aurangzeb even tried to broker an agreement among his sons to partition the empire. This appears to be a reversion to the appanage system and signaled Aurangzeb's resolve to end princely succession struggles for the empire. Significantly, these efforts occurred while he was still in full political charge. According to the contents of a final testament supposedly written in Aurangzeb's own hand and left under a pillow on his deathbed, the emperor implored "whichever of my sons has the good fortune of gaining the kingship" to "not trouble" Kam Bakhsh if he is content to rule over Bijapur and Hyderabad. It goes on to suggest a detailed blueprint for dividing the rest of the empire between Mu'azzam and A'zam.[27] However, as with previous attempts to divide the empire among imperial princes, it gained no traction.[28] Highlighting how deeply engrained the idea and fact of an indivisible empire had become, A'zam rejected any talk of a territorial partition, even writing a verse in which he offered to give Mu'azzam control over the heavens (presumably after he had been killed) in return for his right to be the next Mughal emperor:

Let the territory from the ground floor to the roof [of the palace] be mine

From the roof to the heavens be yours.[29]

Later in the war of succession, in 1708–9, Kam Bakhsh also turned down an offer to divide the empire with Mu'azzam, perhaps realizing that the offer was insincere and not really meant to leave him in peace. In the end, like his brother A'zam, Kam Bakhsh died fighting for the right to rule as the sole Mughal emperor.

Thus we come full circle, with the Mughal succession story ending in the early 1700s not far from where it had been during the latter years of Emperor Akbar's reign when the successful move away from a system of princely appanages had taken place. The idea of a single emperor ruling

---

[27] Aurangzeb, *Dastur-ul-'Amal-i Agahi*, National Library of India, Sarkar Collection 70, f. 49b. Also reproduced in Jadunath Sarkar, *History of Aurangzib*, vol. 5 (Calcutta, repr. 1952), 213.

[28] Ni'mat Khan, *Jangnama*, ed. Khwaja Muhammad Isa (Kanpur, 1884), 14.

[29] Kamwar Khan, *Tazkirat us-Salatin Chaghta*, ed. Muzaffar Alam (Aligarh, 1980), 11–12.

over a unified empire had become too deeply engrained to change. Indeed, even as the effective power of the emperor waned in the eighteenth century and he came under the direct protection or control of other political groups, there was broad acceptance that the political sovereignty of the Mughal emperor was indivisible and to be handed down to only one person from within the imperial family.

## CONCLUSION

The rules and norms of the succession of Mughal princes may have been continuously modulated over the course of the sixteenth and seventeenth centuries, but the principle of an open-ended system was never called into serious question. It was the central dynamic that shaped the lives and activities of generations of Mughal princes. Succession politics formed the backdrop against which all manner of activities – including organizing princely households, building and leveraging networks of friends and allies, and resorting to disobedience and rebellion – occurred. The next chapter turns to the reigns of Babur and Humayun in order to explore in detail how Mughal princes fared before the transformations by which Akbar made the Mughal project truly imperial.

# 2

# The Early Years, 1504–1556

This chapter explores the dynamics of princely households, alliance building, princely disobedience, and succession struggles between 1504 and 1556, corresponding to the reigns of emperors Babur and Humayun. During this early period of the empire, steppe political traditions framed expectations that each adult male family member of a ruler was entitled to some share of the Mughal patrimony. These royals were not so much contenders for a single throne as rivals who ruled over semi-autonomous territories. As such, they ran independent households that drew on their territorial resources, and they enjoyed relative political independence. In this early period, alliance building was crucial, but it often centered on people within individual appanages. A well-networked prince who could draw on allies in times of strife and win friends away from his opponents thrived.

At the same time, because the steppe political tradition invested power across the entire ruling family or clan, the emperor was little more than a first-among-equals, and issues of disobedience or rebellion against the imperial court were not as charged as they became after the 1580s. High-ranking family members would be granted many opportunities to repent their overreaching or other errors of political judgment before being punished. Against this backdrop, princes such as Humayun felt fairly free to express open opposition to imperial authority and to behave in ways that would become unacceptable by the late sixteenth century. Indeed, with this degree of political latitude, princes in this period had little incentive or need to engage in outright rebellion. It was only later, during the reign of Emperor Akbar, when the imperial court began placing real constraints on princely ambition, that the conditions for rebellion were fostered. As this chapter demonstrates, we can see early traces of this shift with Emperor Humayun, who attempted to promulgate a language of obedience and showed gradually diminishing tolerance for challenges from other royals. The conflict between Humayun and his brother Mirza Kamran is illustrative, and Mirza Kamran presents an interesting transitional figure in the emergence of the post-1580s Mughal Prince.

## INDEPENDENT HOUSEHOLDS AND ALLIANCE BUILDING

Adult Mughal heirs prior to Akbar's reign were largely able to finance their own households and thus enjoyed relative political independence and a fairly secure material base. It is only with Akbar's reforms between the 1570s and 1590s that a system emerged wherein all members of the royal family and nobility were ranked numerically, earning a specific stipend, and thus drawn into a centralized imperial hierarchy. Underpinning and enabling the endeavors of the early heirs were the territorial units or appanages (referred to in Timurid sources as *ulus* and in later Mughal historical accounts as *jagir*) over which they exercised permanent and largely unsupervised control.

Thus, after granting Badakhshan as an appanage to his oldest son Humayun in 1519, Emperor Babur abandoned all but nominal authority over the region. Appanages afforded Mughal heirs independent access to a variety of revenue sources. These included taxes on agricultural products or goods passing through their territory alongside individual exactions, gifts, and loans from prominent figures living within their territory (who either willingly or otherwise exchanged money or goods for protection). Beyond these sources, royals also depended on tribute payments from subjugated groups and on military expeditions whose sole purpose was to raise cash. There is little record of what later became the expectation that an emperor would subsidize a prince's day-to-day expenses out of resources drawn from other parts of the empire.[1] Most income raised in a Mughal appanage was the appanage holder's to generate, and to keep or spend as he wished.

---

[1] A late 1520s communication between Babur and Humayun points to one exception: when the emperor was organizing a military campaign that might have placed an inordinate strain on his sons' or brothers' limited resources, he was willing to make a cash payment. Zahir-ud-Din Muhammad Babur, *The Baburnama: Memoirs of Babur, Prince and Emperor*, trans. W. M. Thackston (New York, 2002), p. 423.

No records survive from this period that indicate exactly how money raised in an appanage was dispensed, but it is safe to assume that the bulk of it went to maintaining the prince's household. Household expenses included those of the domestic sphere as well as of administration and military rule. As in other patrimonial kingdoms, and preceding the modern split between public and private, these sets of expenditures were viewed as the normal expenses of a unified royal household enterprise.[2]

Thanks to their appanages and the income generated from them, male royals were relatively independent from the emperor, whose position as first-among-equals was fragile. In this early period, a Mughal emperor could be stymied by a recalcitrant family member: for several years after his conquests in northern India, Babur complained that Humayun had not sent any fresh troops from Badakhshan despite repeated requests; as emperor, Humayun in turn failed to gain Mirza Kamran's crucial support in fending off the threat posed by the Afghan adventurer Sher Khan Suri when the latter directly threatened the continuity of Mughal rule in the late 1530s and early 1540s. Even Akbar spent decades after his accession in 1556 warding off political challenges from his Kabul-based half brother Mirza Hakim; it took a full-scale military campaign and the invasion of Kabul in 1581–2 to finally defang him.

Although early male members of the Mughal emperor's family, both sons and brothers, enjoyed the relative political and economic independence of the appanage system, their independence was hardly secure. They had to be ever vigilant in protecting their territory and faced continual and countless enemies, especially embittered clansmen seeking to expand their own authority. In this milieu, Mughal royals learned the importance of cultivating supporters. Babur himself, during the decades he spent fighting his Timurid clansmen across southern Central Asia, suffered many disappointments and betrayals and came to appreciate the particular importance of winning loyalty.[3] "It was difficult for me," he wrote in his

---

[2] For a fuller discussion of the features of a patrimonial kingdom and its Weberian intellectual antecedents, see Stephen Blake, *Shahjahanabad: The Sovereign City in Mughal India, 1639–1739* (Cambridge, 1991), pp. 17–19. See also Jurgen Habermas, *Structural Transformation of the Public Sphere* (Cambridge, 1989), who argues that the emergence of the modern state in Europe was marked by the gradual separation of household finances from administrative and military finances; thus, an increasingly clean divide between private and public came to replace a more overlapping medieval financial system.

[3] In his memoirs, the *Baburnama*, Babur continuously bemoans the lack of family accord. In the context of a testy visit in 1506 to his cousins in Herat, he wrote, "Although I was young in years, my rank was nonetheless high. Twice by dint of the sword I had recaptured and sat

autobiography, referring to the time when he had been deserted by those he had seen as close supporters, "I wept involuntarily."[4] He further wrote of how, despite these trials, he remained resilient, ambitious, and ultimately optimistic that he could remake his fortunes and grow a new circle of supporters. "When one has pretensions to rule," he went on, "and a desire for conquest, one cannot sit back and just watch if events do not go right once or twice."[5]

Sure enough, following Babur's capture of Kabul in 1504, he honed his expertise at building alliances and managing conflicts. He set about granting fiefs in an effort to win and retain allies. He invited tribes and clans that had been displaced by the surging Uzbeks to come and settle in regions under his control. Babur rewarded his fractious Timurid relatives when they served him well. He cultivated the surrounding Afghan tribes by forging marriage links with the Yusufzai, befriending the ruling clan in Swat, and inviting Dilazai tribal heads to discuss military matters and share in the spoils of his raids into India. Babur also resorted to brutality when opposed. He enslaved women and children, erected skull towers of the defeated, and had his enemies impaled. He destroyed crops and rounded up livestock to starve opponents.[6] Over the next two decades, up to his departure for India in 1525–6, he built up a diverse coalition of allies in Kabul through a combination of benefaction, intimidation, and vengeance. Besides Timurids and Afghans, these allies included Uzbeks, Badakhshanis, Hazaras, Chaghatais, Mughals, sundry other Turko-Mongol groups, Tajiks, Baluch, Ghakkars, Janjuas, and even the occasional Hindu. Kabul offered Babur a fresh start, and he never looked back. Many of the political skills Babur learned during his two decades in Kabul were put to extensive use when he conquered northern India.

---

on my ancestral throne in Samarkand. Who had fought with foreigners and rebels for the sake of the dynasty as I had done? To delay in honoring me was inexcusable." Babur, *The Baburnama*, p. 224. See also Maria E. Subtelny, "Babur's Rival Relations: A Study of Kinship and Conflict in 15th–16th Century Central Asia," *Islam* 66, no. 1 (1989): 101–18.

[4] Babur, *The Baburnama*, p. 67.

[5] Ibid.

[6] One gets the sense that Babur's application of extreme violence in the pursuit of political goals was simultaneously motivated by a desire to crush his enemies as well as to evoke such sanguinary and fearful ancestors as Chingiz Khan and Amir Timur. Regarding the latter and the use of violence as "theatrical demonstrations of power," see Beatrice Manz, "Tamerlane's Career and Its Uses," *Journal of World History* 13, no. 1 (2002): 4–5. See also Manz, *The Rise and Rule of Tamerlane* (New York, 1999).

Babur receiving the capitulation of Kabul in 910 H (A.D. 1504), ca. 1590 or earlier (Freer Gallery of Art, Smithsonian Institution, Washington D.C.: Purchase, F1945.27)

Babur immediately set about rebuilding the same networks of political and military support that had enabled his prior survival in Kabul. Thus, edicts were issued that read as follows:

All those who come seeking our employment will be greatly rewarded but particularly those who have served our fathers and forefathers. If they come, they will receive great favor. And those who are of the lineage of Sahib-i Qiran [i.e., Tamerlane] and Chengiz Khan, let them set out for our court [in Agra]. God has granted the realms of Hindustan (*mamalik-i Hindustan*) to us. Let them come so we may see prosperity together.[7]

But Babur also described tackling new kinds of challenges as he worked to impose and secure his authority over the population. His autobiography reveals the marked distinction he saw between his prior array of allies and the people he met in India. He had "no great reliance upon the people of Hindustan" and described how a "strange antagonism and hatred was felt between our soldiers and the natives."[8] These "natives," however, were a varied population, and in time Babur found allies. Thus, sources reveal several Indian-Afghan and "India officers" (likely non-Afghan Indian Muslims) as well as Indian Muslim religious luminaries in and around the Mughal camps (likely hoping for imperial patronage).[9] Babur's visits to various sacred sites, including the shrines of Nizam-ud-Din Auliya' in Delhi and Shaikh Yahya Maneri in Bihar, and his decision to exempt Indian Muslims from paying certain taxes hint at a growing dependence on sections of this population. Political outreach was not entirely restricted to Muslims, however. We see this in Babur's willingness to reach a political settlement with members of Rana Sangha's Rajput clan following their defeat at the Battle of Khanua in 1527, as well as interactions with other powerful non-Muslim landholding groups including the Baghelas of Bhatta, Bachgotis of Awadh, and Purbias of Malwa.[10]

For help in going further afield in his alliance building exercises, Babur turned early on to his sons. When he presented Badakhshan to Humayun, the expectation was that his oldest son would anchor Babur's authority in that region while also serving as an overlord and patron for politically ambitious locals. Unfortunately, information about Humayun's initial six-year stint in the region is scant. Yet, the inability of Uzbeks to pry the region from Mughal control, the lack of any record of internal revolts, and Humayun's ability to recruit a sizable and loyal contingent of Badakhshanis to serve under him during the early stages of the Indian campaign all speak to the prince's success at winning over the most prominent actors and groups of the region. Humayun's reluctance to leave Badakhshan in the fall of 1525 and his willingness to return in the summer of 1527 also hint at how securely he was ensconced there. Yet in a

---

[7] Gulbadan Begum, *Ahwal-i Humayun Badshah*, British Library, Ms. Or. 166, f. 11a.

[8] Babur, *The Baburnama*, pp. 356, 377.

[9] Ibid., pp. 356, 363.

[10] Iqtidar Alam Khan, "State in Mughal India: Re-examining the Myths of a Counter-vision," *Social Scientist* 30, no. 1–2 (2001): 20.

world of fluid and crosscutting familial and tribal loyalties, gaining influence was a process of continual cultivation. Consequently, there was no question of resting on one's laurels.

Thus, in 1528, when Babur began to receive troubling reports in India that Humayun was neglecting one of his central duties as an appanage holder by withdrawing from the people around him, the emperor became very distressed. (Ishwari Prasad speculates that the young prince was depressed and increasingly addicted to opium.[11]) In a letter – recorded by Babur in his memoirs – the emperor advised his son that "solitude is a flaw in kingship. . . . In kingship it is improper to seek solitude." He went on to encourage Humayun to mingle, consult, and follow through on the advice of certain high-ranking and experienced nobles. Babur concluded by pleading with Humayun: "If you want to make me happy, stop sitting by yourself and avoiding people."[12] Babur's entreaties suggest that for him, Humayun's reluctance to maintain an active public persona posed an immediate and dangerous threat to the Mughals' ability to control Badakhshan in the face of continuing Uzbek threats.

Babur was better served by his second son, Mirza Kamran, who, mostly stationed in Kabul and Multan, built a coalition of Timurid, Chaghatai, and Hazara allies and also brought Afghan and Sindhi chiefs to his standard. As long as Babur was alive, Mirza Kamran worked hard to project the emperor's authority over an extremely turbulent part of the empire. Acknowledging his son's efforts, Babur never expressed any disappointment in Mirza Kamran. The placement of Babur's sons and other close male relatives in regions where he was absent highlights the importance of their efforts to build influence and coalesce power in their appanages. By attending carefully to relations with them, Babur maintained some semblance of control over a rapidly expanding territory to which the term "empire" had become increasingly applicable.

Unfortunately, this skill did not appear to transfer to Humayun, who succeeded his father in 1530. Humayun simply did not inspire the loyalty of his brothers – Mirza Kamran, Mirza 'Askari, and Mirza Hindal or that of their supporters. Compounding Humayun's political difficulties, the Mughal nobility did not treat him with the same regard as they did his father. Given that he had spent a total of only three years at the imperial court between 1519 and 1530, his absence may have impacted his ability to mobilize strong support. In a clear signal of political weakness, he issued

---

[11] Ishwari Prasad, *The Life and Times of Humayun* (Calcutta, 1956), p. 22.

[12] Babur, *The Baburnama*, pp. 423–4.

proclamations allowing his brothers' appanages to continue unchanged or even be expanded. Of the nobility, he said, "Let each keep the office, and service, and lands, and residence which he has had, and let him serve in the old way."[13] These moves did nothing to bolster his influence.

Unlike Babur, Humayun never succeeded in getting the most powerful members of the nobility, his relatives, or his brothers – the most important appanage holders of his empire – to consistently channel local and regional loyalty upward to him. Furthermore – and this is especially true of his three brothers – they only barely acknowledged him as the prime leader among leaders. Consequently, Humayun's access to the most important resources of state formation – money, men, and information – was always more severely constrained and dependent on the goodwill of others than was true for Babur, whose personal charisma and prestige as the founder of an expanding kingdom allowed him to overcome such difficulties.

Humayun's hold on the empire finally collapsed in 1540 after his brother Mirza Kamran refused to provide military assistance in the fight against Sher Khan Suri. Mirza Kamran's refusal led to a showdown with Emperor Humayun over Kabul, the last substantial territory still under Mughal control and the center of Kamran's appanage. Following on the heels of the empire's collapse in India, that struggle lasted more than a decade and temporarily hamstrung any possibility of a return strike against the ascendant Suri dynasty.[14] Indeed, Humayun's initial weakness vis-à-vis Mirza Kamran is a perfect illustration of the importance of allies and the vulnerability of a ruler who was either unwilling or unable to win broad support.

In this early period, as the stories of Babur, Humayun, and Mirza Kamran reveal, a ruler had to be adept at cultivating ties and managing webs of influence. Whereas Humayun showed himself less than capable on this front in the decade after inheriting Babur's position, his brother had steadily built his own power base across the northwestern territories of the Mughal Empire (see the next section in this chapter). Mirza Kamran was able to challenge his theoretical overlord and brother Humayun in 1540 precisely because of his own success in this regard and the emperor's failure.

Humayun ultimately prevailed in the struggle against Mirza Kamran, but he suffered many setbacks before doing so. When Humayun finally stamped

---

[13] Gulbadan, *Ahwal-i Humayun Badshah*, f. 20b. See also Khwandamir, *Qanun-i-Humayuni*, ed. M. Hidayat Hosain (Calcutta, 1940), p. 24.

[14] Iqtidar Alam Khan, *Mirza Kamran* (Bombay, 1964), pp. 18–19.

his authority over Mirza's former appanage in the early 1550s, he did so the old-fashioned way: first by preying on the bases of support his brother Mirza Kamran had spent years building in Kabul, and then by fostering his own alliances and improving his management of social networks.

Given the ever-shifting tenor of relations between Babur and his sons, and between Humayun and other family members, we can identify the foundations of empire taking shape from within a warring and expanding clan system. Over the course of Humayun's reign, as the next section lays out, we see the first systematic attempts to articulate an ideology in support of an empowered emperor. The necessary close supervision of possible royal challengers required a change in relations both between father and son and between royal brothers.

## FROM STEPPE RULE TO AN IMPERIAL DISPENSATION

Babur and Humayun may have enjoyed a warm and loving relationship while the latter was still a child. But any affection evaporated in the years following Humayun's dispatch to Badakhshan (1519). Their drifting apart is apparent from the unusual silences in otherwise loquacious Mughal accounts. It is also attested to by Humayun's decision to temporarily ignore his father's summons to Kabul to participate in the long-planned invasion of India in 1525–6. Babur's anger is clearly registered in his memoir, the *Baburnama*. The emperor noted that he sent his son "harshly worded letters." When Humayun finally did arrive, his father gave him an earful: "I rebuked him quite a lot for being so late."[15] This was not the end of Humayun's misbehavior, however. Although the historical sources are careful to not offer us any examples of Humayun's troublemaking over the next few years, we know that Babur had grown tired enough of his son's errant behavior to transfer him and his contingents out of India and back to Badakhshan in 1527. Although Babur explained his action by claiming that the Badakhshanis were exhausted from constant fighting, that Kabul was undermanned, and that he had made a prior promise to release the Badakhshanis once northern India was successfully conquered, these seem to be nothing more than excuses. For instance, the suggestion that Babur was concerned about Kabul's vulnerability is suspect given that he was sending letters "in all directions" at that time pleading for additional troops to come to India.[16] There clearly was little warmth left between

[15] Babur, *The Baburnama*, p. 310.
[16] Gulbadan, *Ahwal-i Humayun Badshah*, f. 11a.

father and son. Indeed, the *Baburnama* records the emperor's greater interest in exploring the hot springs of Ferozpur than in bidding farewell to Humayun on the eve of his removal from India.[17]

Babur's displeasure toward his son was matched by Humayun's irritation at his father's decision to remove him from India. On his march out, Humayun sacked Delhi's imperial treasury. Babur was shocked at this gross affront. Writing in the *Baburnama*, he exclaimed, "I would never have expected such a thing from him! It was difficult for me to believe. I wrote him some extremely harsh letters of reproach."[18]

Over the next year, relations between father and son deteriorated further as Humayun lurched between quiet petulance and outright disobedience. Humayun not only failed to send any fresh troops to India, but also began stoking tensions with his younger brother Mirza Kamran. By 1529, relations between Babur and Humayun had almost reached a breaking point. Realizing this, Humayun decided to head back to India, presumably to beg forgiveness. There was just one problem: he did so without having been summoned first. Babur did not take kindly to the surprise visit, and beyond noting that Humayun's gifts were put on public display on his arrival at the imperial court in Agra, the *Baburnama* is completely silent about the prince and his reception.[19]

Nonetheless, as on previous occasions of princely disobedience and misconduct, Babur refrained from openly punishing his errant son or undermining his political stature. At its heart, Babur's overall tolerance speaks to the corporate nature of Mughal elite politics in the early sixteenth century. Despite assuming the exalted title of *padshah* (emperor) in 1508, Babur's political behavior was still very much that of a big man in a steppe-based warrior band. He was informal and egalitarian in his leadership and ruled through direct personal relationships. As both Stephen Dale and Ruby Lal have observed, in the early Mughal period, there was an ever-present assumption that political loyalties were fluid.[20] It was the emperor's role to cajole and win support through working toward a common position.

Against this backdrop, it is worth considering, if briefly, the place of the *Baburnama* in the larger exercise of power by Babur. Stephen Dale has

[17] Babur, *The Baburnama*, pp. 396–7.

[18] Ibid., p. 399.

[19] Ibid., p. 458.

[20] Ruby Lal, *Domesticity and Power in the Early Mughal World* (Cambridge, 2005), pp. 71–81; Stephen Dale, *The Garden of the Eight Paradises: Babur and the Culture of Empire in Central Asia, Afghanistan and India (1483–1530)* (Leiden, 2004), pp. 187–246.

suggested that the text's "legitimizing audience" were "Islamized, literate, Turki-speaking Timurid and Chaghatay Mongol elite, and beyond them, the broader society of Turco-Mongol military aristocrats."[21] I fully agree and would add only that the text is also a lecture and series of pronouncements directed at his immediate family and especially his adult sons that derive from Babur's vision of proper imperial leadership. This is evidenced in the powerful didactic quality that hangs over the entire text. Learn from my example, Babur seems to be saying, both to avoid my early mistakes and benefit from my later successes. Then there are the admonishments to be more effective or worthy leaders of men. We see an example of Babur speaking as much to his sons as to the larger audience when he quotes the entire text of a letter to Humayun in the *Baburnama*. It is an irascible letter he wrote toward the end of 1528. In it, he attacked his son personally, chiding that "indolence and luxury do not suit kingship." He also criticized Humayun's choice of a name for a recently born son, dismissed Humayun's complaint about his loneliness in Badakhshan, disapproved of Humayun's writing style as "excessively obscure," and chastised him for his laziness in writing letters.[22] Nonetheless, such episodes in the text offer evidence of Babur's commitment to maintaining an alliance with his son, no matter what. His words and actions together reveal an emperor who, for all his military achievements, fully understood that his power remained extremely fragile and liable to fracture if tested by great demands on loyalty and submission. Ultimately, Babur always restrained himself from wreaking extravagant or public punishments on Humayun despite the fact that his son was repeatedly disobedient and failed him on a number of crucial occasions.

Despite the stench of failure that generally hangs over it, Humayun's reign marks the first real attempt to transition the Mughal Empire from a steppe-inspired approach to unruly family members to a system less tolerant of dissident princes and more interested in the image of a strong dynastic ruler. It is possible that Humayun's efforts grew out of his perception of his political and military weakness in relation to his appanage-holding and independent-minded brothers.

Through the 1530s, Humayun strove to augment his authority vis-à-vis his obstreperous nobles and relatives. Of particular note was his cultivation of Indian Muslims as counterweights to the overwhelmingly Central Asian Mughal nobility. In this effort, Humayun departed from Babur's

[21] Dale, *The Garden of Eight Paradises*, p. 41.
[22] Babur, *The Baburnama*, pp. 422–4.

earlier example. Although Babur willingly accommodated Indian Muslims in his army, he never welcomed them into his inner circle. Babur's idea of empire remained wholly Timurid in its influences, with Mongols and Turks at the political helm, Naqshbandis as the dominant Sufi order, and Heratis and Khurasanis dominating its cultural sphere.[23] By contrast, Humayun enticed prominent Indians such as Shaikh Bahlul into his service. The Shaikh came from a highly respected family and was a prominent member of the India-based Shattari Sufi order. By the late 1530s, he had become Humayun's closest political and religious advisor and was a key enforcer of the emperor's will. The following incident testifies to the emperor's confidence in him: when the emperor received news in 1538–9 that his youngest brother was planning a rebellion, Humayun dispatched the Shaikh to parry Mirza Hindal's machinations. The threat that Shaikh Bahlul posed to Mirza Hindal (and the general resentment the rise of Indian Muslims had stirred among the Mughal nobility) can be gauged by the prince's decision to execute the Shaikh on the false charge of colluding with Humayun's Afghan enemies.[24] Shaikh Bahlul's murder and the collapse of Humayun's rule in India the following year put any further efforts to woo Indian Muslims on hold for more than a decade. And in the end, Mirza Hindal was never punished for Shaikh Bahlul's murder.

From Humayun's accession in 1530 through the remainder of the decade, the emperor was repeatedly confronted by and forced to tolerate blatant princely misbehavior in the form of obstruction of orders, failure to follow orders, desertion from campaigns, attacks on his followers, and disrespect toward his person. Among the princes, Humayun's brother Mirza Kamran was foremost in his display of disobedience and disrespect. As early as 1531, Mirza Kamran struck out, forcibly occupying the Punjab against the express wishes of Humayun and replacing military officers loyal to the emperor with his own appointees. He also stopped most revenue flows to the imperial coffers. Through the 1530s, Mizra Kamran bolstered his credibility as a semi-independent ruler in various ways: he parried a number of Safavid

---

[23] Emphasizing the point that Babur's frame of reference was still largely southern Central Asia (Mawarannahr) was his decision to compose his autobiography in Chaghatai Turkish during the final years of his life in India. As Stephen Dale reminds us, this text makes clear that Babur "envisioned his Indian period as a brief, unpleasant sojourn. ... He always thought of himself as a Turco-Mongol, Central Asian conqueror of India, not as an Indian ruler." Dale, *The Garden of Eight Paradises*, p. 149.

[24] Ahmad Yadgar, *Tarikh-i Shahi*, trans. Saiyid Nazir Niyazi (Lahore, 1985), pp. 153–4; Gulbadan, *Ahwal-i Humayun Badshah*, f. 32b; Shaikh Abu'l Fazl, *Akbarnamah*, ed. Abdul Rahim, vol. 1 (Calcutta, 1878), pp. 154–6.

attacks on Qandahar, attacked northern Rajasthan, tried (but failed) to conquer Kashmir, put down a series of Hazara-led revolts, and prevented a distantly related Timurid rebel (Muhammad Zaman Mirza) from seizing Lahore. As his political stature grew, Mirza Kamran attracted important networks of support – military men such as Mirza Haidar Dughlat and powerful noblemen from Babur's reign such as Khwaja Kalan and Mahdi Khwaja – to himself and away from his brother the emperor.[25]

Mirza Kamran's rising political ambitions are especially evident in his dealings with the Naqshbandi *tariqa* (order), a rich and influential Sufi order whose dominance and involvement in politics extended back to the 1300s. In contrast to most other Sufi orders, and following their own particular doctrine of social immersion and participation (*khalwat dar anjuman*), the Naqshbandis did not hesitate to wield their clout and influence with political leaders.[26] Following in his father Babur's footsteps, Mirza Kamran became a devotee of the order. His ability to stay on good footing with different branches of the Naqshbandi (notably the Ahraris and the Dehbedis) helped cement Naqshbandi support for the prince for a time.

Between 1540 and 1552, Humayun repeatedly attempted to supplant Mirza Kamran in the northwest. The tide began to slowly shift against the prince in the mid-1540s. Humayun's comeback was launched by his military support, in the form of more than ten thousand cavalrymen, provided by Tahmasp I, the ruler of Safavid Iran. With Safavid help, Humayun first broke Mirza Kamran's hold over the strategic fortress of Qandahar and then parlayed his growing strength to seize Kabul, his brother's capital.

After taking Kabul, Humayun moved rapidly to mend relations with the Naqshbandis by confirming their *waqf*s (tax-free charitable holdings). Humayun also ensured future Naqshbandi obedience by removing Khwaja 'Abd-ul-Haq, Mirza Kamran's *pir* (religious preceptor), from his powerful position as the custodian of the Naqshbandi holdings in the region. Khwaja Khawand Mahmud, an older brother and likely rival for control over the Kabul-based Ahrari lineage, was installed in his place. Khwaja Khawand and his sons repaid Humayun's favor by staunchly supporting his efforts to establish his power over the next few years.[27]

---

[25] Khan, *Mirza Kamran*, pp. 8–14.

[26] Hamid Algar, "The Naqshbandi Order: A Preliminary Survey of Its History and Significance," *Studia Islamica* 44 (1976): 137–8.

[27] Mirza Sharaf-ud-Din Husain Ahrari, a grandson of Khwaja Khawand, came to India from Kashgar in 1557. By the early 1560s, he had become one of Akbar's highest ranking nobles and a brother-in-law of the emperor. But he rebelled against Akbar in 1563, and the next seventeen years – until his death – were mostly spent supporting various rebels

Mirza 'Askari submits to Humayun, ca. 1603–4 (British Library, OR 12988, Akbarnama Folio 106r)

Having dismantled Mirza Kamran's Naqshbandi base, Humayun chipped away at his half brother's remaining networks of support. Thus, Humayun targeted the Mirza's supporters within the Mughal family: he executed Yadgar Nasir Mirza, a first cousin, in 1546 after catching him in secret communication with Mirza Kamran, and he sent another half brother, Mirza 'Askari, into exile following his capture in 1550. Mirza

against Akbar. Shah Nawaz Khan, *Maasiru-l-Umara*, ed. Ashraf Ali, vol. 3 (Calcutta, 1891), pp. 232–8. See also Stephen Dale and Alam Payind, "The Ahrari *waqf* in Kabul and the Mughul Naqshbandiyya," *Journal of the American Oriental Society* 119, no. 2 (1999): 221.

'Askari had long colluded with Mirza Kamran against Humayun. To further undermine Mirza Kamran's capacity to resist, Humayun sealed marriage alliances with the Uzbeks as well as the distantly related Mirzas of Badakhshan. He also wooed Hazara and Afghan chiefs with gifts, money, and positions of honor at the reconstituted Mughal court. Finally, in 1553, Mirza Kamran was defeated, captured, blinded, and sent off to Mecca where he died in 1557.[28]

Babur is always called the first Mughal emperor; yet, as we have seen, his rule was fundamentally that of a steppe clan leader, albeit a notably triumphant one. It was during the reign of his son Humayun, and then decisively in the later struggle between Humayun's sons Mirza Hakim and Akbar, that we see an emerging imperial dispensation that would shape future Mughal rulership. Despite Humayun's poor start, chronicles from his reign point to his early attempts at crafting the figure of a dominant emperor. The subsequent conflict between his sons (see Chapter 3) illustrates how, once princes had to compete over an emerging empire, political image and persona increasingly gained in importance. It was during Humayun's reign that we discover the beginnings of this shift. In the next section, we consider important rhetorical projects undertaken by early imperial commentators and supporters to craft an image and ideology of an authoritative emperor who was owed loyalty and service, and against whom dissent and insolence were not to be tolerated.

### EMPIRE AND EMPEROR: THE EMERGING IMPORTANCE OF IMAGE

The outline of Humayun's imperial vision can be gleaned from three important contemporary texts: *Tabaqat-i Baburi* (ca. 1531–2), *Qanun-i Humayuni* (1534), and *Tarikh-i Rashidi* (1546). The *Tabaqat-i Baburi*, written by a nobleman of Babur's court, Zain Khan (d. 1533), was completed in the first years of Humayun's reign. It is full of encomiums for the emperor and deals awkwardly with his poor relationship with Babur, suggesting more concern for Humayun's opinion than for Babur's. Thus, Humayun is variously referred to as the "light of the pupils," "the splendor of the garden of justice," "the bud of the salubrious garden of honor and glory," "the phoenix of the highest point of ascent and preferment and exhilaration," and "the dispeller of the darkness of oppression and insurrection," and so on. The text obfuscates Humayun's failure to arrive on time

---

[28] Khan, *Mirza Kamran*, pp. 28–9.

from Badakhshan on the eve of India's invasion in 1526 (breezily suggesting that Humayun's delay was on account of his efforts to raise more troops for Babur in and around Badakhshan). Indeed, Zain Khan exerts considerable effort to portray the relationship between Babur and Humayun as a close one, detailing the celebrations as everyone awaited the prince's arrival from Badakhshan, the delight when he finally turned up – "all of a sudden the rays of the light of felicity began to shine" – and the warm meeting between father and son. Babur's anger is noted in only a few words.[29] Such gentle treatment of a fraught moment between Babur and his son effectively downplays Humayun's disobedience. Why should there be such embarrassment if Babur was himself unwilling to punish his son? Arguably, the *Tabaqat-i Baburi* is trying to set a higher standard of conduct by this glossing over.

More forcefully than the *Tabaqat-i Baburi*, Mirza Dughlat's *Tarikh-i Rashidi*, composed in the mid-1540s when Humayun's conflict with Mirza Kamran was at its worst, depicts Humayun as Babur's obedient and beloved son, aiming to exonerate him of any wrongdoing or disloyalty. In this spirit, it rewrites what we know to be Humayun's abandonment of Badakhshan in 1529. Dughlat suggests that far from abandoning his appanage, Humayun departed for India because the emperor "summoned" his son to have him near, so that a successor could be quickly nominated in case he died. Humayun is then described as sympathetic to pleas from the people of Badakhshan to remain and stave off a possible Uzbek assault. Yet, the prince ultimately concludes that "a royal command [from Babur] cannot be disobeyed."[30] The *Tarikh-i Rashidi* presents us with a loyal and dutiful prince and son departing to help his father in India.

Not only does Mirza Dughlat's text portray Humayun as an obedient son, it also represents Babur as commanding ultimate authority because he is the Mughal emperor. This depiction of a preeminent emperor vis-à-vis other family members is a key development of the period, one that would later be elaborated under Akbar. Thus, Mirza Dughlat writes of the time when the renowned Naqshbandi saint Khwaja Khwand Mahmud came to India in 1535–6. Although Mirza Kamran supposedly begged the Khwaja to stay with him in Lahore and skip the visit to Humayun in Agra, the author pointedly notes that the Khwaja insisted on paying his respects to

---

[29]  Zain Khan, *Tabaqat-i-Baburi*, trans. S. H. Askari (Delhi, 1982), pp. 7–8.
[30]  Mirza Haydar Dughlat, *Tarikh-i-Rashidi*, ed. W. M. Thackston, vol. 1 (Cambridge, MA, 1996), pp. 319–20.

the emperor first. Even the Khwaja believed, writes Mirza Dughlat, in the importance of giving due deference at all times to the *padshah*.[31]

In contrast to the *Tabaqat-i Baburi* and the *Tarikh-i Rashidi*, the *Qanun-i Humayuni* – commissioned by Humayun in 1533 and written by the court-based scholar Khwandamir – entirely avoids his relations with Babur to focus exclusively on Humayun's power and greatness as an emperor. Neither Babur's autobiography – the *Baburnama* – nor the *Tabaqat-i Baburi* engages the same intensity of panegyrics as this text on Humayun. We can argue that it is with Humayun and in the context of threats to his imperial authority that we see the slow emergence of the ideology of a preeminent and powerful emperor. Against the backdrop of real-life political challenges by the emperor's male relatives and the sundry military challenges facing the empire, the *Qanun-i Humayuni* offers a normative, but – as of its writing – unfulfilled, vision of imperial power.

Following an introduction mostly devoted to laying out the attributes and responsibilities of the perfect king, Khwandamir describes the accession of the "deserving" and "all-conquering" Humayun.[32] No longer referred to as a mere *padshah*, as was Babur, but rather as a *padshah-i khilafat panah* (emperor defender of the caliphate), *padshah-i 'ali* (exalted emperor), *padshah-i 'alam* (emperor of the world), and *shahinshah-i nasl-i adam* (emperor of the human race),[33] the emperor is described as offering his largesse and protection to all classes of subjects, who in turn gratefully accept his kindness and authority. The bulk of the text focuses on all the novel and impressive transformations of court life effected by Humayun, including new classification schemes for ranks of imperial officers; new rituals at court; streamlined bureaucratic operations; new clothing designs for imperial attendants; and the introduction of celebrations using special barges, pontoon bridges, movable palaces, compartmentalized tents, and foods.

In keeping with Humayun's stated justification for commissioning the *Qanun-i Humayuni* ("It is worthy and appropriate that the inventions of my auspicious mind and the improvements of my illumined thoughts should be arranged in a series and written down so that in time their light may shine near and far"[34]), Khwandamir continuously invites the reader to dwell on Humayun's originality, influence, and greatness.

[31] Ibid., p. 345.
[32] Khwandamir, *Qanun-i-Humayuni*, p. 21.
[33] Khan, "State in Mughal India," 21.
[34] Khwandamir, *Qanun-i-Humayuni*, pp. 17–18.

Consider two passages. The first describes the celebrations at the imperial court to mark the day the sun reached its greatest strength (*sharaf*):

> The Emperor, protector of the world, like the shining sun whose light provides Aries joyous tidings of exaltation, took his seat in the pavilion (*khargah*) of the twelve zodiacal signs. He then copiously raised the ranks of members of the court ... with awards of robes of honor and other suitable appointments.[35]

The second captures Humayun's daily ritual of showing himself to his subjects at the crack of dawn:

> Every morning when the Jamshid-like sun raised its head out of the collar (*giriban*) of the heavens and put on the robe of satin of the sky, and the celestial world wore the golden crown of the sun ... the King, whose banners are always victorious, adorned his person with a robe whose color was appropriate to the day, and dressed in a new suit placed on his head a crown of the same color ... and his sun-resembling face appeared [to the people] like the planet Jupiter, which shines in the dark of the night.[36]

With the aid of panegyrists such as Khwandamir, Humayun was determined to project imperial authority and command loyalty even if political reality did not quite support these pretensions.[37]

Humayun's insistence that he be acknowledged as something more than a first-among-equals is underlined in his approach to defiance from his brothers. Although Humayun's efforts resulted in severe setbacks in the late 1530s and 1540s, their general trajectory was toward offering less room for princely defiance. The decisions first to crush any pretensions to independent rule and then to exile and/or blind his recalcitrant half brothers make this point dramatically. Indeed, it is with Humayun (as illustrated in these texts) that we can posit the earliest traces of an emerging model of empowered imperial authority. Because of Humayun's premature death in 1556, the effects of his actions had little impact on his still young sons. However, as Humayun's older son and successor Akbar began to build on his father's imperial vision, the consequences for the following generation of Mughal princes would be dramatic.

---

[35] Ibid., p. 96.

[36] Ibid., pp. 72–3.

[37] For more on Humayun's attraction to solar symbolism, see Eva Orthmann, "Sonne, Mond und Sterne: Kosmologie und Astrologie in der Inszenierung von Herrschaft unter Humayun," in *Die Grenzen der Welt, Arabica et Iranica ad honorem Heinz Gaube*, ed. L. Korn, E. Orthmann, and F. Schwarz (Wiesbaden, 2008), pp. 297–306.

CONCLUSION

We do not speak of rebellion as such in the reign of Emperor Babur. It is only during Humayun's reign and in the context of Humayun's aspirations to a status distinct from the "leader amongst equals" that Mirza Kamran (who saw himself as protecting his own appanage) might be viewed as rebelling. Indeed, it is not until Akbar's chronicles, written decades later and under the post-appanage dispensation, that Mirza Kamran's rebellion is characterized as a demonstration of disloyalty to his brother and not as a defense of his patrimony. Yet, although Akbar's chronicles make a case against Mirza Kamran as ultimately disloyal to the memory and expectations of his father Babur in his campaigns against his brother Humayun, Emperor Babur himself never conceived of one son conceding thus to the other. After all, he had assigned them separate appanages and, in a late 1520s letter to Kamran and Humayun, unequivocally stated the rules by which territories were to be divided. The steppe traditions in which Babur was imbued were less concerned with consolidating territory under a single all-powerful emperor. Instead, as long as his authority was not being repeatedly and directly challenged, he was comfortable with carving up territories among his sons and affording them a fairly free rein to manage their own affairs. With the removal of Mirza Kamran and the death or exile of his other brothers, Humayun finally became the dominant focus for local and regional loyalties in the way that Babur had previously been.

Humayun's newfound confidence and political strength are wonderfully captured in a painting likely commissioned by him and completed some time between 1550 and 1555. Now known as "The Princes of the House of Timur" (and housed in the British Museum), it is considered by Mughal art historian Toby Falk to be "one of the largest, most significant – perhaps *the* most significant, and earliest – perhaps *the* earliest, of all Mughal paintings."[38] In its original form (before it was extensively overworked in the seventeenth century and its meaning expanded to affirm the genealogical connections of the Mughals), the composition focused on Humayun seated in a garden pavilion, flanked by seated courtiers and notables, and attended by servants carrying food and drink. Humayun appears commanding but serene. The hardest battles with his brothers are behind him, and his rising political stock, captured in his perfect control of his surroundings, portends a fresh chapter in his life.

---

[38] Toby Falk, "The Written Record," in *Humayun's Garden Party-Princes of the House of Timur and Early Mughal Painting*, ed. Sheila Canby (Bombay, 1994), p. 8. Emphasis in original. See also J. M. Rogers, *Mughal Miniatures* (London, 1993), pp. 35–6.

With Humayun's victory over his brothers, he was indeed in a position to contemplate winning back his lost kingdom in India. He succeeded in doing so in 1555. He immediately revived efforts, previously undertaken in the 1530s, to broaden his political support beyond its fairly narrow base of Central Asians. As in the 1530s, one of the key groups the emperor targeted was Indian Muslims. In a measure of the seriousness of Humayun's intentions, he married the daughter of one of Hindustan's most powerful Muslim *zamindar*s in the year before his death; he encouraged his nobles to marry other Indian Muslim women as well.[39] He also appointed an Indian Muslim cleric, Shaikh Gadai Kambo, to the highly influential and patronage-rich post of *sadr-us-sudur* (chief of religious endowments). These endeavors supplemented others designed to entice Indians of non-Muslim backgrounds to serve under him as well as to promote large numbers of Iranian-Shiite nobles within the Mughal nobility.[40]

Unfortunately for Humayun, his death in 1556 meant that his plans to establish Mughal imperial authority on firmer foundations went largely unfulfilled. In the year of their father's death, his sons Akbar and Mirza Hakim were thirteen and two years old, respectively. Humayun's demise set these two surviving sons on course for another long fight that would conclusively end only with the death of Mirza Hakim in 1585. Ultimately, it was Humayun's grandsons (born to Akbar) who might be described as the first Mughal princes to step onto a truly imperial stage. No longer allowed or even content to entrench their power over smaller patches of princely territory, Akbar's sons would take their struggle for allies and political advantage across the entire length and breadth of the Mughal Empire.

We turn, in Chapter 3, to a consideration of the structure and workings of the princely household, focusing in particular on the "high" period of the empire when it was especially thriving and robust. The figure of the prince, as he emerges in the reign of Akbar, is increasingly one whose life is almost entirely oriented toward the eventual and inevitable war of succession that will decide which sibling will gain the Mughal throne. Ultimately, the long-term political fortunes of the prince would be deeply reliant on the household that cohered around him.

---

[39] Shaikh Abu'l Fazl, *Akbarnamah*, ed. Abdul Rahim, vol. 2 (Calcutta, 1879), pp. 48–9.

[40] Shaikh Farid Bhakkari relates an especially interesting anecdote in which Shah Tahmasp of Iran, upon learning that the Rajputs and Afghans were competitors for power in northern India, advised Humayun to woo the Rajputs as a counterweight to the Afghans. Humayun followed the advice: "Therefore, when His Majesty Humayun Padshah cast the shadow of kingship upon the heads of the people of India, he began patronizing this group." *Dhakhirat al-Khawanin*, ed. S. Moinul Haq, vol. 1 (Karachi, 1961), pp. 103–4.

# 3

# Princely Households

On a cool morning in January 1709, in the waning years of the princely establishment, Aurangzeb's son Kam Bakhsh led a meager force of fewer than a thousand men against his brother Mu'azzam/Bahadur Shah I's army – numbering in the tens of thousands – outside Hyderabad. It was a suicidal charge, a desperate attack. Kam Bakhsh was mortally wounded and died later that night. Most of his men were massacred. No prominent imperial nobles were in Kam Bakhsh's force; any nobles once on his side had deserted him as his territory shrank and his control over it became only nominal. Who then were these diehard supporters? What made them willing to sacrifice their lives for a futile cause? The names and stories of these hundreds of individuals have largely been lost, but we know that most of them were members of Kam Bakhsh's personal household. True to the expectations of the time, they died as they had lived, serving their master.

The households of Mughal princes have received almost no scholarly attention; they are simply assumed to have operated in exactly the same manner as the emperor's household and served the same purposes. The scattered nature of sources makes any account of princely households a challenge to piece together. As a result of this combination of neglect and difficulty, we know very little about the life cycle of princely households, the nature of everyday life inside them, how they were financed and their organizational structure, the composition of their personnel, and the ways they contributed to overall Mughal state formation. Heretofore there has been no coherent account of their development and transformation over the course of the sixteenth and seventeenth centuries.

These gaps in our knowledge are surprising considering how central such households were to the articulation and projection of princely power, particularly after the 1580s. A weak household, everyone knew, foreclosed any possibility that a prince might attain the Mughal throne. And dire consequences accompanied such failure, which might include physical mutilation or death, and for the household, dissolution. Not surprisingly, individual princes poured enormous energy into recruiting people to serve in their establishments – offering them room and board, training, and protection. Princely retainers mostly responded with unconditional loyalty for their prince's political interests, often even to the point of sacrificing their own lives.

Princely households played an important role in the fortunes of the Mughal Empire. At a basic level, they were personal domains, and generations of Mughal princes (absent the opportunities of the princely appanage post-1585) gained invaluable administrative and political experience managing them. Service in these households, in turn, offered princely stalwarts plenty of opportunities to familiarize themselves with the workings of the empire. This distribution of skills helped a prince prepare the ground for a successful accession.

Before proceeding, a brief word on nomenclature. The imperial sources use a narrow set of terms to denote what I am calling "the princely household." They speak of a *sarkar* (household), *sarkar-i 'ali* (eminent household), or *sarkar-i padshahzadah* (household of an emperor's son). When a prince's political stock was taken, it was an unspoken assumption that his power and reputation were dependent on the quality and strength of his *sarkar*. The physical, moral, and political being of the prince himself and the body of his household at large were two parts of the same entity. Such thinking, as Stephen Blake reveals in his 1991 study of the city of Shahjahanabad, derived from normative conceptions first articulated in Akbar's reign and made especially evident in Shaikh Abu'l Fazl's work, the *A'in-i Akbari*. These works related the organization of the imperial establishment to the work and power of the emperor. In this view, the person of the emperor was the embodiment of the empire and vice versa.[1] So also, for a prince, his person was extended and embodied in his *sarkar*.

---

[1] Stephen Blake, *Shahjahanabad: The Sovereign City in Mughal India 1639–1739* (Cambridge, 1991), pp. 20–1, 97–9.

This chapter begins with an exploration of a young prince's childhood: his education, the rites that marked his transition to adulthood, and his gradual emergence as a prominent figure in the public life of the empire. All these shifts were underpinned by the slow evolution of the princely household, whose numbers grew as the prince advanced in status and developed new and more robust forms of funding. Here the focus is on the people who lived, worked, and thrived in the princely household of the late sixteenth and seventeenth centuries. Finally, we consider how a day in the life of a prince might unfold within the context of his household, noting along the way the ambivalence and wariness of the emperor himself in the face of powerful princely households with loyal supporters.

## THE CHILD PRINCE AND FORMATIVE HOUSEHOLD FIGURES

A prince's birth was an occasion for massive festivities.[2] The Mughals, like all imperial dynasties throughout history, prized the birth of male heirs. "Whoever has no son is not happy," proclaimed Emperor Jahangir (r. 1605–27).[3] The birth of a son signaled God's favor for the continuity of a dynasty and was also a mark of God's special favor toward the father of the newborn baby. In 1615, when Jahangir's grandson Dara Shukoh was born to his then-favorite son Khurram (later Emperor Shah Jahan), the emperor wrote delightedly of his hope that the birth would bring good fortune to both the empire and to Khurram.[4] It was with great fanfare and exuberance that the Mughals welcomed a boy child.

Between the sixteenth and seventeenth centuries, these celebrations grew in lavishness as the empire grew wealthier and the Mughal royal family became ever more politically exalted. Thus Babur notes, a few days after his firstborn son Humayun's birth in 1508, that he threw a single, if "excellent," feast for his nobles.[5] At the time Babur was still the ruler of

---

[2] For a detailed discussion of the music and dancing that accompanied royal births as well as a reading of the illustrations depicting these celebrations, see Bonnie Wade, *Imaging Sound: An Ethnomusicological Study of Music, Art, and Culture in Mughal India* (Chicago, 1998), pp. 75–84.

[3] Ni'matullah Khan Harvi, *Tarikh-i Khan Jahani wa Makhzan-i Afghani*, Asiatic Society of Bengal, Ivanow 100, f. 170a.

[4] Nur-ud-Din Muhammad Jahangir, *Jahangirnama*, ed. Muhammad Hashim (Tehran, 1980), p. 160.

[5] Zahir-ud-Din Muhammad Babur, *The Baburnama: Memoirs of Babur, Prince and Emperor*, trans. W. M. Thackston (New York, 2002), p. 260.

(Baby) Shah Shuja, ca. 1650 (The Art and History Collection Arthur M. Sackler
Gallery, Smithsonian Institution, Washington D.C., LTS 1995.2.98)

only a medium-sized principality with a population of fewer than fifteen
thousand people and centered in Kabul, not the conqueror of northern
India. By contrast, when Khurram's fourth son Murad was born in 1624,
celebrations continued over three days at Khurram's military base camp
along the banks of the River Tons in Bihar, with feasting, poetry, music, and
lavish gifts awarded to his supporters. Meanwhile, in the fort of Rohtas
where Murad was born, and where mother and infant were recuperating
following a difficult delivery, we learn from the nobleman Mirza Nathan –
who was assigned the task of procuring supplies for the festivities – that

celebrations required 30 kilograms of white ambergris (a rare perfume derived from the intestine of a sperm whale), 74 kilograms of poppy seeds, 2,000 pods of musk, 185 kilograms of amber resin, 2,000 bottles of Egyptian willow perfume, 10,000 bottles of rose water (imported from Yazd in Iran), an unspecified number of bottles containing jujube and orange perfumes, and 1,850 kilograms of Kashmiri saffron.[6] The cost of securing and transporting these goods must have amounted to tens of thousands of rupees.[7] Remarkably, these expenses were incurred at a time when Khurram was in active rebellion against his father and hard-pressed by imperial forces. Mughal rulers prior to Akbar could only have dreamed of such extravagance around the birth of a firstborn son let alone a fourth.

By contrast, if a male heir's birth was not marked by special ceremony – and this oversight was always deliberate – it was a clear sign that the princely father was imprisoned or otherwise disgraced. Thus, when Khusrau had a son in 1616, Jahangir's only comment in his autobiography the *Jahangirnama* was, "God gave Khusrau a son by the daughter of Muqim, son of Mehtar Fazil Rikabdar."[8] At the time, Khusrau was under house arrest for having led a rebellion against Jahangir a decade earlier. When a son was born in 1676 to Muhammad Sultan, there is no indication that his grandfather, the Emperor Aurangzeb, even honored his grandson with a visit, and there were neither gifts exchanged nor public celebrations. At that time, Muhammad Sultan was serving a prison term for having rebelled against Aurangzeb in 1659. The next mention of this ill-fated infant relates his death a year later.[9]

A young prince usually lived within his father's extended household until his early teenage years. There were notable exceptions, however. Akbar, for example, spent the first three years of his life, between 1542 and 1545, in his uncle Mirza Kamran's charge in Kabul. Humayun had

---

[6] Mirza Nathan, *Baharistan-i-Ghaybi*, trans. M. I. Borah, vol. 2 (Gauhati, 1936), pp. 735–6.

[7] Khurram continued the tradition of lavish gift giving and expenditures after becoming emperor in 1628. Thus, following the birth of his oldest son Dara Shukoh's fifth and sixth children, Mumtaz Shukoh and Siphr Shukoh in 1643 and 1644 respectively, he bankrolled their birthday celebrations to the tune of Rs. 200,000 each. 'Abd al-Hamid Lahawri, *Padshahnamah*, ed. Abdul Rahim, vol. 2 (Calcutta, 1872), pp. 337, 388–9. Such extravagance continued into the next generation when Emperor Aurangzeb's first grandson Mu'izz-ud-Din was born in 1661. Bhimsen offers us an eyewitness account of the accompanying festivities. As well as a massive feast, valuable gifts were exchanged, dancers and singers performed, and illuminations were hoisted all over the palace and surrounding areas. Adding to the general merriment was an extravagant fireworks display. Bhimsen Saxsena, *Tarikh-i-Dilkasha*, trans. Jadunath Sarkar (Bombay, 1972), p. 39.

[8] Jahangir, *Jahangirnama*, p. 182.

[9] Musta'idd Khan, *Maasir i Alamgiri*, ed. Agha Ahmad Ali (Calcutta, 1871), pp. 155, 161.

been forced to abandon his infant son during his flight out of India to Iran. Likewise, Khurram was handed over to his grandmother Ruqaiya Sultan Begum, Akbar's first and childless wife, immediately following his birth in 1592. Just prior to Khurram's birth, a soothsayer had reportedly predicted to Ruqaiya Sultan Begum that the still unborn child was destined for imperial greatness. By giving her charge of the infant, Akbar fulfilled his aging wife's wish to be remembered for her help in raising a future Mughal emperor. It was not until Khurram had turned thirteen and his father Salim had succeeded Akbar as the Emperor Jahangir that the young prince was finally allowed to return to his father's household, and thus closer to his biological mother.[10] Then there are the cases of Khurram's own sons, Dara Shukoh and Aurangzeb. In early 1626, they were separated from their parents and sent to live as hostages at the imperial court of their grandfather Jahangir. Khurram had been forced to offer them up as part of a settlement aimed at ending his faltering rebellion. The boys were not reunited with their parents until Khurram's accession as Emperor Shah Jahan in January 1628.

Mughal sources offer sporadic insights into the character of the relationship between princes and their imperial fathers. These were, of course, relationships largely framed by absence, especially those of Babur and Humayun, who were constantly away in battle or on the move. They did not necessarily take their young sons with them. Occasionally, however, we do catch glimpses of close and tender moments in imperial father-son relations, especially in the princes' early years before political competitiveness set in following the achievement of adult status. Thus Akbar's devotion to his three infant sons is well documented,[11] as is the love that

---

[10] The decision by an emperor to promise an unborn infant to a senior woman was not unprecedented. In 1519, for example, Babur handed Mirza Hindal over to the infant's stepmother, Maham Begum. She had pleaded for the unborn baby after losing several babies of her own. Babur, *The Baburnama*, p. 267.

[11] Shaikh Abu'l Fazl, *Akbarnamah*, ed. Abdul Rahim, vol. 3 (Calcutta, 1886), p. 75. In contrast to the detachment of earlier rulers from their sons, Abu'l Fazl says, Akbar "kept his children under his own care." As a result, Salim was fully equipped to fulfill his duties as a future king by the tender age of four. Regretfully, according to the Shaikh, "old custom" nevertheless demanded that the young prince be committed to the instruction of tutors in order for him to learn to read, write, and understand the Islamic scriptures. A Jesuit traveler to Akbar's court, Fr. Monserrate, had a slightly less benign view of Akbar's treatment of his sons: "The king's nature was such that, though he loved his children very dearly, he used to give them orders rather roughly whenever he wanted anything done; and he sometimes punished them with blows as well as harsh words." Fr. Monserrate, *The Commentary of Father Monserrate, S.J., On His Journey to the Court of Akbar*, trans. J. S. Hoyland (Oxford, 1922), p. 53.

Aurangzeb's third-born son A'zam demonstrated to his teenage sons Wala Jah and 'Ali Tabar.[12]

A young prince's daily needs, however, were not met by his father or other men in the imperial household; it fell to his mother, along with other household women, to take care of his food, care, and entertainment. The mother's role was central. Barring an event beyond her control – her own death, the desire of a senior woman to adopt an infant, the need to offer a child as a political hostage, or a forced flight that necessitated abandoning a child – a mother was rarely separated from her infant sons. Stories of close and lifelong mother–son bonds are plentiful. But mothering a prince was a very special kind of maternal role, since the woman also had to be a bodyguard – necessarily suspicious and paranoid, ever vigilant to threats against her son's life and always apprehensive about possible traitors and enemies close by. Thus, in 1548, when the six-year-old Akbar complained of a toothache, his stepmother Haji Begum went in search of a remedy. Recounting the episode years later, Akbar recalls that his mother, Maryam Makani, showed immediate "vigilance and caution." According to Akbar, she was in agony that the medicine might turn out to be poison. For fear of offending Haji Begum by refusing it, Maryam Makani instead tried to spirit the child away to the safety of her own quarters. The boy Akbar was reluctant to go, however, and in the end it was only after Haji Begum tasted the medicine herself that "the minds of those present were set at rest ... and also my pain soothed."[13]

The prince's mother usually had many helpers both in life and in the case of her death. We know for instance that Jahangir's wife Nur Jahan helped Mumtaz Mahal, her niece, and her husband Khurram/Shah Jahan to raise one of their sons, Shuja' (b. 1616), who suffered from epilepsy.[14] Older sister Jahan Ara (b. 1614) took charge of the seven-year-old Murad following their mother Mumtaz Mahal's untimely death in 1631. Likewise, Zeb-un-Nisa (b. 1638), the daughter of Aurangzeb and Dilras Banu Begum, served as a surrogate mother to her one-month-old brother Akbar following their mother's demise in 1657.[15]

---

[12] Mughal news bulletins (*akhbarat*) tell of the warmth with which A'zam greeted his own young sons on their birthdays or following successful hunts, his solicitousness in getting them desirable presents, acceding to requests to ride favored animals or to visit interesting places, and in awarding imperial honors to their close companions. *Akhbarat-i Darbar-i Mu'alla*, National Library of India, Sarkar Collection 41, pp. 33–4, 67, 88, 89, 93, 98–9, 108, 112, 113, 127–8, 131, 137, 141, 148, 164, 190, 194, 205, 209.

[13] Fazl, *Akbarnamah*, vol. 3, pp. 77–8.

[14] Jahangir, *Jahangirnama*, p. 281.

[15] In fact, out of this sibling bond emerged an abortive plot in 1680–1 to overthrow their father Aurangzeb and place Akbar on the Mughal throne. (Akbar eventually fled India for

Assisting in the managerial and political aspects of the Mughal mother's tasks was a team of foster mothers (*anaga*s) who nursed, clothed, and cleaned the baby and kept him safe from bodily harm. This team was very carefully picked. According to Akbar's panegyrist Shaikh Abu'l Fazl, a foster mother was required not simply to supply plentiful breast milk; her milk should be a conduit for her necessarily good temperament and spiritual inclinations.[16] Of course, she was also required to be a loyal supporter of the royal family, and sometimes her appointment, like a marriage, could be a vehicle for forging ties between her family and the royals. When Humayun chose Jiji Anaga – who was married into the prominent Ghazni-based Atga clan – to nurse Akbar, he did so in the context of contention with his younger brother Mirza Kamran over parts of eastern Afghanistan, including Ghazni. Just less than thirty years later, Akbar appointed a number of women from the family of Shaikh Salim – a member of the renowned pan-Indian Chishti Sufi order – to nurse his first son, Salim. Over the next few years, other women from the same family served as foster mothers for his two other sons, Murad and Danyal. In so doing, Akbar added a material and bodily attachment to the spiritual ties he had already tried to forge with the Chishtis, an order that upheld his political ambitions to become a specifically Hindustani Muslim emperor.

After the 1580s, we see a shift in foster mother selection, as the political alliance aspect faded. Henceforth it was a foster mother's personal qualities that were emphasized. Underlying this shift may have been the memory of Akbar's own *anaga*, Maham, who had made an unsuccessful grab for political power in the early 1560s. Perhaps for fear of the ambitions of high-profile *anaga*s, women of modest backgrounds and no particular social or political significance were increasingly employed to nurse Mughal princes through the seventeenth century. Regardless of the foster mother's status, ties between a prince and his *anaga* could run deep. Akbar, for example, only twice shaved off his moustache to mourn someone's death: once, when his mother died and, four years before that, when his foster mother Jiji Anaga died.

In his early years, the child prince also forged close friendships with other young boys. Most were the children and wards of his *anaga*s. With them, he shared childhood experiences: playing games, mastering fighting

---

Safavid Iran, but Zeb-un-Nisa was caught and spent the last twenty years of her life under house arrest in Delhi.)

[16] Shaikh Abu'l Fazl, *Akbarnamah*, ed. Abdul Rahim, vol. 1 (Calcutta, 1878), p. 43. For a longer discussion, see Ruby Lal, *Domesticity and Power in the Early Mughal World* (Cambridge, 2005), pp. 188–94.

skills, going on hunting expeditions, attending court celebrations, or playing truant when they should have been in school. These were the prince's
foster brothers (*kokas*), and, indeed, for a young boy who soon came to
view his biological siblings as political rivals and potential murderers, his
*koka*s were for all intents and purposes his true "brothers." As such, the
prince and his *koka*s shared the entire gamut of sibling relations, from
rivalry to love, framed by unquestioned brotherly bonds that were rooted
in shared childhood memories. The strength of these ties was such that
*koka*s sometimes were the only people who could speak – as Khan Jahan
Bahadur Koka repeatedly did to Emperor Aurangzeb – with "audacity and
recklessness."[17] However annoyed emperors might become with their
*koka*s, they usually indulged them on account of what Akbar once lyrically
described as the "river of milk" (*juy-i shir*) that flowed between him and his
own favorite *koka*, Mirza 'Aziz Koka.[18]

There were also instances when a child prince's male servants developed
relationships with the prince that, although not comparable to those
between a prince and his *anaga*s or *koka*s, shared something of their close-
ness. A story from 1553 tells of Humayun ordering one of his retainers,
Mihtar Jauhar Aftabchi, to bathe, dress, and bring the eleven-year-old
Akbar before him. As recounted many years later by Jauhar, Akbar pro-
tested, "I cannot get naked in your presence ... I am embarrassed to show
myself," and he would comply only when Jauhar brought in Rafiq, one of
the prince's own servants.[19] The adult prince would sometimes fondly
remember his childhood dependence on a retainer. Thus Aurangzeb's son
A'zam recalled with affection the food tasting, the playing, and the home-
made remedies for hurts and illnesses provided him by a long-deceased
servant, Ghulam Muhammad.[20] On occasion, gratitude for their services
was made concrete, as when Emperor Jahangir, fifteen years into his reign,
turned over all the tribute offerings for a single day in April 1619 to
Mahmud, his water steward during his infancy and early childhood.[21]

We can quite safely assume that all these individuals in a prince's
childhood household, who served him in such minute detail every minute

[17] Saxsena, *Tarikh-i-Dilkasha*, p. 202.
[18] Motamad Khan, *Iqbalnamah-i Jahangiri*, ed. Abdul Hai and Ahmad Ali (Calcutta, 1865),
pp. 230–1. See also Shah Nawaz Khan, *Maasir-ul-Umara*, ed. Abdur Rahim, vol. 1
(Calcutta, 1888), p. 675.
[19] Jauhar Aftabchi, "Tadhkiratu'l-waqiat," in *Three Memoirs of Humayun*, ed. W. M.
Thackston (Costa Mesa, 2009), p. 197.
[20] *Akhbarat-i Darbar-i Mu'alla*, vol. 41, p. 198.
[21] Jahangir, *Jahangirnama*, p. 305.

of the day, smothered him with attention. At the same time, the vagaries of illness and disease also meant that these royal children, like any other children of their era, were viewed as fragile and under continual threat of injury or death. Nor was any caregiving entirely error proof. For example, the four-year-old Shuja' fell headlong off a fifteen-foot-high palace balcony in 1620, presumably when his caregiver's head was turned the other way, and, just over two decades later, a minor son of Shuja' was killed when a fire broke out in his palace. Moreover, young princes could not be entirely protected from imperial political drama. Mirza Kamran used his three-year-old nephew Akbar as a human shield to prevent Humayun from bombarding and storming Kabul's ramparts where the young prince was held hostage. Similarly, during Khurram's rebellion in the 1620s, his youngest son Murad was nearly killed when a cannonball hit his mother's tent and set it ablaze during a battle outside Thatta.

We can only wonder how such an upbringing – with its multitude of relationships and all the attention, danger, and drama of an imperial domestic setting – might have shaped the dispositions and capacities of these future leaders. The Mughal chronicler Bayazid Bayat wrote that a prince's attendants needed to keep in mind that the treatment they meted out to young princes "remains in their memories (*khatir*)," with possibly severe consequences for the attendant should the prince become king.[22] Might this explain the unwillingness of Mun'im Khan, one of Humayun's most powerful noblemen, to turn down young Akbar's request to skip his lessons one day? (This despite knowing that the prince's father would be furious if he learned his son had missed school.[23]) Might it explain the earnest reproaches directed toward the Italian adventurer/traveler/servitor Manucci by matrons and eunuchs when he instructed Aurangzeb's grandson Mu'izz-ud-Din to control an angry outburst upon getting hurt?[24] Let him act it out, they seemed to suggest, for he could be emperor one day.

It is against this backdrop that we must place the final key figure in the prince's early household, his *ataliq* (guardian/tutor/surrogate father).[25]

---

[22] Bayazid Bayat, *Tadhkira-i-Humayun wa Akbar*, ed. M. Hidayat Hosain (Calcutta, 1941), p. 148.

[23] Ibid., pp. 147–8.

[24] Niccolao Manucci, *Mogul India or Storio do Mogor*, trans. W. Irvine, vol. 2 (New Delhi, repr. 1996), p. 324.

[25] A term formed by joining the Turkish adjectival and relative suffix *liq* to *ata*, meaning "father." Although *ataliq* refers to the title and post of someone serving as a prince's guardian or tutor, it also engages a powerful notion of honorific kinship akin to that of a surrogate father. For the role of the *ataliq* in the post-Mongol Central Asian political context, see Yuri Bregel, "Atalik," in *Encyclopaedia of Islam* II, Brill Online.

As with Babur's son Hindal, an *ataliq* could be selected within months of a prince's birth. Generally, however, *ataliqs* were chosen around the time a prince reached school age, when he was four or five years old. *Ataliqs* were usually temporary appointments – Salim had at least three, Akbar four, and Kam Bakhsh at least five. As in Akbar's case, princes occasionally had overlapping *ataliqs*. If the first was dispatched on another imperial duty, then a second was appointed as a stand-in.[26]

Like *anagas*, *ataliqs* were carefully chosen. These were men who commanded great respect – the better to rein in an errant prince – and were revered for their bravery and loyalty, as well as for their willingness to die to protect their young charges.[27] The prince's *ataliq* was ideally a figure of fierce authority, perhaps the most important such male figure in his life. Invariably a powerful noble, the *ataliq* also anchored a minor prince in the political landscape of the time. Not surprisingly, the list of men who served at one time or another as *ataliqs* reads like a who's who of the imperial nobility.[28]

The *ataliqs'* position was unenviable. They had to carefully balance their own political interests alongside not only those of their princely charge but also those of the emperor, their ultimate patron and employer. Compounding this delicate juggling act, an *ataliq* was often closely monitored, and sometimes obstructed, by more long-standing members of a princely household (for example, *anagas* or *kokas*). Possibly fearing a recession of their own influence in the face of a forceful *ataliq*, members of a princely household were often determined to adopt a maximalist position when it came to protecting a prince's political interests.[29] If the relationship between prince and *ataliq* soured,

---

[26] Thus Khwaja Jalal-ud-Din Mahmud was temporarily appointed to be Akbar's *ataliq* after Humayun detained Mun'im Khan at the imperial court. Bayat, *Tadhkira-i-Humayun wa Akbar*, p. 165.

[27] Miram Beg did precisely this for Mirza 'Askari after Hazaras ambushed and encircled the prince's household on the road between Qandahar and Kabul. Although the Beg died fighting off the Hazaras, his actions won Hindal enough time to escape. The respect accorded Miram Beg's action can be judged by the characterization of his death as "martyrdom" (*shahadat*) by one observer. Bayat, *Tadhkira-i-Humayun wa Akbar*, p. 170.

[28] A short list of the high-ranking nobles honored between Akbar and Aurangzeb's reigns include Mun'im Khan, Shams-ud-Din Khan, Bairam Khan, 'Abd-ur-Rahim Khan-i-Khanan, Sa'id Khan Chaghatai, Qutb-ud-Din Khan, Shaikh Faizi, Qulij Khan, Mirza Yusuf Khan, Raja Man Singh, Asaf Khan, Khan Jahan Lodi, Mahabat Khan, Mir Jumla, Wazir Khan, Sha'ista Khan, and Khan Jahan Bahadur Koka.

[29] In 1597, on the eve of Danyal's departure for Allahabad, Akbar appointed Qulij Khan as the prince's *ataliq*. Over the next year, Qulij Khan's goading of the prince, on behalf of the emperor, to be a more proactive administrator resulted in deteriorating relations. Danyal

which it occasionally did, the latter was often deemed the worst kind of betrayer.[30]

The relationship of a prince with his *ataliq* was necessarily awkward. Indeed, the guardian's term was deliberately restricted to a few years to minimize the possibilities of forming deep affection or ties deemed too close. Growing distance between *ataliq* and charge, moreover, measured the latter's transition from boy to adult. As a young prince came to anticipate his full adult status, marked in part by freedom from an *ataliq*'s supervision, the prince-guardian script, so to speak, had the prince straining at the end of his guardian's leash. The *ataliq*'s oversight eventually ceded to the advantage of bonds formed by his charge such that, by the time he attained adult status, a prince was often well on his way to establishing an independent network of friends and allies.

### RITES OF PASSAGE FROM CHILDHOOD TO MINOR STATUS

Two separate ceremonies – circumcision and the start of formal education – launched the prince into his boyhood. Both generally occurred when he was between four and five years old. Barring some notable exceptions,[31] these events tended to occur in close succession, and both were colossal and boisterous affairs that introduced the otherwise sequestered imperial child to the public eye.

was more interested in conserving his resources for a looming succession struggle than following his *ataliq*'s biding. He was encouraged in his stance by unnamed members of his household. Ultimately, Qulij Khan conceded defeat and returned to Agra. Fazl, *Akbarnamah*, vol. 3, 744.

[30] Thus when Khusrau Shah deceived and then blinded his princely charge – a distant relative of Babur's – Babur wrote: "A hundred thousand curses upon anyone who performs or has performed such a despicable act! Until the dawn of doomsday let anyone who hears of the deeds of Khusrawshah curse him! Anyone who hears of this and does not curse him deserves to be cursed himself!" Babur seems to have been particularly disturbed by the fact that Khusrau Shah allowed his personal ambition to be a powerbroker overtake his responsibilities to a prince "whom he had taken care of and raised from childhood." Babur, *The Baburnama*, p. 70.

[31] For instance, Akbar's son Murad was eight years old when he began his education. The delay, we are told, was on account of successive medical problems that had held him back. Fazl, *Akbarnamah*, vol. 3, p. 267. Another Murad – this one Khurram's son – was also almost eight years old when a formal tutor was first appointed to take charge of his education in 1632. Although none of the imperial sources explains the reason for the delay, it may be that the unsettling effect of his father's princely rebellion, the more pressing need to consolidate political power following Khurram's accession in 1628, and the unexpected death of Murad's powerful mother Mumtaz Mahal in 1631 delayed matters.

Akbar's circumcision occurred soon after he was reunited with his father Humayun, after spending three years as a hostage of his uncle Mirza Kamran. Powerful nobles from across the region were invited, and Akbar's mother and other senior members of the imperial family were recalled from Qandahar to Kabul. On the day itself, tent halls were set up, grandly decorated, and lit with lamps; there were separate halls for men and women. Surrounding gardens, the town's central market, and its main thoroughfares were also decorated. At the evening gatherings, food and alcohol were consumed and massive gifts exchanged between the nobles and the prince's proud father. On the next day, residents of Kabul – young and old, powerful and weak, rich and poor, learned and illiterate – were drawn into the celebration as food and money were given out in honor of the occasion.[32] By some accounts, the festivities continued for days.[33] Indeed, the following centuries of Mughal rule saw little change in the special ostentation of celebrations around a male heir's circumcision.[34]

The start of the prince's schooling was celebrated in similarly grand and lavish style with feasts, prayers, and gift giving, although this occasion was more solemn. Akbar's court chronicler Shaikh Abu'l Fazl lays out for us the goals of an ideal princely education: it should impart the importance of listening to and obeying a father's/emperor's instructions; it must also train a prince to administer a kingdom justly. Most crucially, however, a prince's education must train him to select and groom the most capable men to help him run the empire; he had to learn how to enable such men to "emerge from the defile of limited means" and to confer "abundance and general comfort upon them" so they might serve him and the empire well and wisely.[35] Ultimately, a well-educated prince combined the best qualities of a man of the pen (*ahl-i qalam*) and a man of the sword (*ahl-i saif*).

Khurram/Shah Jahan, for example, studied the Quran; Islamic sciences (*ulum*), which included rhetoric, epistolary style, proper speech, prosody, and other forms of literary learning; and Turkish. He was also taught military strategy and tactics as well as the correct use of various weapons including daggers, swords, pikes, and muskets. Aurangzeb's sons,

---

[32] Gulbadan Begum, *Ahwal-i Humayun Badshah*, British Library, Ms. Or. 166, ff. 66a-b.
[33] Bayat, *Tadhkira-i-Humayun wa Akbar*, pp. 59–60.
[34] For an account of the celebrations and gift giving accompanying Aurangzeb's fourth son Akbar's circumcision in 1662, see Muhammad Kazim, *Alamgirnamah*, ed. Khadim Husain and Abdul Hai, vol. 2 (Calcutta, 1868), pp. 663–4.
[35] Fazl, *Akbarnamah*, vol. 3, pp. 75–6.

Humayun celebrates Akbar's circumcision, ca. 1603–4 (British Library, OR 12988, Akbarnama Folio 114)

the sources suggest, covered the same general terrain, but they spent a little more time on Arabic, historical studies, and biographies of the Prophet and influential religious figures, likely in keeping with the emperor's own greater interest in these subjects. In general, art appreciation and a mastery of calligraphy also had important places in a prince's education. Mirza Khan wrote the manual *Tuhfat-ul-Hind* in the 1670s to aid student princes' learning. It suggests that the curriculum was by this time further expanded to engage an appreciation for Hindavi, the Nagari script,

Master and Pupil (perhaps Prince Salim with his tutor), late 16th century (Harvard Art Museums/Arthur M. Sackler Museum, The Stuart Cary Welch Collection, Gift of Edith I. Welch in memory of Stuart Cary Welch, 2009.202.204)

Indian music and indigenous Indian sciences.[36] According to Bindraban Das Khushgu, author of *Safina-i Khushgu* (an early eighteenth-century anthology of Persian poets), Emperor Aurangzeb's third son, A'zam, was fully versed not only in the arts of fighting and governing but also in the principles of music, dance, poetry, and speech.[37] With such learning and

---

[36] Muzaffar Alam, *The Languages of Political Islam in India* (Delhi, 2004), pp. 178–9.

[37] Bindraban Das Khushgu, *Safina-i-Khushgu*, ed. S. S. M. Ataur Rahman (Patna, 1959), pp. 40–1. For more on the patronage extended by A'zam and other members of Aurangzeb's family to Braj poets and poetry, see Allison Busch, "Hidden in Plain View: Brajbhasha Poets at the Mughal Court," *Modern Asian Studies* 44, no. 2 (2010): pp. 297–8.

skills, a prince was well positioned to operate across a wide social land-scape and in any company. If his political success depended on his capacity to draw men to himself, his education was intended to enhance that prospect. No wonder Shaikh Abu'l Fazl spoke of the significance of a prince's education in reverential tones.

Many people were recruited to teach this diverse curriculum. In Khurram's case, they numbered at least eight; some were imperial nobles, others religious scholars.[38] According to one count, his son and successor Aurangzeb had nine different tutors.[39] Occasionally tutors taught more than one prince. Thus, whereas Mulla 'Abd-ul-Latif Sultanpuri separately instructed Shah Jahan's sons Aurangzeb and Dara Shukoh in the Quran, Dara Shukoh and Murad shared the noted Islamic legal scholar Mulla Mirak Harvi as their tutor. Judging from the Mughal sources, princely tutors – unlike *ataliqs* or *anagas* – were selected not on the basis of affiliation to powerful groups or networks but rather on the presumption of their mastery of a particular discipline or skill. There also was little expectation that tutors would play a significant role in a prince's life following the completion of his education.[40]

There probably is no better indication of the importance the Mughals attached to their princes' education than the anger expressed toward bored or truant princes. Thus, after learning that his son Kam Bakhsh had been skipping his tutorials, Aurangzeb furiously reprimanded him: "A person without knowledge (*bi-ilm*) is a beast (*haiwan*). A prince, in particular, should have a refined mind." After reproaching Kam Bakhsh, Aurangzeb ordered him confined to his personal quarters for a month and a half.[41] A prince whose education was considered lacking was likewise stigmatized and shunned. Aurangzeb's grandson Buland Akhtar, for example, spent much of his youth in the care of rebellious Rajputs after being abandoned by his father Prince Akbar following the latter's failed rebellion in 1681.

---

[38] Salih Kambo Lahori, *'Amal-i Salih*, ed. Ghulam Yazdani, vol. 1 (Lahore, 1967), pp. 26–7.

[39] S. Moinul Haq, *Prince Awrangzib: A Study* (Karachi, 1962), pp. 2–4.

[40] Aurangzeb's thrice-a-week meetings, even as king, with one of his childhood tutors, Saiyid Muhammad Qanauji, offer a rare example of a truly resilient relationship. The same Saiyid, along with another tutor, Mulla Abu'l Wa'iz, is said to have participated in the compilation of the *Fatawa-yi 'Alamgiri*, a manual of Islamic jurisprudence commissioned by Aurangzeb in the late 1660s.

[41] Ishwar Das Nagar, *Futuhat-i-Alamgiri*, ed. Raghubir Singh and Qazi Karamatullah (Vadodara, 1995), pp. 308–9. See also Humayun's reprimand to Akbar. Quoting the poet Nizami, Humayun writes: "Sit not idly, it's not the time for play/It's the time for knowledge and for endeavor (*ghafil munshin na waqt-i bazi ast/waqt-i honar ast wa karsazi ast)*." Fazl, *Akbarnamah*, vol. 1, p. 316.

Upon his reunion with Aurangzeb and the Mughal court in the late 1690s, Buland Akhtar was deemed uneducated and uncivilized; one contemporary described him as possessing no restraint of speech or habit.[42] It was a reputation that he was never able to shake.

It is only after his circumcision and the start of his education that a prince would warrant a public celebration following recovery from sickness or begin to have his name appear on lists of recipients of imperial gifts. These two rites marked the end of a prince's infancy. They signaled that both his social standing and his physical body were now of imperial significance and symbolic as they had not been when he was a mere infant. The prince was now an integral part of the life of the empire, and he might march in imperial processions, accompany his father or grandfather during military campaigns or royal hunts, participate in royal weddings and other imperial-sponsored religious festivals, and make public appearances at the Mughal court. Other functions that increasingly devolved to young princes included welcoming or sending off favored imperial guests, condoling powerful noble families on a death in their household, and making an offering to a Sufi shrine or religious luminary. In one unusual episode, in 1583, the Emperor Akbar even temporarily handed over the management of key imperial duties – among them royal weddings and feasts, and the administration of justice, religious affairs, and the Mughal household – to his three non-adult sons.[43]

Even so, at this point, a prince was still considered a child. He remained subservient to the emperor, a fact demonstrated by his continued receipt of a daily stipend (*yaumiya*). Most princes began receiving daily stipends directly following their circumcision and/or schooling ceremonies. On rare occasion, stipends were offered even to newborn princes, as in the case of at least two of Aurangzeb's grandsons, Wala Jah (b. 1684) and Muhiy-us-Sunnat (b. 1696). The amount of the initial stipend varied. For instance, whereas the infant Wala Jah started with a daily stipend of Rs. 80 (roughly $1,200 in 2009 dollars[44]), Shah Jahan ordered stipends of Rs. 1,000 for Dara Shukoh (b. 1615), Rs. 750 for Shuja' (b. 1616), Rs. 500 for Aurangzeb (b. 1618), and Rs. 250 for Murad (b. 1624) following his

[42] Nagar, *Futuhat-i-Alamgiri*, p. 393.
[43] Fazl, *Akbarnamah*, vol. 3, p. 404.
[44] This calculation is based on M. N. Pearson's calculation that one rupee was equivalent to four dollars in 1976. A currency converter, in turn, suggests that four dollars in 1976 would be equal to $15.10 in 2009. See M. N. Pearson, *Merchants and Rulers in Gujarat: The Response to the Portuguese in the Sixteenth Century* (New Delhi, repr. 1976), p. 155, and www.measuringworth.com.

accession in 1628.[45] Besides being the sons of a newly crowned emperor, each was also considerably older than Wala Jah. Incremental increases – ranging from Rs. 10 to Rs. 100 – followed over subsequent years until a prince was accorded full adult status. Most princes received full adult status well before hitting what seems to have been an upper ceiling of Rs. 1,000.[46]

Princes usually received daily stipends until such time as they were considered ready to be offered an independent source of revenue that, after the 1580s, came to be known as a *mansab* (referring to a rank or office; the person who held that rank was known as a *mansabdar*). *Mansab*s were mostly bestowed on a prince around the time that he was transitioning to adult status. A *mansab* had two components. The first indicated an individual's place within the imperial hierarchy (*zat*) and the second the number of cavalry he was expected to maintain out of his income (*sawar*). In a handful of cases, emperors assigned a *mansab* while still keeping a minor prince on a stipend. This suggests the possibility that the *mansab* was occasionally used to signal a minor prince's rising importance since it gave him a clear place in the imperial hierarchy. It may also have been part of an effort to indicate a line of succession in the event of an imperial mishap or a decision to set aside the claims of more senior princes. There is little evidence, however, that minor princely *mansab* honorees ever maintained the required cavalry contingents, much less paid for them.

Take the case of Prince Khusrau, who received a single *mansab* rank of 5000 in 1594 from his grandfather Akbar (the system of double ranks, *zat/sawar*, was introduced a couple of years later). At the time of this award, Khusrau was only seven years old. His appointment placed him on par with the highest ranking Mughal nobles. Unlike them, however, he was not required to maintain the imperially mandated number of cavalry corresponding to his new rank; the emperor assigned troops to him instead. We may assume that Akbar was motivated to promote young Khusrau as a counterweight to his restless father, Salim, who would become Emperor Jahangir. On the eve of Akbar's death in

---

[45] In 2009 dollars, these amounts translate to daily stipends of $15,100, $11,325, $7,550, and $3,775.

[46] For a comprehensive discussion of the weight and value of the Mughal rupee between Akbar and Aurangzeb's reigns, see Irfan Habib, *The Agrarian System of Mughal India, 1556–1707* (New Delhi, repr. 1999), pp. 432–44. By way of comparison, the imperial administration calculated the average rate of pay for a qualified cavalryman at roughly twenty rupees per month or less than a rupee a day. Shireen Moosvi, *The Economy of the Mughal Empire c. 1595: A Statistical Study* (New Delhi, 1987), p. 216.

1605, the now eighteen-year-old Khusrau still received a daily stipend of Rs. 1,000, even though his original *mansab* had doubled to 10000. The markedly small size of his personal cavalry – roughly 350 men – in April 1606, six months into Jahangir's reign, points to the still largely honorific nature of his *mansab*. The same seems to have been true for other princes who received *mansab*s as minors.[47]

Whether or not minor princes were accorded a *mansab* rank, they remained in their father's residence and were thus closely supervised, with their father, the emperor, their mother, their tutors, *ataliq*s, and senior royal women all taking a keen interest in their development. Emperor Aurangzeb appears to have been particularly fastidious in his supervision as indicated in a note advising his oldest son Muhammad Sultan on his daily regimen:

Whether you are in residence or on a march, get up from bed seventy-two minutes before sunrise. After spending forty-eight minutes in bathing and getting ready, come out of your rooms for the morning prayer. After saying the prayer and reciting set passages, read one section of the Quran. Breakfast in the inner apartments comes next. If you are on a march, take horse (i.e., ride) forty-eight minutes after sunrise. Should you hunt on the way, take care to reach the halting place appointed for that day punctually. . . . The principal meal and some repose will fill your time till two hours before sunset, when the *asar* prayers should be said. But if the meal alone suffices to refresh you, spend the interval in improving your handwriting, composing letters, or reading Persian prose and poetry. After the *asar* prayer, read Arabic for a short time, and then, some twenty-four minutes before sunset, hold a "select audience," at which you should sit till forty-eight minutes after nightfall. Then leave the chamber and read a section of the Quran, retiring to the inner apartments, go to bed at nine p.m.[48]

Surely any prince would eagerly anticipate his attainment of adult status and the accompanying release from such close supervision.

---

[47] Included among the ranks of princes who received *mansab*s prior to reaching adult status were Akbar's three sons, Salim, Murad, and Danyal. They were aged eight, seven, and five when Akbar bestowed this honor on them in 1577. In Aurangzeb's reign, we see similar types of *mansab* grants for his fourth son Akbar and two grandsons, Bidar Bakht and Wala Jah, among others. Their ages were ten, nine, and ten respectively. In Aurangzeb's son Akbar's case, a contemporary chronicler even remarks that he was the only imperial prince who was given a *mansab* without any prior "service." Khafi Khan, *Muntakhab al-Labab*, ed. Kabir-ud-din Ahmad, vol. 2 (Calcutta, 1874), p. 209.

[48] Jadunath Sarkar, *Studies in Aurangzib's Reign* (Calcutta, repr. 1989), pp. 27–8.

## THE TRANSITION FROM MINOR TO ADULT

The transition from partial to full adulthood – from minor to adult prince – was slow and often encompassed many years. The process varied over the span of the Mughal Empire but changed in important ways after the 1570s with the gradual development of the *mansab* system.

Prior to the 1570s, a prince took his first step toward adulthood when the emperor deemed it necessary and/or appropriate to grant him a significant administrative or military assignment. Thus Akbar was nine years old when Humayun appointed him to take charge of his princely appanage of Ghazni in 1551.[49] To fulfill their independent duties, princes could initially expect substantial help from their fathers, especially in the form of experienced personnel. In Akbar's case, all of his recently deceased uncle Hindal's retainers were assigned to him. Over the years that followed, however, princes were fully expected to build up their own households by recruiting in the regions in which they served. We know this to be the case from Humayun's active recruitment of Badakhshanis to serve in his princely establishment during the early to mid-1520s. Even so, in this early period, full adult status did not come until a prince was in his mid to late teenage years, and nowhere is this more strongly suggested than in the continued presence of powerful *ataliqs* in the prince's emerging household as he took on his first assignments.

After the 1570s, two distinct and increasingly formalized rituals marked a minor prince's advance into adulthood. The first entailed graduating the prince from a relatively meager daily stipend to a full-fledged *mansab*, and – unlike during the earlier period – this might happen with or without a provincial or military assignment that moved a prince from the imperial court into a separate residence.[50] A prince's marriage was the second key marker.

Typically, *mansab* grants preceded marriage, although the examples of Shah Jahan's older sons Dara Shukoh and Shuja' offer exceptions.[51]

---

[49] In Humayun's case, he was eleven years old when his father Babur gave him the governorship/appanage of Badakhshan in 1519. His younger brother Kamran was thirteen when he received the governorship/appanage of Qandahar in 1522.

[50] Prominent examples of princes who remained largely court based for long periods after receiving their *mansab* include Akbar's son Salim, Jahangir's son Shahryar, Shah Jahan's son Dara Shukoh, and Aurangzeb's son Kam Bakhsh.

[51] In contrast, both of Shah Jahan's younger sons, Aurangzeb and Murad, received their initial *mansab*s two and three years before their first marriages in 1637 and 1642, respectively.

Inasmuch as the path toward adult status was variable, so too was the age at which princes began their respective journeys. Although none of the princes in the post-1570s period were as young as Akbar or Humayun when they began, the transition tended to occur sometime between thirteen and nineteen years of age. Contemporary sources offer us no insight as to why there was such variation. Likewise, neither a prince's status as a favored or older prince, nor whether or not he was permanently based at the imperial court, brings further clarity to the matter.

Even if marriage and a full *mansab* grant were key indicators that a prince was on the cusp of full adult status, it is crucial to remember that he was still not fully independent. Consider Aurangzeb's example. Despite getting his first *mansab* at the age of sixteen in 1634, being assigned to command a major military expedition against refractory Bundelas in 1635, and being awarded the governorship of the Deccan in 1636, Aurangzeb continued to be closely supervised by an *ataliq*, his maternal uncle and imperial nobleman Sha'ista Khan. Over the next couple of years, Sha'ista Khan traveled everywhere with him and even counter-signed all of Aurangzeb's princely orders. It was only in 1638, one year after Aurangzeb's first marriage, when he had already turned twenty, that Sha'ista Khan's supervision was finally lifted. The prince was now considered a full adult. The age at which *ataliq*s were no longer appointed to supervise varied greatly in the post-1570s period. For instance, Akbar's younger sons – Murad and Danyal – continued to be supervised by their powerful *ataliq*s well into their mid-twenties.

Because the process of attaining full adult status invariably stretched over years, it was never marked by a single coming-of-age celebration. Instead, the life of an imperial prince – especially after the 1570s – was punctuated by a number of important life-stage celebrations including the grant of his initial *mansab*, his marriage(s), the birth of his children, and his first send-off on a provincial or military assignment. The retirement of his *ataliq*, perhaps the single most important sign that he was truly considered an adult, occurred with no major accompanying ceremony. Marriage celebrations, on the other hand, attracted by far the most attention and incurred the greatest expense. The broad outlines of a marriage celebration varied little over the latter half of the sixteenth and seventeenth centuries. Dara Shukoh's first marriage to his cousin Nadira Begum in 1633 is illustrative of what generally transpired.[52]

---

[52] 'Abd al-Hamid Lahawri, *Padshahnamah*, ed. Kabir-ud-din and Abdul Rahim, vol. 1 (Calcutta, 1867), pp. 452–60.

Following months of preparations and the exchange of lavish gifts between members of both families, various ceremonies and celebrations unfolded over the course of several days at venues around the imperial court. These included processions, royal audiences, music and dance performances, fireworks and other light displays, and open-court viewings of the gifts exchanged. The high point was the actual wedding ceremony, officiated by a senior Muslim clergyman.

In a discussion about princely households, it is significant that, at the time of his marriage, Dara Shukoh had not been granted a *mansab* but rather still received a daily allowance, which in comparative terms was very small. This was despite the fact that he already had his own personal residence, albeit one on the grounds of the emperor's palace. We know this because the most important chronicle of Shah Jahan's reign, the *Padshahnama*, describes how he was escorted from his house to the court for the wedding ceremony. After the night's festivities were concluded, he and his bride were escorted back to his residence.[53] One week later, the emperor honored Dara Shukoh by visiting him there.[54] At the time, the prince was almost eighteen years old. He had likely been living in a physically separate residence since his father Shah Jahan's accession in 1628 when he was around thirteen years old.

Judging from this and the examples of other Mughal princes, such as Khurram in Jahangir's reign and princes Akbar and Kam Bakhsh in Aurangzeb's, emperors' sons were usually given the right to set up a separate personal residence some time around puberty. Until then, however, they were expected to be content with a personal apartment within or contiguous to their father's harem. Grandsons of a reigning emperor often continued to live in their father's establishment until well into their twenties. This was certainly the case with Aurangzeb's numerous grandsons. In this manner, the dynasty restricted both the proliferation of princely households and the cultivation of political ambitions on the part of immature princes. Princes of collateral imperial lines tended to be restricted to rooms in a single sprawling and overcrowded establishment (sometimes referred to as the *deorhi-i salatin*) specifically built to accommodate them and their families. They often lived there for the duration of their lives. With fewer princes and princely households strutting across the imperial stage, Mughal political energy could remain focused.

---

[53] Ibid., pp. 457–60
[54] 'Inayat Khan, *Shahjahannama*, trans. A.R. Fuller (Delhi, 1990), pp. 91–2.

Upon the prince's move to a separate, stand-alone residence at the imperial court, we begin to see the earliest outlines of an emerging adult princely household. Broadly, it was composed of two albeit often over-lapping spheres. The first had a domestic-oriented quality (it was largely female along with some eunuchs), and the second focused on administra-tive and military matters. These two parts were constituted, respectively, at the prince's marriage and at his attainment of a proper (versus honorary) *mansab*.

After the 1580s, marriage brought a major infusion of new people into the princely household. Among them was a select group of women whose job was to oversee the workings of an emerging princely harem. These women were appointed either by the emperor himself or by the mother of the prince. A matron known as the *mahaldar* directed them. Since the emperor usually paid all their salaries, these women were typically answer-able to him alone. They acted as his eyes and ears both within and outside the princely harem. For example, when Prince A'zam behaved recklessly, going too close to the imperial entrenchments during the siege of Panhala in the early 1700s, his *mahaldar* reported this to his father Aurangzeb.[55] Not surprisingly, princes did not always enjoy smooth relations with their *mahaldar*s. In one instance, Aurangzeb severely reprimanded A'zam for deliberately abandoning his *mahaldar* while on a march with the rest of his household. As well as humiliating his son by calling him "short-sighted," "base-minded," and "foolish," Aurangzeb fined A'zam the substantial sum of Rs. 50,000 (around $750,000 in 2009 dollars).[56]

A second major group of women, including every social rank, tended to the daily needs of the wife, or wives, of the prince. At the higher end of the social spectrum were tutors who instructed their royal charges in reading the Quran, composing poetry, appreciating literature, painting, and sometimes even handling a weapon. The slowly growing princely household also included a wife's childhood friends and female relatives as well as the prince's foster sisters. Most of these women lived in the prince's household until their own marriage. Their numbers were relatively small, however, compared to the vast phalanx of female servitors responsible for bathing, clothing, dressing, feeding, and entertaining the mistress and her wards. Among the ranks of this last group were likely individuals with specific

---

[55] Aurangzeb, *Anecdotes of Aurangzib*, trans. Jadunath Sarkar (Calcutta, repr. 1988), p. 49. For a separate episode involving a *mahaldar* spying on Mu'azzam, see Sarkar, *Studies in Aurangzib's Reign*, p. 41.

[56] Aurangzeb, *Anecdotes of Aurangzib*, p. 50.

artisanal and medicinal skills. Their presence allowed a princely harem to be fairly self-contained.

Rounding out the harem was a third important group of women: female guards. The female guards were responsible for protecting the inner precincts against uninvited intruders. Central Asian women were particularly prized in this role because of their skill with weapons, their supposed no-nonsense temperament, and their strong physical frames. It is important to note that princes generally had only incidental contact with the vast majority of the women living in their households. The senior women (including perhaps the emperor's representative, the *mahaldar*) orchestrated meetings between the prince and his wives, even determining which wife the prince could meet on any particular evening. Their decisions were informed by the status of the different wives and also by concerns about an uncontrolled proliferation of imperial heirs. In the imperial family, relations between husband and wife, copulation, pregnancy, childbirth, and childrearing had significant political consequences. Although Mughal sources never mention birth control practices or other attempts to limit the number of children born to a prince, Manucci (the Italian traveler and sometime "doctor" to Prince Mu'azzam's harem) suggests that princes were not allowed to have more than four sons. To keep within that number, women were forced to abort unwanted fetuses.[57]

The two parts of an imperial household – whether that of a minor prince, an adult prince, or the emperor himself – were gendered: the domestic realm, the realm of the harem, was considered female, whereas the administrative and military part was considered male. The imperial household thus depended on eunuchs to serve as hinges between its female domestic and male public parts. Although all Mughal emperors from Akbar down to Aurangzeb made gestures toward forbidding the castration of young boys (most eunuchs came from Bengal and Orissa), their dependence on eunuchs meant that these injunctions were rarely followed. An important role of the eunuchs was administration of the harem, and they complemented female servitors at every level including the *mahaldar*.

We do not know if eunuchs served princes when the royals were still children. Only with a prince's first marriage are they brought into prominence. For instance, we know that Khwaja Talib/Khidmatgar Khan (d. 1704), chief administrator of Aurangzeb's imperial harem in the last decades of his reign, had first joined the emperor's household when he was

---

[57] Manucci, *Mogul India*, vol. 2, p. 384.

a prince, at the time of his marriage to Dilras Banu Begum in 1637. The Khwaja was a gift from Shahnawaz Khan Safavi, Dilras Banu's father.[58] In similar fashion, Navid, the chief eunuch (*khwajasara*) of Mu'azzam's senior wife and a key co-conspirator in his mistress and master's attempts to subvert the Mughal conquest of Golkonda in 1687, joined Mu'azzam's household at the time of the prince's first marriage in the early 1660s.[59]

Years of loyal service often led individual eunuchs to accrue great wealth, honor, and prestige. Some did so exclusively within the narrow context of the princely harem, but others graduated to important administrative and military positions in the larger princely household. Khwaja Shahbaz, for example, was Murad's right-hand man during the 1657–9 war of succession. In the same conflict, Khwaja Basant and Khwaja Maqul continued to serve Murad's brother and foe Dara Shukoh with military distinction, even after his political cause was all but lost and almost everyone else had deserted him. A distinct corporate identity, forged through a shared physical condition, the sometimes negative reaction of others, and strict hierarchies among their own ranks, made the eunuchs a force to reckon with in any princely household.

If marriage boosted the development of the princely household's domestic realm, it was the grant of an adult *mansab* that initiated and shaped its administrative and military sphere. With true adulthood came wealth and the obligation to meet important imperial duties. The growth of these administrative and military elements is taken up in much greater detail in the next two sections in this chapter.

Decades might pass between granting a prince the right to maintain his own household – not just a separate residence within the imperial court, but a separate household in another region of the empire – and the time his father, the emperor, vacated the throne. In Humayun's case it was eleven years, a mere four for Akbar, twenty for Salim/Jahangir, twenty-one for Khurram/Shah Jahan, twenty-three for Aurangzeb, and forty-eight for Mu'azzam/Bahadur Shah I. For these men, as well as other politically less successful princes, those years were filled with frenetic and unrelenting household growth; it was a period when their households took concrete shape and grew in size. Failure to build a strong household meant certain death, and success depended to a large extent on access to money. The ways in which princely households were funded over the life of the empire and implications of the money chase for princes, households, and empire alike are the subject of the next section.

---

[58]  M. Khan, *Maasir i Alamgiri*, p. 481.
[59]  K. Khan, *Muntakhab al-Labab*, vol. 2, p. 334.

## FUNDING THE PRINCELY HOUSEHOLD, 1585–1680S

Money was the lifeblood of all princely households. Without relatively easy access to wealth, they could not expect to grow, retain the people they had, meet their master's imperial obligations, or face down potential political or military threats. Not surprisingly, adult princes did everything in their power to ensure that their households collected the money to which they thought they were entitled.

In Chapter 2, we saw how the appanage system offered a fairly focused target – a specific region – for raising princely income. In the post-1585 period, with the end of appanages, princes were forced to do things differently. Not only did this development spawn princely entrepreneurship and creativity in search of money, but princely endeavors across the empire also drove the expansion and deepening of Mughal regional influence and authority through the end of the seventeenth century. Although lacking the degree of autonomy enjoyed by an appanage holder, the Mughal Prince of the post-1585 period still learned valuable lessons for governance and administration in this new setting. The task of securing income brought princes and their households into contact with the various ethnic groups and political formations that comprised the empire, forcing on them the experience of governing in a complicated landscape and providing opportunities to improve and transform revenue collection within it. This practical education in household building and maintenance was of long-term political and administrative significance and benefit to the empire.

In 1577, eight years before he finally put an end to the institution of the appanage at the death of his brother Mirza Hakim, Akbar had already made it clear that his own sons would never control appanages. Instead, those sons represented a new generation of Mughal princes whose income was to be derived through a complex and interconnected system of *mansab*s (imperial ranks) and temporary land assignments called *jagir*s. The *jagir* system was specifically devised to replace the old system of appanage-based princely authority and autonomy.

Following two decades of tinkering, the *mansabdari* system had assumed by the mid-1590s a form that it largely maintained until the eighteenth century.[60] It had two broad aims: to confer on its holder a

---

[60] My understanding of the *mansab* system depends heavily on the following accounts: M. Athar Ali, *The Mughal Nobility under Aurangzeb* (Delhi, repr. 1997), pp. 38–62; Shireen Moosvi, "Evolution of *Mansab* system under Akbar until 1596-7," *Journal of the Royal Asiatic Society* 2 (1981): 175–83; Irfan Habib, "Mansab System, 1595–1637," *Proceedings of the Indian History Congress* 29 (1967): 221–42; Jos Gommans, *Mughal*

rank (*zat*) within a larger imperial hierarchy and to provide a salary that covered both household expenses (indistinct from personal expenses) and the costs of maintaining a specified number of cavalry. By this, Akbar effectively quantified and graded the power of the various important figures beneath the Mughal emperor, including that of the princes. Whereas the old system relied on the emperor's personal management of the many figures within his court, the *mansabdari* systematized that task within a bureaucratizing apparatus.[61]

To reckon the overall amount due to a *mansab* holder, two sets of calculations were required. The first focused on status rank (*zat*) and was geared toward defraying the cost of a personal establishment. A fairly straightforward table was used to calculate exactly what amount might be expected. Thanks to the figures provided in the *A'in-i Akbari* (compiled in the mid-1590s), we know that princes with *zat* ranks between 5000 and 7000 received a monthly payment of Rs. 45,000; those between 7000 and 8000, Rs. 50,000; and those between 8000 and 10000 received Rs. 60,000. This translates to annual salaries in the range of Rs. 540,000 to Rs. 720,000 ($8,154,000 to $10,872,000 in 2009 dollars).[62] By the early 1640s, and with continuous upward adjustments, annual amounts earmarked for a prince's household expenses ranged from Rs. 300,000 for someone holding a lower *zat* of 6000 to Rs. 1,000,000 for a *zat* of 20000 or above ($4,530,000 to $15,100,000 in 2009 dollars).[63]

The second amount due a *mansabdar* – an amount referred to in the sources as *sawar* (cavalry) – was meant to help him maintain a prescribed number of troops. Without going into the complexities of all the possible upward adjustments in *sawar* payments – including such items as salary accommodations for onerous assignments, additional services rendered (*mashrut*), and extra pay for especially valued types of horses and soldiers – individuals received a base sum derived from a simple formula. It entailed

*Warfare: Indian Frontiers and Highroads to Empire, 1500–1700* (London, 2002), pp. 84–88.

[61] This development, Stephen Blake has argued, points to the evolution of a new model of empire, from a previously patrimonial state (where state and household officials were virtually indistinct) to an emerging patrimonial-bureaucratic one (in which, for instance, officials who were neither "dependents nor bureaucrats, worked in an organization intermediate between the household apparatus of the patrimonial kingdom and the highly bureaucratized system of the modern state"). Blake, *Shahjahanabad*, pp. 17–20. See also Stephen Blake, "The Patrimonial-Bureaucratic Empire of the Mughals," *Journal of Asian Studies* 39, no. 1 (1979): 77–94.

[62] Shaikh Abu'l Fazl, *Ain-i-Akbari*, ed. H. Blochmann, vol. 1 (Calcutta, 1872), p. 180.

[63] *Selected Documents of Shahjahan's Reign*, ed. Yusuf Husain Khan (Hyderabad, 1950), pp. 79–80.

multiplying the number of a person's cavalry rank (*sawar*) by a unit cost per cavalryman. According to Jos Gommans, the latter remained fairly stable for most of the seventeenth century, around Rs. 20 per month.[64] As a result, a prince such as Khurram, who had received a *sawar* rank of 5000 at the beginning of his princely career in 1607, could expect to receive roughly Rs. 100,000 per month. A decade later, when Khurram had attained a *sawar* rank of 20000 (of which half was now calculated at double rates, as a mark of Jahangir's favor), he could expect around Rs. 600,000 per month. When this sum is added to the entitlement from his *zat* rank of 30000, Khurram may have been entitled to a staggering annual salary of more than 8 million rupees (or $120,800,000 in 2009 dollars).[65] To put this in a broader context, the total tax revenues of the independent Uzbek-ruled kingdoms of Balkh, Badakhshan, Bukhara, and Samarkand in the 1640s amounted to no more than a few million rupees annually.

Such extraordinary entitlements were met in two ways. One was through direct cash grants (*in'am*). This mode was generally discouraged, however, and remained infrequent until the last years of Aurangzeb's reign. Instead, preference was given to offering *mansabdars* a time-bound salary claim (*talab*) on the assessed income of a fiscal unit called a *jagir*, to which the following section is devoted.

### *Jagirs* as sources of revenue in the *mansabdari* system

On average, an appointee could claim the income of an awarded *jagir* for three years, after which it was transferred to someone else. In most instances, the *talab* of princes was not met from a single *jagir* but rather from an array of different-sized *jagirs* of varying quality. Although princes were occasionally given clusters of *jagirs* in the region where they served or had a particular political interest, the imperial court tended to prefer scattering their *jagirs* across the empire. Kam Bakhsh's predicament in 1694 was fairly typical. His *jagir* portfolio included holdings in at least five imperial provinces including Delhi, the Punjab, Malwa, Awadh, and the Deccan.[66] Needless to say, this made the prince's task of collecting his *jagir* salary

---

[64] Gommans, *Mughal Warfare*, p. 87.

[65] In the late 1640s, Shah Jahan's oldest son, Dara Shukoh, held a *mansab* rank of 20000/20000 (of which 10000 was calculated at enhanced rates). This entitled him to the extraordinary pay of Rs. 10 million ($150,000,000 in 2009 dollars). Habib, *The Agrarian System of Mughal India*, p. 325.

[66] *Akhbarat-i Darbar-i Mu'alla*, vol. 17, no. 36/16; vol. 19, pp. 48, 110, 329, 330.

very complicated and forced him and his household to focus considerable energy and attention on this critical task.

Because princes held mostly scattered and transferable *jagir*s, they confronted two difficulties.[67] First, they often lacked specific and detailed knowledge about the revenue-paying capacity of a given *jagir*. They were also not always attuned to the minutiae regarding local political and social realities. They relied on two sets of locally based officials (notably these were the emperor's, and not princely, appointees) to help them overcome these deficits.

The first group was composed of permanent, often hereditary officials (local and usually Hindu) who handled most of the lower-level and day-to-day operations of the imperial revenue machinery. The second group included higher-ranked imperial employees, most often Muslims. Usually *mansab* holders themselves, this latter group manned the upper echelons of a region's political, military, and administrative government. On occasion, they were drawn in to help *jagir* assignees maintain order and collect their money. They also might serve as a bulwark against abuses by *jagir* holders. Interfacing with these two groups of imperial officials were designated members of a prince's household.

Since access to sources of revenue was crucial to the solvency of a princely household, powerful princes tended to send representatives to a given *jagir* immediately upon receiving the all-important certificate confirming their claim. In 1652, for example, upon learning that his *jagir*s had been consolidated in the Deccan following his reappointment as governor of the region, Aurangzeb immediately ordered one of his leading servitors, Muhammad Tahir Khurasani, to head south from the city of Multan where he was stationed to take charge of them.[68] In June 1695, when Aurangzeb's son A'zam learned that he had been awarded Ratlam, he ordered one of his household servants and a sizable contingent of troops to proceed there without delay.[69] Similarly, urgent orders are scattered across the historical record.[70] Pending the arrival of princely representatives, separate orders were often sent to local officials commanding them, as in Aurangzeb's case in 1652, to appoint "intelligent and honest" revenue collectors ('*amil*s) in the hope that "there is no shortfall in revenue

---

[67] This account is largely derived from Habib, *The Agrarian System of Mughal India*, pp. 316–18.

[68] Aurangzeb, *Adab-i 'Alamgiri*, ed. Abdul Ghafur Chaudhuri, vol. 2. (Lahore, 1971), pp. 676–7.

[69] *Akhbarat-i Darbar-i Mu'alla*, vol. 19, p. 537.

[70] Aurangzeb, *Raqa'im-i Kara'im*, Asiatic Society of Bengal, Ivanow 383, f. 198b; *Akhbarat-i Darbar-i Mu'alla*, vol. 25, p. 53.

collection and that the peasants are not oppressed."[71] Such commands reflect the anxiety of *jagir* holders that transitional moments offered opportunities for malfeasance and general troublemaking.

To maintain a *jagir*, the prince relied most heavily on two occasionally overlapping groups of princely retainers. The first was composed of men with specialized accounting and administrative skills; the second were military men.[72] These two groups complemented each other, and they often lived and worked together in a *jagir* over a few years, separated from their master's court while they managed his affairs.

As Irfan Habib has observed, it was not uncommon for princes to sometimes grant sub-assignments out of their own *jagir*s to such employees. Besides providing monetary compensation, this may well have provided an incentive to these employees to maintain a well-oiled revenue collection apparatus.[73] In some cases, the servant of a prince was directly inserted into the local bureaucracy through an imperial assignment. Such was the case with 'Ali Sher Quli, who was made the chief police official (*kotwal*) of Banaras. He was a longtime servant of Aurangzeb's son A'zam, and at the time of his appointment, Banaras lay within A'zam's *jagir*.[74]

The job of princely officials on *jagir* assignments was never an easy one. In the course of ensuring that the assessed amount of *jagir* income flowed into their master's coffers, they often faced peasants unwilling to pay up, intermediary figures eager to profit themselves, mismatches between central assessments and the actual revenue a *jagir* was able to generate, fluctuating revenues resulting from weather or political disturbances, and various other complications arising from the nature of their task. Sometimes a prince's manager was deemed so inept that the emperor himself stepped in to reprimand him.[75] Other times a prince's managers were so overwhelmed by the challenges that they saw fit to call for military backup from more experienced individuals based outside the *jagir*.[76]

---

[71] Aurangzeb, *Adab-i 'Alamgiri*, vol. 2, pp. 675–7.

[72] The broad outlines of these two groups are apparent in the personnel who were sent to take charge of Mu'azzam's *jagir*s as he was gradually rehabilitated into the imperial system in late 1694 following a long stint in prison for plotting to undermine Aurangzeb's war objectives in the Deccan. *Akhbarat-i Darbar-i Mu'alla*, vol. 19, pp. 19, 324, 327, 370, 379.

[73] Habib, *The Agrarian System of Mughal India*, p. 326.

[74] *Akhbarat-i Darbar-i Mu'alla*, vol. 17, no. 36/26. See also vol. 41, pp. 74, 141.

[75] Aurangzeb, *Ruq'at-i 'Alamgiri*, ed. Saiyid Muhammad Abdul Majeed (Kanpur, 1916), p. 14; *Akhbarat-i Darbar-i Mu'alla*, vol. 29, p. 58.

[76] *Akhbarat-i Darbar-i Mu'alla*, vol. 17, nos. 36/16, 37/2; Aurangzeb, *Adab-i 'Alamgiri*, vol. 1, pp. 189–92.

There are also notable instances when the efforts of princely officials led directly to improvements in the administrative machinery of a *jagir*, and these enhanced the Mughal state's powers of extraction from its subject population. A series of revenue documents relating to one area, Dhar, in the province of Malwa, offer insight into how this process worked. Dhar was a part of Shah Jahan's son Murad's *jagir* between 1653 and 1657. Upon receiving certification, Murad sent his representative Dianat Khan to the region. Dianat Khan's work there appears to have had transformative effects: he clarified the rights and obligations of a powerful family of lower-level officials; he intervened to untangle disputes around village water rights; and he combated what he deemed illegal taxes being levied by a group of lower-level officials. The year 1656 saw a bumper harvest, but, more importantly, increased tax receipts – an achievement perhaps attributable to Dianat Khan.[77] His efforts were not popular among the local *zamindar*s, however, and in 1657–8 these hereditary and non-imperial landholders rebelled against the Mughals just as the *jagir* was being transferred away from Murad.[78] At that time, an imperial war of succession was also underway, and, perhaps in the ensuing political uncertainty, the local Dhar landlords sought to regain their previous and more favorable social and financial position. Their failure, and the continued extension of imperial revenue collection into Aurangzeb's reign, is suggested in a 1661 document. It contains an official call for a fresh assessment and presumably an upward revision in the revenue demands placed on every village in Dhar, as well as a continuation of the efforts of the previous decade when Murad held this *jagir*.[79]

Also in the 1650s, Prince Aurangzeb, Shah Jahan's other son, similarly undertook creative imperial management as governor of the Deccan, returning to a post he had previously held between 1636 and 1644. The Mughal elite had long complained that the Deccan's *jagir*s' revenue was woefully low. The Deccan was considered so scrawny an assignment that nobles were unwilling to serve there. One Shah Jahan–era *mansabdar*, Mirza Owais Beg, quipped, "*Jagir*s in the Deccan, aside from abandoned villages, have nothing." He continued, playing on the double meaning of the word *dam*: "Your *lakh* [i.e., 100,000] *dam*s [equal to Rs. 2,500] is the equivalent of a *dam* [a weight measure] in

[77] Islamic Art Museum/Dar al-Asar al-Islamiyyah, Kuwait, LNS 235, docs. b, c, d, j, k, l. I am grateful to Professor Irfan Habib for generously sharing these documents with me.
[78] Ibid., doc. i.
[79] Ibid., doc. mm.

which there is not a single grain."[80] When given this assignment a second time, Aurangzeb deployed officials from his household, as well as Deccan-based imperial administrators (such as Murshid Quli Khan), to institute broad reforms.

In the prevailing system, the Deccan's revenue was assessed on the basis of the number of plows counted. To replace this, Aurangzeb first introduced a system based on crop sharing (in which peasants handed over a percentage of their crop to the state). A few years later, that system was also phased out in favor of one based on payments in cash determined by complex calculations based on crop prices and yields versus payments in kind as under the previous systems. This final version remained in place into the eighteenth century.[81]

Aurangzeb marched out of the Deccan in late 1657 to wage a war of succession. By this time, we can assume that his revenue collection had improved considerably given that he was able to independently raise and pay for the imperial forces under his command and maintain a strong personal army as well. Speaking to the agricultural transformation of parts of the Deccan, especially around the eponymously named city of Aurangabad, in the late 1650s, Bhimsen Saxsena, a contemporary historian, notes that the region "is very thickly populated and not a single piece of land was to be found which was without cultivation." He goes on to praise the relative affordability of wheat, millet, pulses, sugar, and unrefined oil.[82]

Making these changes, however, had not been easy. When he was first sent back to the Deccan from Multan in 1652, Aurangzeb complained to Shah Jahan that his transfer had cost him the not inconsiderable amount of Rs. 1.7 million in lost *jagir* income. Aurangzeb was incensed when Shah Jahan refused to either grant him a cash salary or assign him revenues from more productive *jagir*s in northern India to make up the difference. In a letter to the emperor, he declared:

If His Majesty wishes that I should be put in charge of such an important province, then I should have the means to manage such a large and disturbed province in a manner that does not embarrass me before the nobles and the rulers of the Deccan.[83]

---

[80] Shaikh Farid Bhakkari, *Dhakhirat al-Khawanin*, ed. S. Moinul Haq, vol. 3 (Karachi, 1974), p. 75.

[81] Habib, *The Agrarian System of Mughal India*, pp. 234, 268–9.

[82] Saxsena, *Tarikh-i-Dilkasha*, p. 20.

[83] Aurangzeb, *Adab-i 'Alamgiri*, vol. 1, pp. 95–8.

Shah Jahan stood his ground, however, and ordered his son to make do with what resources this *jagir* offered. To this, Aurangzeb replied:

I have always tried to extend tillage and increase the number of houses; but since I am not a vain man I have reported it [i.e., the difficulties] to you. A country that has been desolated by various calamities cannot be made flourishing in two or three years. ... How can I, in one or two seasons, bring back cultivation to a *pargana* [a revenue and administrative unit] that has been monetarily unproductive for twenty years?[84]

Aurangzeb viewed his Deccan assignment as a sign that Shah Jahan considered him irrelevant to imperial politics and sought to undermine his claims to a properly royal future. In response, starting in 1653, he began complaining to his powerful sister Jahan Ara, who lived with Shah Jahan at the imperial court:

If His Majesty [i.e. Shah Jahan] wishes that of all his servants I alone should spend my life in dishonor and die in obscurity, I cannot but obey ... it is better that by order of His Majesty, I should be relieved from the disgust of such a life so that no harm may reach the state and other people's hearts may be at rest. Ten years before this I had realized this fact and, knowing my life to be threatened, had resigned my post so that I might cause no worry to other people.[85]

Finally, in 1655, Shah Jahan gave in to Aurangzeb's pestering. He seems to have been under considerable pressure from the prince's strong lobby of supporters, including Prime Minister Sa'dullah Khan, at the imperial court. Aurangzeb was also using his penury as an excuse to refuse taking direct charge of at least ten key forts across the Deccan (including Ahmadnagar).[86] The emperor finally agreed to subsidize a large part of Aurangzeb's household and gubernatorial expenses from the treasury of Malwa.[87] This made all the difference to Aurangzeb's Deccan projects. His financial position was less precarious and his land-revenue reforms began to take effect. And of special note: where previously he had struggled to retain household members, repeatedly losing them to the imperial court and rival Deccani courts, now he was able to slowly lure them back. Thus a former household member and later loyalist Mir Malik Hussain returned, and others – including close princely advisors such as Muhammad Tahir

---

[84] Quoted in Jadunath Sarkar, *History of Aurangzib, Volumes I & II* (Bombay, repr. 1973), p. 112. See also Aurangzeb, *Adab-i 'Alamgiri*, vol. 1, pp. 140–3, 163–4.

[85] Quoted in Zahir-ud-Din Faruki, *Aurangzeb and His Times* (Delhi, repr. 1972), p. 17. See also Aurangzeb, *Adab-i 'Alamgiri*, vol. 2, pp. 807–8.

[86] Aurangzeb, *Adab-i 'Alamgiri*, vol. 1, pp. 505–6.

[87] Ibid., pp. 165–8, 506–7.

Khurasani and Shaikh Mir – turned down lucrative offers of employment outside the Deccan. Each of these figures would play a significant role in Aurangzeb's successful struggle for the Mughal throne in 1658.

Princely dependence on *jagir* income led Aurangzeb to improve his revenue collection; such was also the case with his brother Shuja', who extended and improved the revenue collection apparatus in Bengal on the eve of the 1657–9 war of succession. Likewise, Salim's Allahabad-based rebellion between 1599 and 1604 not only resulted in significant long-term improvements in imperial revenue collection in Allahabad, Bihar, and Awadh, but also consolidated imperial authority across the region. Perhaps the most significant efforts unfolded on the geographical margins of the empire, in regions such as Thatta, the Deccan, or Bengal, leading to their closer incorporation.

### Gifts, trade, and military campaigns as revenue sources

Even though it remained absolutely central to household financial security, *jagir* income came to be supplemented by money that flowed from new sources to post-1580s Mughal princes. Three of these are especially noteworthy.

The first included gifts in cash or kind from a huge cast of characters, ranging from the emperor to other members of the royal family, the nobility, foreign rulers and visitors, merchants, imperial officials, religious figures, and down to humble supplicants. As might be expected, the most valuable gifts tended to come from the emperor, usually in celebration of every conceivable occasion. A short list of the more important dates might include imperial birthdays (both lunar and solar), the date of accession, weddings, births, religious holidays, and military victories. In this manner, princes might receive many millions of rupees worth of gifts from their fathers during their lifetimes.[88] Yet it is likely that the gifts received from all the other people and groups that directed their generosity toward imperial princes far outweighed those of the emperor himself. Princes would in turn re-gift much of this largesse within their own practices of patronage and munificence, although some went toward paying household expenses. If especially cash strapped or junior, a prince would even request that the

---

[88] Perhaps the most extraordinary case of imperial largesse occurred in 1526. After seizing the Lodi capital of Agra, Babur gave his oldest son Humayun Rs. 2 million plus another room of uncounted money from Agra's treasury; his second son Kamran received Rs. 1.7 million, and his younger sons 'Askari and Hindal got Rs. 1.5 million each. Babur, *The Baburnama*, p. 356.

cash equivalent of a valuable item be substituted to pay the salaries of people working for him.[89]

Some princes further supplemented their income with trade. Certainly, those who came of age between 1605 and 1658 actively tapped into the trade of agricultural goods and luxury products. They built ships to ply the most lucrative routes between northern India, the Persian Gulf, the Red Sea, and the Bay of Bengal; they established bazaars, towns, and ports; and they worked out lucrative deals with both Indian and foreign merchants. Akbar's sons of the earlier era may also have done so, but we have no evidence of it. Jahangir's son Khurram, however, made a fortune in commerce, and a wealth of East India Company records and European personal accounts survive to tell the tale.

Khurram was actively involved in buying and selling goods, and he could get rough when thwarted. He demanded that Europeans offer his representatives the right of first refusal on anything that landed in Surat, Mughal India's most important port city and part of Khurram's *jagir* through the 1610s and early 1620s. When they balked, set their own prices too high, or refused to extend lines of credit, Khurram was not above sending a detachment of cavalry to physically intimidate them or embargo their warehouses; he might stop their caravans from going in and out of Gujarat or prevent them from buying goods elsewhere in Mughal India.[90]

Khurram maintained his own fleet of ships to enable direct dealings with foreign traders and to actively shape the flow of goods into his territories. Parlaying his power as Jahangir's favored son, Khurram sometimes demanded European protection for his ships against other European pirates and renegades. He tried to establish a princely monopoly on the import of coral from the Red Sea, and he endeavored to prevent Europeans from selling Indian-produced goods in the port city of Mocha (Yemen). On one occasion, he even forced the English to help him refloat one of his ships that had run aground in Gujarat. As well as importing coral, precious metals and jewels, coffee, and tobacco, Khurram exported cloth, rice, dyes, and an assortment of manufactured goods.[91]

---

[89] *Akhbarat-i Darbar-i Mu'alla*, vol. 17, nos. 36/24, 36/26.

[90] W. Foster, *The English Factories in India, 1618–1669*, vol. 1 (Oxford, 1906), pp. 121, 134, 321; W. Foster, *The English Factories in India, 1618–1669*, vol. 2 (Oxford, 1908), pp. 189, 316; Sir Thomas Roe, *The Embassy of Sir Thomas Roe to India, 1615–1619* (Delhi, repr. 1990), p. 120. Farhat Hasan, "Mughal Records on the English East India Company: A Calendar to 1740," unpub. M.A. thesis, Aligarh Muslim University (1987), pp. 3–6.

[91] Foster, *English Factories in India*, vol. 1, pp. 106, 117, 131, 135, 167–77, 204, 321; Foster, *English Factories in India*, vol. 2, pp. 173, 218, 219, 230.

By all accounts, the prince earned rich profits from his trading activities. Like all other income sources, this one fed the overall expenses of his household, be they domestic, administrative, or military. Attesting to his household's place at the heart of powerful political and economic networks is the presence of figures such as Muhammad Taqi. A member of Khurram's inner circle and a scion of a trading family, Muhammad Taqi seems to have served as a hinge between Khurram and various commercial groups up until his capture and execution by imperial forces during Khurram's rebellion in the 1620s.

All the sons of Khurram (now Emperor Shah Jahan) were similarly energetic and enterprising. Even so, Aurangzeb stands out. In addition to maintaining a personal fleet of ships, contracting English ships to carry goods for him, and at one point trying to corner the market on lead and saltpeter, Aurangzeb cultivated close links to men such as Mir Jumla, the prime minister of Golkonda, with whom the prince shared important political and commercial interests. Most significantly, over the course of his princely career, Aurangzeb constructed two new towns – Aurangabad in the Deccan and Aurangabandar in Thatta. Both were marked by their proximity to commercial traffic. Aurangabad lay astride key trading routes linking the Deccan Plateau to the Konkan coast to the west and Gujarat and Malwa to the north. Aurangabandar was a seaport in an estuary of the River Indus; from here Aurangzeb hoped to tap into the wealth flowing in and out of the thriving Punjab region as well as that moving between Mughal India and the Persian Gulf. Aurangzeb not only held a stake in trade routes moving westwards, he was also deeply involved in running ships toward Southeast Asia, to Aceh in particular.[92]

Outside the small group of Mughal princes who spent most of their lives at the imperial court, princes in the post-1580s period generally enjoyed access to a fourth (after *jagirs*, gifts, and trade) source of income. This was money derived from their participation in successful military campaigns. Immense sums were sometimes accumulated in this manner, usually in the form of tribute payments, cash settlements, and gifts. Over the first half of the seventeenth century, the Deccan was a particularly lucrative arena. For instance, following a successful 1617 campaign against an alliance of Deccan-based kingdoms, Khurram collected Rs. 2 million from Bijapur, Rs. 1.2 million from Ahmadnagar, and

---

[92] S. Arasaratnam and A. Ray, *Masulipatnam and Cambay: A History of Two Port Towns, 1500–1800* (New Delhi, 1994), p. 67.

Rs. 1.8 million from Golkonda (roughly $30 million, $18 million, and
$27 million respectively in 2009 dollars). Around the same time,
Khurram strong-armed various Rajas in the Gondwana region into dis-
gorging hundreds of thousands of rupees in owed tribute and offering
large numbers of valuable elephants. These payments were all collected
by princely household retainers, not imperial officers. Khurram either
directly pocketed the income or his grateful father Jahangir offered it
back to him. Between 1620 and 1621, Khurram replenished his coffers
with another campaign in the Deccan. This income helped fund the first
stage of his princely rebellion in 1622.

Aurangzeb, too, drew heavily on funds raised through military campaigns to meet his household and military expenses. In the late 1630s, he
forced states including Jamra and Portuguese-held Goa to make annual
tributary payments. In 1645, after crushing a Koli rebellion in Gujarat, he
forced their chiefs to pay a large cash indemnity. The same fate awaited the
Nahmardis, Karanis, Jukiyas, Hotis, and the Jam of Hala after they
opposed Aurangzeb's authority following his appointment as governor
of Thatta-Multan in 1647. Aurangzeb also raised millions of rupees in his
campaigns against Bijapur and Golkonda in 1656–7. In fact, his success
prompted terrible recriminations from his father Shah Jahan. The latter
suspected him of hoarding his gains and shortchanging the imperial
treasury. And sure enough, in 1657, Aurangzeb – always perennially
cash strapped prior to this – suddenly had sufficient financial resources
to raise a large army to fight and win the Mughal throne. Even though he
was likely helped by improving returns from his *jagir*s in the Deccan, the
money squeezed out of Bijapur and Golkonda proved pivotal to
Aurangzeb's political fortunes.

If the political vision of Mughal princes prior to the 1580s was anchored in fixed appanages, post-1580s princes looked out upon the entire
empire as their stage and their land of opportunity. It was incumbent
upon them to raise money across the empire – whether from scattered
*jagir* holdings, trading ventures, or military campaigns – to fund their
households and foster their political ambitions. For their success, the
princes depended entirely on the presence of experienced, knowledge-
able, and loyal individuals in their households. They also depended on
their households being militarily robust. We now turn to the composition
and roles of adult princely households. Without a clear picture of these,
we cannot appreciate the absolute centrality of his household to the life
and fate of the Mughal Prince.

## THE STRUCTURE OF A MATURE PRINCELY HOUSEHOLD

Every adult Mughal Prince – barring the disgraced or imprisoned – possessed his own household. These varied in size from a few individuals for princes of collateral imperial lines to the mega-households of the direct heirs of an emperor. Such grand princely households could encompass thousands of individuals. After the 1580s, exercising their tentacled presence across the entire empire, these households exerted enormous political influence. Their strength, size, and combined capabilities helped determine the political fortunes of the small group of princes jockeying to be the next emperor. On the basis of his household wealth and the effectiveness of his retainers, a prince might establish his reputation as a general, project his power in times of peace and war, accomplish delicate political missions, build ties to powerful individuals or groups, and broadly make the case for his suitability to be the next emperor to imperial subjects of every status.

From its nascent beginnings around the time a prince turned four or five, the process of building a full-fledged and independent household unfolded slowly and in stages. As we have seen, key early growth spurts occurred around a series of firsts: *mansab* grant, marriage, and administrative or military assignment. Until a prince was granted full adult status, however, households continued to be fairly small. They also generally lacked the military and administrative capacities of mature princely households. Instead, they continued to depend heavily on court-appointed imperial servants or others appointed by a princely father or the emperor.[93] Such reliance invariably meant that outsiders with primary loyalties to someone else dominated the households of young princes. Until they had gained sufficient confidence in their own political abilities and built a rudimentary administrative and military apparatus that was answerable to them alone, they tended to accept this situation. Princes had a powerful incentive to get on with the task of imprinting their authority on their households, however. For until an emperor was convinced that a prince was up to the challenge of handling

---

[93] Thus Prince Aurangzeb's sixteen-year-old son Muhammad Sultan was made to rely on officials temporarily assigned by his father to help him collect Rs. 92,000 from one of his own *jagir*s in 1655. Aurangzeb, *Adab-i 'Alamgiri*, vol. 1, pp. 189–92. Similarly although A'zam's son Wala Jah was eighteen years old in 1702 (he already had a *mansab* of 7000/ 2000 in November 1693), the young prince relied on his father's princely employees to provide him with security during hunting expeditions. *Akhbarat-i Darbar-i Mu'alla*, vol. 41, pp. 89, 128, 131.

Young Prince, ca. 1650–60 (Arthur M. Sackler Gallery, Smithsonian Institution, Washington D.C.; Purchase – Smithsonian Unrestricted Trust Funds, Smithsonian Collections Acquisitions Program, and Dr. Arthur M. Sackler, S1986.425)

the pressures that came with full adult status and relative independence, this ultimate favor was withheld.

Aurangzeb's example offers some insight into this process during the period between quasi-adult and full adult status. When he assumed the governorship of the Deccan in 1636, Aurangzeb was surrounded by a powerful coterie of court-appointed officials. They included tutors such as Mulla Jewan Amethi, Saiyid 'Ali Tabrizi, Muhammad 'Arif, and Mir Hashim Gilani, who were charged with completing the eighteen-year-old prince's formal education. Other officials included the prince's maternal uncle, Sha'ista Khan, as *ataliq*; Mir Asadullah Khan, who became the paymaster (*bakhshi*) of Aurangzeb's princely household; and Fazil Khan and Habash Khan, who served as advisors-at-large. These individuals initially dominated the prince's household and helped minimize any countervailing influence exercised by the small group of foster brothers (*kokas*) and childhood companions who also accompanied the young prince down to the Deccan.

Although much of the early expansion in Aurangzeb's Deccan-based household occurred through appointments by his father Shah Jahan, it is clear that by 1637, Aurangzeb was actively recruiting his own men. We know, for example, that Aurangzeb succeeded in attracting Muhammad Tahir Khurasani (a former household official of the prince's maternal grandfather Asaf Khan) as well as Shaikh Mir (a recent immigrant from Khwaf in Iran) into service around this time. Both men proved loyal and served with distinction over the next two decades. They were joined by many lesser-known figures including, for example, in November 1637, a contingent of cavalrymen who came recommended by Sha'ista Khan.[94] The prince's growing household and salary obligations may be divined from the involvement of dozens of personal retainers in massive birthday celebrations that same November and approval for a large payment to household servants the following month.[95] Another key piece of evidence comes from early 1638 when Muhammad Tahir Khurasani commanded 3,000 cavalrymen drawn from the prince's own household in an expedition against the kingdom of Baglana. Following the successful conclusion of that campaign, Aurangzeb ordered Muhammad Tahir Khurasani to undertake a land survey of the region and assume personal charge of Auranganagar, the renamed capital of Baglana. Thus Shah Jahan's withdrawal of Sha'ista Khan's supervision in 1638 was a sign that he saw Aurangzeb as now deserving of full adult status. Aurangzeb was twenty years old at the time. Other imperial appointees, such as the prince's tutors, began to fade into the background. Although some chose to remain in Aurangzeb's service, others simply returned to the imperial court or took up other assignments.

Once the princes attained full adult status, their households generally experienced explosive growth. The largest among them – such as that of Shah Jahan's son Dara Shukoh – took up entire neighborhoods in imperial cities (in some cases lending their master's name to that section of the city, as with Darapur in Allahabad). On marches outside the cities and towns, princely troops were the bane of peasants, who feared damage to their

---

[94] *Mughal Archives: A Descriptive Catalogue of the Documents Pertaining to the Reign of Shah Jahan, Vol. 1*, ed. M. Z. A. Shakeb (Hyderabad, 1977), p. 155.

[95] Ibid., pp. 161, 163, 164, 167, 169, 179, 183.

crops, theft of livestock, strain on local resources, and price spikes in basic commodities. It is impossible to estimate the size of the largest post-1580s princely households because no records survive, but it is not unlikely that they could number in the tens of thousands of people at any given time.

At the apex of the princely household, of course, was the prince himself. He was the focus of all attention. Each person's place in the household's hierarchy depended on judgments about the social and physical distance that separated him or her from the prince.

At the outermost edges were those who had no access to his ear, never came in contact with his person, and were not permanently employed by him or any other powerful figure in his household. Their primary function was to serve those who did receive an emolument from the prince or some other high-ranking individual within his inner circle. Every conceivable profession, licit and illicit, was represented on these outermost edges. This was a highly transient population that recycled itself depending on economic opportunity, physical safety, and geographic location. Princes felt little if any obligation regarding the well-being of this group. In turn, this group's loyalty to a given prince was ephemeral at best. And yet in times of political strife, rebellion, or an actual war of succession, it was to individuals with military skills in this group that princely intermediaries occasionally turned if they needed to rapidly fill their ranks. As might be expected, they were also the first ones to peel away when the going got tough.

Moving in from this outer fringe was a second band of individuals who were connected through some combination of shared familial, ethnic, tribal, or religious ties to someone within the prince's inner circle. Whatever form their remuneration took, the key point is that it came directly from the hand of this patron, not from the prince. They also depended on this intermediary to use his resources and influence to protect them and their dependents. In return, this person received their primary loyalty. Therefore, when such a person decided to leave a prince's household, he inevitably took most of his clients with him. If he died, these dependents might drift toward another high-ranking individual within the same princely household, end up joining the ranks of the outermost group, or completely detach themselves.

Closer to the inner core of the household, we can identify a third group that received its salaries directly from the prince. These people usually had some glancing contact with their royal master, and princes may have recognized many of them by sight, if not necessarily by name. Princes seem to have felt a fair degree of responsibility for the welfare, comfort, and security of these retainers and their families. They in turn often felt a deep sense of loyalty and obligation to the prince. They celebrated his successes and anguished over his losses. All among them likely prayed that their master would become the next Mughal emperor.

This third circle included almost every existing profession to preserve the self-containment and mobility of the princely household. Barbers, gatekeepers, gardeners, mahouts, carpenters, tentmakers, tailors, ironsmiths, palanquin bearers, tanners, water carriers, diggers, scribes, knife sharpeners, bookbinders, astrologers, accountants, metal workers, animal trainers, entertainers, fanners, huntsmen, sweepers, lamplighters, jewelers, launderers, cooks, perfumers, cloth and carpet weavers, masseurs, runners, and masons all had a place. These employees enjoyed higher social status and incomes than people who undertook even the very same work in the other two groups. As a result, the competition to get and then hold on to these jobs was keen. Extended family and caste clusters tended to monopolize them.

Reflecting organizational arrangements at the imperial level, princely employees involved in manufacturing goods were often clustered into specialized workshops called *karkhana*s. In addition to items produced for immediate consumption in the household, *karkhana*s produced vast quantities of goods to supply the massive gift exchanges in which the prince participated. Princes viewed the *karkhana*s and the people working in them as their responsibility and pride, and the distribution of the work thus produced as their prerogative. Thus, when Shah Jahan began to place excessive demands on Aurangzeb's *karkhana*s, requesting that they produce cloth for the imperial court in the 1650s, the prince at first was evasive. Aurangzeb claimed that he did not have enough artisans and that the quality was not sufficiently high.[96] When the emperor did not let up in his demands, Aurangzeb complained that the emperor should just take over the prince's cloth-weaving *karkhana* because it did nothing but supply the emperor's needs.[97] So also in the early 1700s, Mu'azzam delegated a substantial force of household troops to rescue his *karkhana*s after a group of Afghan tribesmen had seized them and taken them to their stronghold.[98] In 1702, Kam Bakhsh made a priority of rescuing his *karkhana*s after massive floods inundated the area where his household was pitched.[99]

---

[96] Aurangzeb, *Adab-i 'Alamgiri*, vol. 1, p. 147.

[97] Ibid., vol. 2, pp. 463–4.

[98] *'Ara'iz-o-Faramin*, National Library of India, Sarkar Collection 46, p. 1.

[99] *Akhbarat-i Darbar-i Mu'alla*, vol. 25, p. 111. If *karkhana*s failed to produce the necessary product or if the final good was judged to be too shoddy, princely agents often went onto the open market to meet their demands. *Akhbarat-i Darbar-i Mu'alla*, vol. 21, no. 40/38;

The other invaluable constituency within this third group – indeed, this one in a class all its own – was composed of the prince's professional soldiers. These men were reasonably well paid and often received payment before anyone else in their peer group. Unlike other groups belonging to the princely household, soldiers may have resided outside its confines. Many of them accompanied the princely household wherever it went, and many also served in the prince's *jagirs* or helped fulfill his military obligations elsewhere in the empire. We know, for instance, that Dara Shukoh's personal contingents were widely dispersed all over the empire in 1657–8. As a result, on the eve of the pivotal battle at Samurgarh that decided who among Shah Jahan's sons would succeed to the Mughal throne, Dara Shukoh was – perhaps fatally – forced to recruit contingents of mercenaries and poorly trained part-time soldiers of questionable loyalty.

Princes normally put a high premium on recruiting the right kind of soldier. Each recruit had to present his mount for inspection, demonstrate his military skills, and relate his background and story before the prince and accompanying audience. Some soldiers came directly recommended by members of a prince's inner circle or someone else of high standing; some were poached from rival imperial or noble households; some were invited to join following the dissolution of another major household; and – in rare cases – some were offered employment after performing stellar acts of bravery. The process of inducting professional soldiers, like any other category of servant for that matter, never really ceased. It just waxed and waned depending on a host of factors including general attrition, anticipated conflicts, and the financial abilities of a given prince at a given time.

Closer to the prince than any of the preceding groups (the outermost edge, the employees of princely officials, and the large third group of professionals) was the small inner core of close supporters and advisors whom we might place in two further categories. The first was composed of imperial officials who had been assigned to assist a prince. Although their importance as a group faded once a prince attained full adult status, individual officials nonetheless maintained an important presence. In some cases, they assumed administrative and military tasks for which the prince had not as yet found a suitable retainer.[100] It was not unusual for

---

vol. 23, p. 301. Fierce competition occasionally ensued between different sets of imperial agents. In 1653, for example, Aurangzeb was accused by the superintendent of the emperor's *karkhana* in Burhanpur of obstructing the supply of good yarn. Aurangzeb, *Adab-i 'Alamgiri*, vol. 2, p. 463.

[100] Snapshot documentation for both A'zam's princely establishment in October 1693 and Mu'azzam's in December 1694 reveals large numbers of imperial appointees holding a

princes to request that a specific individual be transferred to his household. Such requests invariably had a strategic quality. To offer one example, in the early 1620s, Jahangir's son Shahryar asked that an imperial official named Sharif-ul-Mulk, a noted loyalist of his stepmother and mother-in-law the Empress Nur Jahan, be appointed to manage his household. It is interesting and not incidental that, at the time, Shahryar and Nur Jahan were locked in an intensifying power struggle against another of Jahangir's sons, Khurram. Sharif-ul-Mulk was to serve as a key political bridge between Shahryar and Nur Jahan.

Sharif-ul-Mulk managed Shahryar's princely establishment for six years, a relatively long stint for someone who was also an imperial employee. In most other cases, imperial officials rotated fairly rapidly in and out of a prince's employ. Such transience distinguished them from other dependents, for instance, foster brothers, who rarely moved to outside jobs. Not only were they transient, but their primary loyalty was elsewhere, upward to the emperor, although they appear to have taken care to always acknowledge the authority of a prince while serving in his household. In times of father-son strife, however – as between Akbar and Salim, Shah Jahan and Aurangzeb, and Aurangzeb and Akbar – it was not uncommon for princes to doubt the loyalty of their imperial employees. They knew that these officials could prove to be the Achilles heel of their households, and they were a group to be watched and cultivated with extreme care and caution lest they destabilize the household.

The second category of the inner core – indeed, its very heart – were the high-ranking princely dependents whose salaries were paid by the prince himself. A dependent's salary was typically paid in cash grants, land assignments (prebends), and/or the right to tap into other sources of the prince's overall income.[101] This group included everyone from foster brothers, longtime advisors, and military commanders, to a variety of non-imperial allies. They were the true nerve center of the princely household. It is also within this group that we must situate the most senior women of the princely harem, itself a highly complex space and institution that came into its own only in the 1580s, following the first marriages of Akbar's sons.

Ruby Lal has suggested that supporting hundreds if not thousands of women from diverse backgrounds allowed the Mughals to symbolically demonstrate their protection and dominion over all imperial subjects and

wide range of important administrative positions. *Akhbarat-i Darbar-i Mu'alla*, vol. 17, no. 37/10; vol. 19, pp. 347, 354, 359, 361, 364, 365, 366.

[101] Habib, *The Agrarian System of Mughal India*, p. 326.

every part of the empire.[102] In turn, the most important women in the harem served as links between the royal household and the families, clans, rulers, and regions from whence the women came. Khurram's example offers insight into the reach a prince might attain from his wives alone. His primary wife, Mumtaz Mahal, offered crucial access to the influential faction within the Jahangir-era nobility led by her father Asaf Khan. Another wife, the granddaughter of 'Abd-ur-Rahim Khan-i Khanan, enabled Khurram to tap into a separate cluster of powerful imperial nobles. And a third wife, an unnamed Rathor princess, helped smooth her husband's ties not only to the Rathors but to other Rajput groups as well.

Aurangzeb's son Prince A'zam received active support from his redoubtable senior wife, Jahanzeb Banu Begum. A daughter of his dead uncle Dara Shukoh, Jahanzeb Banu Begum played multiple roles in her husband's household. Two of them in particular stand out. The first can be broadly defined as military in nature. In 1679, it was Jahanzeb Banu Begum who led A'zam's military contingents for more than three weeks when the prince was forced to move ahead on an urgent summons from his father, Aurangzeb. Three years later, in 1682, Jahanzeb Banu Begum mounted her own elephant to encourage a lagging Mughal counterattack on a Maratha army. She is said to have personally handed out spears and *paan* (a South Asian delicacy that combines, at a minimum, betel leaf, areca nut, and lime) and promised to commit suicide if the Mughal army was overrun.[103] She went into battle again in 1685–6 when A'zam's forces had lost all hope during the invasion of Bijapur and is credited with whipping up morale.

Less dramatic, but just as critical, Jahanzeb Banu Begum maintained harmonious household relations by cultivating a strong spirit of camaraderie and shared struggle among key members of the princely household. Her skill at this came to the fore in the winter of 1702 when a spat between A'zam and his chief huntsman and *koka* Mir Hedayatullah occurred as the men were on a hunt. Because of a strong wind, falcons trained by Mir Hedayatullah failed to perform properly. Frustrated, A'zam lashed out at his foster brother, and Mir Hedayatullah responded by impertinently asking the prince if he could share any wisdom that might train the wind. This made A'zam furious, and he immediately threw his *koka* out of his household. It fell to Jahanzeb Banu Begum to persuade her husband to

---

[102] Lal, *Domesticity and Power*, pp. 167, 171–4.
[103] Sarkar, *Studies in Aurangzib's Reign*, pp. 45–6.

forgive Mir Hedayatullah, which she was able to do. After a few days, Mir Hedayatullah rejoined A'zam's household in his old position.[104]

The princess was also responsible for managing relations between A'zam and their son Bidar Bakht (b. 1670), who emerged as one of Aurangzeb's favorite grandsons in the 1690s. Unfortunately, imperial favor poisoned relations between Bidar Bakht and his father. When Bidar Bakht was appointed governor of Malwa (contiguous to Gujarat where A'zam was serving) in the early 1700s, Jahanzeb Banu Begum petitioned Aurangzeb to permit Bidar Bakht to come and visit her since she had not seen him in a long time. The young prince was granted seven days to visit his mother.[105] Judging by the movement of men and information between Gujarat and Malwa in the months that followed, a temporary reconciliation between father and son seems to have been effected during that short visit. It would last at least until Jahanzeb Banu Begum's death in 1705.

The political activities of women in the royal households could also backfire. In 1687, it was discovered that Mu'azzam's senior wife, Nur-un-Nisa Begum, was using her own eunuchs and agents to support her husband's attempts to undermine imperial policy against Golkonda. As a result, Mu'azzam was imprisoned for seven years in the Deccan and Nur-un-Nisa and the rest of Mu'azzam's harem were exiled to Delhi. They were not reunited with the prince for another five years.

A multilayered virtual citadel, the household was never apart from the prince; it traveled with him when he was on the move, an extension of his royal person. Over the decades, Mughal princes deployed the power they accrued in the context of building their households in various ways. None was more important than the capacity of the household to transform itself into a powerful fighting organization. This is the focus of the next section. We will explore the military aspect of the princely household through a close examination of the household of Salim/Emperor Jahangir's son, Khurram. Khurram's household became so vast and powerful that it increasingly collided with and overshadowed the imperial establishment. Tensions came to a head between father and son in the spring of 1622, and by the middle of the summer, Khurram was actively trying to seize the Mughal throne.

---

[104] *Akhbarat-i Darbar-i Mu'alla*, vol. 41, pp. 122, 124.
[105] Ibid., p. 77.

## A PREDATORY HOUSEHOLD: THE ACTIVITIES
## OF PRINCE KHURRAM, 1614–1621

In 1607, Jahangir granted the fifteen-year-old Khurram his first *mansab*: 8000 *zat* and 5000 *sawar*. Khurram subsequently emerged as his father's favored heir, eclipsing his formerly dominant older brother Parvez. Although Khurram remained based at the Mughal court for the next five years, he received rapid *mansab* promotions during this time. By 1613, Khurram's rank had reached 12000/6000. Going by imperial regulations, Khurram likely maintained anywhere between 20 percent and 33 percent of his *sawar* rank in cavalry (1,500–1,980 men).[106] Furthermore, as his father's favored son with expanding access to financial resources, he could increase his household troops at short notice even as he built a strong inner core of loyalists.

Khurram demonstrated his household's growing military capacity and prowess in his first major campaign. In 1614, he successfully went up against the long recalcitrant Rajput kingdom of Mewar. Of Mewar, Jahangir once wrote, "They have bowed their heads in submission to none of the [Muslim] kings of Hindustan and for most of the time have been refractory and rebellious."[107] And yet in 1614, Khurram deployed the military forces of his household alongside imperial forces, and, after a few months of vicious fighting, the kingdom of Mewar sued for peace. It was a stunning, if brutally won, victory and noteworthy especially since it had long eluded the Mughals. Furthermore, it is possible to make a case for the pivotal role played by members of Khurram's princely household in this success.

Among the standout commanders of the Mewar campaign were Muhammad Taqi and Ra'i Sundar Das. The former is spoken of as terrorizing the local population with scorched earth tactics, whereas the latter was tasked with pursuing the royal family of Mewar from one hideout to the next. The sources indicate that another princely official, Hakim 'Alimullah, was also commended later for his work as superintendent of the camp (*diwan-i buyutat*). Separately, Jahangir ennobled Muhammad Beg, at the time on Khurram's payroll, with the title of "Zulfiqar Khan" for his standout performance as Khurram's personal emissary to Jahangir throughout the campaign. It fell to yet another

---

[106] Habib, *The Agrarian System of Mughal India*, p. 308.
[107] Jahangir, *Jahangirnama*, p. 142.

The Maharana of Mewar submitting to Prince Khurram, ca. 1618 (© Victoria and Albert Museum, London, 2006BF9922–01)

princely retainer, Mulla Shukrullah, who had served as the chief judicial officer (*mir-i ʿadl*) of the expedition, to hammer out a peace settlement.

Khurram's victory raised his political profile. He used it to expand the reach of his household. Some of his retainers – including Raʾi Sundar Das, Mulla Shukrullah, and Muhammad Beg – moved on to imperial appointments, with the prince's blessing. This was a noteworthy development. The hitherto sharp lines demarcating service to the emperor and his sons were being deliberately blurred. We might speculate that rather than the emperor using imperial employees to maintain a hook in his son's household, the reverse was now happening: Khurram was using his own followers to extend a tentacle into the imperial apparatus. And as imperial appointees, their *mansab*s and *jagir*s no longer strained the prince's resources.

The capabilities of Khurram's princely household were such that post-1614, he confidently deployed them in a number of full-scale military campaigns. Thus he did not hesitate to place his retainers in command of campaigns against the Deccan sultanates (1616–17 and 1621–2) and Kangra (1618). Prior even to the onset of these campaigns, however, the prince's retainers were being deployed to ensure their prince's success.

Consider the activities that occurred prior to the 1616–17 Deccan campaign as an example. Khurram assigned his foster brother Mirza Makki Koka and Ra'i Jadu Das with the diplomatic mission of enticing Golkonda into an anti-Ahmadnagar alliance. He also sent Ra'i Sundar Das (now "Raja Bikramajit") and Mulla Shukrullah (now "Afzal Khan") on a similar mission to Bijapur. On receiving the news that their respective missions had been successful, Khurram sent his own *parwarda* (protégé) Saiyid 'Abdullah Khan Barha with the good news to the imperial court at Ajmer.

Following the constitution of the invading Mughal army, Khurram's retainer Bairam Beg Turkman was appointed the chief paymaster (*mir bakhshi*) of the imperial contingents. It was his job to ensure that all Mughal soldiers were properly paid and that the rolls and branding regulations were followed. He also oversaw organizing all the district police chiefs (*thanadar*s) and military commandants (*faujdar*s) for the defense of the entire Deccan. Through Bairam Beg Turkman, Khurram was increasingly able to co-opt the entire imperial establishment in the south.

After Raja Bikramajit's success in storming Ahmadnagar, the prince sprinkled his household members across command positions in the Deccan. For example, Sipahdar Khan was designated fort commandant (*qiladar*) of Ahmadnagar and Jan Sipar Khan was assigned as *thanadar* of Jalnapur. Around the same time, Raja Bikramajit was ordered to escort Bijapur's tribute payments back to the imperial court, and Hakim Khushal and Afzal Khan were appointed ambassadors to Bijapur and Golkonda, respectively. Bairam Beg Turkman, another household member, was appointed to lead an imperial army against the principality of Baglana, and Rustam Khan Shighali was deployed to invade western Gondwana. In an unprecedented manner, the prince's retainers had effectively taken charge of running the Deccan and had done so bypassing other high-ranking imperial officials and nobles. As a result, resentment toward them ran high among imperial commanders.

In early 1618, the visiting English ambassador to Mughal India, Sir Thomas Roe, commented that although Jahangir was the reigning emperor, Khurram in fact was the "absolute king."[108] Increasingly, Jahangir turned to Khurram to run his military campaigns, permitting him to draw on his own loyalists and retainers to man them. Thus it was Raja Bikramajit who led the imperial expedition against the fortress of Kangra in 1618. As with the previous Deccan expedition, the high command of this one was also stacked with current and former princely retainers including Muhammad Taqi, Shahbaz Khan Dalumani, Jamal Khan Afghan, Rustam Afghan, and Saiyid Nasib Barha. It was the same with the empire's next major campaign in 1620–1, once again in the Deccan.

Khurram awarded command of the army's vanguard to Bairam Beg Turkman and made Raja Bikramajit responsible for all logistics; two of the five imperial divisions were placed under the command of Raja Bikramajit and Raja Bhim Singh Sisodia. Following the campaign's successful conclusion, Khurram appointed his own stalwarts to build police stations (*thana*s) and forts all over the newly conquered region. These strategic posts – although technically under imperial control and not a part of Khurram's *jagir* holdings – were largely garrisoned by troops loyal to the prince. It was also Khurram's household retainers, not imperial officials, who collected the agreed tribute payments from the three defeated states. Thus Hakim 'Abdullah Gilani was sent to Bijapur, Ra'i Kunhar Das (brother of Raja Bikramajit) was dispatched to Ahmadnagar, and Qazi 'Abd-ul-'Aziz was ordered to Golkonda. Simultaneously, Raja Bhim Singh Sisodia was awarded command of a substantial army aimed at collecting back payments of tribute from the Rajas of Gondwana. Once all these matters had been satisfactorily arranged, Khurram designated his longtime retainers, Afzal Khan and Hakim 'Alim-ud-Din, to convey the news of his victories to the emperor.

A predatory princely household such as Khurram's, however, was the exception rather than the rule. Although all Mughal princes strove to build solid and extensive households, none – barring Khurram – seem to have actively plotted, let alone successfully achieved, the infiltration of the imperial machinery while the emperor still ruled. Certainly Khurram/Shah Jahan's sons Aurangzeb and Dara Shukoh drew on their

---

[108] Foster, *English Factories in India*, vol. 1, p. 17.

households to run military campaigns, but neither did so on the scale their father had.[109] By its very nature, princely household building had its limits. Once they had been deprived of their semi-independent territorial appanages, mature Mughal princes were on an uncertain and unstable footing – at once royal and adult, but not yet emperor. And of course the emperor carefully monitored his sons and grandsons using spies and informants and strategically placed imperial officials. Still, it was only a matter of time before a perversion of such an unstable system evolved, as it did with Prince Khurram and the Emperor Jahangir.

As the example of Khurram's household attests, shared military and political experiences, played out over decades, usually produced a coherent household of retainers who learned to work together in times of war. Not only military and diplomatic experience but also experience with collecting taxes, reforming revenue collection methods, and managing the everyday running of the mobile princely household all contributed to ensuring that a prince such as Khurram was poised, ready, and capable of assuming these same responsibilities once he became emperor. From this perspective, it is no stretch to argue that princes who ran successful households in fact served the empire in a most stellar way, even if the pursuit of their own interests sometimes set them on violent collision courses with the emperor.

### A DAY IN THE LIFE OF A PRINCE AND HIS HOUSEHOLD

To further demonstrate the centrality of the princely household in the life of the Mughal Empire after the 1580s, it is useful to consider how its structure and management shaped the daily activities of a Mughal Prince. Such an exercise must necessarily generalize and so cannot be the story of any particular prince, although this section draws heavily on the news bulletins (*akhbarat*) that document A'zam's princely spell in Gujarat in the

---

[109] Aurangzeb relied heavily on his own retainers in the course of difficult campaigns in Balkh (1647) and the Deccan (1656–7). Likewise, Dara Shukoh depended heavily on generals and troops drawn from his own household during his abortive attempt to take Qandahar in 1653. Later, in Aurangzeb's reign, we see his sons and grandsons repeatedly turning to their own households to accomplish all sorts of critical missions. Among them were conducting difficult diplomatic missions, leading the final stages of siege operations, protecting valuable supply lines, conducting intelligence-gathering missions, pursuing the enemy, transporting badly needed treasure, rescuing imperial troops from defeat, and guarding the imperial court from attack.

early 1700s. Even so, it will trace broadly how princely household activities fed into the life of the empire.[110]

A prince's household began stirring a couple of hours before sunrise. Servants – eunuchs as well as other members of an inner core of trained domestics – lit candles and incense sticks; heated coals for heating water, portable furnaces, and preparing food; and laid out the prince's clothing. If an early morning hunt was on the schedule, swords and daggers would be sharpened, bowstrings tightened, muskets primed, saddles cleaned, princely flags and insignia gathered, horses and elephants brushed, and lists of dependents accompanying the prince prepared. By the time the prince was awakened, his household was already a hive of activity.

Emerging from his sleeping quarters (alternatively referred to in the sources as *khalwatgah*, *khwabgah*, *shabkhana*, or *shabistan-i iqbal*), where he might have slept alone, with one of his wives or concubines, or surrounded by a small group of close personal companions who may have included his *koka*s, the prince got dressed and performed his morning ablutions. Judging by Aurangzeb's 1654 order to his oldest son Muhammad Sultan, such routines were highly regularized. Aurangzeb specified that exactly forty-eight minutes were to be spent on them.[111] During this time, the prince may have looked to his closest male companions for some early morning mirth, possibly his first *paan* of the day, or – as in Aurangzeb's case – a coffee.[112]

At this time, the atmosphere around a prince was likely still relaxed, maybe even a little informal. The prince would have received the latest news from around his household as well as any fast-breaking political or military intelligence from his closest advisors and confidants. He would also most certainly have set aside a little time to meet with his personal

---

[110] The daily routine that follows draws on the following primary materials: *Akhbarat-i Darbar-i Mu'alla*; Aurangzeb, *Dastur-ul-'Amal-i Agahi*, National Library of India, Sarkar Collection 70; Aurangzeb, *Ruq'at-i Alamgiri*; Chandar Bhan Brahman, *Chahar Chaman*, trans. Muhammad Murtaza Qadiri (Hyderabad, 1992); Lahawri, *Padshahnama*; and Kazim, *'Alamgirnama*. Among the secondary sources consulted: Ibn Hasan, *The Central Structure of the Mughal Empire* (New Delhi, repr. 1980), and Sarkar, *Studies in Aurangzib's Reign*.

[111] Sarkar, *Studies in Aurangzib's Reign*, pp. 27–8.

[112] Aurangzeb may have picked up the habit during his first stint as governor of the Deccan (1636–44). His fondness for coffee stayed with him for the rest of his life as seen in a 1695 report in which he is shown to enjoy the drink. *Akhbarat-i Darbar-i Mu'alla*, vol. 19, p. 462. In 1705, he is also seen receiving a gift of coffee beans from the deputy-governor of Bijapur, vol. 30, p. 51.

astrologers. With fully prepared charts at their disposal, these astrologers would be expected to answer any question the prince might throw at them: what activities might meet with success or failure this day, what time to commence an activity, what foods to consume or avoid, whether to issue a particular order or wait. Such guidance, privately delivered in the context of his household, always had the potential to cause last-minute changes in a prince's schedule, such as the cancellation of imperial functions or putting off administrative or political decisions. Regardless of his astrologers' findings, however, a prince would likely never have missed his early morning prayers (*fajr*).

Whether a prince was on the march or permanently stationed somewhere, he always had a choice of venues for prayer, including his private apartment, a mosque within his household, or the local congregational mosque. His choice determined who got to pray with him. Thus, if he decided to stay in his apartment, he prayed with his very closest companions. If the prince wished to cultivate an important religious group in the surrounding region or to make a public statement of his religiosity, he would have invited members of the *'ulama'* (Islamic religious scholars) to join him and his household retainers in one of the area mosques. Thus in 1702, A'zam decreed that whenever he was in Ahmadabad, his household would conduct all Friday prayers at the mosque attached to the tomb of the renowned Sufi saint Shaikh Ahmad Khattu Ganj-Bakhsh.[113]

Following prayers, a prince returned to his private chamber for a working breakfast. His guests might include high-ranking imperial officers and nobles not necessarily attached to his household. During this time, the prince might administer judgments or sign military orders that could not wait until later in the morning. After issuing orders to the relevant imperial official, it was not unlikely that a prince would then turn to a retainer and entrust him with the responsibility of ensuring that his orders were carried out to the letter.

This breakfast session usually lasted about an hour. The atmosphere around the prince was now formal and ceremonial because of the presence of non-household members. In this context, his retainers maintained a careful, yet discrete, watch over the person of the prince as well as the imperial officers around him. Any sign of inappropriate behavior – whether in the form of quiet political dissent or breaches in

---

[113] *Akhbarat-i Darbar-i Mu'alla*, vol. 41, p. 210. For more on the significance of this saint to the history of Ahmadabad and Gujarat, see Z. A. Desai, "The Major Dargahs of Ahmadabad," in *Muslim Shrines in India*, ed. Christian Troll (Delhi, 1992), pp. 77–83.

imperial etiquette such as spitting, hacking, letting off gas, not main-taining an appropriate distance from the person of the prince, fidgeting, dozing – was noted and, depending on the gravity of the offence, reported immediately or shared with the prince later on. Inasmuch as imperial employees often spied on a prince on behalf of the emperor and served as a counterweight to members of a prince's household, princely retainers played the same role vis-à-vis the emperor's repre-sentatives. The surviving news bulletins for A'zam's court in Gujarat are full of examples of princely servitors and imperial employees team-ing up to investigate cases of administrative mismanagement and finan-cial corruption, assess the prospects for a hunting expedition, arrange for the transportation of horses and tribute, hunt down rebels, order nobles to present themselves with their contingents, and requisition grain for the imperial establishment.[114]

Roughly an hour or so after sunrise, the prince would proceed with an entourage to a vantage point – a raised platform, a window in his apart-ment, or the battlement of a fort – to be viewed and greeted by a gathered crowd of imperial subjects, a ceremony usually referred to as *jharoka darshan*. Some in the crowd were supplicants, others well wishers, and the rest simply present to see the prince. Here, the prince might administer justice (if only perfunctorily) to a number of complainants. He might inspect imperial and princely household troops, elephants, and horses. In the process, he would have been able to observe their overall battle read-iness, and it was not uncommon for the prince to then command their immediate deployment for an administrative or political task, and com-mandeer still others to accompany him on a morning hunt.

In the case of emperors, a *darshan* session rarely lasted more than forty-five minutes. Presumably, it was about the same for princes. Afterward, the prince either went off to hunt or proceeded to the public audience hall (*Diwan-i 'Am*). Judging from orders issued by Aurangzeb to Muhammad Sultan in 1654 as well as the examples of A'zam's sons Wala Jah and 'Ali Tabar in the early 1700s, minor princes were permitted to skip the *Diwan-i 'Am* to go hunting, whereas older princes were expected to preside.[115] Some princes, such as A'zam, Aurangzeb's third son, tried to get out of it as often as they could. Indeed, even in his fifties and notwithstanding the onset of arthritis that hit during his stint as governor of Gujarat in 1701–5, A'zam often shirked his public audiences in favor of a hunt. It was not

---

[114] *Akhbarat-i Darbar-i Mu'alla*, vol. 41, pp. 22, 41, 46, 50, 69–70, 72, 135, 212.

[115] Aurangzeb, *Dastur-ul-'Amal-i Agahi*, ff. 7a-8a.

uncommon for him to regularly devote between four and five hours a day to hunting. His close household retainers (*bandegan-i padshahzada*) always accompanied him.[116]

Hunts provided members of a princely household with a chance to unwind while forging friendships and honing shooting, riding, and tactical skills. These skills had to be keen if a prince were to successfully deploy his household contingents to fulfill various imperial duties as well as to possibly fight for the Mughal throne at short notice. A hunt also brought princes and their households into direct contact with local populations, thus exposing them to intelligence they could scarcely glean ensconced in a formal court setting. In A'zam's case, while hunting he received complaints about corruption among imperial officials, flood damage to crops, enemy movements, banditry, the flight of peasants, instances of usury, and other misfortunes that demanded his attention. Such information permitted Mir Hedayatullah (A'zam's foster brother and chief huntsman), on at least one occasion, to reprimand local imperial officers (*mansabdars*), telling them that if they wanted an audience with A'zam, they had better pay more attention to improving affairs in the areas under their jurisdiction.[117]

If not out on a hunt, the prince repaired with his mixed entourage of imperial officials and household employees to the *Diwan-i 'Am*. When the household was on the march, his personal retainers would have set this

---

[116] *Akhbarat-i Darbar-i Mu'alla*, vol. 41, p. 33; vol. 30, pp. 125–6. A'zam's interest in hunting ultimately took him across the length and breadth of Gujarat – from Kutch to Dohad, from Ahmadabad to Cambay – and the *akhbarat* painstakingly list every manner of bird and animal caught or killed on these occasions. All told, they number in the thousands. As well as demonstrating Mughal control over the land and resources needed to undertake successful hunts, such careful record keeping points to how hunts offered a critical venue for not only the very important gift-giving activity so integral to the patronage networks that underpinned imperial power but also, on account of their character as leisure-cum-sports activity (comparable perhaps to golf today), individual displays of princely graciousness and magnanimity as well. For instance, while in Dabhoi in the third week of November 1702, A'zam gave permission to some of the highest-ranking officials in the province – including the paymaster (*bakhshi*), the treasurer (*diwan*), the military commanders of Dohad and Khirki, and a couple of other senior nobles – to ride elephants while hunting with him. Two weeks later, after arriving in the town of Sarkhej, A'zam released all imperial *mansabdars* from their duties at his court for two to three days to spend a little time in their own homes and establishments. When he met with high-ranking individuals, A'zam often promised imperial promotions for them or their dependents. Ultimately, A'zam was loath to give up hunting even in the face of powerful reprimands from his father to take care of other state business including a Maratha invasion of Gujarat. Ibid., vol. 41, pp. 9, 13, 39–40, 53, 54, 90, 106, 119, 189, 190, 195.

[117] Ibid., vol. 41, p. 72.

A prince holding an audience, 18th century (The Bodleian Library, University of Oxford, MS. Douce Or. b.3 fol. 17a)

chamber up at the center of the traveling household. Already gathered would be serried ranks of officers, soldiers, and any number of distinguished individuals. Beyond them, standing somewhere outside the canopy, were lower-ranked imperial, princely, and noble employees. Seniority determined proximity to the prince. Most of the assembly stood in complete silence.[118] Princes usually remained there for a couple of hours quietly transacting all manner of business.

[118] For more details, see Sir Thomas Roe's accounts of his visits to the courts of Parvez and Khurram, *The Embassy of Sir Thomas Roe in India*, pp. 70–1, 293–4.

Some business related to the management of the empire. In A'zam's court, for example, this entailed issues such as the following: the prince listened to requests for imperial military promotions and interviewed the candidates; he offered stipends to poor supplicants and to religious institutions, administered justice, interviewed prisoners, met visiting imperial officials or foreign dignitaries, inspected and responded to imperial correspondence, received and gave gifts, issued administrative or military orders to local officials, and read or listened to imperial communiqués. The last category included reports about his son and rival Bidar Bakht's stellar military performance during the successful siege of Khelna, the death of his disgraced sister Zeb-un-Nisa in Delhi, and the accession of Zulfiqar Khan and 'Inayatullah Khan to the posts of imperial *bakhshi* and deputy *bakhshi* at Aurangzeb's court at Islampuri.[119]

A'zam also attended to the affairs of his own household while seated in the *Diwan-i 'Am*. The lines between imperial and princely business were not sharply demarcated, since the business of one often coursed into the other. A'zam admitted as much when he noted in open court that there was little distinction between his own work (*kar-i huzur*) and that of the emperor (*kar-i padshahi*).[120] Thus, imperial duties would not have precluded A'zam from also inspecting products produced in his workshops (*karkhana*s); examining animals that he wished to buy; reviewing household horses, elephants, and troops; promoting or demoting people in his household; giving or receiving gifts from princely retainers; meting out punishment or justice among his household members; and offering condolences on deaths or congratulations on marriages or births. A'zam is also seen issuing commands to his princely troops to collect tribute and *jagir* income, escort treasure convoys, chase down rebels, firm up imperial resistance to Maratha incursions or Koli depredations, ferry communications to his son Bidar Bakht or the emperor, and set out for administrative duties in other parts of the country.

Sessions in the *Diwan-i 'Am* also provided an opportunity for the prince to interview and recruit potential retainers. Thus the *bakhshi* (paymaster) in the household of A'zam's son Wala Jah recommends a group of eunuchs for employment by the prince; Afzal Khan (the treasurer of Gujarat) recommends two men who have recently returned from the Hajj; an imperial *mansabdar* named Khwaja Muhammad Yar introduces seven men from "his nation" (*watan-i khud*) to serve with A'zam; Musavi Khan, an imperial

[119] *Akhbarat-i Darbar-i Mu'alla*, vol. 41, pp. 10–11, 13, 69, 102.
[120] Ibid., p. 180.

noble and the *bakhshi* of Gujarat, offers six Delhi-based Central Asians suitable to be princely overseers (*mushrif*); various imperial nobles recommend contingents of cavalrymen who have recently arrived from foreign lands (*wilayat*) to serve among the prince's troops; and the *sadr-us-sudur* (official responsible for religious endowments) of Ahmadabad proposes a relative who has served him with distinction for princely employment.[121] Recommendations by imperial officials demonstrate how princes and the empire could conspire to co-opt groups that were militarily, politically, or socially significant and upwardly mobile.

A private session to wrap up any remaining business that could not be transacted in the full glare of public observation usually followed the session in the *Diwan-i 'Am*. This would be held in the prince's private apartment or another inner chamber. If the routines of the emperors Shah Jahan and Aurangzeb or Prince A'zam are anything to go by, the number of individuals allowed to participate in these deliberations was strictly limited. Only high-ranking imperial officials and a prince's closest companions and advisors attended – the latter, as always, to safeguard the prince's interests and offer a non-imperial perspective.

After lunch, often followed by a siesta, the prince would almost always head to his harem for up to three hours. It was during these afternoon hours that the women of the harem gained access to the prince's ear. A prince rarely traveled without his entire or at least parts of his harem – no matter if he was hunting, fighting, or marching between assignments. These women were not only instrumental to the prince's political network, but the harem also afforded the prince a measure of privacy and refuge. When he was ill, members of the harem would certainly be close at hand. One episode from the early 1690s, when A'zam was thought to be dying from dropsy, describes him prostrate in his quarters, his family and certain intimates of his harem weeping and praying all around the ailing prince. Suddenly, according to one contemporary historian's account, A'zam had a vision that the Caliph 'Ali promised him immediate recovery, and his condition began to improve. He sat up and informed his favorite wife, Jahanzeb Banu Begum, and the others that he was on the mend. His miraculous cure sparked rejoicing across the harem and the princely household. In thanks, Jahanzeb Banu Begum gave a present of Rs. 60,000 to the Shiite shrines at Najaf and Karbala, more than any other member of the princely householder.[122]

---

[121] Ibid., pp. 51, 53, 54, 58, 66, 88, 89, 166, 222–3.
[122] M. Khan, *Maasir i Alamgiri*, pp. 362–4.

The fate of the women of the harem was wrapped up with that of the prince. Were he to die, the harem would be broken up and scattered. The sources report widespread weeping among harem inmates when they believed a prince was about to be imprisoned by the emperor. Some stories relate futile attempts by harem women to protect their master after he was marked for death following an unsuccessful battle to ascend the throne, and others tell of celebrations in the harem to mark a prince's birthday or the birth of a son. Much happiness was expressed in response to generous gift giving by a prince.

During his afternoon hours in the harem, a prince dealt with its day-to-day management, which included handling recommendations for employment there and in the princely establishment at large, listening to appeals in favor of princely or imperial officials he had shunned, approving audiences or the exchange of gifts between his senior women and imperial officials, signing off on requests for subsistence allowances for indigent women or widows, working out the harem's arrangements for traveling or hunting expeditions, granting promotions for men who had served the harem with distinction, and possibly listening to political or military intelligence gathered through networks linked to his harem.[123]

The remainder of the prince's day was variable. Communicating to his young son Muhammad Sultan, Aurangzeb prescribes that minor princes spend most of the afternoon and early evening in their personal quarters. Here the prince might pursue his studies. If the prince were on the march and without a more senior prince around, he might visit the private audience chamber attached to his room just before sunset. There he would wrap up any remaining imperial business. After less than an hour, he was permitted to retire for the night. An older prince tended to maintain a more rigorous work schedule over the latter part of the day. He might emerge from his harem; attend congregational prayers; and then go, to quote Aurangzeb's instructions to A'zam, with "prayers on lip and rosary in hand"[124] to the *Diwan-i 'Am* or one of the more intimate private chambers. The choice of venue usually reflected the kind of work to be transacted. Thus matters that required greater secrecy were usually transacted in a smaller, more intimate, setting. As in morning court sessions, imperial and princely business often overlapped. Formal work usually

---

[123] *Akhbarat-i Darbar-i Mu'alla*, vol. 41, pp. 8, 67, 77, 93–4, 95, 124, 138, 162, 173, 182–3, 185, 197.

[124] Aurangzeb, *Dastur-ul-'Amal-i Agahi*, ff. 7a–8a.

continued until either the evening prayers (*'isha'*) or eight in the evening, whichever came later.

The rest of the evening was generally given over to various forms of entertainment. The prince might choose music, dance, poetry recitations, story telling, readings, magic shows, or interviews with people who had interesting life stories or experiences. Invariably, good food and alcohol were served alongside these diversions. Although Aurangzeb ended alcohol consumption at the imperial court, the households of his sons and grandsons did not refrain from consuming large quantities of alcohol. The harem occasionally served as the venue for entertainments – in such cases, the performers were always women, as per custom. Mostly, however, entertainments unfolded in one of the private audience halls attached to a prince's sleeping quarters. This slightly more public setting allowed a prince to accommodate politically important men or others connected to a his household while still offering members of his harem the chance to sit behind the privacy of a curtain and observe the proceedings.

Surrounded by entertainers, non-imperial allies, household retainers, imperial officers, clergymen, and other important figures, a prince could represent himself as a sophisticated patron as well as a generous one. Only someone who saw a rosy future for himself would refuse to hoard his wealth against a rainy day and would generously indulge in lavish entertainment. Texts on social etiquette – such as the *Mirzanama* from the 1660s – emphasized the importance of generosity even if expenses outweighed income. Another text, the *Mau'izah-i Jahangiri*, written in the 1610s and dedicated to Jahangir, explains: "There are no better qualities, especially for the nobility (*ashraf*) and the rulers, than benevolence (*jud*) and generosity (*sakhawat*)." According to its author, generosity is "the virtue that conceals all defects" and enables "fame, prosperity and ultimate success." It is the key to drawing people "into bonds of loyalty (*ata'at*) and affection."[125] Once someone has partaken of someone else's generosity, "eaten their salt," to use a favorite Mughal phrase, he becomes indebted.

Stephen Dale's work suggests further that entertainments offered a relaxed and convivial context in which princely retainers could get to know one another and build friendships and loyalties.[126] Even if the context were different from that of the battlefield or a hunt, the outcome

---

[125] Muhammad Baqir, *Advice on the Art of Governance, Mau'izah-i Jahangiri of Muhammad Baqir Najm-i Sani*, trans. Sajida Alvi (Albany, 1989), pp. 47–50.

[126] Stephen Dale, *The Garden of the Eight Paradises: Babur and the Culture of Empire in Central Asia, Afghanistan and India (1483–1530)* (Leiden, 2004), p. 182.

in terms of building camaraderie and social cohesion was remarkably similar. We see hints of precisely this during a magic performance held at A'zam's court in Gujarat in the early 1700s. According to the report, following the conclusion of the show, individuals laughed and talked to one another for a long time; they marveled at their luck at being present at such a remarkable event.[127]

In stark contrast, however, another entertainment at A'zam's Gujarat-based court turned sour. A'zam accused one of his musicians of losing his mind from too much alcohol (*az sharab diwanah shudeh*). Insulted, the musician (one Ajab Singh Raja) and his sister (who was employed as a musician in the princely harem) complained in turn that it was the prince who had drunk too much. A brawl ensued and, afraid for their lives, the musician and his sister threatened to lodge a complaint with Aurangzeb (*hazrat pur-nur*) if they were further mistreated. An infuriated A'zam immediately sacked them and forbade them from ever appearing in his princely camp (*urdu-yi 'ali*) again. According to a subsequent news report, the episode led to lingering resentment and fissures among the prince's followers, with some supporting A'zam and others presumably feeling that he had been too harsh.[128]

Evening entertainments could also be an occasion in which individuals and groups might be "housetrained," or taught to appreciate and emulate Mughal cultural tastes. Consider the story of Mir Yadgar, a recent recruit to A'zam's household in Gujarat. On his arrival at a performance in pants deemed too tight and a shirt too long, A'zam proclaimed before the entire assembly that his attire was unacceptable. Mir Yadgar promptly left and returned in changed clothing, presumably much embarrassed.[129] Indeed, the households of the Mughal elite exerted remarkable and enduring influence on the fashions of northern and central India.

At exactly what time a prince and his household finally retired for the night depended on the length of the evening entertainments and the mood of the prince. Even as a prince, Aurangzeb is said to have kept his evening entertainments to a minimum. He generally spent the last several hours before going to sleep chatting with his companions, reading, or praying. His orders to A'zam offer some indication of the kind of stories he may have enjoyed listening to or reading as a young prince: fantasy and

---

[127] *Akhbarat-i Darbar-i Mu'alla*, vol. 41, p. 11.

[128] Ibid., p. 198.

[129] Ibid., pp. 85, 87. For another episode involving A'zam reprimanding a servant for wearing clothes that did not conform to princely expectations, see Khushgu, *Safina-i-Khushgu*, p. 41.

fairytales, the actions of kings, the behavior of the wise, and the life and times of the prophets and saints.[130] A prince could choose to sleep in his own chambers or join one of his wives or concubines. If the former, he was likely undressed by a chosen group of personal attendants. If the latter, he was likely undressed by eunuchs appointed to the harem. Even in sleep, a prince was never alone. In his own quarters, he may have had one of his *koka*s or a small group of close companions (*chela*s) nearby. If in the harem, he was likely watched over by a senior woman or eunuchs or specially recruited female bodyguards.

The post-1580s princely household was the stage on which individual princes built and exercised their power. At no point in any given day was a prince ever far removed from members of his household. They accompanied him everywhere, guarding him, entertaining him, serving as his eyes and ears, assisting him in governing or fighting, and helping him cultivate powerful political, economic, and social connections that extended well beyond the household. The life of the princely household continuously intersected that of the larger empire. These establishments trained countless individuals for service to the empire, they were symbols of Mughal might and wealth, and they remained a key interface between the dynasty and Indian society. Still, as mentioned earlier, too powerful a princely household could threaten the delicate balance on which the imperial machine was based. To ensure that their sons' households did not overreach, emperors continually found ways to undermine their operation, just as princes endeavored to defend them against such interference.

## PROTECTING AND UNDERMINING PRINCELY HOUSEHOLDS, 1580s–1680s

How did princes try to insulate their households from imperial meddling? And how and to what extent did emperors from Akbar to Aurangzeb try to undermine them? Prior to Aurangzeb's reign, unless a prince went into active rebellion, he could more or less protect his household. Imperial interference was usually undertaken in the spirit of a controlling parent keeping an eye on his child, but it could lead to overreaching. Emperor Shah Jahan undertook a particularly vengeful campaign to destroy the political and military effectiveness of Prince Aurangzeb's household. The broader political context involved the emperor's desire to enhance the accession prospects of his oldest and favorite son Dara Shukoh (see

---

[130] Aurangzeb, *Dastur-ul-'Amal-i Agahi*, ff. 7a–8a.

Chapter 1). But even so, Aurangzeb managed to retain sufficient resources to launch a fight that would finally overthrow his father in 1658.

The ties that bound household retainers to their prince were invaluable, and a successful prince cultivated them skillfully and carefully. Retainers knew they had special access to the person of the prince, and they also frequently benefited from his generosity, as in 1644 when Aurangzeb gave his *koka* Mir Malik Husain all the presents sent by the state of Bijapur following a successful diplomatic mission. After victories over Golkonda and Bijapur in 1656–7, Aurangzeb redistributed large amounts of the booty among his householders. His brothers – Dara Shukoh, Shuja', and Murad – were similarly celebrated for their generosity toward their householders.

A prince also stood to gain loyalty by his solicitude toward his household. During the 1656 siege of Golkonda, for instance, Aurangzeb personally dressed the wounds of some of his soldiers and household members. Roughly ten years prior, he had led a dangerous rescue mission to save Muhammad Tahir Khurasani, one of his most senior officers, and a contingent of household troops from encirclement by Uzbeks during the Balkh-Badakhshan campaign. Given that the beginning of heavy winter snows was threatening to cut off the Mughal retreat through the treacherous Hindu Kush mountains, the major detour required for the mission and the delay of two days' march underscored the risks Aurangzeb ran to defend the members of his household.[131] A protective Dara Shukoh battled an imperial nobleman, Mahabat Khan, after the latter was accused of killing one of the prince's householders.[132] The prince also angrily defended his household treasurer Pahar Amal in the face of accusations of financial misconduct by Shah Jahan's highly respected prime minister Sa'dullah Khan.[133]

Loyalty and service even in the face of great personal danger were highly valued in the milieu of the princely household. An imperial nobleman said of one retainer who was decapitated while fighting in Khurram's service and whose head was placed on a pike: "There is no greater deed than a man laying down his life for his master. See, even now his head is higher than all others."[134] Princes condemned and sometimes severely punished those who failed to live up to such expectations. Indeed, as the example of Rustam

---

[131] 'Inayat Khan, *Shahjahannama*, p. 389.
[132] Manucci, *Mogul India*, vol. 1, p. 216.
[133] Aurangzeb, *Raqa'im-i Kara'im*, f. 204a; Aurangzeb, *Ruq'at-i 'Alamgiri*, pp. 21–2.
[134] Jahangir, *Jahangirnama*, p. 469.

Khan Shaghali demonstrates, loyalty was so valued a personal characteristic that a perceived lapse could mean a devastating loss of reputation.

Rustam Khan was first employed as a simple cavalryman in Khurram's household in the early 1610s. Within a decade, he had risen to become the prince's representative in Gujarat. During Khurram's rebellion, however, Rustam Khan betrayed his master, bringing about the collapse of the prince's authority over the Deccan. The vituperative account in the *Ma'asir-i Jahangiri*, a near-contemporary source written shortly after Khurram had succeeded to the Mughal throne as Emperor Shah Jahan, is stinging. Rustam Khan is condemned for not knowing right from wrong, for being traitorous, and for having corrupt thoughts.[135] A later commentary states that the Khan "ignored what was due from him as a loyal and cherished servant." It goes on, "When the Prince [i.e., Khurram] experienced such disloyalty and effrontery from someone he had so greatly favored, what hope could he have from anyone else? On whom could he rely? The Prince no longer trusted anyone."[136] Although Rustam Khan likely expected to be richly rewarded by Jahangir after deserting Khurram, he quickly found that his treachery and disloyalty had damaged his reputation at the imperial court as well. He was treated "with contempt and scorn."[137] When Khurram ascended the Mughal throne in 1628, he stripped this former retainer of all his worldly possessions and status. In the end, the Khan was reduced to such poverty that he was said to be without horse, servant, or home. He died in abject poverty.[138] From Shah Jahan's reign onward and until the writing of *Ma'asir-ul-Umara* in the latter half of the eighteenth century, Rustam Khan's name was synonymous with the miseries that awaited those who failed their princely masters.[139]

But the sources abound in praise of loyal service by princely retainers. When Shuja' fled toward Arakan and almost certain death after losing the war of succession to Aurangzeb in 1659–60, a core group (numbering perhaps forty to fifty) was respectfully referred to as continuing to discharge "the obligations of friendship and devotion to him."[140] Likewise,

[135] Kamgar Husaini, *Ma'asir-i-Jahangiri*, ed. Azra Alavi (Bombay, 1978), p. 376.

[136] Shah Nawaz Khan, *Maasiru-l-Umara*, ed. Abdur Rahim and Ashraf Ali, vol. 2 (Calcutta, 1890), p. 201.

[137] Ibid.

[138] Ibid.

[139] Shaikh Farid Bhakkari, *Dhakhirat al-Khawanin*, ed. S. Moinul Haq, vol. 2 (Karachi, 1970), p. 307; S. Khan, *Maasiru-l-Umara*, vol. 2, pp. 199–201.

[140] K. Khan, *Muntakhab al-Labab*, vol. 2, pp. 109–10. Even Hatim Khan, a close supporter of Aurangzeb and author of the *'Alamgirnama*, offers words of sympathy and admiration

sources refer to the "faithful followers" who accompanied Prince Akbar into a life of exile in Iran in the mid-1680s after Emperor Aurangzeb managed to turn back his rebellion.[141] Other instances of singular devotion are captured in various episodes: in the decision by roughly two hundred of A'zam's "most faithful household troops" (led by his foster brother Mir Hedayatullah) to continue to fight and die to protect the prince's body following his death in the Battle of Jaju in 1707;[142] in Shuja''s servant Wali Farghuli's resolve to commit suicide rather than surrender to Aurangzeb; in the choice by one of Dara Shukoh's concubines to permanently disfigure her face with a knife so that she would not be absorbed into Aurangzeb's harem; and in the willingness of one of Mu'azzam's servants to bear torture and eventual death in 1687 rather than implicate his master in a treasonous plot to undermine Mughal war aims against Golkonda.

In the face of the fidelity and sacrifice that knit together all and not just the largest and most powerful post-1580s princely households, the emperor's tasks and dilemmas are noteworthy. Every emperor from Akbar to Aurangzeb took care to maintain a balance between enabling and controlling a prince's reach and authority, lest it overwhelm his own. The *ataliq* represented the subordination of prince to emperor, but what was an emperor to do once a prince was deemed fully adult and the *ataliq*'s services dismissed, usually with, although in a few instances without, the emperor's blessing?

The most accepted and widespread practice was to place imperial loyalists inside princely households to serve as spies. In the late 1670s, for example, Aurangzeb heard about Mu'azzam's drinking habits through one of the prince's tutors. Some years later, Aurangzeb demanded that Manucci (who was at that point serving as one of Mu'azzam's physicians) report to him about the prince's condition every time he bled him. We know that various *mahaldars* (administrative heads) of both Mu'azzam's and A'zam's harems were also imperial spies. Commenting on the extent to which princely households were riddled with imperial informants, Manucci stated that Aurangzeb maintained a "vigilant eye" on his sons.[143]

But princes also had considerable success in subverting the loyalties of their minders. Jahangir's son Parvez was able to enter into political

---

for the men who remained true to their salt even as the political fortunes of Shuja' collapsed. British Museum, Add. Or. 26233, ff. 97b, 100a, 101b.

[141] K. Khan, *Muntakhab al-Labab*, vol. 2, p. 285.

[142] Kamraj, *A'zam al-Harb*, British Museum, Ms. Or. 1899, ff. 397, 402, 406–7, 408.

[143] Manucci, *Mogul India*, vol. 2, pp. 366, 369.

alliances with two of the most powerful nobles in the empire – Khan Jahan Lodi and Mahabat Khan – who served under him in various capacities. In both instances, Emperor Jahangir's concern that his nobles' trustworthiness had been compromised led him to reassign them. Likewise, both princes Mu'azzam and A'zam managed to become very close to some of the highest-ranking nobles sent to monitor them by Aurangzeb. In Mu'azzam's case, the threat posed by his friendship with Bahadur Khan Koka (the emperor's foster brother) caused Aurangzeb to hastily recall the latter out of the Deccan. Aurangzeb may have moved in similar fashion against an emerging friendship between A'zam and Dilir Khan had the latter not suffered an untimely death.

When all other measures to protect their political authority and households had failed, princes did not hesitate to resort to murder. We are told that Mu'azzam ordered the assassination of the tutor who informed Aurangzeb about his drinking. We also know that Mu'azzam's son 'Azim-ud-Din made several attempts to kill Kartalab Khan/Murshid Quli Khan, the most senior imperial official in Bengal and the treasurer of his household in the early 1700s because he considered him an Aurangzeb loyalist. Perhaps few princely assassination plots matched the brutality of Murad's against 'Ali Naqi. The latter was simultaneously the treasurer of the provincial administration of Gujarat and of the prince's household. As such, he was a member of Murad's inner circle; even so, he turned out also to be a spy for Dara Shukoh and Shah Jahan. When this was revealed to Murad in the fall of 1657 from intercepted secret correspondence, the prince went into a fury and called the nobleman before him; right there, in open court, he drove a spear into his chest with his own hand, killing him on the spot. (Six years later, Emperor Aurangzeb would use this as a pretext for sentencing Murad to death and having him executed.)

Having spies in their sons' establishments was not the only way by which emperors sought to maintain oversight of their sons. They could also undermine their sons' households by removing or transferring princely partisans away from their master's service. Although all emperors from Akbar to Aurangzeb did this, Shah Jahan's use of this tactic against his third son Aurangzeb drew the strongest reaction. To clip the prince's growing powers in the early 1650s, Shah Jahan began targeting men in the prince's inner circle of dependents. Although the emperor failed to entice either of Aurangzeb's leading commanders, Muhammad Tahir Khurasani or Shaikh Mir, into leaving the prince's service, he had much greater success with the second rung of leadership in the prince's household.[144] The biggest prize of all – even if only a temporary one because he eventually returned to be near Aurangzeb in the Deccan – was Mir Malik Husain Koka, Aurangzeb's own foster brother. By 1657, Shah Jahan had extended his efforts to luring away entire military contingents within Aurangzeb's personal cavalry. Anywhere between three and four thousand men were removed in this manner in 1656.[145] The prince lost similar numbers on the cusp of the war of succession of 1657–9. In many cases, these men had been carefully selected, groomed, and trained by the prince. Many were veterans of Aurangzeb's campaigns in Balkh-Badakhshan, Qandahar, and the Deccan.

Aurangzeb felt their loss acutely. He may have even thought his chances to be the next Mughal emperor had suffered an irrevocable blow. In 1657, he penned a furious letter to his sister Jahan Ara:

If this practice continues and the officers serving under me are called to the [imperial] center and given promotions higher than they deserve, no one will remain with me. The band of workers whom I have been able to bring together over a period of twenty years will be dispersed. In that case, it will not be possible for me to discharge my duties in a satisfactory manner. If, however, this is considered necessary then orders should be issued so that I might willingly ask all my capable officers to proceed to the court, thus fulfilling the purposes of my "well-wishers."[146]

The very next year, Aurangzeb referred to Shah Jahan's efforts to undermine his household as one of the justifications for overthrowing his father.

However much Aurangzeb or any other prince may have complained about his father's attempts to keep a tight rein on his household, at no point – barring moments of rebellion – were princely households fundamentally compromised by imperial actions prior to the 1680s. Princes always seem to have had sufficient access to money and manpower resources to maintain relatively cohesive, loyal, and powerful households.

## CONCLUSION

Mughal records are rich in information about the imperial household, but the same is not true for households lower in the royal family. Sadly, we

[144] Among those he succeeded in luring into the imperial service with its promise of greater and immediate rewards were Dattaji, Krishnaji Bhasker, Mirak Ataullah Khwafi, Zahid Khan, Muhammad 'Aqil Barlas, and Muhammad Yusuf Husain.

[145] Aurangzeb, *Adab-i 'Alamgiri*, vol. 1, pp. 401–4.

[146] Ibid., vol. 2, pp. 828–31; Aurangzeb, *Muqaddama-i Ruq'at-i 'Alamgiri*, ed. Saiyid Najib Ashraf Nadvi, vol. 1 (Azamgarh, 1930), pp. 249–52.

cannot create a comprehensive list of *jagirs* for any post-1580s prince, and it is hard to know either how princes parceled out their *jagirs* among supporters or the mechanics of these transfers. Gaps remain in our knowledge of the administrative structure of princely households and the workings of a princely harem, and we know only very little about the countless individuals who ensured a functioning household. Working with disparate sources, this chapter has pieced together a broad account of the princely household, from the time of a prince's birth until the occasion that a prince might become the next emperor.

Princely households were profoundly shaped by a new kind of mobility after the retirement of the appanage system. As well as becoming administratively more complex, they also evolved into self-reliant units with an extensive knowledge of the workings of the empire. Households also served as the first and last line of a prince's defenses if intra-familial strife erupted.

If the 1580s marked a crucial shift in the life of princely households, the 1680s inaugurated another one. Large, powerful, and structurally complex, households had come to depend on huge amounts of money to function at a time when the empire's access to income was increasingly compromised by deteriorating law and order conditions across vast swathes of the Mughal Empire. Princes desperately sought to raise money from any available source and became dependent on the emperor for help in maintaining their households. The earlier cohesiveness and élan of the princely household took a turn for the worse. As the princely household foundered, so also its dynamic role in extending the empire was diminished (Chapter 7 will explore this in detail). If princely households offer a key arena in which to judge the shifting fortunes of the Mughal Prince, the other is the world of alliance building, of winning friends and allies. It is to this subject that we turn in the next chapter.

# 4

# Friends and Allies

Up to the 1980s, Mughal studies were dominated by arguments for the modernity of Mughal administrative structures.[1] In 1959 and 1966, respectively, Satish Chandra and M. Athar Ali published groundbreaking books that, although not directly challenging the view of the Mughal Empire as highly centralized and bureaucratic, shifted the focus to the social relations between, on the one hand, different groups and regional entities and, on the other, the imperial dynasty.

What followed in the 1970s with the work of John Richards, Peter Hardy, Michael Pearson, Karen Leonard, and Philip Calkins, and in the 1980s and 1990s with the scholarship of Muzaffar Alam, Richard Barnett, C. A. Bayly, André Wink, Douglas Streusand, Stephen Dale, Dirk Kolff, and Sanjay Subrahmanyam, to name a few, was a new appreciation of the Mughal Empire as an alliance-state, the sum total of many constituent parts. In 1986, Muzaffar Alam described the empire as deriving its success from "balancing" and "coordinating ... between conflicting communities" for which service to the empire promised the best path for political, social, or economic advancement.[2] Also in 1986, André Wink argued that alliance making and breaking (processes he controversially described as *fitna*) rather than the outright destruction of one's opponents through sustained military action was the central dynamic undergirding the

---

[1] See W. Irvine, *The Army of the Indian Moghuls* (Delhi, repr. 1994); Ibn Hasan, *The Central Structure of the Mughal Empire* (Delhi, repr. 1980); Irfan Habib, *The Agrarian System of Mughal India, 1556–1707* (Delhi, repr. 1999). The work of F. W. Buckler provides a notable exception: *Legitimacy and Symbols: The South Asian Writings of F.W. Buckler* (Ann Arbor, 1985).

[2] Muzaffar Alam, *The Crisis of Empire in Mughal North India* (Delhi, repr. 1997), p. 5.

sovereignty of the Mughals as well as all other Indian dynasties.[3] Unlike previous generations of Mughal historians who argued that compromised and/or overreaching administrative institutions eventually caused the empire's collapse, these revisionist scholars instead located imperial failure in the decision by different groups to either abandon or co-opt Mughal imperial authority while striking out on their own.

More recently, in a series of books published between 2004 and 2005 – *The Mughals of India* by Harbans Mukhia, *State and Locality in Mughal India* by Farhat Hasan, and *Domesticity and Power in the Early Mughal World* by Ruby Lal – we see affirmed the view that Mughal success depended on Mughal skill in forging and managing diverse sets of alliances and interests. Cementing these processes was a willingness to share what Hasan describes as the "privileges and perquisites of sovereignty."[4] The result, again, was quite similar to what historian of early modern Europe Nicholas Henshall identifies as the "side-by-side operation of absolute and shared power."[5] Hence, behind the Mughal façade of autocracy, there existed practices of kingship that privileged co-optation and consent over coercion, resulting in an imperial system in which broad swathes of society were persuaded to participate, and where the nature and composition of the Mughal state was continuously being reshaped by shifting relationships and alliances. What this book overall and this chapter in particular describe is the key role of the Mughal princes in forging these relationships and alliances. Even though the emperor and the imperial court stood at the heart of wide-ranging networks of influence and activity, the princes too played a role (distinct in each case, and in each generation, yet always crucial) in embedding the imperial system throughout expanding territories. In this chapter, I demonstrate how the vitality of the princely institution and its alliance building endeavors shaped, in no small measure, the destiny of the Mughal Empire itself.

Whereas Chapter 2 described such kingship practices for the pre-1556 period, this chapter relates how much more important alliance building became during and after Akbar's reign. Deprived of the patrimonial right to an appanage, Mughal princes were forced to embrace the shaping of their own fates, an enterprise founded on their initial willingness to patronize standout individuals and/or groups. Given the general preference for

---

[3] André Wink, *Land and Sovereignty in India: Agrarian Society and Politics under the Eighteenth Century Maratha Svarajya* (Cambridge, 1986), pp. 26, 34.
[4] Farhat Hasan, *State and Locality in Mughal India* (Cambridge, 2004), p. 119.
[5] Nicholas Henshall, "The Myth of Absolutism," *History Today* 42, no. 6 (1992): 46.

men not already committed to competing princes or the emperor, princely efforts routinely functioned as a vehicle through which political, ethnic, and class outsiders were first embraced, and by which these outsiders learned to interact and carve out a place for themselves in the Mughal system. The process of drawing new groups into the ambit of Mughal politics effectively embedded the empire's authority along the ever-shifting political and geographical frontiers.

This chapter also emphasizes how each prince's sets of alliances spoke to his particular political image. In building alliances and loyal supporters, princes shaped and projected political personas. Since the post-1585 Mughal system never presumed that a favored prince would stand unchallenged, all princes expended great energy in making the case for their own accession to the throne. For the empire's subjects, political neutrality was never an option, especially in times of princely conflict or during the inevitable war of succession; it was thus to and through them that a prince made his case. This chapter considers, then, how the prince, going beyond the rules and obligations of loyalty in his household, grappled with the wider and less reliable but equally crucial realm of friends, well wishers, and allies without whom neither the princely institution nor the Mughal Empire could survive. In the end, as they fortified their own power, Mughal princes in effect did the same for the dynasty as a whole.

## AKBAR'S HINDUSTANI EMPIRE, 1556–1605

If his grandfather Babur had dismissed "Hindustanis" as a strange and unfamiliar race of people and remained steadfastly Timurid and Central Asian in his orientation, Akbar's father was determined to lay the foundations for a Mughal empire in which those very Hindustanis had some stake. When Humayun appointed a tutor for his young son Akbar, his duty was to coach the prince in the "manners and customs of Hindustan" and introduce him to Indians (*ahl-i Hind*). As a consequence, the *Akbarnama* (ca. 1598) tells us, Akbar learned to enjoy Indian ways.[6] We can only speculate about the relationship between such enjoyment and the will to build and expand an empire in Hindustan. For we do know that Akbar went on to grab the turbulent but richer parts of the empire centered on the Punjab and Delhi upon his father's death in 1556. Over the next five

---

[6] Shaikh Abu'l Fazl, *Akbarnamah*, ed. Abdul Rahim, vol. 1 (Calcutta, 1878), p. 347.

decades, Akbar would succeed in melding the Central Asian Mughal presence with the social landscape of Hindustan, a project his father had imagined but not achieved.

There was a telling moment in 1582, when Akbar's only brother Mirza Hakim,[7] the appanage holder of Kabul, made a passionate appeal to the Central Asian officers within Akbar's attacking army. He begged them not to help Akbar occupy Kabul but instead to turn on "the natives of Hindustan" (*Hindi nazhadan*), their fellow soldiers and officers recruited in India.[8] (Akbar's imperial army included high-ranking Central Asian, Iranian, Indian Muslim, and Rajput generals.) Mirza Hakim's plea proved futile; his attempt to manipulate anti-Hindustani sentiment among the Central Asians simply did not work. The army ultimately occupied Kabul, and Mirza Hakim's efforts to keep his threatened appanage from being folded into the Delhi-based Mughal Empire failed.

Akbar crafted a Hindustani image for himself most pointedly to portray his difference from Mirza Hakim. We will consider here briefly how Mirza Hakim, in turn, took pains to contrast his image with Akbar's. From his base in Kabul and over eighteen years after achieving political maturity in 1564–5, Mirza Hakim positioned himself and his kingdom as a counterpoint to the emerging hybrid Hindustani Mughal court centered on Akbar's new capital of Fatehpur Sikri. Hakim promoted himself as the only true legatee and guardian of Central Asian and Chaghatai-Timurid political and religious ideals, implying that Akbar had betrayed those ideals by becoming more "Indian." Mirza Hakim offered his kingdom as a safe haven to mostly ethnic Central Asian rebels who opposed Akbar's efforts to diversify the Mughal nobility. Long after it had been abandoned elsewhere in the region, Mirza Hakim continued to occasionally apply a version of the *tura-i Chaghatai* (customs of the Chaghatai), a Turco-Mongol tribal-nomadic code, to judge particular kinds of crimes. Furthermore, the Mirza retained the *shahrukhi*, a Timurid/early Mughal coin, as Kabul's main currency, while banning Akbar's Hindustan-based imperial coinage from circulation.

Finally, as Muzaffar Alam has discussed, the language of political Islam in Kabul starkly contrasted with that emanating from Fatehpur Sikri.[9] In a

---

[7] For an extended discussion of the contest between Mirza Hakim and Akbar and its implications for the Mughal Empire, see Munis D. Faruqui, "The Forgotten Prince: Mirza Hakim and the Formation of the Mughal Empire in India," *Journal of the Economic and Social History of the Orient* 48, no. 4 (2005): pp. 487–523.

[8] Shaikh Abu'l Fazl, *Akbarnamah*, ed. Abdul Rahim, vol. 3 (Calcutta, 1886), pp. 364, 366.

[9] Muzaffar Alam, *The Languages of Political Islam in India* (Delhi, 2004), pp. 69–80.

late 1570s book, *Akhlaq-i Hakimi*, written at the Mirza's court by his chief secretary and dedicated to the prince, the Kingdom of Kabul affirmed its commitment to the supremacy of Islam and Muslims.[10] By contrast, the Mughal court was inching toward an imperial Islamic commitment to tolerate difference and protect people of all religious faiths.

Alongside his Central Asian credentials, Mirza Hakim proclaimed fealty to his grandfather Babur, thus positioning himself as the true heir to Mughal familial traditions. By contrast, Akbar embraced their father Humayun's legacy. Mirza Hakim's decision to attach himself to Babur's legacy made sense given that the latter continued to enjoy great prestige as the founder of the Mughal dynasty, and his tomb was located in Kabul. The Mirza spent large sums of money to maintain the tomb, and each year he presided over celebrations to mark his grandfather's death anniversary. Following Babur, he portrayed himself as a *ghazi* (Islamic frontier warrior) with a rough-and-ready Turkish steppe identity, a staunch Sunni, and a bold risk taker. Like Babur, he swore allegiance to the Naqshbandi *tariqa* (order) and helped transform Kabul into an important center of Naqshbandi authority, scholarship, and training in the 1570s. In 1570–1, the Mirza moved against the Roshaniyya – a popular Islamic revivalist and millenarian movement with strong roots among some Afghan tribes in the eastern parts of his kingdom. Drawing a page from Babur's book, Mirza Hakim succeeded by playing the Afghans against one another.[11] These and other successes drew widespread attention to Mirza Hakim's rising political star. In 1576–7, he was approached by Shah 'Ismail II of Iran to seal an alliance aimed at strengthening the Shah's efforts to reconvert Iran back to Sunni Islam.

By posing as a stark contrast to Akbar, Mirza Hakim became a powerful focus for anti-Akbar rebels in India. In 1566 and again in 1581, they invited the Mirza to invade India, dethrone Akbar, and restore Central Asian dominance there. But Mirza Hakim had only limited appeal for the vast majority of Akbar's Indian subjects, few of whom supported his invasions of northern India.

---

[10] The author Hasan 'Ali ibn Ashraf al-Munshi explicitly states that the first custom/obligation (*shi'ari*) of good governance in this world and the next is to enable Islam's spread and protection for the Prophet's descendants (*millat-i Hazrat*). This can be achieved by extirpating Islam's enemies (*mukhalafan-i din*). *Akhlaq-i Hakimi*, British Library, Ethe 2203, f. 96a.

[11] See Ni'matullah Khan Harvi, *Tarikh-i-Khan Jahani wa Makhzan-i-Afghani*, ed. S. M. Imam-ud-Din, vol. 2 (Dhaka, 1962), p. 580.

When Akbar finally defeated Mirza Hakim in 1582, he knew that he had to simultaneously undermine the Mirza's networks of support and, where possible, reconstitute them under his own authority. Toward this end, Akbar ordered the Mirza's key supporter, and long-standing prime minister, Khwaja Hasan Naqshbandi (a direct descendant of Khwaja Baha'-ud-Din, the fourteenth-century founder of the Naqshbandi order) banished forever from Kabul. In the process, Akbar struck at the heart of the Naqshbandi *tariqa*'s close alliance with Mirza Hakim. Rather than simply weakening the Mirza's allies, however, Akbar moved more importantly to build on his brother's attempts to cultivate his own power. Akbar's efforts intensified after Mirza Hakim's death from alcohol poisoning in 1585, the permanent removal of his sons to India, and the end of his princely appanage. Thus, even as Akbar accommodated himself to the Naqshbandis through the late 1580s and early 1590s, he continued Mirza Hakim's policy of co-opting Hazara political and military support and recruiting extensively among resident Uzbeks and Badakhshanis. He also appointed senior Mughal nobles or locally influential figures to the governorship of the region. These included his foster brother Zain Khan Koka; Shah Quli Khan (who had earlier undergone castration in order to serve both in Akbar's harem as well as in the court); and Hasan Beg Badakhshi, a leading Badakhshani noble. Despite initial misgivings, Kabul's population eventually embraced the Hindustan-based Mughals and remained remarkably loyal until the first decades of the eighteenth century. However troublesome Mirza Hakim may have been to Akbar during his lifetime, his extensive efforts to win friends and allies with an eye toward entrenching his own power proved crucial to long-term Mughal control over the entire arc of territory extending from the Punjab to Kabul.

Mirza Hakim's defeat signaled two key shifts in the story of the Mughal Empire. The first entailed a clear move toward a vision of empire that acknowledged and transcended India's diversity, a multiethnic empire in which narrowly sectarian or ethnic appeals could gain little purchase. The second was a shift away from territorial appanages (such as those held by Mirza Hakim and, before him, by Humayun and his brothers) toward a different, more nebulous role for princes and family members in the imperial enterprise. Akbar had been building toward this for some decades already.

It took Akbar a long time to inculcate the solidarity that his army displayed in 1582 outside Kabul. When he ascended the throne in 1556, enemies – hostile nobility, many of them Central Asian, and Afghan and

Rajput coalitions beyond the court – surrounded him. Early on, and perhaps drawing inspiration from Humayun's own efforts to address his narrow base of support, Akbar was determined not to restrict his inner circle of friends and allies to individuals of Central Asian origin. In the early to mid-1560s, his efforts to broaden the composition of the Mughal nobility led Timurid relatives and Central Asian nobles to revolt, but Akbar successfully crushed this opposition. He also worked harder to ingratiate himself among Indian Muslim clerics, Chishti saints, military and service lineages such as the Barhas and Shaikhzadas, caste-based scribal groups such as the Kayasths and Khatris, Hindu temple networks, and Rajput chiefs, among others. The Mughal nobility was gradually transformed by these initiatives.[12]

The remarkable changes Akbar wrought among the Mughal nobility are recorded in Shaikh Abu'l Fazl's *A'in-i Akbari* (ca. 1598). A perusal of earlier comparable Mughal texts reveals little or no attention afforded to any individual or group lacking a Central Asian lineage. In the *Baburnama* (ca. 1529–30), for example, Emperor Babur boasts of all those who benefited from his largesse when he raided the massive Lodi treasury in Agra:

All the Afghan Hazaras, Arabs, and Baluch in the army ... every merchant and student, indeed every person who was along with the army ... Large portions of the treasury even went to those who were not in the army... Many gifts went to the beggars and soldiers who were on the other side. To Samarkand, Khurasan, Kashgar, and Iraq went gifts for relatives and kinfolk. Offerings went to the shaykhs in Samarkand and Khurasan; one was even sent to Mecca and Medina. There was a shahrukhi of largesse for every living soul, male and female, bondsman and free, adult and child alike, in the province of Kabul and the district of Wersek.[13]

The list is long, but it does not include a single Indian group. By "everyone," this text and others of the period meant only Central Asians and groups to the northwest of India. Babur's almost total silence about the

---

[12] Between 1555 and 1580, the percentage of nobles of Central Asian origin had dropped from 52.9 percent to 24.2 percent, Iranians dropped from 31.3 percent to 17.2 percent, and Indian Muslims and Rajputs (and other Hindus) rose from none to 16.1 percent and 15.8 percent respectively. Iqtidar Alam Khan, "The Nobility under Akbar and the Development of His Religious Policy, 1560–80," *Journal of the Royal Asiatic Society* 1–2 (1968): 35.

[13] Zahir-ud-Din Muhammad Babur, *The Baburnama: Memoirs of Babur, Prince and Emperor*, trans. W. M. Thackston (New York, 2002), p. 356.

people who inhabited his "vast and populous kingdom"[14] becomes all the more astounding in the face of his lengthy descriptions of the animals, birds, reptiles, and flora of Hindustan. So also, the historical accounts *Tabaqat-i Baburi* (ca. early 1530s) and the *Qanun-i Humayuni* (1534) project a Central Asian/Timurid-Muslim imperium in India in which the existence of (never mind dealings with) subject populations is barely acknowledged. The contrast between these early Mughal accounts versus Shaikh Abu'l Fazl's late sixteenth-century writings speaks to the transformation wrought by Akbar and undoubtedly justifies the reputation he continues to hold in present-day India as an inclusive and truly great Indian ruler.

Before Shaikh Abu'l Fazl's profuse praise of Akbar's accomplishments, we can consider a transitional text such as 'Arif Qandahari's *Tarikh-i Akbari* (ca. 1580). Qandahari, an ethnic Central Asian himself, represents an earlier moment, one that affords no more than a lukewarm recognition of Akbar's incorporation of Indians into the Mughal system. It was one of the earliest major histories of Akbar's reign. In it, Qandahari openly acknowledged the diversity of Akbar's empire. The emperor's success in incorporating and reconciling the many nations under his control is broadly admired, as is his capacity for justice and good administration.[15] Important Hindu nobles are occasionally mentioned by name, although Qandahari almost never recounts actual instances of imperial patronage of non-Muslims (such as the Rajput chiefs whom Akbar inducted into the nobility starting in the 1560s). Nor is any mention made of the emperor's (unprecedented) marriages with Rajput women or the inclusion of non-Muslims in imperial-sponsored religious debates in Fatehpur Sikri. Crucially, Indian Muslim nobles, clerics, and administrators also receive short shrift at the hands of Qandahari. Since there is no doubting Qandahari's admiration for Akbar, *Tarikh-i Akbari* offers an excellent example of the rhetorical lag between the reforms Akbar initiated and the language of the empire. Shaikh Abu'l Fazl's endeavors helped close this gap in the following decade.[16]

---

[14] Ibid., p. 330.

[15] 'Arif Qandahari, *Tarikh-i-Akbari*, ed. Imtiaz Ali Arshi (Rampur, 1962), pp. 4–7, 9–11.

[16] This discussion draws on the insights of Alam, *The Languages of Political Islam*. See also John F. Richards, "The Formulation of Imperial Authority under Akbar and Jahangir," in *Kingship and Authority in South Asia*, ed. John F. Richards (Madison, 1978), pp. 252–85; K. A. Nizami, *Akbar and Religion* (Delhi, 1989); M. Athar Ali, "The Perception of India in Akbar and Abu'l Fazl," in *Akbar and His India*, ed. Irfan Habib (Delhi, 1997), pp. 215–24.

The Shaikh was one of Akbar's closest political advisors from the 1570s onward. He led efforts to generate the intellectual scaffolding needed to move the Mughal Empire away from its Central Asian and exclusively Muslim roots. To this end, Shaikh Abu'l Fazl pursued a two-pronged strategy.

The first part entailed a powerful affirmation of the multiethnic and multireligious character of the Mughal Empire. Nowhere is this explained in greater detail than in the third volume of the *A'in-i Akbari*, a work that showcases the Shaikh's skillful and innovative framing of Akbar's reign. In it, Shaikh Abu'l Fazl introduces the primarily Muslim imperial elite to the literary, philosophical, religious, and scientific achievements of Hindus. He also offers Hindu nobles a sweeping view of the most famous prophets and Islamic kings, saints, and Sufi orders who have, in turn, made India their home. The introduction to this volume explains that the project was undertaken to alleviate religious ill will by providing insights into one another's civilizational and religious attainments. With this knowledge before them, the Shaikh hopes, everyone will step back from engaging in religious disputations and conflicts and instead focus on his own spiritual well-being.[17] Celebrating the empire's diversity, alongside pleas for individuals to respect one another's cultural differences, is a major theme running through the Shaikh's other works as well.[18] This was not Shaikh Abu'l Fazl's end goal, however.

The second part of the Shaikh's strategy aimed at presenting Akbar as the guardian of India's diversity. What unfolds – reading his two major works, the *A'in-i Akbari* and the *Akbarnama*, together – is a complex theory of sovereignty. It begins by addressing the importance of a strong and righteous ruler who can protect the four worldly "essences" – access to wealth, life, honor, and religion.[19] It is a rare ruler, the Shaikh argues, who is capable of fulfilling these obligations because most are not recipients of the "divine light" (*farr-i izadi*) that is directly communicated by God to kings. Without this benediction, a king does not have access to divine wisdom and cannot therefore be a Perfect King.[20] Akbar, Shaikh Abu'l Fazl insists, is an exception.

---

[17] Shaikh Abu'l Fazl, *Ain-i-Akbari*, ed. H. Blochmann, vol. 2 (Calcutta, 1877), pp. 3–4.

[18] Shaikh Abu'l Fazl's introduction to the Persian translation of the *Mahabharata* offers a superb example. For an English translation, see Carl Ernst, "Muslim Studies of Hinduism? A Reconsideration of Arabic and Persian Translations from Indian Languages," *Iranian Studies* 36, no. 2 (2003): 180–2. See also Fazl, *Akbarnamah*, vol. 1, pp. 49–52.

[19] Shaikh Abu'l Fazl, *Ain-i-Akbari*, ed. H. Blochmann, vol. 1, Part 1 (Calcutta, 1872), p. 290.

[20] Ibid., p. 2.

The Shaikh offered two proofs to corroborate Akbar's status as a "godly ruler" (*farman-i haqiqi*).[21] The first described the chain of transmission of the divine light over fifty-two generations of ancestors down to Akbar. This was coupled with stories of miracles surrounding Akbar's birth and his infancy. The Shaikh's second proof drew attention to Akbar's religious policies. According to Abu'l Fazl, only a godly ruler could alleviate the religious discord that grew from a false consciousness that the world was divided into two competing spheres: the spiritual and temporal. Since Akbar had made the idea of universal peace (*sulh-i kul*) the centerpiece of his ruling ideology and actually succeeded in alleviating religious discord across his empire, he must be a Perfect King. What emerges from this often strained but nonetheless innovative exposition is a vision of Akbar's patronage and protection as guaranteed to everyone regardless of race or religion.[22] So we go from an early Mughal Empire under Babur whose rhetorical allegiance was largely focused on Central Asians to Akbar's empire wherein Indian Muslims and non-Muslims alike are an integral part.

As Akbar's sons came of age in this brave new world, the wide-ranging nature of their search for friends and allies set them apart from previous generations of territorially anchored princes. Even if Akbar's seventeenth-century imperial successors largely abandoned his precise rhetoric, they retained an imperial ethos that stressed an inclusive vision of empire.

## SALIM, THE FIRST GREAT MUGHAL PRINCE, 1569–1605

In Akbar's vanquishing of Mirza Hakim and his cultivation of his first son, Salim, we see a focus on the immediate family of the emperor himself, and a clear shift away from the idea of an extended ruling family co-sharing in imperial power. What becomes apparent is that an empire was being grown and protected, and Akbar intended to pass it along intact to one of his sons. This remained Mughal custom right to the end of Farrukh Siyar's reign in 1719. If Humayun, working in his appanage of Badakhshan, built his princely network of support largely in that area, princes who came of age during Akbar's reign – of whom the first and

---

[21] Ibid.

[22] This vision manifested itself in, among other things, new court rituals, festivals, and even a new imperial calendar. Stephen Blake, "*Nau Ruz* in Mughal India," in *Rethinking a Millennium: Perspectives on Indian History from the Eighth to the Eighteenth Century. Essays for Harbans Mukhia*, ed. Rajat Datta (Delhi, 2008), pp. 121–35.

perhaps the most exemplary was Salim – embodied larger and wider aspirations. It was Akbar who first confronted the question of what to do with grown princes who were no longer automatically entitled to an appanage.

Judging from his actions in the 1580s, Akbar sought at first to keep his sons close at hand. Although not averse to occasionally sending them to manage administrative or military duties away from the imperial court,[23] Akbar wished to remain intimately involved in their training and in their initial alliance building. He surrounded each of his three sons with people of influence, but he focused especially on embedding Salim in several far-flung networks of symbolic and real imperial power. Akbar thus simultaneously groomed the first generation of post-appanage imperial princes, even as he clearly signaled to powerful and ambitious nonroyals in the empire that the best they could do was to hitch their fortunes to one from among this small group of princely candidates.

Salim was the quintessential post-Akbar prince and the first great Mughal Prince. In his story we see both evidence of Akbar's careful grooming and – given the threat it posed to the imperial court itself as the prince grew from child to adult – the tensions inherent in such a project. First with direction and help from his father the emperor, and then on his own, Salim forged extensive networks of support. In some cases, these were anchored squarely within his own household. Other alliances, however, such as those with powerful nobles or members of the imperial harem, were forged outside the context of the princely household. This section describes alliance building both in the prince's early years, as engineered by Akbar and as concretized in the substance of Salim's household, and also later on, as built by Salim himself. The section thus collapses themes from both the previous chapter on households and this present chapter. As evident from Salim's example, the process of extending a prince's influence never ceased. He pursued his goals with single-minded determination and did so whether he was in residence at the Mughal court or in rebellion against his father. Ultimately, in Salim's case, his alliance building brought him into conflict with his father, the emperor.

---

[23] Besides exercising nominal command over the army that fought Mirza Hakim in 1582, Akbar's son Murad was also initially tapped to avenge the Yusufzai massacre of an imperial army in 1586. The difficulty of that task, however, finally persuaded Akbar to listen to Raja Man Singh's advice to rescind the order. Akbar later considered sending his third son Danyal but decided against that as well. See Fazl, *Akbarnamah*, vol. 3, pp. 485–7, 491.

Rejoicing at the birth of Prince Salim, late 16th century (© Victoria and Albert Museum, London, 2006AP2507–01)

Yet, starting from the very birth of the young prince, Akbar was meticulous in his grooming. In 1569, Akbar took his pregnant wife Maryam-uz-Zamani to the small village of Sikri, the home of the Chishti *pir* (religious preceptor) Shaikh Salim Chishti to give birth. The Shaikh had previously told the emperor of a dream in which Akbar, who had no male heirs despite being in his late twenties, had not one but three sons. When a boy was born, a grateful emperor named the infant Salim after the *pir* who had predicted his birth. Casting Shaikh Salim Chishti as his son's protector, the emperor also appointed a daughter and daughter-in-law of the Shaikh to be the prince's wet-nurses.[24] A number of the Shaikh's grandsons thus became Salim's foster brothers (*koka*), and in his early years many of the Shaikh's family members lived with and attended to the prince. In 1577, Akbar appointed the Shaikh's second son and a foster father of Salim – Shaikh Ahmad – to be one of the prince's tutors.

The *Akbarnama* describes other ways in which Akbar entwined Salim's future with the Chishti lineage, paving the way for his son to be a future patron of the order. Soon after Salim's birth, Akbar undertook a pilgrimage to the shrine of the founding Chishti saint, Khwaja Mu'in-ud-Din Chishti (d. 1230), fulfilling his vow to walk the two hundred and twenty odd miles from Agra to Ajmer if granted a son.[25] Some years later, Salim accompanied his father to the same shrine, on which occasion, we are told, he was ordered to bow before the saint's grave and then circumambulate the shrine.[26] Just as Khwaja Mu'in-ud-Din Chishti encapsulated an expansive spiritual vision that extended its blessings to everyone in India, so too Salim embodied for the emperor the future of his imperial vision, which also encompassed all of India.[27]

By all accounts, Akbar celebrated milestones in Salim's life with unprecedented pomp and ceremony, making of them occasions to honor the Mughal nobility as well as to draw them into the ambit of the prince's early years. In 1573, Akbar ordered all "the amirs and the great officers of the state" to attend the circumcision of Salim (and his brothers).[28] After the ceremony, massive gift giving and raucous celebrations ensued, building much goodwill toward the young prince.[29] To mark the beginning of Salim's formal education, large numbers of nobles were invited to watch as the Quran was placed in the lap of the then four-year-old prince. Following a short prayer, the assembly erupted in such a roar of congratulations that the foundations of the assembly hall shook (according to *Tabaqat-i Akbari*, one of the sources for this event). Mir Kalan Harvi, the

---

[24] Nur-ud-Din Muhammad Jahangir, *Jahangirnama*, ed. Muhammad Hashim (Tehran, 1980), p. 442.

[25] Shaikh Abu'l Fazl, *Akbarnamah*, ed. Abdul Rahim, vol. 2 (Calcutta, 1879), p. 350.

[26] Khwaja Nizamuddin Ahmad, *The Tabaqat-i-Akbari*, trans. Brajendranath De, vol. 2 (Calcutta, repr. 1996), p. 429.

[27] Bruce Lawrence has argued that Akbar had sought to set himself as a latter-day political counterpart to Shaikh Mu'in-ud-Din Chishti. I'd extend this argument to include Salim in the equation. Bruce B. Lawrence, "Veiled Opposition to Sufis in Muslim South Asia," in *Islamic Mysticism Contested*, ed. Frederick de Jong and Bernd Radtke (Leiden, 1999), p. 438.

[28] Ahmad, *The Tabaqat-i-Akbari*, vol. 2, p. 423.

[29] Fazl, *Akbarnamah*, vol. 3, pp. 74–5.

prince's newly appointed tutor, then raised Salim onto his shoulder amidst a shower of coins and even more acclaim.[30]

Akbar was deliberate and strategic in his selection of the prince's *ataliqs* (guardians), anointing ever more important individuals to this post as Salim approached adulthood. At first, Akbar had favored religious scholars such as Mir Kalan Harvi and Shaikh Ahmad. But in 1579, with Salim then ten years of age, Akbar appointed Qutb-ud-Din Khan, a high-ranking noble and member of the powerful Central Asian Atga clan. (Sure enough, during a revolt the following year led by nobles and officers of Central Asian origin, the Atgas remained faithful.) When Qutb-ud-Din Khan was later needed in Gujarat in 1582, Akbar replaced him with another high-ranking noble, 'Abd-ul-Rahim Khan-i Khanan.

'Abd-ul-Rahim Khan-i Khanan was the son of Bairam Khan (d. 1561), Akbar's own *ataliq* and first prime minister. He had grown up under Akbar's direct charge and had been given the honorific of "son" (*farzand*) by the emperor.[31] Akbar was married to 'Abd-ul-Rahim Khan-i Khanan's maternal aunt as well as his former stepmother (Salima Sultan Begum). Large numbers of his father Bairam Khan's former retainers also populated the ranks of Akbar's nobility.[32] Moreover, 'Abd-ul-Rahim Khan-i Khanan's father-in-law Mirza 'Aziz Koka was a scion of the Atga clan, a foster brother of Akbar, and a nephew of Qutb-ud-Din Khan. He was fluent in Arabic, Persian, Turkish, and Hindavi; admired as a most generous patron; and famed as a consummate gatherer of rumor, gossip, news, and intelligence. As such, he was a perfect choice to teach the young prince the workings of the empire.[33] His selection as tutor suggests the value Akbar placed on passing along such wisdom to Salim.

The imperial harem, which had taken on a distinct corporate identity and grown in importance during Akbar's reign,[34] was dominated by a small group of women, including the emperor's mother, several aunts, and

[30] Ahmad, *The Tabaqat-i-Akbari*, vol. 2, pp. 423–4.
[31] 'Abd-ul-Baqi Nihawandi, *Ma'asir-i Rahimi*, Asiatic Society of Bengal, Ivanow 140, f. 307a.
[32] Shah Nawaz Khan, *Maasir-ul-Umara*, ed. Abdur Rahim, vol. 1 (Calcutta, 1888), pp. 375, 382.
[33] For more on the colorful 'Abd-ul-Rahim, see C. R. Naik, *'Abdur-Rahim Khan-i-Khanan and His Literary Circle* (Ahmedabad, 1966); Annemarie Schimmel, "Khankhanan Abdur Rahim and the Sufis," in *Intellectual Studies in Islam*, ed. Michel Mazzaoui and Vera Moreen (Salt Lake City, 1991), pp. 153–62; Eva Orthmann, *'Abd or-Rahim Khan-e Khanan: Staatsmann und Mäzen* (unpub. M.A. thesis, University of Tubingen).
[34] Ruby Lal, *Domesticity and Power in the Early Mughal World* (Cambridge, 2005), pp. 140–213.

a few senior wives, all of whom liked and respected one another. This made for a rare unanimity of purpose in the harem. Steadfast in their loyalty to Akbar, these senior women were also united in their support for Salim. Much of this had to do with Akbar's encouragement. Compared to his younger brothers, Salim had many more opportunities to meet, fete, and cultivate relationships with the senior women of the imperial harem. For example, in 1578, on the eve of a hajj expedition by senior ladies of the harem, Salim held a special farewell audience with them. This occurred as another order for his younger brother Murad to accompany them to Gujarat was canceled. When the women sailed off, they did so in a boat named "Salimi," likely not a coincidence. In the same year, when Akbar's mother, Maryam Makani, decided to visit the emperor in the Punjab, Salim was given the honor of welcoming her on her arrival at the imperial camp. A few years later, on the return of the royal women from Mecca, Salim was the first member of the imperial family to greet them. He did so outside Ajmer, and afterward Salim and the women gave thanks at the shrine of Khwaja Mu'in-ud-Din Chishti. The deliberate symbolism of Salim and the ladies of the harem united under the protection of the saint would not have been lost on anyone. In 1583 and again in 1585, Salim was the preferred choice among the princes to welcome his grandmother and other senior ladies when they arrived at the imperial camp in Allahabad and Kabul, respectively.

Such extensive contact meant that the harem showed great concern when Salim fell ill in 1577. So also, in 1581, Maryam Makani requested that the emperor take her grandson Salim with him on the expedition to crush Mirza Hakim instead of leaving him behind in Hindustan, against the prince's wishes. Sure enough, when Salim arrived at the imperial camp and paid his respects to Akbar, Shaikh Abu'l Fazl noted that the women of the harem were especially happy.[35] Over the next few years, the harem directed birthday celebrations for Salim (1582) and a newly born daughter (1586). Neither of Akbar's other sons, Murad and Danyal, ever enjoyed the same degree of attention. The harem continued to be a powerful pillar of support for Salim over the remaining decades of Akbar's reign. Senior women such as Salima Sultan Begum and Ruqayya Begum played crucial roles in negotiating a settlement between Akbar and Salim when father-son relations turned sour in the early 1600s, eventually helping to pave the way for Salim's accession to the Mughal throne.

---

[35] Fazl, *Akbarnamah*, vol. 3, p. 369.

But Akbar did not fail to introduce his other sons into circles of influence of imperial scope. He appointed high-ranking and loyal Mughal nobles as *ataliqs*: Sa'id Khan Chaghatai and Shaikh Faizi for Danyal (1577 and 1579), and Sharif Khan for Murad (1580). He also offered Murad and Danyal opportunities to participate in a range of imperial functions and activities. Some were quite significant, as when Danyal was delegated to visit Ajmer and pray at Khwaja Mu'in-ud-Din's shrine on his father's behalf in 1580 or when Murad was given nominal command over the imperial forces that defeated Mirza Hakim outside Kabul in 1582. Generally, however, the spotlight never shone as brightly on them as it did on Salim. We may never know if this was because Akbar simply favored his firstborn son or if it was a necessity in a post-appanage system that one son be specially groomed so that attention to the empire's future remained clear and focused.

In 1585, Akbar granted Salim full adult status. Over the next two decades until Akbar's death in 1605, and even as his relations with his father deteriorated through the 1590s and during his rebellion between 1599 and 1604, Salim worked indefatigably to build a cohesive core of household retainers, the first step in consolidating his base of loyal supporters and a necessary one for all subsequent far-flung alliance building. Accordingly, the prince appears to have recruited into his household at least three (overlapping) groups of individuals: (i) political opponents of Akbar, (ii) outsiders to the Mughal system, and (iii) individuals entrenched in key social networks.

Many former supporters of Akbar's half brother Mirza Hakim, whom Akbar fought for years and whose Kabul-based kingdom he annexed in 1585, gravitated toward Salim after the annexation. The prince welcomed them and their networks into his household in stark contrast to Akbar, who largely shunned them. Thus men such as Lala Beg Kabuli, Khwaja Dost Muhammad, and Zamana Beg achieved high positions in Salim's princely household and eventually assisted him in his rebellion and then rose to high ranks in the imperial nobility following Salim's accession to the Mughal throne. Salim also lured the notorious Vir Singh Bundela, who had fought Akbar through most of the 1590s on the grounds that Akbar had favored his older brother to succeed to their father's kingdom of Orchha (in Central India). Vir Singh joined Salim in the city of Allahabad at a time when the prince was already in rebellion against Akbar. In 1602, Vir Singh Bundela assassinated Shaikh Abu'l Fazl (who was Akbar's closest advisor as well as a sworn enemy of Salim). When Salim became emperor, Vir Singh was made one of the richest and highest-ranking imperial nobles in the Mughal Empire and ruled a broad swathe of semi-autonomous territory in central India until his death in 1626. In this fashion, the Mughals were temporarily able to assert their authority over the perennially restive region.

Like Vir Singh, Raja Basu of Ma'u and Patan (located in the foothills of the Punjab), was a perennial rebel who moved in and out of Salim's ambit through the 1590s and early 1600s. Raja Basu too was rewarded with control over his ancestral territories after Salim's accession in 1605.

Salim reached out to groups we might consider outsiders to the Mughal imperial system, groups that had long opposed Akbar. In this regard, Salim's recruitment of Afghans was especially significant. Steadily displaced as the dominant political and military group in northern India with the spread of Mughal rule after the 1550s, most Afghans deeply resented the Mughals. Akbar in turn largely refused to incorporate them into the Mughal nobility. By contrast, Salim drew prominent Afghans to himself through the 1590s, offering them honor and rewards. One such person, Shaikh Rukn-ud-Din Rohilla, was later admiringly characterized by Salim/Jahangir as "the head of a tribe and a very brave man who, while in the service of nobles, lost an arm to a sword."[36] Salim also wooed other Afghan notables such as Pir Khan – a scion of the Lodi dynasty whose defeat by Babur in 1526 paved the way for the founding of the Mughal Empire. Although Pir Khan ultimately decided against forging an alliance with Salim, the prince's interest in the Khan persuaded other Afghans to flock to his rebellious standard in Allahabad. Following the Emperor Jahangir's accession to the throne in 1605, we see the beginnings of large-scale Afghan participation in the Mughal enterprise. No one rose higher than Pir Khan, who won the title of Khan Jahan Lodi and remained a committed imperial loyalist until Jahangir's death in 1627.

Salim also reached out to alienated Kashmiris. They had been conquered by the Mughals in 1586 and rebelled against them over the ensuing years. When Akbar sought to increase Kashmir's tax burden in 1592, Salim openly opposed the plan. Salim became a patron of Kashmiri holy men such as Wahid Sufi and Ganga Rishi. After 1599, Salim attracted an influential core of Kashmiris into his service in Allahabad. One of them was Amba Khan Kashmiri. A descendant of the recently displaced Chak royal family, he proved crucial in mobilizing a network of supporters for Salim in Kashmir and in the eastern parts of the Mughal Empire (where large numbers of Kashmiris had been exiled by Akbar in the 1590s). These connections were crucial in helping Salim consolidate his hold over Bihar during his princely rebellion. Following Salim's accession to the imperial

---

[36] Jahangir, *Jahangirnama*, p. 11.

throne, his Kashmiri connections also ensured that Kashmir, once a hotbed of anti-Mughal activity, emerged as one of the most quiescent parts of the empire and, over the course of the seventeenth century, the primary summer playground of the Mughal court.

The third group identifiable within Salim's household included men who, through their own status and friendships, afforded him access to significant social networks. Among them were notable religious leaders from the Naqshbandi order, as well as dons of locally embedded ethnic groups such as the militarily powerful Saiyids of Barha and the learned *shaikhzadas* of Kairana. Salim greatly valued his association from 1594 onward with Khwaja 'Abdullah, a lineal descendant of the famous Naqshbandi saint Khwaja Ahrar (d. 1490), and a nephew of Khwaja Hasan Naqshbandi, Mirza Hakim's

Prince Salim with a courtier and attendants in a tent, ca. 1600 (Freer Gallery of Art, Smithsonian Institution, Washington D.C.: Purchase, F1960.27)

prime minister from 1565 to 1582. Khwaja 'Abdullah's recruitment to Salim's household created a link to the prominent Naqshbandi order that Akbar had largely ignored in favor of other Sufi orders, such as the Chishtis. Sure enough, nobles with ties to the Naqshbandis provided critical military support during Salim's struggle to succeed his father in October 1605 and in his 1606 conflict with his son Khusrau.[37]

The Saiyids of Barha, a group that traced its origins to a thirteenth-century Arab immigrant to India, were a force to be reckoned with across an arc of territory northwest of Delhi. Ignored by the previous Lodi rulers of north India, the Barhas became a key constituency within the Mughal military establishment after Akbar's accession in 1556. Although the Barhas were considered rustic in habit, simple, and boorish,[38] every Mughal emperor from Akbar onward treated them as especially loyal Mughal supporters within the general population and placed them at the honored head of the Mughal vanguard (*harawal*) in battle. Salim/Jahangir once described them as "the bravest men of their time,"[39] and Akbar and Salim wrestled for influence among them.[40] Saiyid 'Ali Asghar Barha, Salim's childhood friend and confidant, remained by the prince's side even through his rebellion. Saiyid 'Ali Asghar was the son of Saiyid Mahmud Barha – the first major Barha figure to accommodate himself to the Mughals in the 1550s and a high-ranking imperial noble during Akbar's reign.

Shaikh Hassu, son of Shaikh Bina (of Sirhind), was a surgeon as well as an elephant doctor at the Mughal court and had also been a childhood friend of Salim.[41] His clansmen, the *shaikhzada*s of Kairana (in present-day western Uttar Pradesh), were firmly allied with various other *shaikhzada* lineages in the region through marriage and friendship and were respected as educated landholders, albeit with small landholdings. In the early 1590s, when Shaikh Hassu introduced two '*alim*s (religious scholars), Shaikh Muqim-ud-Din and Shaikh Ahmad, to Salim, the prince immediately recommended both men for subsistence grants (*madad-i ma'ash*).[42] The Shaikhs were founders of *madrassa*s (Islamic religious

---

[37] K. A. Nizami, "Naqshbandi Influence on Mughal Rulers and Politics," *Islamic Culture* 39 (1965): 46–7.

[38] Shah Nawaz Khan, *Maasiru-l-Umara*, ed. Abdur Rahim and Ashraf Ali, vol. 2 (Calcutta, 1890), p. 377.

[39] Jahangir, *Jahangirnama*, p. 38.

[40] Saiyid Roshan Ali, *Saiyid-ul-Tawarikh* (Delhi, 1864), pp. 24–6.

[41] 'Abd al-Qadir Badauni, *Muntakhab al-Tawarikh*, ed. Ahmad Ali, vol. 3 (Calcutta, 1869), pp. 169–70.

[42] Shaikh Ali Mushtaqi, *Gulistan-i Kairana* (Amroha, 1888), p. 49.

schools) in Kairana[43] and became useful conduits of influence in their *qasba* settlements as a result of their roles as educators of local landholders (*zamindars*), dispute resolvers, and marriage matchmakers.

Like every other important Mughal Prince, Salim reached out as well to cultivate scholars and artists. The list of well-known poets who were patronized at one point or another by Salim include Saiyid Muhammad 'Itabi, Mulla 'Ali Ahmad Nishani, Akbar Isfahani, Khusraui Qa'ini, Ra'i Manohar, Sultan Afshar, Mirza Hasan, Tifli, Maqsud 'Ali Tabrizi, Rukn-ud-Din Masih Kashani, and Muhammad Hashim Sanjar Kashani. Many were recent immigrants from Safavid Iran. Salim's early education under men such as Shaikh Faizi, Akbar's poet laureate, and Muhammad Husain Zarin Qalam (one of the greatest calligraphers of his generation) seems to have prepared him well for the role of literary and artistic patron, a man of both the pen and the sword – the perfect Muslim ruler and a worthy son to Akbar.

Salim's atelier, his artistic establishment, projected this precise motif both before and after he rebelled against his father in 1599. Salim laid the foundation of his atelier some time in the mid- to late 1580s with the decision to employ Aqa Reza Herati, a recent immigrant from Herat, as its artistic director. Aqa Reza remained in the prince's service after he rebelled, removing himself from the imperial court to Salim's base in the city of Allahabad. Aqa Reza's body of work was, as expected, dominated by the figure of Salim.[44] He depicted a youthful, energetic prince, drinking, hunting, carousing with companions; studying; conversing with old men; and holding court.[45] So also the works of other artistic luminaries in Salim's household including Mirza Ghulam, Nanha, Bishan Das, Quli, Mir 'Abdullah Katib Mushqin Qalam, Abu'l Hasan and Nadira Banu highlighted their master's charisma, his religiosity, his divine favor, his Chaghatai roots, his authority over the people around him and their loyalty through service to him, and his administrative and judicial experience.[46] Through their art, the members of Salim's atelier emphasized how the prince

[43] Ibid., pp. 49–50.
[44] S. P. Verma, *Mughal Painters and Their Works: A Biographical Survey and Comprehensive Catalogue* (Delhi, 1994), pp. 62–9.
[45] Ibid., pp. 64–9.
[46] Asok K. Das, *Mughal Painting during Jahangir's Time* (Calcutta, 1978), pp. 45, 47, 50, 54, 57, 62; Verma, *Mughal Painters and Their Work*, pp. 66, 65, 69; Ellison B. Findly, "Jahangir's Vow of Non-Violence," *Journal of the American Oriental Society* 107, no. 2 (1987): 246; L. Binyon et al., *Persian Miniature Painting* (Oxford, 1933), p. 149.

Prince Salim at a hunt, Folio from a Shikarnama (Hunting Album) ca. 1600–4 (Los Angeles County Museum of Art, Los Angeles, U.S.A. Digital Image © 2012 Museum Associates/LACMA/Art Resource/Art Resource, NY)

was a serious contender for imperial power.[47] The importance of such work earned Aqa Reza Herati his place in the inner circle of Salim's household.

---

[47] In light of Salim's known fascination with Christian iconography, we might assume that he was fully aware of the power of pictorial representations in focusing loyalty in the person of an individual. Father Jerome Xavier, writing in 1597, noted that Salim was "so anxious for things imported from Portugal … and especially for pictures of Our Savior and the Blessed Virgin, the Queen of Angels (to whose care he commends himself) that he excites our wonder." E. D. Maclagan, "Jesuit Missions to the Emperor Akbar," *Journal of the Asiatic Society of Bengal* 65 (1896): 67. In the following year, Father Xavier found Salim busy directing the work of two painters who were "tracing out by the application of colors" some pictures with Christian themes. Ibid., 74.

The Mughal Prince Parvez and a holy man, early 17th century (Freer Gallery of Art, Smithsonian Institution, Washington D.C.: Purchase, F1929.3)

A powerful household such as that built by Salim depended on casting a broad and inclusive net for recruitment and also on building a cohesive inner core. Work in this vein never ceased until the fateful day a prince either achieved his ambition to become the next Mughal emperor or died in the attempt. In the interim, a powerful household also served a prince who turned to rebellion against the imperial court, as did Salim against Akbar in 1599, following years of growing tension.

As early as the late 1580s, the wisdom of Akbar's decision to keep his sons at the Mughal court began to appear increasingly suspect. The relatively close living quarters, increasing conflicts over precedence, and rising tensions among the princes' supporters engendered an environment of competition and hostility. The marriage of Mirza 'Aziz Koka's daughter to Murad in 1587, for example, seems to have placed this powerful nobleman and foster brother of the emperor on a collision course with Salim. To prevent conflict from breaking out at court, Akbar finally separated his sons geographically. In 1591, Murad was appointed provincial governor of Malwa, then Gujarat, and finally the Deccan where he died in 1599. In 1597, deteriorating relations between Salim and Danyal forced the latter's removal to Allahabad. Danyal mostly stayed away from the Mughal court as long as Salim remained there.

The father–son feud between Akbar and Salim, however, continued to simmer. Salim systematically heaped favor on precisely those individuals Akbar had sidelined or from whom he suffered a slight. Thus, when Akbar imprisoned the poet Saiyid Muhammed Etabi for his satires of certain Mughal nobles, Salim petitioned for his release. Akbar then ordered the poet's exile to the Hejaz, but Salim helped him flee to the Deccan instead. When Akbar imprisoned an imperial nobleman, Yusuf Khan Rizvi, for colluding with Kashmiris in a rebellion, Salim recommended Rizvi's reappointment as governor of Kashmir. Just as Akbar was in the midst of yet another standoff with Raja Basu of Mau (who had already rebelled against the Mughals on a number of occasions), Salim sought a royal pardon for the Raja.

Akbar retaliated by bringing pressure to bear on Salim's supporters and by undermining their loyalty. For example, in 1594, he married one of Salim's strongest supporters in the harem, Shakr-un-Nisa Begum, to a distantly related Timurid cousin Mirza Shahrukh (the former ruler of Badakhshan). Immediately following this marriage, the emperor contracted a second one between another daughter and supporter of Salim, Khanum Sultan, and Muzaffar Husain Mirza. Both men harbored strong political ambitions that rendered them unlikely to kowtow to Salim; in the process, Salim lost two powerful supporters in the harem.

The poet Khwaja Muhammad Shirazi, more commonly known as 'Urfi, may have been among the best-known victims of this intensifying father-son struggle. Although only one from a large stable of poets patronized by Salim, 'Urfi was one of the greatest exponents of the *qasida* (ode) during the Mughal period. 'Abd-ul-Qadir Badauni, his contemporary, notes that the poet's *divan* (collection of poems) was not only one of the most popular works of its day but also was considered an auspicious possession by literate Persian speakers.[48] In a context in which highly regarded poets

[48] Badauni, *Muntakhab al-Tawarikh*, vol. 3, p. 285.

often had their poems transcribed for private circulation, read aloud in private and public assemblies, recited on the streets, and used as templates to tutor individuals in the art of poetic composition, a single *qasida* by a poet of 'Urfi's stature could draw his patron to the attention of a large number of people. 'Urfi deployed some of his considerable ode-writing talents in favor of Salim.[49] Rosalind O'Hanlon best captures the value of an endorsement by someone of 'Urfi's stature in her observation that

[I]t was people, rather than land, which constituted the scarcer resource . . . [it was] people therefore that these states needed to work hard to attract. In this setting, literary and aesthetic modes of appealing to loyalties, attracting clients and cultivating forms of identity may well have made more sense than strategies of direct coercion.[50]

For Salim, 'Urfi's value lay also in his indirect animosity to Akbar, itself derived from 'Urfi's early snub in 1585 by Shaikh Abu'l Faiz, "Faizi," Akbar's chief poet and the brother of the powerful Shaikh Abu'l Fazl. Faizi rarely patronized poets himself but rather maintained a "long-standing habit" of being "friendly with everybody for a week."[51] This short association was usually sufficient for him to gauge whether an individual was worthy of being introduced to the imperial court. In skill and talent, 'Urfi Shirazi clearly passed this test; yet, on account of a bitter falling-out with Faizi, 'Urfi never gained a full-time position in Akbar's household. As a result, for the next few years, 'Urfi had to content himself with being an employee of the high-ranking Mughal nobleman Hakim Abu'l Fath Gilani, who was known for his dislike of Shaikh Abu'l Fazl. It was upon the death of the Hakim in 1589 that 'Urfi turned to Salim as his new patron, along with the noblemen Zain Khan Koka and 'Abd-ul-Rahim Khan-i Khanan.

Not only did Salim thus gain an ally in 'Urfi, he also was privy to the goodwill of 'Urfi's other two patrons between 1589 and 'Urfi's premature death in 1591. Joint patronage of 'Urfi was not merely about highlighting a shared platform of cultural appreciation; more importantly, it signaled the

---

[49] In one famous composition, for example, 'Urfi speaks of Salim's omniscience, his ability to remove injustice and tyranny from the world, his ability to cure the infirm, his philanthropy, his benevolence, his gentle nature, his qualities as the perfect son, and, significantly, the attributes of sovereignty he shared with his father. Abdul Ghani, *Persian Language and Literature at the Mughal Court*, vol. 3 (Westmead, repr. 1972), p. 105.

[50] Rosalind O'Hanlon, "Cultural Pluralism, Empire and the State in Early Modern South Asia – A Review Essay," *Indian Economic and Social History Review* 44, no. 3 (2007): 368. O'Hanlon's insights are substantially supported by Allison Busch, "Hidden in Plain View: Brajbhasha Poets at the Mughal Court," *Modern Asian Studies* 44, no. 2 (2010): 267–309.

[51] Badauni, *Muntakhab al-Tawarikh*, vol. 3, p. 285.

growing political ties among Zain Khan Koka, 'Abd-ul-Rahim Khan-i Khanan, and Salim. Linking these men was their shared dislike of the brothers Shaikh Abu'l Fazl and Faizi, whose arrogance and abrasiveness, proximity to the emperor, and role in formulating some of Akbar's more controversial policies (especially their attempt to help Akbar fashion a new imperial cult, the *Tauhid-i Ilahi*) had made them notorious and unpopular figures at the imperial court. Ultimately, as the eighteenth-century historian Khafi Khan wrote, the poet 'Urfi Shirazi fell to the machinations of this duo; "it is well known," Khafi Khan asserts, "that Faizi and Abu'l Fazl, out of jealousy, had him murdered by administering poison."[52]

Salim's partisans and networks were attacked in other ways as well: by being removed from imperial posts and being disgraced and publicly humiliated. Yet despite all the bad blood between father and son, we might argue that their struggle in no way hurt the dynasty – on the contrary. For, regardless of whether you chose Akbar or Salim (or any of Akbar's other sons), your ultimate choice was still a core member of the Mughal dynasty. In the earlier appanage system, competition for loyalties resulted in factions that supported different territorial pieces belonging to different family members and undermined the consolidation and extension of the empire over generations. The system instituted by Akbar, which involved alliance building as an integral part of a prince's grooming, actually augmented the growth of the empire. We see in the following section how these processes continued through Salim's rebellion and how the struggle between father and son took both of them far afield in pursuit of supporters. The prince was no longer territorially limited, nor could he afford to limit his pursuit of alliances to fellow Central Asians.

### Salim's Allahabad-based Rebellion Extends the Reach of Empire

Salim's rebellion provides a good example of how princes forged new social networks beyond the confines of the imperial court. This point holds despite the ultimate failure of Salim's rebellion.[53] Salim's five-year stay (1599–1604) in Allahabad resulted in his firmly establishing dynastic authority in this region because of the manner in which the prince attracted support to his cause. Whereas prior to the 1580s Allahabad was reputed to

---

[52] Khafi Khan, *Muntakhab al-Labab*, ed. Kabir-ud-din Ahmad, vol. 1 (Calcutta, 1869), p. 241.

[53] As laid out in Chapter 5, Salim's long rebellion failed because, being based in Allahabad, outside the major zones of power, he was unable to get any real traction against Emperor Akbar.

be an area of fierce anti-Mughal sentiment, after 1604 this was no longer the case, nor did such resistance return until a century or so thereafter. Salim's stay played no small part in this transformation and can be taken as a great demonstration of how the spread of imperial power was helped, and not hindered, by the friendships and alliances forged in the context of a dramatic rebellion.

When Salim and his entourage relocated to Allahabad in 1599, he brought imperial courtly life to a region that had never encountered it in any sustained manner. During the next five years, he extended his authority over a swathe of territory between the cities of Patna in the east and Qannauj in the west. In early 1600, in a throwback to the appanage-centered past, he pronounced himself *sultan* (king) to assert his independence from Akbar.[54] In the summer of 1602, he appropriated the even more exalted title of *padshah* and began issuing coins in the name of "Sultan Salim *Padshah Ghazi*" (Warrior Emperor). Before long, his new power center in northern India began to lure individuals from the imperial court who had been unable to attain high positions in that establishment. Salim's "little kingdom" offered fresh opportunities for professional and economic advancement.

Abu'l Hasan Mashhadi was one of many talented individuals whose migration to Salim's court transformed Allahabad's place in the Mughal Empire. Prior to the death of Akbar's son Murad in 1599, Abu'l Hasan had served as that prince's personal secretary and *diwan* (treasurer) in the Deccan. Abu'l Hasan, however, was not an imperial officer, and his hopes of entering the larger imperial system appeared to die with Murad. Although he could have remained in the Deccan and attempted to gain employment with Danyal – Murad's brother and replacement – or even waited for an opportunity to join Akbar's imperial establishment, he instead moved northward to Allahabad where he entered Salim's service. His noted administrative skills in no small measure helped the prince consolidate his control over the region, and Abu'l Hasan remained with the prince for the duration of Salim's estrangement from Akbar.[55]

Allahabad's growing attractiveness as a counterpoint to service under Akbar or Danyal is also suggested in the example of Pir Khan (later Khan Jahan Lodi). Between 1600 and 1603, he continually threatened to leave Danyal's employment in the Deccan and decamp to Allahabad. In the end,

---

[54] Fazl, *Akbarnamah*, vol. 3, p. 773; Kamgar Husaini, *Ma'asir-i-Jahangiri*, ed. Azra Alavi (Bombay, 1978), p. 24.
[55] Shah Nawaz Khan, *Maasiru-l-Umara*, ed. Ashraf Ali, vol. 3 (Calcutta, 1891), pp. 163–8.

only his powerful social connections within the Deccan-based nobility and massive gifts from Danyal kept him from joining Salim.[56]

Alongside his efforts to entice imperial employees to his own service, Salim worked very hard to forge links with regional leaders, including Indian Muslim figures. Salim's princely court at Allahabad proved extremely hospitable for men such as the distinguished religious scholar Miran Sadr-i Jahan, who hailed from the town of Pihani in the region of Qannauj, and administrators such as Muhammad Muqim/Wazir Khan and Shaikh Khubu/Qutb-ud-Din Khan, who shared links to the north Indian town of Badaun. Others such as Shaikh 'Ala-ud-Din, Shaikh Bayazid, Shaikh Kabir, Shaikh Yusuf, and Shaikh Hassu were tied into various *shaikhzada* communities in Fatehpur, Mau, Kairana, Gopamau, Khairabad, Daryabad, Bihar Sharif, and Mustafabad. The mass desertion of pro-Akbar imperial officials at the outset of Salim's rebellion strengthened the hand of the Indian Muslim *zamindar* and *qasba* elites in Salim's domain, since their main competitors in local patronage systems had left. Many of these individuals went on to become high-ranking Mughal nobles following Salim's accession in 1605, thus making available to the dynasty their extensive social networks and connections in Allahabad and beyond.

Below the level of the princely court, Salim's administration in the *suba*s (provinces) of Allahabad, Awadh, and Bihar provided disparate communities with many professional opportunities. Again, the example of Indian Muslim groups is instructive. The departure of imperial officials following Salim's arrival in Allahabad seems to have accelerated their induction into all levels of administration in the princely state. Although there is no definite information regarding the ethnicity of officials such as Nurullah, Mu'in-ud-Din, Shaikh Nurullah, and 'Abd-us-Salim,[57] nor of Shaikh Ahmad,[58] their names suggest that they were Indian Muslims. Indeed, it is noteworthy that of the eighteen names of lower-ranking officials that have survived in a variety of records from Salim's years in Allahabad, fourteen were likely so. Although it is not possible to track the subsequent careers of these men, the experience and training garnered while running a princely administration would have undoubtedly enabled them to find work within the imperial service once the region reverted to direct imperial control.

---

[56] Harvi, *Tarikh-i-Khan Jahani*, vol. 2, pp. 486, 491.
[57] *Mughal Farmans*, ed. K. P. Srivastava (Lucknow, 1974), pp. 14–15.
[58] *Mughal Documents 1526–1627*, Vol. I, ed. S. A. I. Tirmizi (Delhi, 1989), p. 75.

Salim's success with Indian Muslims was replicated with groups of regionally powerful Bundelas and Purbiyas as well. Based on their support for the prince during his rebellion, many individuals – most notably Vir Singh Bundela (mentioned earlier) – rose to become high-ranking imperial noblemen after 1605. Just like their Indian Muslim counterparts, certain non-Muslim groups were integrated into the Mughal Empire through their participation in Salim's rebellion, which set up their eventual accommodation as loyal subjects.

Individuals drawn from the *qasba*s of the Allahabad region did more than simply fill out the ranks of Salim's administration or army. They also served as local contacts and conduits for demonstrations of Salim's largesse and powers of adjudication. This is apparent from a 1602 case in which Saiyid 'Abd-ul-Khalil, a resident of Qannauj, petitioned Salim, "the just prince" (*shahzada-i 'adil*), for help after he had been cheated out of some land. During his audience with Salim, the Saiyid complained about his own misfortune, and he also warned the prince that unrest (*shorish*) was sweeping Qannauj on account of the corruption (*fasad*) of local officials. Salim responded by restoring Saiyid 'Abd-ul-Khalil's lands and punishing a host of local officials.[59] Such actions – facilitated by the proximity and accessibility of Salim's court in Allahabad – likely contributed to Salim's later success, in 1602, in mobilizing a sizable army of just fewer than 40,000 men for a (failed) push against Agra.

Salim also actively reached out to local *shaikhzada* notables and religious figures by issuing numerous new land grants and confirming many older ones. In some cases, the prince reached out to individuals who had received prior favors from the Mughal state. Invariably, his actions deepened ties between the recipients and the dynasty. In other cases, however, Salim's generosity helped forge new relationships, extending the breadth of imperial connections across the region. Among the recipients of the prince's largesse were local figures such as Shaikh Jahan, Shaikh Muhammad, and Shaikh Nasir – descendants of Hazrat Makhdum Abkash Daryabadi who had originally founded the important settlement of Daryabad.[60] Pir Jalil, the founder of a large Suhrawardi *khanaqah* in Awadh and a member of a very distinguished religious family, was similarly honored with a *madad-i ma'ash* grant (tax-free lands given in charity to religious or worthy individuals).[61] Likewise, in 1601 and again in 1604,

---

[59] Mulla Khairullah, *Tarikh-i Khandan-i Rashidi*, KU Mss. 15/2, f. 22a-22b.
[60] Brij Bhukan Lal, *Tarikh-i Daryabad* (Daryabad, 1924), p. 100.
[61] Agha Mehdi, *Tarikh-i Lucknow* (Lucknow, 1976), p. 342.

the family of Pir Damaria of *suba* Bihar received large land grants from Salim.[62] Salim also issued land grants to representatives of the family of Makhdum Saiyid Hasan, the founder of the settlement of Hasanpura in District Saran. This Indian Muslim family was dominant in the large and densely populated districts of Saran, Muzaffarpur, Patna, and Bhagalpur (*suba* Bihar).[63] The archival record also reveals the prince's largesse percolating down to a number of lesser individuals and families. Among them were an aged and unnamed widow and her son, who received a small land grant in district Sandila after she petitioned the prince for pecuniary help.[64] On account of Salim's willingness to issue extensive land grants to both *madad-i ma'ash* holders and disparate *shaikhzada* groups, earlier trends favoring the creation of a powerful new class of Indian Muslim landholders in the countryside of Awadh and Allahabad gathered pace in the early 1600s. Salim's efforts and his determination to carve out an independent area for his rule – harnessing, if you will, the energies of the earlier nomadic appanage warrior-ruler system to the emerging post-Akbar dispensation – extended his own and ultimately Mughal dynastic authority into new areas.

## COMPETING ALLIANCES AND PRINCELY STYLES: DARA SHUKOH AND AURANGZEB

The example of Salim demonstrates how the fate of the empire became more closely entangled with the interpersonal dynamics – both intimate and public – of the royal family itself. This had profound implications for the relationship between father/emperor and sons/princes, and also for the sibling relations among the princes. From the perspective of the emperor, the dilemma was which prince to groom and how. Should all efforts focus on one expected heir? Should all sons be given some degree of preparation? Should they be equally groomed? Should the prince remain at the court or be sent out to the provinces? From the prince's point of view, as he grew older and became aware of his possible destiny, he became necessarily hostile to his competitor brothers and, indeed, developed a certain level of paranoia regarding every symbolic and concrete extension of influence the emperor might offer to one or the other. Each prince's story was distinct,

---

[62] R. R. Diwakar, *Bihar through the Ages* (Patna, 1958), p. 491.

[63] S. H. Askari, "Documents Relating to an Old Family of Sufi Saints in Bihar," *Procs. Ind. Hist. Rec. Com.* 26 (1949): 1.

[64] NAI 2672/2, National Archives of India (Delhi).

and each generation of princes grappled with different circumstances, different court intrigues, and a whole new set of noble and regional players. All of them, including every Mughal emperor after Akbar, had to be adept at managing webs of interrelationships, garnering support from a wide section of the population, and even befriending and gaining the loyalty of those with whom they did not always agree. These qualities of kingship were appreciated well before Akbar (Babur, as noted in Chapter 2, warned Humayun that a king must know how to enjoy and be constantly in the company of others). Yet their importance came into sharper focus and their attainment became ever more of a challenge as the empire grew bigger and more diverse.

By the time Emperor Shah Jahan's sons, Dara Shukoh and Aurangzeb, competed for the throne in the late 1650s – a contest Aurangzeb eventually won – the importance of managing large networks of crosscutting alliances had become critical. Such management and the specific allies one gained together shaped a prince's public image and presaged the style of kingship he might one day assume. And in the event of a prince's failure to build allies, his image and his rulership did indeed come under question, as happened to Humayun, who lost his throne in the early 1540s. Ali Anooshahr goes so far as to blame this loss on Humayun's "indifference or failure to realize the importance of exerting direct control over his image."[65] Observing the careers of generations of Mughal princes, it is clear that each worked hard, often over decades, to fashion his image through strategic alliance building. Crucially, there was no single template on which a prince modeled himself. Rather, depending on the situation at hand, the maneuverings of one's major political rivals, and the mood of the empire, each prince had to create his own niche.

This section focuses on the infamous contest between the brothers Dara Shukoh and Aurangzeb, noting their distinct approaches to alliance building and the contrasting public image produced, wittingly and unwittingly, by each. The contest is fascinating because even though Dara Shukoh was the oldest and favored son of Shah Jahan and even though, like Salim, he was mostly kept at the court and carefully groomed for the throne, Dara Shukoh's bid for the empire failed. In part, his failure can be put down to the fact that he served only one stint leading an army (an abortive campaign in 1653 to retake the Safavid-held city of Qandahar) and had never built up credible military experience. This is in sharp contrast to his brothers Shuja',

---

[65] Ali Anooshahr, "The King Who Would Be Man: The Gender Roles of the Warrior King in Early Mughal History," *Journal of the Royal Asiatic Society* 18, no. 3 (2008): 328.

Aurangzeb, and Murad, each of whom undertook a variety of military and gubernatorial assignments in the provinces. But Dara Shukoh's candidacy failed for another reason: he never worked as hard as his brothers – especially Aurangzeb – to cultivate wide-ranging and diverse sets of allies across the empire. As a result, it was Aurangzeb's superior alliance building and corresponding strong public image that won out over the controversial and comparatively isolated public figure struck by Dara Shukoh.

### Prince Dara Shukoh's Alliances

Over the course of his princely career, Dara Shukoh did successfully build some relationships with powerful people. After Emperor Shah Jahan, no one was more openly supportive of Dara Shukoh's imperial aspirations than his older and unmarried sister Jahan Ara (b. 1614). After her father and Dara Shukoh, she was likely the third most influential person in the Mughal Empire between the 1630s and the end of Shah Jahan's reign in 1658. She was certainly one of the richest people in the empire, with an annual income that may have reached up to 10 million rupees. With so much wealth at her disposal, the princess is said to have maintained a massive household that included large contingents of administrators and soldiers.[66] Whenever possible, Jahan Ara tried to help Dara Shukoh. Most notably, in 1658, during the war of succession, she not only gave him money and jewels to help him flee Aurangzeb's advancing forces, but she also offered an unsuccessful proposal to partition the empire between the rival brothers following Dara Shukoh's defeat at the Battle of Samugarh. It is very possible that Jahan Ara's strong contacts in the Punjab, Gujarat, and Ajmer/Rajasthan played a role in directing Dara Shukoh's flight in 1658–9.

Dara Shukoh also nurtured close ties with prosperous and expanding merchant networks including those of the Jain community. He seems to have largely done so through the head of Surat's merchant guild, the merchant and tax farmer Shanti Das. Under Dara's protection, Shanti Das gained complete freedom of movement for his property across the entire empire in 1642 and was granted permission to restore a temple site

---

[66] Niccolao Manucci, *Mogul India or Storio do Mongor*, trans. W. Irvine, vol. I (Delhi, repr. 1996), p. 212. In case anyone doubted Jahan Ara's power, one look at some of the buildings endowed by her during the construction of Shah Jahan's new capital in Delhi would have sufficed. These included the largest bazaar in the city and one of the city's largest gardens. Jahan Ara also sponsored the construction of the main congregational mosque in Agra, the second largest Mughal city, in the late 1640s.

in Ahmadabad that had been confiscated and destroyed by Aurangzeb.[67] Nor was Dara unhappy to have the right of first refusal, via this powerful merchant, on the valuable jewels imported into India. These were often passed on as gifts to Shah Jahan, whose gratitude confirmed Dara Shukoh's importance. Although Shanti Das was coerced into financially supporting Dara Shukoh's younger brother Murad at the beginning of the war of succession in 1657 (Murad was serving as governor of Gujarat at the time), there are indications that he remained loyal to Dara Shukoh. When the prince arrived in Gujarat in 1659 after being on the run for more than a year, Shanti Das helped him raise funds to recruit a fresh army. He may have also been one of the unnamed "merchants of Gujarat" who provided Dara Shukoh crucial intelligence about Aurangzeb's difficulties in overcoming Shuja' in eastern India.[68] This information may have steeled Dara Shukoh's resolve to strike toward Ajmer and the heart of the empire in one final push to defeat Aurangzeb.

Dara Shukoh's ties to sections of the Jain community were matched by links to certain Hindu religious communities. In 1643, for example, Dara Shukoh affixed his seal to an imperial order (*farman*) confirming a grant in Gokul and Gopalpur to Goswami Vithal Ra'i. The stated purpose was to encourage the Goswami to "continue to offer prayers for the perpetuity of this eternity-allied kingdom." This was confirmed in three successive princely orders between 1646 and 1647.[69]

For all his well-known disillusion with and scorn for the mainstream Islamic establishment, Dara Shukoh occasionally did confer or confirm land grants for Muslim religious figures across the empire.[70] His princely patronage also extended to building a mosque – aptly named "Masjid-i Dara Shukoh" – for the *'ulama'* of Jaunpur,[71] making a gift of a religious school in Thanesar,[72] and providing employment opportunities in the imperial service for religious scholars from such diverse parts of the empire

---

[67] *Mughal Documents A.D. 1628–59*, Vol. 2, ed. S. A. I. Tirmizi (Delhi, 1995), p. 71.

[68] Bindraban Das Ra'i, *Lubb-ut-Tawarikh*, Asiatic Society of Bengal, Ivanow 161, f. 136a.

[69] *Imperial Farmans (AD 1577 to AD 1805). Granted to the Ancestors of His Holiness the Tikayal Maharaj*, ed. K. M. Jhaveri, (Bombay, 1928), n.p.; *Mughal Documents A.D. 1628–59*, ed. Tirmizi, pp. 81, 87.

[70] Lachman Singh, *Tarikh-i Zila'-i Bulandshahr* (Bulandshahr, 1874), p. 237; M. M. U. Bilgrami, *Tarikh-i Khat-i Pak-i Bilgram* (Aligarh, 1958), p. 175; Shams-ud-Din Belgaumi, *Tarikh-i Mukhtasar-i Dakhan* (Belgaum, 1944), pp. 122, 126; *Mughal Documents A.D. 1628–59*, ed. Tirmizi, p. 102.

[71] S. I. A Jaunpuri, *Tarikh-i Salatin-i Sharqi aur Sufiya-yi Jaunpur* (Jaunpur, 1988), p. 609.

[72] Abul Hasnat Nadvi, *Hindustan Ki Qadim Islami Darsgahain* (Azamgarh, 1936), p. 30.

as Bilgram and Thatta.[73] In 1656, Dara Shukoh made several extraordinary gifts. He not only paid for a massive and expensive prayer rug for the Prophet Muhammad's mosque in Medina, but he also ordered that Rs. 100,000 worth of goods and cash be distributed in Mecca.[74] Efforts to patronize other significant Muslim religious groups also led the prince to endow cash and land grants for important Chishti shrines and lineages in Ajmer, Delhi, and Khuldabad (in the Deccan), among others. Given the central importance of Sufi shrines as hubs for all manner of political, economic, religious, and sociocultural networks, the prince's patronage was almost certainly aimed at generating positive publicity well beyond the immediate confines of the shrine.[75]

Reaching out also to Sufis who were not clearly identified with any established *tariqa*, Dara Shukoh welcomed the famous antinomian and naked *qalandar* (mystic) Sarmad in his court and kept him by his side through most of the 1650s. He likewise made overtures to men such as Shah Fath Muhammad Qalandar of Jaunpur as well as Punjab-based saints such as Shaikh Sulaiman Misri Qalandar, Shah Muhammad Dilruba, and Shaikh Bari. The prince ordered his officers to provide Sulaiman Misri a warm welcome whenever he visited the city of Multan. Following the death of Shaikh Bari in 1652, Dara Shukoh commissioned a dam to protect his tomb from periodic flooding by the River Ravi.

Dara Shukoh's backing of such lone figures likely emerged from his antipathy toward the mainstream Islamic religious establishment and his interest in spiritual experiments, and certainly it earned him the loyalty of those who revered these local saints. Ultimately, however, his most sincere devotion was reserved for the Qadiri *tariqa*, in whose company he reports

---

[73] Ghulam Hasan Siddiqui, *Sharaif-i 'Usmani*, Asiatic Society of Bengal, Ivanow 277, ff. 60a, 66a; Bilgrami, *Tarikh-i Khat-i Pak-i Bilgram*, p. 174; Nabi Hadi, *Dictionary of Indo-Persian Literature* (New Delhi, 1995), p. 249.

[74] K. Khan, *Muntakhab al-Labab*, vol. 1, p. 731.

[75] Muhammad Ismail, *Sufi Literature in India during the 17th Century*, unpub. M.Phil. thesis, Aligarh Muslim University, 1986, pp. 93–4. Elsewhere the historical record shows Dara Shukoh playing the role of patron for Chishti intellectuals such as 'Ala-ud-Din Muhammad Chishti Barnawi. Barnawi dedicated an anthology named *Chishtiya-i Bihistiya* (ca. 1655–6) to the prince. It includes notices of famous saints from the Prophet Muhammad to Shaikh Nasir-ud-Din Chiragh-i Dilli (d. 1356). More significantly, it contains notices of local saints of Barnawa and Rapri in the Punjab. At the time, both towns were part of Dara Shukoh's *jagir*. The prince's patronage for such a work was likely a source of some pride for the local residents. It may have even won him some political support in the region.

finding "God's grace in this world and the next."[76] He assumed the pen name "Qadiri" and wrote verses praising the founder of the order, Saiyid 'Abd-ul-Qadir Gilani (d. 1166), and his own teachers Miyan Mir (d. 1635) and Mulla Shah Badakhshi (d. 1661).

Despite all the ties he cultivated, Dara nonetheless can be described as ultimately failing in the task of alliance manager because of serious

Dara-Shikoh with Mian Mir and Mulla Shah, ca. 1635 (Arthur M. Sackler Gallery, Smithsonian Institution, Washington D.C.; Purchase – Smithsonian Unrestricted Trust Funds, Smithsonian Collections Acquisitions Program, and Dr. Arthur M. Sackler, S1986.432)

[76] Dara Shukoh, *Sakinat-ul-Auliya'*, ed. Tara Chand and Reza Jalali Naini (Tehran, 1965), pp. 5, 6.

missteps. He became altogether too personally involved with the Miyan Mir lineage of Qadiri Sufis. Not only was this exclusivity alienating to other Qadiri lineages, not to mention other Sufi orders, it also drew Dara into highly corrosive debates about religious precedence. It was missteps such as these that seem to have paved the ground for Aurangzeb to eventually charge his brother with heresy.

Dara Shukoh also seems to have had an absolutely unrivaled propensity for making enemies among the highest echelons of the Mughal nobility, alienating in turn Mir Jumla, Sa'dullah Khan, Mahabat Khan, Khalilullah Khan, 'Ali Mardan Khan, Qasim Khan, Sha'ista Khan, Afzal Khan, Raja Jai Singh, and Saiyid Miran Barha. Alarmed, Shah Jahan reminded his son to try and improve his behavior, to "not be ill-disposed or suspicious of royal grandees ... [to] treat them with favor and kindness."[77] Yet the emperor's entreaties were in vain. Later on in life, Aurangzeb claimed that Dara Shukoh's capacity to be an "enemy of good men" and his unwillingness to listen to the advice of Shah Jahan were important factors in his political downfall.[78]

## Prince Aurangzeb's Alliances

It is telling that four generations of Mughal emperors, from Jahangir to Bahadur Shah, had been princes who spent substantial stints away from the court in the years leading up to their accession. Favored sons such as Dara Shukoh, who stayed at the imperial court, did not, it seems, pose an insurmountable obstacle. Indeed, the example of Aurangzeb demonstrates precisely the advantage held by the prince who was made to venture farther afield.

Yet life away from the imperial court was not easy for princes, especially in their early years. Jahangir's son Prince Parvez asked to return to court shortly after his first major appointment as commander of the Mughal forces against Mewar in 1606. The rigors of the campaign as well as the presence of a host of domineering Mughal nobles came as a shock to the young prince. Less than forty years later (in 1644), Aurangzeb simply abandoned his governorship of the Deccan and returned to court without permission. It seems he was exhausted and longed to be back in the imperial court. In 1646, Aurangzeb's brother Murad also deserted his

---

[77] Aurangzeb, *Ruqa't-i 'Alamgiri*, ed. Saiyid Muhammad Abdul Majeed (Kanpur, 1916), p. 18.

[78] Aurangzeb, *Raqa'im-i Kara'im*, Asiatic Society of Bengal, Ivanow 383, f. 204b. See also Aurangzeb, *Anecdotes of Aurangzib*, trans. Jadunath Sarkar (Calcutta, repr. 1988), pp. 26, 27; Aurangzeb, *Ruqa't-i 'Alamgiri*, pp. 18, 22, 36.

command in Balkh on the northwestern frontier. But despite the draw-backs of being and feeling out of touch with events at court, princes sometimes learned that in the bitter competition for the throne, certain advantages accrued to having relative independence. Thus, for a time, Akbar's son Murad evaded his father's efforts to bring him back to court from his command in the Deccan. As tensions with his father and step-mother, Emperor Jahangir and Nur Jahan, increased in the early 1620s, Prince Khurram willingly left for the Deccan. In 1645, after realizing how unwelcome he was at the imperial court, Aurangzeb begged his father's chief minister Sa'dullah Khan to assign him anywhere so long as it was far removed from the court.[79]

A decade before, when Aurangzeb was seventeen, Shah Jahan did send him far away. Following a successful military campaign in Bundelkhand, the young prince was assigned to manage the Deccan provinces. By this distant assignment, Shah Jahan tried early on to nullify his younger son's potential challenge. Aside from an eight-month stretch in 1644–5 and three short visits in 1647, 1649, and 1651, Aurangzeb spent all the rest of his post-1635 princely career away from the imperial court. He under-took two stints as governor of the Deccan (1636–44 and 1652–8) and also held the governorships of Gujarat (1645–7) and Multan (1648–52). He led campaigns in Bundelkhand (1635), Balkh (1647), and Qandahar (1649 and 1652). In the long years of these assignments, Aurangzeb learned to work with and to accommodate unfamiliar and sometimes hostile groups, most of whom, unlike himself, had deep roots in these regions.

Mughal sources abound with accounts of how Aurangzeb specifically sought out local Muslim clerics. Likely consulting with religious leaders in Burhanpur and Khuldabad, traditional centers of Islamic learning in the Deccan, he is known to have maintained lists of individuals to whom he then reached out. When he built the city of Aurangabad in the 1630s, he filled its mosques and *madrassa*s with these individuals.[80] In September 1641, Aurangzeb granted Shaikh Ibrahim of Bir just over six acres of land plus a stipend to buy oil to light the lamps of a mosque.[81] He also ordered a small stipend provided to one Bibi 'A'isha, the granddaughter of a minor religious scholar.[82] In the 1640s, when the imperial court moved

---

[79] Aurangzeb, *Anecdotes of Aurangzib*, p. 25.

[80] *Mughal Archives: A Descriptive Catalogue of the Documents Pertaining to the Reign of Shah Jahan*, Vol. 1, ed. M. Z. A. Shakeb (Hyderabad, 1977), pp. 90–1; *Selected Documents of Shah Jahan's Reign*, ed. Yusuf H. Khan (Hyderabad, 1950), p. 184.

[81] *Mughal Archives*, ed. Shakeb, p. 20.

[82] Ibid., pp. 24–5; *Selected Documents of Shah Jahan's Reign*, ed. Y. Khan, p. 186.

to investigate imperial *madad* grants (of land) for suspected large-scale malfeasance, Aurangzeb stonewalled, perhaps to curry local favor for himself and against Shah Jahan. During his governorship of Multan, he gave large cash gifts to repair the shrines of at least three Suhrawardi saints, and he issued or confirmed *madad* grants for a number of Shaikh Baha'-ud-Din Zakariya's Suhrawardi descendants in Multan. Many Shattari disciples of Shaikh 'Abd-ul-Latif Burhanpuri as well as Dihbidi Naqshbandis were also granted employment in Aurangzeb's own household or else recommended by the prince for imperial service.

Unlike Dara Shukoh, Prince Aurangzeb never narrowed his religious commitments beyond a general association with Hanafi-Sunni Islam. In fact, he is described as spending long hours in conversation with all manner of Muslim religious figures. Thus we know that he spent a great deal of time with Deccan-based Shah Waliullah Husaini, a direct descendant of the Chishti saint Khwaja Saiyid Muhammad Gesu Daraz (d. 1422), a custodian of the saint's tomb, and a locally influential figure. While in the Deccan, Aurangzeb also regularly met with the famous Shattari *pir* Shaikh 'Abd-ul-Latif Burhanpuri and the Qadiri *pir* Saiyid Sher Muhammad Qadiri Burhanpuri. In Gujarat, he repeatedly called on the Chishti notable Shaikh Muhiy-ud-Din and cultivated a number of prominent Qadiri lineages, including those of Saiyid Hasanji Qadiri of Patan and the descendants of Saiyid Muhammad al-'Aydarus of Ahmadabad – bitter rivals of the Hazrat Shah 'Alam lineage favored by Shah Jahan and Dara Shukoh. The steady correspondence between Aurangzeb and the Naqshbandi master Khwaja 'Abd-ul-Ghaffar in the late 1640s includes communication about presents received and bestowed, military campaigns, and the comings and goings of specific traveling notables.[83] Just as such outreach efforts proved crucial in enabling Aurangzeb to govern effectively, they also undoubtedly laid the groundwork for his successful bid for the throne.

Thus, when Dara Shukoh lost the Battle of Samugarh, no amount of supplication (he offered Rs. 25,000 to Shaikh Baha'-ud-Din Zakariya's shrine) could bring Multan's religious communities to his aid. Meanwhile, the Naqshbandis provided Aurangzeb with soldiers and also imported horses and camels as expressions of their support. In Gujarat, too, Dara Shukoh encountered a lack of support among some of the big Qadiri shrines in Patan and Ahmadabad. As in Multan, Aurangzeb's earlier

[83] Aurangzeb, *Adab-i 'Alamgiri*, ed. Abdul Ghafur Chaudhuri, vol. 1 (Lahore, 1971), pp. 616, 619, 619–21, 630–1, 632–3; 'Inayat Khan, *'Inayatnama*, British Library, Ethe 411, ff. 44a-47a, 47a-50a.

patronage and personal associations in this region plus powerful intra-Qadiri rivalries effectively thwarted the hapless older prince.

Aurangzeb had more in his arsenal than the backing of locally powerful religious groups. He had cultivated strong support among Afghans, Dakhnis, and Marathas during his time in the Deccan. Consider the Afghans. Every important Afghan tribal group was present among the troops that marched out of the Deccan with Aurangzeb in 1657–8, including Ansari, Khweshgi, Niyazi, Lodi, Tarin, Kakar, Bakhtiyar, Ghauri, Sarwani, Daudzai, Orakzai, Masud, Mohmand, and Wilakzai. An addendum to the chronicle, *Tarikh-i Khan Jahani wa Makhzan-i Afghani*, in fact tells the story of thirteen poverty-stricken brothers from a single unnamed Afghan family who joined Aurangzeb's forces as they left the Deccan in 1657.[84] The prince's army provided attractive employment to Afghans, and they helped ensure his ultimate success. Yet, sources suggest that it took a good deal of work on Aurangzeb's part to cultivate his relations with Afghans and other ethnic groups, especially when they had not fought for the Mughals before.

Moreover, the imperial court seemed wary of granting advancement to Afghans. Nonetheless, during his first stint in the Deccan, Aurangzeb cultivated close ties with men such as Hadidad Khan (d. 1656), his sons, and their Ansari clan. The Rohillas were also among the Afghans whom Aurangzeb counted as friends. In 1653, Aurangzeb increased Usman Khan Rohilla's *mansab* rank to 1000/1000 and appointed him the *faujdar* (military commandant) of Sultanpur and Nandurbar.[85] Meanwhile, between 1653 and 1655, Usman Khan's nephew, Fath Khan Rohilla, received three rapid promotions to reach a *mansab* of 1000/1000.[86] In a 1657 letter, responding to imperial disquiet about granting such rapid advancement to Afghans, Aurangzeb demanded to know why a further increase in the *mansabs* of Fath Khan Rohilla and his brother Hayat Rohilla had been rejected. They must be rewarded, he declared, for their sterling actions during a recent military campaign against Golkonda, adding that promoting Afghans did not violate imperial norms.[87]

---

[84] Harvi, *Tarikh-i-Khan Jahani*, vol. 2, p. 873.

[85] Aurangzeb, *Adab-i ʿAlamgiri*, vol. 1 pp. 120–2; Shaikh Farid Bhakkari, *Dhakhirat al-Khawanin*, ed. S. Moinul Haq, vol. 3 (Karachi, 1974), p. 116.

[86] M. Athar Ali, *The Apparatus of Empire: Awards of Ranks, Offices and Titles to the Mughal Nobility, 1574–1658* (Delhi, 1985), p. 277; *Selected Documents of Shah Jahan's Reign*, ed. Y. Khan, p. 197.

[87] Aurangzeb, *Adab-i ʿAlamgiri*, vol. 1, pp. 604–5.

Thus, in his role as Mughal Prince and governor of the Deccan, Aurangzeb fought for groups otherwise overlooked by the court. We see the same pattern with Sidi Miftah Habash Khan, a *Habshi* (African, former slave) leader whose first imperial appointment was to Aurangzeb's nascent household in 1636.[88] Aurangzeb heaped favors and patronage on Habash Khan in recognition of his influence in the Deccan. Habash Khan's daughter was married to the son of Malik Ambar, the greatest *Habshi* warrior-statesman in the region and de facto ruler of Ahmadnagar for almost two decades until his death in 1626. A second daughter was married to Hasan Khan Habshi, the son of yet another well-known *Habshi* clan leader, Yaqut Khan Habshi. Habash Khan augmented these impeccable familial and political connections by encouraging the immigration of Arab Saiyids to the Deccan, accommodating them as servitors, and helping them in various ways. Habash Khan and his family repaid the many kindnesses of Aurangzeb by fighting with great loyalty during his campaign against Dara Shukoh, alongside many other *Habshi*s.[89] Large numbers of these men – again, many who had never previously served under the Mughals – fought on Aurangzeb's side. They joined the ranks of other non-Habshi Dakhnis who had been similarly cultivated and recruited by Aurangzeb during his military campaign to win the Mughal throne. Some, such as Ghazi Bijapuri and 'Abd-ul-Rahman Khan, were richly rewarded with imperial titles and subsequently inducted into the Mughal nobility.[90] In the process, an important source of opposition to imperial rule in the Deccan was gradually neutralized.

The Marathas were another group to play an important part in Aurangzeb's winning coalition. Although the Deccan's political elite was primarily Muslim and included *Habshi*s, and recent Iranian and Turkish immigrants, locally raised armies were mostly non-Muslim and often heavily Maratha. The Marathas were especially renowned for their skills as guerilla fighters. Fairly detailed records of Aurangzeb's activities in the month of November 1637 highlight the prince's early recognition of their

---

[88] The Habshis (individuals with African familial roots) were one of the many groups that comprised the larger Dakhni population. Others included descendants of Circassians, Turks, Iranians, and local converts to Islam. Often, different Dakhni groups fought one another for political domination of the Deccan. Yet, they also shared some tenuous bonds, among them their ties to the geographical space of the Deccan, their adherence to Islam, and their more than occasional opposition to Mughal power.

[89] S. Khan, *Maasir-ul-Umara*, vol. 1, p. 582; Muhammad Kazim, *Alamgirnamah*, ed. Khadim Husain and Abdul Hai, vol. 1 (Calcutta, 1868), p. 45.

[90] Kazim, *Alamgirnamah*, vol. 1, pp. 62, 76.

important role within the Deccan's politics. For example, as part of the celebrations around his nineteenth birthday, Aurangzeb held an audience with a Maratha commander called Linguji Bhonsle.[91] Linguji was a member of the Bhonsle clan that included Shahuji, perhaps the most powerful Maratha commander of the 1630s. Shortly after, Aurangzeb had another audience, this time with a much larger group of Maratha chiefs.[92] Several days later, Marathas constituted more than half of the important individuals invited to attend Aurangzeb's nineteenth birthday celebration in Aurangabad. Included on this list were almost all the high-ranking Marathas within the imperial service in addition to an assortment of powerful Maratha allies.[93] Many of them would participate in the successful Mughal expedition against Baglana in 1638. They also played a critical role in Aurangzeb's efforts to crush a *zamindari* revolt prior to his transfer in 1644.

Aurangzeb's efforts to cultivate Maratha support intensified following his return to the Deccan in 1653. Although none seems to have held a visibly important position in his princely household, Aurangzeb held regular audiences with Maratha luminaries.[94] Aurangzeb also recommended Maratha imperial officers, such as Maluji, to participate in key Mughal military campaigns, including the one against the kingdom of Deogarh in 1655–6. In 1657, Kartalab Khan (originally Jaswant Rao prior to his conversion to Islam) was placed in command of a force ordered to collect back payments of tribute from Deogarh. The decision to appoint a Maratha to handle such a delicate task was a sign of great favor.

Aurangzeb seems to have won broad support among the most important Maratha military networks by 1657, and many Marathas accompanied him to confront Dara Shukoh. Among them were imperial officers such as Kartalab Khan, Jadu Ra'i, and Rustam Ra'i. His forces also included a significant number of Maratha chiefs such as Damaji, Natuji, Netuji Bhonsle, Babaji Bhonsle, Dadaji, Dakuji, Beas Rao, Betuji, and Manuji, who were not imperial employees. In an apparent attempt to cement his support across this group, Aurangzeb offered most of them high-level *mansabs*.[95] The Marathas with their large contingents proved a bastion of support for the prince both prior to and during the battles of Dharmat and Samugarh; they assisted in the subsequent occupation of

[91] *Selected Documents of Shah Jahan's Reign*, ed. Y. Khan, p. 32.
[92] *Mughal Archives*, ed. Shakeb, pp. 148–50, 151, 152, 153.
[93] *Selected Documents of Shah Jahan's Reign*, ed. Y. Khan, pp. 42–3.
[94] *Mughal Archives*, ed. Shakeb, pp. 108, 123.
[95] Ibid., pp. 47, 48, 54.

Agra and Delhi as well. Such service, however, laid the grounds for a vicious internecine war in the 1660s that pitted pro-Mughal Marathas against a rising Maratha commander by the name of Shivaji . . . but this is another story.

As in the Deccan, so also in Gujarat, Balkh, Multan, and Qandahar – local imperial administrators and scribal groups; merchants and grain carriers (*banjaras*); Afghan, Uzbek, Hazara, Rajput, Bundela, and Baluch tribal chiefs; Sindhi and Koli *zamindars* all drifted in and out of the prince's world. In some cases, Aurangzeb succeeded in drawing people to himself; in others, he was thwarted by local rivalries, competition from his brothers, or just a lack of interest among certain individuals or groups in becoming part of the Mughal system. Nonetheless, Aurangzeb's networking experiences in the provinces prepared him superbly for his struggle for the throne, both in terms of his learning political leadership and the skills to manage alliances and also very practically in cultivating sources for troops and material support. With no exceptions, until the eighteenth century, the candidate with the broadest backing across the empire became the next emperor.

### The Devout Warrior-Prince Versus the Court-based Scholar-Prince

During Aurangzeb's various governorships and more than two decades from his first military mission in 1635, he largely won the goodwill and respect of the people who served under him as well as those he was responsible for governing. During that period, Aurangzeb commanded at least six major campaigns. Even in failure, he usually managed to salvage his military reputation. Thus, despite his inability to conquer Balkh in 1647, he was credited with saving the imperial army from complete annihilation at the hands of the enemy Uzbeks and Almans. When Aurangzeb returned from this fight, the court-based imperial poet 'Alvi wrote a panegyric he named *Iftitah-i Sultani* or "The Beginning of Kingship." In it 'Alvi lauded the prince for his manliness, his bravery, his quick judgment, his steadiness under attack, and his military skills. Aurangzeb's marvelous performance, 'Alvi suggests, was a sign that God and the Prophet Muhammad were on his side.[96]

Even after two further military failures in wresting Qandahar from Safavid control, Aurangzeb's military reputation again emerged more or less unscathed. The failures were effectively pinned, in fact, on Shah

---

[96] 'Alvi, *Iftitah-i Sultani*, National Library of India, Buhar Collection 394, ff. 9b, 13a-b.

Jahan's efforts to micromanage both campaigns and then on his decision to prematurely call off the second expedition even as Aurangzeb pleaded for more time to force a positive result.[97] On the eve of the 1657–9 war of succession, there is no question that Aurangzeb was perceived as the most militarily and administratively experienced Mughal Prince ever. It was a powerful reputation, one that he deployed to devastating effect, first against his brother and later his father.

Descriptions of Aurangzeb the prince depicted a heroic individual in the spirit of earlier Persian and Islamic rulers. In one episode at the age of fifteen, Aurangzeb fought a rogue elephant at the imperial court, earning the title "Bahadur" (brave) from his father. Later during the Balkh campaign, at the height of a battle with the Uzbeks, Aurangzeb is said to have dismounted from his elephant to say his prayers. The opposing commander is recounted as saying in amazement: "To quarrel with such a man brings ruin upon yourself."[98] Aurangzeb was indeed a man to be reckoned with.

In addition to his courage, Aurangzeb cultivated a reputation for great generosity and selflessness. Although the contemporary French traveler François Bernier offers an unfavorable impression of Aurangzeb based on his political ruthlessness during the succession struggles with his brothers and father, Bernier also grudgingly concedes that Aurangzeb gave to others "with a liberal hand."[99] The prince is elsewhere described as loyal and thoughtful toward his supporters and household members. During campaigns, he was known to dress the wounds of men under his command and to make little distinction between their personal safety and his own. Far from living the life of ease typical of other Mughal princes, Aurangzeb was reportedly as hard a taskmaster on himself as on others.[100] In contrast to most other Mughal princes, he seems to have found no detail too small for his attention. In the surviving correspondence from his days as a prince, we read of him tackling everything from high administrative and political matters to the provision of thread to the imperial *karkhana* (workshop). According to the correspondence, Aurangzeb even personally oversaw

---

[97] Aurangzeb, *Adab-i 'Alamgiri*, vol. 1, pp. 33–4, 35–7, 42–4, 44–7, 47–8, 64–6, 67–70.

[98] 'Abd al-Hamid Lahawri, *Padshahnamah*, ed. Abdul Rahim, vol. 2 (Calcutta, 1872), p. 704.

[99] François Bernier, *Travels in the Mogul Empire*, trans. A. Constable (Delhi, repr. 1983), p. 10.

[100] This is evident, for example, in his extraordinary instructions to his oldest son Muhammad Sultan in 1654 detailing how the young prince should spend his day. Jadunath Sarkar in *Studies in Aurangzib's Reign* (Calcutta, repr. 1989), pp. 27–8.

efforts to ensure that Burhanpuri grapes and mangoes arrived in good shape at his father's court by having them packed in paper.[101]

Aurangzeb's manner of dress and his habits of eating and entertainment were the very antithesis of other Mughal princes. He strenuously avoided all excesses of food and drink and strove to speak in a quiet and calm voice. It was widely believed that his behavior was shaped by his personal religiosity; the prince seems to have been consciously modeling his life and manners on the first four Rightly-Guided Caliphs of Islam. Although Shah Jahan and Dara Shukoh occasionally lampooned Aurangzeb and even suggested that he was a hypocritical dissimulator, his behavior won him admirers within the Muslim religious establishment. There were certainly members of the Mughal nobility, whether Hindu or Muslim, who also appreciated his restraint. Aurangzeb talks about how as a prince "he used to treat the nobles in such a way that they were pleased and always praised him whether he was present or absent."[102] We read of Shah Jahan advising Aurangzeb to drop his "meekness of spirit" or face the possibility of the nobles' contempt; yet Aurangzeb cited a Prophetic saying in response: "Whoever humbles himself, God bestows honor on him."[103]

By contrast, Dara Shukoh, the favored older brother, had a reputation as arrogant and brash. In contrast to Aurangzeb's military achievements in the Deccan, Dara Shukoh displayed his urbanity, sophisticated tastes in literature and philosophy, and a generally scholarly and sedentary leadership style. Indeed, Dara Shukoh appeared to disavow Mughal expansionism in favor of his well-known, if controversial, scholarly adventures and his long and impassioned study of the relationship between Islam and Hinduism. When it came to relations with Hindus, Aurangzeb, on the other hand, preferred forming political alliances while maintaining his own mainstream Muslim religiosity.[104] And whereas Dara Shukoh patronized the arts and literature, Aurangzeb showed no public interest in either.

The story of Dara Shukoh's self-fashioning is an extraordinary one. No other major Mughal Prince evinced less interest in the empire's administrative or military affairs than he did. Not surprisingly, his one and only military enterprise ended in absolute disaster. In a contemporary and anonymously written account of the 1653 Qandahar campaign,

---

[101] Aurangzeb, *Adab-i 'Alamgiri*, vol. 1, pp. 119, 146–7; vol. 2, pp. 806, 819, 821–2.

[102] Aurangzeb, *Ruq'at-i 'Alamgiri*, p. 4.

[103] Aurangzeb, *Anecdotes of Aurangzib*, pp. 26–7.

[104] M. Athar Ali, "The Religious Issue in the War of Succession, 1658–59," in *Mughal India: Studies in Polity, Ideas, Society, and Culture* (New Delhi, repr. 2006), pp. 245–52.

*Lata'if-ul-Akhbar*, Dara Shukoh variously comes across as stubborn yet also easily swayed by flattery and abusive when thwarted, eager to resort to astrology or magic for guidance, insensitive to reports of suffering by Mughal troops, and thoroughly incompetent as a military commander. For example, in more than one episode, he places his trust in groups claiming they could force Qandahar's submission through magic incantations or secret flying objects from which the prince's soldiers might lob exploding devices.[105] One man even went so far as to demand two dancing girls, two thieves, two gamblers, a dog, a sheep, a buffalo, and five chickens as part of a sacrifice to create a special potion that when applied to the blade of a sword, the man assured, could cut through steel. In the end, perhaps because the human subjects escaped, the potion proved useless.[106] Elsewhere in the text, Dara Shukoh's unwillingness to honor anyone but his own household retainers and the disregard and contempt he showed toward the imperial noblemen serving under him undermined Mughal field operations.[107] All in all, the account of the prince's actions in *Lata'if-ul-Akhbar* stands in stark contrast with *Iftitah-i Sultani*, the poem commemorating Aurangzeb's equally difficult 1647 Balkh campaign.

Dara Shukoh's behavior seems mystifying: how did he expect to win the throne without any interest or experience in fighting and winning military campaigns? Was he uninterested in the throne, or did he have some alternative and unusual plan of his own? Perhaps Dara Shukoh presumed that loyalty to Shah Jahan would automatically translate into loyalty to him. Besides, he was vastly wealthier than his three brothers; his income equaled all of theirs combined, and he probably had a similar advantage in terms of military contingents. The sources also suggest, however, that Dara Shukoh enjoyed a sense of his own omnipotence, a certain spiritual exaltedness, and an entitlement to the Mughal throne ordained by God himself. Whether or not he did so consciously, he differentiated his leadership from that of his brothers through the religious adventures that dominated his life.

Dara Shukoh appears to have seen links between his religious proclivities and his political fate as emperor, and to have envisioned himself as a

---

[105] Anon., *Lata'if-ul-Akhbar*, Center of Advanced Study Library (Aligarh Muslim University), Persian Ms. 15, ff. 121–2.
[106] Ibid., f. 128.
[107] Ibid., ff. 27, 33, 104, 112, 120, 134–5, 156, 175–7, 183, 190–1, 194.

saint-king.[108] In his second book, *Sakinat-ul-Auliya'*, for example, he describes a dream from his youth in which an angel appeared before him and repeated four times: "Those things that have not been made apparent to any earthly kings, God has bestowed upon you."[109] The same episode was recounted a few years later in his next book, *Risala-i Haqnuma*.[110] Later still, according to the record of a conversation with the Hindu ascetic Baba Lal Vairagi, Dara Shukoh digresses to ask a series of political and ethical questions. Why, for instance, must the king of a large country (i.e., the Mughal Empire) arrest, imprison, and execute people? How does a king who was once a *yogi* (ascetic) remain true to his earlier vocation? Is it acceptable for a king who is also a *faqir* (ascetic) to not require his courtiers to dress like dervishes?[111] Through the early to mid-1650s, Dara Shukoh and his followers cultivated an aura of inevitable political success around this "prince of the world," an aura that enfolded at once his religious and political aspirations.[112]

There is no doubt that Dara Shukoh's intellectual endeavors were driven by abiding spiritual interests and a quest that likely began when he was a teenager. As the sense of his spiritual importance increased, however, so too did the belief, as his older sister Jahan Ara put it, that he was the heir apparent (*wali 'ahd*) to both the "esoteric" (*batin*) and "exoteric" (*zahir*) kingdoms.[113] With Shah Jahan's acquiescence, any expectation of normative Mughal princely conduct seems to have been set aside for Dara Shukoh. His religious perfection became the platform from which he differentiated himself from his brothers and staked his claim to the imperial throne. Ultimately, he lost to Aurangzeb in the war of succession. If Mirza Hakim's political failure (versus his half brother Akbar) arose from his appeal to only a narrow Central Asian constituency, Dara Shukoh's lay with how little his claims to special spiritual insight resonated with anyone beyond his household or Shah Jahan's staunchest loyalists.

---

[108] This question is explored in greater detail in Munis D. Faruqui, "Dara Shukoh, Vedanta, and the Politics of Mughal India," in *Religious Interactions in Mughal India*, ed. Vasudha Dalmia and Munis D. Faruqui (New Delhi, forthcoming 2012).

[109] Shukoh, *Sakinat-ul-Auliya'*, pp. 5–6.

[110] Shukoh, *Risala-i Haqnuma*, National Library of India, Zakariya Collection 177, f. 7b.

[111] Cl. Huart and Louis Massignon, "Dara Shikoh's Interview with Baba La'l Das at Lahore," in *On Becoming an Indian Muslim*, ed. and trans. M. Waseem (Delhi, repr. 2003), p. 115.

[112] Zulfiqar Ardistani, *The Religion of the Sufis: From the Dabistan of Mohsin Fani*, trans. David Shea and Anthony Troyer (London, repr. 1979), p. 78.

[113] Jahan Ara Begum, "Risala-i Sahibiya," ed. Muhammad Aslam, *Journal of the Research Society of Pakistan* 16, no. 4 (1979): 96.

CONCLUSION

In 1705, a Mughal nobleman named Mubarakullah Wazih/Iradat Khan was appointed commandant (*qila'dar*) of the fort of Mandu in Malwa. As such, he was a subordinate of Aurangzeb's grandson Bidar Bakht, who was serving as governor of Malwa at the time. In keeping with proper etiquette, sometime after his arrival in Malwa, Iradat Khan visited Bidar Bakht's court in the city of Ujjain. According to Iradat Khan's memoir (written in the mid-1710s), the two men hit it off instantly. "By the grace of God, in very little time," writes Iradat Khan, "a friendship resulted between me and him that was inconceivable between ruler and subject/ servant (*naukar*)."[114] According to Iradat Khan, Bidar Bakht demanded that they spend as much time together as possible. The prince extended his favor by also generously sharing his own food and undertaking no important decision without consultation. When Iradat Khan finally left to take charge of his position in Mandu, Bidar Bakht made him promise to write once a week. In return, the prince promised to do the same. Over the next few years, the two men stayed in constant contact.

When Aurangzeb died in 1707 and a war of succession was upon the empire, Bidar Bakht immediately commanded Iradat Khan to leave his post and join him in Ujjain. Tapping into Iradat Khan's network of support, the prince sent a separate invitation to the Khan's son, then the military commander of a district near Ujjain with a few thousand troops at his disposal, to join him.[115] Over the years, Bidar Bakht had built an intricate web of friendships and obligations on which he could prevail when needed. And so it was with generations of other Mughal princes. They spent most of their lives striving to build friendships or positioning themselves to cajole support, often in preparation for the time that they might need them in combat against one another.

No doubt, Mughal administrative acumen played a key role in the empire's success between Akbar's reign and the end of Aurangzeb's. A second, less studied, but even more fundamental source of Mughal success, however, was the dynasty's extraordinary capacity to build and sustain alliances in bewilderingly diverse geographic and social settings. This is an imperial practice that the Mughals shared with other contemporary entities including the Ottomans and the Safavids. What sets the Mughals

---

[114] Mubarakullah Wazih, *Tarikh-i Iradat Khan*, ed. Ghulam Rasul Mehr (Lahore, 1971), p. 9.
[115] Ibid., pp. 10, 20, 22.

apart, however, is the central and long-standing role that princes played in alliance building across the empire.

As princes pursued friendships and alliances, they drew groups already subject to Mughal power into deeper relations with the dynasty. Competition between members of the royal family also fostered ties to powerful individuals and groups who were on the political margins or even opposed to the dynasty. As we will see in the next chapter, such efforts received a powerful fillip in the course of princely rebellions.

# 5

# Disobedience and Rebellion

In the spring of 1616, during an imperial tour, Emperor Jahangir (r. 1605–27) stopped off at the central Indian town of Mandu, once the capital of an independent Muslim sultanate but now incorporated into the Mughal Empire. After admiring the town's main mosque, Jahangir visited the tombs of the region's former rulers. In his autobiography, Jahangir describes how he became fixated on one of the tombs: that of Nasir-ud-Din Sultan (dead for more than a century). It bore the traces of a previous act of desecration. Jahangir wrote approvingly of this sacrilegious act and recounted how he himself then proceeded to kick the grave. He ordered those present with him to do the same. According to Jahangir, "This didn't satisfy me." He therefore commanded that the former ruler's grave be opened and his "crumbling bones" thrown into a fire. Immediately, the emperor appears to have had a change of heart, fearing his actions might be inauspicious. He then decreed that the remains of the "eternally damned" Nasir-ud-Din Sultan be thrown into the nearby River Narbada instead.

The reader might be struck by Jahangir's bizarre and somewhat scandalous behavior, and perhaps no less by his recounting of it in his autobiography. Yet we can offer some explanation for why he harbored such contempt for Nasir-ud-Din Sultan. This ruler, it turns out, had murdered his own father in order to ascend the throne of Malwa. Jahangir describes his act as so "odious" (*shani'*) that, even in death, Nasir-ud-Din Sultan's remains were considered "impure" (*na-pak*).[1]

---

[1] Nur-ud-Din Muhammad Jahangir, *Jahangirnama*, ed. Muhammad Hashim (Tehran, 1980), pp. 208–9.

By desecrating this sultan's tomb publicly, and then committing this act to history by recounting it in his autobiography, Jahangir proclaimed his allegiance to the ideals of filial duty and loyalty to a reigning king. His actions also bespeak the deep fear of the Mughal emperor that he himself might fall victim to a similar fate. No Mughal emperor yet had suffered patricide or regicide; still, Jahangir had good reasons to fear for his personal safety. He had himself rebelled against his own father, Akbar, during the waning years of the latter's reign, and by the mid-1610s, he had already survived one rebellion by his oldest son, Khusrau, and a plot by Khusrau's supporters to kill him.

Ultimately, no Mughal emperor would escape some level of noncompliance and even outright rebellion from one or another royal son or relative, but neither was an emperor ever killed by a prince. Between 1526 and 1707, over 181 years, the Mughal Empire witnessed seven significant princely rebellions. The first two, in the early period, included the revolt by Humayun's brothers (1540–53) and the rebellion of the Mirzas against Akbar (1560s). The latter five, the subject matter of this chapter, include Salim against Akbar (1599–1604); Khusrau against Jahangir (1606); Khurram against Jahangir (1622–7); Muhammad Sultan against Aurangzeb (1659); and Akbar against Aurangzeb (1681).[2] All of these were major rebellions, yet none of them succeeded.

Such frequent upheaval belies the official depiction of the Mughal emperor as absolute in his power, against whom any disobedience, never mind violent rebellion, was unimaginable. This image is mostly a fantasy put forth in imperial propaganda. In their overstatement, official records mask the degree to which the entire Mughal political edifice was riven, in the best of times, by dissent and opposition and, during the worst, by violence and conflict. Challenges to the authority of the emperor and to the smooth functioning of the empire were continual, coming from diverse quarters including the Mughal nobility, *zamindari* subjects, ethnic and tribal groups, and even peasant formations. None of these, however, was a greater source of turmoil than challenges from within the Mughal family itself. In fact, other sources of opposition to the emperor were often subsumed under the banner of princely rebellions. When other

---

[2] I choose not to count the conflict between Aurangzeb and his brothers (1657–9) as a rebellion. This is an arguable choice since the conflict started out as a rebellion against Shah Jahan but then morphed into a succession struggle once Shah Jahan had been forced to abdicate his throne in the summer of 1658. For a counterargument maintaining that this conflict counts as a "rebellion" rather than a "war of succession," see S. M. Azizuddin Husain, *The Structure of Politics under Aurangzeb 1658–1707* (Delhi, 2002), pp. 13–48.

groups joined forces with refractory princes, the potential for the empire to tear itself apart in an orgy of uncontrollable violence was never far from the horizon. And yet, this book argues, it is precisely in the capacity of princes to co-opt non-imperial sources of sedition and conflict that enabled the Mughals to parry many of the threats to their rule.

This chapter explores the wide spectrum of oppositional behavior, and ultimately rebellion, resorted to by the post-Akbar Mughal princes. Arguing that over time, emperors became less tolerant of noncompliance and princes correspondingly more defiant, I will lay out the forces arrayed against the prince that constrained him from scaling up, unless greatly pressed, to an open challenge. Princes nonetheless continued to rebel. As the stakes grew higher, how princes justified their rebellions and how the imperial chroniclers reported on them later become more fascinating. Thus, whereas Mirza Kamran saw little need to explain his opposition to Humayun in the 1540s, subsequent generations of princes developed a language of rights and obligations: their right to possibly ascend the throne and the emperor's obligation to treat all his sons equally during his lifetime.

At the same time, princes leveraged energy and urgency for their rebellions by grafting them on to preexisting local or regional grievances. The rapidity with which princes were able to repeatedly build massive armies points to the importance of this dynamic. It also points to the presence of a massive surplus military labor force in the Indian subcontinent and the importance of tapping into it. But this source of support was fickle and often vanished in the face of a superior imperial force, financial inducements from the other side, or a prince's inability to raise sufficient funds. Nevertheless, princely rebellions were the prompt that renewed links between the thousands of male imperial subjects willing to fight and the apparatus of empire. This offered an avenue for particularly enterprising military brokers to transition into imperial service, while also breeding a pervasive Mughal-centered ethos of service-patronage. Even as princely actions focused attention on the imperial dynasty, the emperor's counterattack did the same, playing a crucial role in deepening the hold of the Mughal imperium across its territories.

It is important to note that any attempt to classify attitudes toward princely defiance and the forms and outcomes of princely rebellions is complicated by particular father-son relations, the distinct personalities of emperors and princes, and specific historical circumstances. In other words, it is difficult to tease apart precisely where the historical process of evolving imperial formation ends and where family dramas begin.

Nonetheless, this chapter tries to do so within certain constraints; it offers a general account of the creative tensions between Mughal emperors and subordinate members of the imperial family between 1556 and the 1680s.

## NORMS OF LOYALTY, COMMITMENT TO A COSMIC ORDER

At the heart of most Mughal accounts of princely rebellion lies a basic tension: although the absolute power of the emperor – his place at the core of a divinely ordained natural order – is repeatedly affirmed, violent strife within the royal family persists. How did imperial chroniclers iron over this embarrassing paradox? Furthermore, how did princes justify their rebellion against the cosmic order, despite the widespread idiom of loyalty to one's father and deference to one's elders?

The idiom of loyalty is present in widely disparate sources. They include popular (as attested by the large number of extant manuscripts from the Mughal period) tales like *Rustam and Sohrab* – in which a father unwittingly battles with and kills his son. Certain Sufi treatises pick up on similar ideas; *Ganj-i Sa'adat* is an example. Written in the mid-seventeenth century by an adherent of the Naqshbandi *tariqa*, it describes the duties of a king, including maintaining law and order, promoting justice, protecting the powerless, and enforcing religion. Alongside, the author notes that sons (*farzandan*) must obey their fathers. Eternal damnation, we are told, will be the fate of the disobedient.[3] Elsewhere the Chengizid *yasa* (code), cited in Jahangir's autobiography but more generally held by the Mughals to be a part of their Central Asian heritage, promotes notions of respect toward the old.[4] And when the Safavid monarch Shah Husain Safavi turned down a request by Prince Akbar to help fight his father Aurangzeb, he cited the *shari'a*'s condemnation of disobedient sons.[5] In Mughal court vocabulary itself, emperors would occasionally address a senior nobleman as *baba* (father) or *ammu* (uncle), using kinship terms to demonstrate how respect for elders also informed a normative imperial hierarchy.[6]

The Islamic juristic maxim "Sixty years of tyranny are better than an hour of civil strife" is often cited to highlight the deep political

---

[3] Mu'in-ud-Din bin Siraj-ud-Din Khawand Mahmud, *Ganj-i Sa'adat*, Asiatic Society of Bengal, Ivanow Coll. 1275, f. 550a.

[4] Jahangir, *Jahangirnama*, p. 61.

[5] Khafi Khan, *Muntakhab al-Labab*, ed. Kabir-ud-din Ahmad, vol. 2 (Calcutta, 1874), p. 450.

[6] Harbans Mukhia, *The Mughals of India* (Malden, MA, 2005), pp. 54–5.

conservatism of Islamic law. It, along with numerous *hadith* (Prophetic sayings) and centuries of legal judgments condemning civil strife (*fitna*) and corruption (*fasad*), suggests that Islam itself encourages unconditional obedience to those in power. Khalid Abou el Fadl's 2001 study of rebellion and violence under Islamic law, however, offers a compellingly nuanced understanding of this norm. Although Muslim jurists "affirmed a general legal principle: those in power must be obeyed," el Fadl notes, they went on to "riddle the field with qualifications, exceptions, and provisos so as to render the general principles quite complicated, and to elicit the classic legal response to many legal issues – 'It depends.'"[7] Such ambiguity notwithstanding, the bar for potential challengers to political power remained high. In fact, the Hanafi School of law, dominant in Mughal India, was generally less tolerant of rebels than other Sunni schools.[8] Mughal princes labored to come up with juridically acceptable justifications for engaging in *fitna*.

A similar predilection to order, stability, and obedience to the ruler is articulated in *akhlaq* literature – the influential corpus of ethical thinking that informed Mughal rule after the 1580s. As Muzaffar Alam and Harbans Mukhia have detailed, the king's place in society was not merely that of a political figurehead. Rather, he was considered the lynchpin of his subjects' everyday existence as well as the maintainer of social harmony and justice.[9] His influence and significance extended beyond the merely political to the cosmological. Thus *Akhlaq-i Padshahan* – an anonymous text commissioned by an unnamed prince and completed in 1645 – offers a grandiose vision of kingly power and duties. In it, the king is responsible for maintaining order in the universe, guarding all living things, upholding justice by rewarding the deserving, and upholding truth.[10] The *Akhlaq-i Padshahan* goes on to state that the king's laws and the *shari'a* "are like two sons born from the womb of the same mother, like two rings on the same finger." Obedience to one entails obedience to the other.[11] Those who are God fearing and wish for a just and good society, therefore, are

---

[7] Khalid Abou el Fadl, *Rebellion and Violence in Islamic Law* (Cambridge, 2001), p. 22.

[8] Ibid., p. 190.

[9] Muzaffar Alam, *The Languages of Political Islam in India, c. 1200–1800* (Delhi, 2004), pp. 46–80; Mukhia, *The Mughals of India*, pp. 43–4, 51. For an exhaustive treatment of "advice literature" in the larger Islamic context, see L. Marlow, "Advice and Advice Literature," in *Encyclopaedia of Islam* III, Brill Online.

[10] Anon., *Akhlaq-i Padshahan*, Asiatic Society of Bengal, Ivanow 1391, ff. 264a-266b.

[11] Ibid., f. 265b.

enjoined to obey the king. "Chaos and disorder and civil strife/rebellion" are not to be tolerated. Violators are to be mercilessly punished.[12]

These norms speak to a popular and scholarly discourse that vilified princely defiance against the imperial court. A prince, therefore, offered justifications for his decision to rebel both to the wider public and especially to the nobility and the *'ulama'* (Islamic religious scholars). The following subsection explores in detail how princes from Akbar's reign onward variously justified their decision to rebel and demonstrates how the expectation of an appanage haunts these justifications.

### Justifying Princely Rebellion

Although imperial chronicles saw fit to portray rebellious princes as young, impulsive, and irrational, we know that princes in fact deliberated carefully and prepared extensively for any rebellious move. The decision to risk life and limb in opposition to the emperor was never taken lightly and usually marked the culmination of years of growing tension. Before 1585, princes were simply expected to protect their territory and their alliances if faced with imperial encroachment. The situation became more complex after 1585 (starting with Akbar's sons), since princes now felt compelled to cite some "legitimizing notion" and to explain their just defense of traditional rights and prerogatives.[13]

Although Akbar put a conclusive end to the patrimonial right of all royals to an appanage, the question of what precisely remained of a prince's entitlement was not fully settled until the 1610s. Thus, despite Akbar's own intentions, he relented; his initial responses to Salim's 1599 rebellion were tentative; and he did not immediately crush Salim's political pretensions in Allahabad. For almost five years, Salim maintained a separate political existence until his rehabilitation in 1604, when his Allahabad-based kingdom reverted to Akbar's authority. However, princely dreams of controlling distinct territories did not die easily: it took the third major rebellion of this middle period (1556–1680s) – Khusrau's against his father Salim (now Emperor Jahangir) – to remove from the table once and for all the right to an appanage as a legitimate reason to rebel. (See a full discussion of Khusrau's rebellion and Jahangir's retaliations in a later section of this chapter.) With the crushing of Khusrau's rebellion, any last chance that

---

[12] Ibid., ff. 266b, 269b–270a.
[13] E. P. Thompson, "The Moral Economy of the English Crowd in the Eighteenth Century," *Past and Present* 50 (1971): 78.

some version of the appanage system might have survived into the seventeenth century was put to rest. Despite having surrendered their right to control a distinct area within the larger empire, princes nonetheless continued to jealously guard the other foundations of their political strength, especially their households and alliances. They incessantly jockeyed to assert their political importance within the new imperial dispensation, and they greeted any attempt to sideline them with suspicion. When Jahangir's third son Khurram rebelled in 1622, it was in the context of this new, more volatile, and increasingly competitive political culture. Indeed, the occurrence of two rebellions so close together and within the era of a single emperor suggests the tumult that resulted from deep political transformation.

If the appanage system had granted every son an actual piece of his father's realm, the end of that system introduced the new expectation that each prince had an equal claim on the entire kingdom on the death of the emperor. If that right were interfered with, as Khurram believed had been the case, then a prince felt entitled to rebel. Just as Khurram's rebellion was stoked by resentment at his father's failure to protect his political interests in the face of his stepmother Nur Jahan's efforts to elevate his teenage brother Shahryar,[14] so subsequent princely rebellions – Muhammad Sultan's in 1659 and Akbar's in 1681 – were driven by similar complaints.

Anxiety and ambivalence surrounding a prince's political future brought into focus other unanswered political questions. Who decided which son should succeed as emperor? The current emperor? Or did that question have to be decided through a pitched battle among the sons? Given the high stakes, jealousy and aggrievement between father and sons and between brothers were inevitable. Decades earlier, under the appanage system, Mirza Kamran had rebelled against Humayun because the emperor was seen as not respecting his appanage; subsequent princes rebelled because everything was now up for grabs.

By claiming patrimonial rights and expressing outrage at imperial malice or unfair dealings, princely justifications of their rebellions flew in the face of the norms of loyalty to emperor and imperial court. The imperial chronicles, for their part, offered what might best be described as post-rebellion apologetics. Official court chronicles take great pains to exonerate the rebellious prince by reclaiming him in the imperial family. Each of the five major rebellions of the high period of Mughal rule (1585–1680s) is handled carefully to mask any serious crisis within the royal family.

---

[14] Kamgar Husaini, *Ma'asir-i-Jahangiri*, ed. Azra Alvi (Bombay, 1978), pp. 352–3; Shah Nawaz Khan, *Maasir-ul-Umara*, ed. Abdur Rahim, vol. 1 (Calcutta, 1888), pp. 146–7.

## Imperial Chronicle Depictions of Princely Rebellion

In the spirit of upholding the royal family's reputation in the cosmic order, imperial accounts tend to downplay the role of princes in instigating and leading rebellions. In some cases, blame is placed on individuals within the prince's circle who instigated young and impressionable princes into rebellion. In other instances, fault was pinned on individuals in an emperor's inner circle for fomenting trouble and forcing a prince to fight to protect his interests.

Accounts of Khusrau's 1606 rebellion against Jahangir provide excellent examples of the first kind of exonerative narrative. A range of texts written between the 1620s (*Jahangirnama*) and the 1730s (*Muntakhab-ul-Lubab*) reveal a clear pattern of assigning blame on individuals close to Khusrau. They are variously called "mischief-makers," "well-wishers," "close companions," "enemies of friendship," and "creators of discord" (*fitna angez*). Throughout most of these accounts, Khusrau invariably comes across as someone easily manipulated because of his youthfulness. He is often described as "short-sighted," "inexperienced," "easily misled," and even "simple-minded." The *Jahangirnama* suggests that the prince had "no choice" but to participate in the rebellion in order to "placate these dogs" – especially his Badakhshani supporters. So also, the *Muntakhab-ul-Lubab* blames Muhammad Sultan's rebellion against Aurangzeb in 1659 on the "tricks and treachery" of his uncle Shuja', "opportunists," "flatterers," and servants and eunuchs. It goes on to identify the prince's youth and inexperience as the cause of his downfall:

[Y]oung men (*jawanan*) tend to hate the friendship, conversation, and advice of experienced old men, preferring instead the company of unaccomplished people who then become the cause of a loss of judgment, wealth, and self-respect.[15]

In a similar vein, *Mir'at-ul-'Alam* (ca. 1680s) accounts for Muhammad Sultan's actions by claiming that he was easily "beguiled" on account of his youthfulness and ignorance. Although the *'Alamgirnama* (ca. 1680s) – an officially sponsored history of the first decade of Aurangzeb's reign – is especially harsh in its condemnation of Muhammad Sultan's rebellion, it too assigns much of the blame for the prince's "route of opposition and disobedience" (*tariq-i mukhalafat wa 'isyan*) to his immaturity and ignorance. The rebellion by Akbar in 1681 is treated in similar fashion. Thus,

---

[15] K. Khan, *Muntakhab al-Labab*, vol. 2, p. 91.

even as Akbar is denounced as "the greatest of the worst" (*akbar-i abtar*), his actions are depicted in *Muntakhab-ul-Lubab* as driven by "ill-fated companions." Aurangzeb's own correspondence blames the "devilish-natured" (*iblis kirdar*) and treacherous Rajputs. Akbar is described as a victim of "beguilement" on account of his inexperience and simple-minded nature. The *Fatuhat-i 'Alamgiri* (ca. 1730s) blames some of Akbar's closest advisors for infecting the prince with "vain ambitions," asserting that he was unable to resist these enticements on account of the "intoxicating vanity of youth" that led him astray from the "path of obedience."

Some imperial accounts honed in on a specific villain who influenced the prince, causing the rebellion. Thus, in the *Ma'asir-i Jahangiri*, Salim's rebellion is blamed quite squarely on the emperor's advisor Shaikh Abu'l Fazl, who is repeatedly described as a *baghy* or "rebel." Had the Shaikh not poisoned the emperor's mind, according to the *Ma'asir-i Jahangiri*, father and son would have been more easily reconciled. In this account, Salim comes across as a reluctant rebel. A number of Shah Jahan–era chronicles, including the *Ma'asir-i Jahangiri*, *Iqbalnama-i Jahangiri*, *Shahjahannama*, and *Ahwal-i Shahzadagi*, point accusingly to Nur Jahan in their discussions of Khurram's rebellion against Jahangir. She is variously depicted as driving wedges between father and son, taking advantage of Jahangir's ill health to consolidate her power, and forcing Khurram into rebellion. In similar fashion, the story of Aurangzeb's succession struggle in the late 1650s would play off the image of the innocent prince reluctantly forced to challenge the emperor on account of powerful forces at the imperial court working to destroy him.

Imperial sources are as wary about calling conflict rebellion as they are about stating the culpability of the prince. We see great care taken to avoid using the especially incendiary term *fitna* to refer to a princely rebellion. The symbolism of this term derived from its first use in describing the tumultuous late 650s and early 660s, a period of epic intra-Muslim civil strife in Arabia that generated a massive corpus of Islamic juridical rulings condemning such conflict. Mughal chronicles step gingerly around the term, finding a variety of alternatives that downplay the threat to imperial order posed by princely rebellions and devising other ways to make sense of the aggrieved prince and his antagonistic moves and postures. Consider Jahangir's account of the Khusrau and Khurram rebellions. Although *fitna* is used on three occasions in the *Jahangirnama* – twice in conversations about Khusrau and once about Khurram – the emperor shows a marked preference for less incendiary terms such as *mukhalafat* (opposition), *fasad* (mischief/corruption), and *shorish* (rebellion/revolt). Later accounts of Khusrau's and Khurram's rebellions also generally steer clear of using the term *fitna*, preferring instead terms such as *zalalat* (disobedience/misbehavior), *hangama* (outbreak), *bagha* (rebellion), and *ashob* (destruction).[16]

But the word *fitna* was routinely deployed against non-princely actors – whether princely supporters or princely opponents. The *Ma'asir-i Jahangiri* reports only one instance when Akbar described Salim as engaged in *fitna*; yet, this chronicle is replete with proclamations of *fitna* to describe the anti-Salim maneuverings of Shaikh Abu'l Fazl, unnamed individuals in the imperial circle, and Mirza 'Aziz Koka and Raja Man Singh. The same discretion is also apparent in the *Ma'asir-i Jahangiri*'s treatment of Khusrau's rebellion. Despite the fact that its author, Khwaja Kamgar Husaini, was unfavorably inclined toward Khusrau, he still prefers to call Khusrau's action a *shorish*. He uses *fitna* only to describe the rebellious character of Khusrau's Badakhshani supporters and a later plot by the prince's partisans to kill Jahangir. Likewise, while taking pains to avoid applying the term to Khurram's rebellion, the *Ma'asir-i Jahangiri* characterizes Nur Jahan's actions against Khurram as *fitna*. So also the *Iqbalnama-i Jahangiri* (ca. 1632) characterizes Khusrau's Badakhshani supporters as being inclined to *fitna*, *shorish*, and *fasad*,[17] but it avoids using the term with regard to the prince himself. Even a pro–Nur Jahan source – the *Fathnama-i Nur Jahan Begum* (ca. 1626–7) – terms Khurram's rebellion a mere *shorish*, while using *fitna* to describe another unrelated but simultaneous rebellion by the nobleman Mahabat Khan. The same pattern is repeated in the handling of princes Muhammad Sultan's and Akbar's rebellions during Aurangzeb's reign.

The care taken not to deploy *fitna* in descriptions of princely aggression against the empire suggests recognition that princes, at the end of the day, were an integral part of the imperial body. Thus, when the *Jahangirnama* describes Khurram's 1620s rebellion, yes, Khurram is castigated – Jahangir orders that Khurram be henceforth referred to as the "wretch" (*bi-daulat*); he is described as "rash" and lacking in the "scent of goodness" (*bu-yi khair*); and his actions are characterized as "full of effrontery" (*jurat namudeh*), "belligerent," filled with "ignorance and error," and no longer on the "highway of propriety" (*jadeh-i maqul wa shahrah-i adab*) – yet we do not see here the vituperative language that will be used in the

---

[16] Here I have consulted a number of popular seventeenth-century chronicles including *Ma'asir-i Rahimi*, *Tarikh-i Khan Jahan wa Makhzan-i Afghani*, *Ma'asir-i Jahangiri*, *Iqbalnama-i Jahangiri*, and *Khulasat-ul-Tawarikh*.

[17] Motamid Khan, *Iqbalnamah-i Jahangiri*, ed. Abdul Hai and Ahmad Ali (Calcutta, 1865), p. 10.

later description of the failed 1626 rebellion against Jahangir by the noble-man Mahabat Khan. This rebellion is documented by Mulla Kami Shirazi in the *Fathnama-i Nur Jahan*, dedicated to Nur Jahan, Jahangir's powerful wife and reflecting her view on the Khan's rebellion. In it, Mahabat Khan is variously reviled as "full of deceit," "unfaithful," "disloyal," an "evil thinker" (*bad-khwa*), a "villain," of "ignoble/ugly character" (*zisht kirdar*), filled with "malice," "ill-starred" (*bad-akhtar*), the "source of deceit and deception," a "beast" (*dad*), "malicious," without "honor," a "tyrant" (*jufakesh*), a "monster" (*div*), "without faith" (*bi-din*), filled with "pride and arrogance," "black-hearted" (*dil-siyah*), a "wicked leper" (*bis-i tadbir*), a committer of "wicked deeds," and a "dog" the likes of which the world has never seen. In addition, the Khan is denounced as a non-Muslim (*na-Musalman*) whose "faith and belief are both faulty" (*nah din-i tu durust ast wa na iman*); he is compared to "the accursed Satan," with the "wicked habit of Satan"; the commander of a "Satanic army" (*lashkar-i iblis*) whose Rajput soldiers are "bloodthirsty"; and a member of a "Satanic nation" (*qaum-i shaitan*) and engaged in "heresy" (*bid'at*) and, of-course, *fitna*.[18]

In sharp contrast to Jahangir's allowances for Khurram's actions, the furious rhetoric of *Fathnama-i Nur Jahan Begum* suggests that there can be no tolerating a noble-led rebellion. Although Jahangir was deeply disappointed in Khurram, he conveys a sense of resignation that his son was not acting entirely out of character as a Mughal Prince. And so imperial accounts reveal an acceptance of princely rebellions as an almost inevitable part of the jostling for power between adult males in the Mughal royal family. By generally avoiding the language of *fitna*, the Mughals seem to reflect both a tacit acceptance of the right of princes to rebel as well as a desire to foreclose this option for anyone else.

Although princes were tacitly permitted the option of rebellion, that option was nonetheless severely constrained. Rebellion was an enormously disruptive affair all around. Yet sibling rivalry for the throne and for the emperor's favors being unavoidable, sidestepping rebellion required that the Mughal princes resort to adaptive strategies and stances in their family relations. The following section studies the full range of these strategies and stances developed by princes to cope with their unenviable situation, and it also explores how the outbreak of rebellion itself was constrained.

---

[18] See Mulla Kami Shirazi, *Fathnama-i Nur Jahan Begum*, Center of Advanced Study Library (Aligarh Muslim University), Rotograph 10.

### PRINCELY DEFIANCE, IMPERIAL CONSTRAINTS

The popular notion of the Mughal Prince is one of a figure caught up in bloody and brutal rebellions or wars of succession. For the prince, however, armed rebellion was only a last resort. That only five major rebellions took place between the 1580s and 1680s suggests powerful constraints – including imperial surveillance, relatively poor resources, and norms of loyalty – operating on most princes at most times. Disaffected princes tended to register their defiance and anger in ways that stopped just shy of outright rebellion, expressing what, inspired by James Scott, we might call princely disobedience.[19] The Mughal Prince during and after Emperor Akbar's reign lived a life structured by subordination to his father. Like Scott's peasants, Mughal princes were forced to disguise their ambitions given the larger compact of rule and the elaborate rituals of loyalty and obedience imposed on them.

Public acquiescence to their subordinate status was matched by behind-the-scenes defiance. This "infrapolitics" of the Mughal prince[20] included false compliance, grumbling, foot dragging, political sabotage, and other forms of private disobedience. Even if these do not exactly count as "weapons of the weak" when wielded by Mughal princes, they were similarly indirect means by which princely disquiet could be signaled in the face of a commanding emperor. Princely infrapolitical strategies intensified as the Mughal Empire sought to constrain its princes' autonomy, and greater constraints produced greater disobedience and deceit and, in the case of Prince Aurangzeb, intense paranoia. Moreover, as the following discussion demonstrates, imperial tolerance of even defiance would lessen over the course of the period in question.

### Akbar's Diminishing Tolerance for Disobedience

Between the 1560s and 1580s, as he did away with semipermanent appanages, Akbar, Humayun's son and successor, dramatically empowered the position of the emperor. With this, the near political and military parity that had once existed between Emperor Humayun and his brothers

---

[19] James Scott's focus on peasants and the socially disenfranchised could not be further removed from this study's focus on princes in the Mughal Empire. Nonetheless, his framework is suggestive for the trajectories traveled by several Mughal princes in their bids for the throne.

[20] James Scott, *Domination and the Arts of Resistance: Hidden Transcripts* (New Haven, 1990), p. xiii.

vanished. By the time Akbar's sons reached adulthood in the mid-1580s, the gap between the emperor's power and that of his sons was significant, and reflecting this new reality were three new developments. One was a clear willingness on the part of the emperor to emphasize his superior authority through public orders to his adult sons. The second entailed the willingness of Akbar's sons to generally maintain a façade of public obedience to the emperor. The third was the princes' increasing preference for making oblique, rather than direct, challenges to the emperor's authority. We can look to Akbar and his second son Murad (b. 1570) for the sorts of troubles emperor and prince encountered as they negotiated their relationship under this new dispensation.

In a document prepared for Murad before he left the imperial court on his first major assignment as governor of Malwa (1591), Akbar offered extremely detailed instructions as to how the prince should comport himself. Besides recommending "correct behavior" in all matters pertaining to food, drink, and personal behavior, Akbar commanded the prince to exercise political restraint at all times. This meant avoiding tyrannical actions, not promoting unqualified individuals, and guarding against sycophants and other troublemakers. It also entailed listening to the advice of experienced councilors, maintaining the dignity of his office, keeping a close watch on the administrative machinery of the state, and rewarding good service. Toward the end of the document, Murad is commanded to always remain God fearing, even keeled, and above all loyal. The day after this epistle was delivered to the prince, Akbar ordered his confidant and political advisor Shaikh Abu'l Fazl to make sure that Murad had understood the meaning of the document and also to remind him that father and son were bound by a spiritual union that transcended physical separation.[21] Murad was being publicly enjoined while away in Malwa to remain a faithful and obedient Mughal Prince, and as such this exercise unequivocally set forth both imperial authority and expectations.

Unlike Humayun who had responded to Babur's decision to send him away from the center of power by sacking Delhi in 1527, Murad accepted Akbar's order to transfer away from the imperial court without public fuss. Akbar is described as being delighted upon learning of Murad's acquiescence.[22] Once removed from the imperial court, however, the prince became progressively less manageable. It is crucial to note that

---

[21] Shaikh Abu'l Fazl, *Akbarnamah*, ed. Abdul Rahim, vol. 3 (Calcutta, 1886), pp. 598–9.
[22] Ibid., p. 600.

although he never rebelled against Akbar, he followed a policy of persistent, if indirect, disobedience.

Thus two nobles – Ismail Quli Khan and Sadiq Khan – sent in succession by Akbar as *ataliqs* for his son, found their charge impossible to control. Not only did they fail to rein in Murad's "bad conduct in all relations of life" and his "excessive pride and arrogance," they watched helplessly as he began to mutter about his readiness to ascend the Mughal throne.[23]

Following the transfer to his next assignment as governor of the Deccan in 1594, the prince's defiance deepened. Although he never openly challenged Akbar, Murad repeatedly picked fights over strategy and tactics with 'Abd-ul-Rahim Khan-i Khanan and Shahbaz Khan Kambo, Akbar's leading noble commanders in the region. The Mughal war effort in the Deccan began to falter under the weight of these feuds; to pacify the prince, Akbar eventually removed 'Abd-ul-Rahim Khan-i Khanan from his command. Yet Murad remained unwilling to wage the campaign in the Deccan according to Akbar's orders. He found ways to secretly undermine imperial objectives by making overtures to various enemies, displaying a distinct lack of military initiative, and picking arguments with Akbar's other generals. In a final bid to rein in his son, Akbar sent Shaikh Abu'l Fazl to the Deccan in 1598–9 to recall Murad to the imperial court in Agra. To evade control, Murad shifted camps while never officially rejecting a meeting with the Shaikh. By so doing, he likely reasoned, he could not be accused and possibly punished for ignoring his father's summons. Murad died of alcohol poisoning shortly thereafter, and we could say that even under the new dispensation of a powerful emperor and the expectation of an obedient prince, Murad's final communication to his father was a snub. In the face of escalating imperial demands for loyalty and (sometimes) desperate efforts to project unanimity of imperial purpose, princes such as Murad highlight the chinks in the façade.

Murad's recalcitrance inspired enough anxiety in the emperor to deem it worthy of mention, if in passing, in the *Akbarnama*, the official court-sponsored chronicle of Akbar's reign. When Shaikh Abu'l Fazl completed the bulk of the *Akbarnama* in 1596, Murad's death was still three years off. Remarkably, Shaikh Abu'l Fazl chose to include Akbar's 1591 letter to the prince in the volume as a clear reminder of imperial expectations of a son dispatched from the court. Yet Murad failed to live up to most of the letter's ideals, as recounted over the succeeding pages of the *Akbarnama*.

---

[23] 'Abd al-Qadir Badauni, *Muntakhab al-Tawarikh*, ed. W. N. Lees and Ahmad Ali, vol. 2 (Calcutta, 1865), p. 379.

The prince is variously depicted as inconstant in his friendships, mercurial, arrogant, vulnerable to flattery, and undisciplined. So too is his alcoholism hinted at. His military achievements after Malwa are described as negligible. Any claims to popularity among powerful nobles are turned aside by episodes that show him fighting with imperial commanders or abandoning them on the eve of crucial battles.

This pushback against Murad occurred even as the emperor was beginning to experience similar difficulties with Salim, who was more careful and determined than Murad in his defiance (see Chapter 4 for a fuller discussion). Through the 1590s, Salim picked fights with his brothers and imperial officials such as Shaikh Abu'l Fazl, who were closely associated with key aspects of Akbar's rule. He petitioned the emperor to forgive rebels against the empire and engaged in dilatory tactics when commanded to lead military expeditions. Over time, Salim had begun to view himself not as a supporter of the emperor's authority but rather more as an oppositional force.

A 1589 story in the *Akbarnama* provides a glimpse of Akbar's frustration in face of Salim's behavior. Akbar had commissioned the prince to escort the imperial harem through a treacherous stretch of mountainous terrain on the road to Kashmir. Inexplicably, the reader is told, Salim abandoned the harem and marched onward to join up with his father. Akbar was furious on the arrival of his son. According to Shaikh Abu'l Fazl's retelling, the emperor immediately dismissed his son, mounted his own horse, and, in a cold and driving rain, retraced his son's route back to where the harem had been left behind. Shaikh Abu'l Fazl suggests that in so doing, he meant to highlight his own fortitude and sense of duty as compared to Salim's failings on those fronts. Later, Akbar lambasted Salim's companion and supporter 'Abd-ul-Rahim Khan-i Khanan for failing to keep the prince on the right path. Akbar also publicly castigated his son for his "destructive intentions" (*khwahish-i tabah*).[24]

As discussed in Chapter 4, Akbar sought to actively undermine Salim by compromising his networks. He would also eventually pit Salim against his own son, Akbar's grandson Khusrau. Nonetheless, expressions of princely disobedience during Akbar's reign were a great deal more restrained and indirect than they were during Humayun's reign. Though oblique, however, princely unrest and ambition were such that no player in this arena could afford complacency. Even a highly respected and powerful emperor such as Akbar had to worry about the actions of his sons. This constant and reciprocal vigilance injected a restless energy and dynamism, and

---

[24] Fazl, *Akbarnamah*, vol. 3, p. 542.

perhaps even viciousness, deception, and tragedy, into Mughal succession dramas that continued through the reigns of Akbar's successors.

## Jahangir's Intolerance Fosters Princely Deceit

Emperors wholeheartedly sought to reinforce their unquestionable authority as fathers and emperors. The case of Jahangir (formerly Salim) is exemplary. From the very beginning of his reign, Jahangir endeavored to overcome the stain of his rebellion against Akbar. His autobiography, the *Jahangirnama*, speaks pointedly of this effort. In addition to eschewing any responsibility for his actions by blaming "short-sighted men" within his own princely circle, Jahangir credits himself for coming to his senses:

> In the end, their words and advice did not seem reasonable to me at all, for I knew how long a reign based on contention with my father would last. I was not led astray by the advice of these weak-minded people but rather, putting into practice what was required by intelligence and knowledge, went to pay homage to my father, my guide, my metaphorical *qibla* [axis] and lord.[25]

Having deemed rebellion against one's father and emperor unacceptable, Jahangir goes on to declare his son Khusrau's 1606 rebellion indefensible – "the vexing part of this affair was that my son, without reason or cause, became an enemy and opponent."[26]

The *Jahangirnama* is particularly keen to highlight moving accounts of loyalty toward Jahangir the father, husband, and emperor. Those that stand out include the decision by Khusrau's mother to commit suicide because she could not bear that her son had challenged his father, the instance of the nobleman Islam Khan praying to God to take his life instead of that of a very sick Jahangir, and the story of Nur Jahan selflessly nursing a gravely ill Jahangir back to health. It talks too of ingratitude and disloyalty revolving around instances of princely disobedience and rebellion.

After Jahangir's third son Khurram launched a rebellion in 1622, he is subjected to harsh treatment:

> Of the patronage and favors I showered upon him I can say that until now no monarch has ever showered upon any son. The favors my exalted father showed my brothers I showed his liegemen . . . so it is no secret to the readers of this register of prosperity how much attention and favor he has been shown.[27]

[25] Nur-ud-din Muhammad Jahangir, *The Jahangirnama: Memoirs of Jahangir, Emperor of India*, trans. W. M. Thackston (New York, 1999), pp. 55–6.
[26] Ibid., p. 32.
[27] Ibid., p. 387.

In addition to the chronicled word, Jahangir sought to reinforce his authority as father and emperor in public deed. Besides his public desecration of the grave of the early sixteenth-century patricide and regicide Nasir-ud-Din Sultan in 1616, Jahangir cultivated a very public devotion to Akbar's memory in an effort to reinvent himself as a dutiful son. Invariably these endeavors took their sharpest form when he was under political pressure from his own sons.

In the arena of father-son relations within the Mughal family, however, Emperor Jahangir's blinding of his oldest son Khusrau in 1607 stands out for its unprecedented severity. Humayun's earlier blinding of his brother Mirza Kamran – the only previous incident of princely blinding in Mughal history – occurred after decades of hostility and might even be viewed as an expression of the rage of one emperor against a semi-independent ruler. By contrast, Khusrau was blinded after a failed assassination plot by some of his supporters (possibly without the prince's knowledge) against the emperor. Jahangir's vicious response stands in sharp contrast to his own father Akbar's unwillingness to punish Salim for either a plot to poison the emperor in the early 1590s or even his five-year-long rebellion.

I think of Jahangir's retaliatory physical violence as marking a more authoritative relationship between emperor and prince – a style of relationship that began with Akbar but was increasingly consolidated under Emperor Jahangir. Throughout his reign, Jahangir worked hard to contain his ambitious sons by forcefully reminding them at every opportunity of his greater authority. Thus, when Parvez was found to be subverting Jahangir's plans for expansion in the Deccan, the emperor's reaction was swift, public, and draconian. He removed Parvez from his command and dismissed him to the relative backwater of Allahabad in 1616. For almost four years thereafter, the prince was denied an imperial audience or even a visit to the court.

The lesson of Jahangir's intolerance for and determination to severely punish princely dissent was not lost on his third son Khurram. Even as relations between Jahangir and Khurram deteriorated after 1620, the prince was extremely careful to avoid provoking his father. Instead, he seemed to acquiesce to Jahangir's authority while he quietly marshaled his own power and waited for an opportunity to strike a much deadlier blow in the form of a massive princely rebellion (more on this in a later section of this chapter). Sir Thomas Roe – a visiting English ambassador to Jahangir's court – sensed that something was terribly awry in the relationship between Jahangir and Khurram when he noticed the prince (whom he calls a "sly youth") engaging in unnamed "ambitious practices" aimed at securing power at the Mughal court.[28] The short-term success of Khurram's strategy (short term in that his rebellion eventually failed) is attested by Jahangir's surprise when he learned in 1622 that his son was marching up from the Deccan to try and overthrow him.

Emperor Jahangir weighing Prince Khurram (Shah Jahan) against gold and silver, ca. 1615 (British Museum, London, ME OA 1948.10–9.069)

When Khurram eventually ascended the Mughal throne on his father's death in 1628 (as Emperor Shah Jahan), he too demonstrated little tolerance

---

[28]  Sir Thomas Roe, *The Embassy of Sir Thomas Roe to India, 1615–19*, ed. W. Foster (Delhi, repr. 1990), p. 244.

for dissent from his sons. Indeed, Khurram/Shah Jahan's tight grip was such that his reign ended with an unprecedented event: the loss of his throne to a son. In 1658, Aurangzeb overthrew Shah Jahan after a bitter war of succession among the aging emperor's four sons. We might speculate that the growing intolerance for any form of dissent pushed resentments between father and sons and tensions among competitor brothers underground. The eventual explosion, like the gases and molten rocks of an erupting volcano, was far more violent for having been repressed.

## The Deceit and Paranoia of Prince Aurangzeb

The increased intolerance of princely disobedience during the first half of the seventeenth century led to extraordinary princely deceit. Aurangzeb, the third son of Shah Jahan and brother to the greatly favored eldest son Dara Shukoh epitomized the art of princely dissimulation. He was at once the most paranoid, the most deceptive, and the most effective contender for the throne, perhaps because of his father's fervent wish that it go to Dara Shukoh. In the course of his princely career, Aurangzeb undertook various forms of "hidden resistance" while maintaining an almost perfect record of public obedience.

From early on in Aurangzeb's princely career, Shah Jahan thwarted his son's political ambitions at every turn. Having sent him off to serve as governor of the Deccan in 1636, the emperor refused his repeated requests to return to the court. In 1644, when Aurangzeb's older sister Jahan Ara was seriously burned in an accident that nearly took her life, the prince leapt on this pretext to return to the imperial court without Shah Jahan's permission, claiming he wanted to be near his ailing sister. The emperor did not believe him and when Aurangzeb appeared before him in court, Shah Jahan promptly placed the prince under house arrest and stripped him of rank and title. Shah Jahan's severe reaction suggests how much imperial attitudes had stiffened since Humayun's uninvited return to Babur's court in 1529.[29]

After a year in political oblivion, Aurangzeb was rehabilitated by the emperor but sent far away from court again to be the governor of Gujarat.[30] Thereafter, Aurangzeb perfected a mode of overt submission

---

[29] Shah Jahan was similarly harsh with Aurangzeb's younger brother Murad, who was also placed under house arrest and had his household disbanded following his decision to abandon the Balkh-Badakhshan campaign without imperial permission in 1646.

[30] 'Inayat Khan, *Shahjahannama*, trans. A.R. Fuller (Delhi, 1990), pp. 313, 318–19. For similarly ambiguous accounts see Salih Kambo Lahori, *'Amal-i Salih*, ed. Ghulam

and covert resistance. He became, in the words of François Bernier, a contemporary French traveler in Mughal India, "a complete master of the art of dissimulation. When in his father's court, he feigned devotion which he never felt ... while clandestinely endeavouring to pave the way to future elevation."[31] So also a March 1651 communication in the English East India Company archives offers the following: "This is certayne ... Prince Oran Zeab beares the eldest Prince [Dara Shukoh] a great deale of respect, and verey submissive he is unto him, but that may (be) in outward shewe before the Kinge."[32] Indeed, this opinion agrees with that of Manucci, the Italian adventurer/traveler/servitor, who confirms that Aurangzeb operated during the last decades of his father's reign "in great secrecy, with much craft."[33]

Aurangzeb's private imperial correspondence, anecdotal records collected posthumously, and accounts written by visiting foreigners ever so infrequently offer a glimpse of the prince's hostility toward his father. Here we see Aurangzeb mocking Shah Jahan's favoring of Dara Shukoh.[34] There we read of Aurangzeb attacking the court as out-of-touch with the daily realities of the empire.[35] In a privately recorded conversation with a Deccan-based Sufi master, he decried the court's irreligiosity.[36] He also indirectly questioned Shah Jahan's military skills.[37] Was such a whispering campaign, begun by Aurangzeb and his partisans, ultimately responsible for the widespread rumors recorded by contemporary European travelers such as Bernier of debauchery at the Mughal court? Of Shah Jahan engaging in the despicable act of incest with his oldest daughter Jahan Ara?[38] It is not unlikely.

Sometimes, we can discern Shah Jahan's unease about Aurangzeb. The emperor seems to have sensed his son's defiance if never openly witnessing

---

Yazdani, vol. 2 (Lahore, 1967), pp. 336–7, 346; 'Abd al-Hamid Lahawri, *Padshahnamah*, ed. Abdul Rahim, vol. 2 (Calcutta, 1872), pp. 376, 398.

[31] François Bernier, *Travels in the Mogul Empire, AD 1656–1668*, trans. A. Constable (Delhi: repr. 1997), p. 10.

[32] *The English Factories in India, 1618–1669*, ed. W. Foster, vol. 9 (Oxford, 1906–27), p. 52.

[33] Niccolao Manucci, *Mogul India or Storia do Mogor*, trans. W. Irvine, vol. 1 (Delhi, repr. 1996), p. 220.

[34] Aurangzeb, *Adab-i 'Alamgiri*, ed. Abdul Ghafur Chaudhuri (Lahore, 1971), vol. 1, pp. 98–100; vol. 2, pp. 828–31; Aurangzeb, *Muqaddama-i Ruq'at-i 'Alamgiri*, ed. Saiyid Najib Ashraf Nadvi, vol. 1 (Azamgarh, 1930), pp. 65–8.

[35] Aurangzeb, *Adab-i 'Alamgiri*, vol. 1, pp. 140–3, 183–5, 463–4, 537–8.

[36] K. Khan, *Muntakhab al-Labab*, vol. 2, pp. 553–4.

[37] Aurangzeb's resentment is subtle, if ever-present, in his communications with Shah Jahan during the second expedition against Qandahar (1652), see *Adab-i 'Alamgiri*, vol. 1, pp. 44–7, 47–8, 55–6, 64–6, 67–70, 81–5, 85–7, 87–9, 93–4.

[38] Bernier, *Travels in the Mogul Empire*, p. 11.

it. Consider an event in 1644–5 when the princes accompanied Shah Jahan to a newly constructed underground chamber belonging to Dara Shukoh. During the visit, Aurangzeb chose to sit far removed from the others, at the entrance to the room, in a public breach of imperial etiquette. Midway through the celebration and without imperial permission, Aurangzeb left the party and returned to his own house. When an angry Shah Jahan later demanded an explanation, Aurangzeb replied that he had behaved in this fashion to ensure that Dara Shukoh would not be tempted to murder everyone – including the emperor – and thus secure the Mughal throne. Although preposterous on its face, Aurangzeb frames and justifies his actions as motivated by concern for imperial well-being. Likely gritting his teeth, Shah Jahan was forced to confer unstated gifts on Aurangzeb for his loyalty and devotion.[39]

Of some interest is what this anecdote suggests of the heightened tension and drama surrounding all interactions among these competing royal sons in the mid-seventeenth century. Even if Aurangzeb's claim to have acted as he did to discourage an attack on the emperor is hard to swallow, we can imagine that the ceremony did indeed bring intensely hostile brothers into unbearably close contact. Aurangzeb it seems could no longer tolerate the tension in the air.

A cat-and-mouse game between father and son ensued through the 1640s and 1650s. When Aurangzeb failed in a second attempt to take the fort of Qandahar in 1652, he asked to accompany a third expedition under the command of Dara Shukoh. The emperor was dismissive: "Everyone is made for a job. Wise men have said: 'He who has been tried (and found inadequate) should not be tried again.'" Yet whose failure was it? Aurangzeb is said to have retorted that, after all, he owed all his training to the emperor.[40]

Efforts by Shah Jahan to goad his son to say or do something for which he could be punished always failed. So it was with the Zainabadi episode. Here, Aurangzeb became the object of public ridicule by Dara Shukoh and Shah Jahan upon their hearing that he had fainted, overcome by emotion, following his first encounter with a particularly beautiful concubine in his maternal aunt's household.[41] Aurangzeb might outwardly profess great religiosity, the mocking suggested, but he was not immune to the lure of courtly or even

---

[39] Aurangzeb, *Raqa'im-i Kara'im*, Asiatic Society of Bengal, Ivanow 383, f. 203a; Aurangzeb, *Anecdotes of Aurangzib*, trans. Jadunath Sarkar (Calcutta, repr. 1988), pp. 24–5.

[40] Aurangzeb, *Adab-i 'Alamgiri*, vol. 1, pp. 98–100.

[41] S. Khan, *Maasir-ul-Umara*, vol. 1, pp. 890–2; Aurangzeb, *Anecdotes of Aurangzib*, p. 30.

corporeal pleasure. The sources indicate that Aurangzeb remained silent in response, refusing to defend himself. Yet clearly resentment was building. This is further attested in the correspondence through the 1650s between Aurangzeb and Shah Jahan that survives in the *Adab-i 'Alamgiri*. At various junctures, the prince obliquely accuses his father of undermining his honor, obstructing his ability to administer the Deccan effectively, and being oblivious to the real state of affairs in the south.[42]

Ultimately, Shah Jahan's inability to stop his son's off-stage antics and challenges may have played a key role in sowing doubts about the emperor's capacity to rule. Questions about his political and military judgment percolated to the surface in 1658 and helped justify Aurangzeb's toppling of his father. The almost total absence of opposition to the emperor's overthrow – especially from within the ranks of the powerful imperial nobility – following the battles of Dharmat and Samugarh, and the notable lack of attempts to restore him, speak to the success of Aurangzeb's long-term program to delegitimize his father. By driving princely disobedience deep underground, Shah Jahan had helped create the perfect environment for secret threats to his rule; ultimately, these proved beyond his capacity to counter.

### THE MOMENT OF REBELLION

What happened when a prince went into rebellion? What ultimately tipped off the five significant rebellions between 1585 and the 1680s, and with what consequences? This part of the prince's story features military tactics, elite networks, the politics and intrigues of loyalty and betrayal, and the deployment of public image to drum up support from larger populations. Subsequent to an overview of how a rebellion unfolded, we will look closely at one of them – that of Khurram's against Jahangir in 1622, a rebellion against an emperor who had come down extremely hard on all shows of defiance by princes. Recall that it was Jahangir who in 1607 blinded his rebellious son Khusrau, Khurram's brother.

Princes knew that under most circumstances, rebellions had little chance of success thanks to an emperor's ability to marshal superior political and military resources. In every rebellion, the prince therefore picked a moment when the emperor was in some way politically or physically compromised. Whereas Khurram (in 1622) hoped to benefit from Jahangir's ill health and

---

[42] Aurangzeb, *Adab-i 'Alamgiri*, vol. 1, pp. 96, 100, 118–19, 120–2, 131–4, 136–7, 141–3, 144–5, 146–7, 148–50, 156–8, 165–8, 183–5, 206–7, 216–18, 218–19.

aversion to the heat, Khusrau (in 1606) and Muhammad Sultan (in 1659) chose to strike when their respective fathers had only just ascended the throne and thus before they had firmly established their authority.

In Salim's case, his decision to rebel in 1599 drew on a slightly different set of calculations. Foremost among them was Akbar's heightened political vulnerability in the wake of the death, from alcohol poisoning, of his second son Murad. Responding to Murad's demise – the prince had after all been the supreme commander of all Mughal troops in the Deccan – Akbar decided to remove himself, the Mughal court, and large contingents of troops drawn from all over northern India to take charge of the faltering Deccan campaign. With northern India drained of imperial forces and the emperor absent, Salim knew that there would be little resistance to his decision to come out in open rebellion in a leisurely march to Allahabad, his main stronghold over the next five years.

### First Reactions to the Outbreak of Rebellion

Panic invariably accompanied a princely rebellion. When Khusrau went into rebellion against Jahangir on the night of April 16, 1606, he had first to escape from his captors. The contemporary source *Tarikh-i Khan Jahani wa Makhzan-i Afghani* reports, "tumult gripped the city, and fear and panic spread in every direction."[43] As far as the average person in Agra was concerned, his or her well-being was threatened from every direction. Not only had Khusrau's troops already looted sections of the city to raise money and obtain supplies, people also feared that imperial troops would be unleashed to root out princely supporters, resulting in further mayhem.

But Agra was spared the worst strife in 1606, when the rebellion moved farther west as Khusrau fled toward Lahore. On the way, his supporters robbed travelers and looted traders on the busy Agra-Lahore highway. They burnt caravan stops (*sarai*s), engaged in massive theft of money and horses, and attacked and looted the city of Mathura. Although Khusrau had hoped to take Lahore by surprise, word of his rebellion preceded him by a couple of days, giving imperial officials there sufficient time to force some of the city's leading merchants and bankers to provide supplies and money, and also to prepare the city's citadel for a siege. Anticipating food shortages and rapid price increases, merchants began hoarding goods. By

---

[43] Ni'matullah Khan Harvi, *Tarikh-i-Khan Jahani wa Makhzan-i-Afghani*, ed. S. M. Imam-ud-Din, vol. 2 (Dhaka, 1962), pp. 675–6.

the time Khusrau arrived outside Lahore, he found a city already in panic. The city was temporarily abandoned by the imperial authorities, and Khusrau was met by a delegation of Lahore's leading citizens. They agreed to surrender and raise money for the prince on the condition that he ensured order.[44] But Khusrau was unable to prevent local gangsters and their followers from looting and plundering at will for a couple of weeks.[45] Their violence abated only with Jahangir's arrival following his victory over Khusrau at the Battle of Bhaironwal in late April.

Just as things were beginning to look up for Lahore's beleaguered residents, Jahangir decided to unleash his forces on the city to punish it for complicity in Khusrau's rebellion. Thus caught in the middle, the people there suffered terribly. Imperial soldiers conducted house-to-house searches looking for the prince's partisans. Over several days, according to a contemporary Dutch observer, many people were rounded up for interrogation and a large number of houses were sacked.[46] Fear and panic again gripped the city; citizens claimed that the Day of Judgment had finally arrived.[47] Conditions did not begin to ease until after hundreds of people had been impaled or hanged and their bodies left to rot in the burning summer heat.

As Lahore's residents suffered, so too did the inhabitants of other imperial cities. Mughal sources variously attest to the miseries of Kabul's citizens in the 1540s; of Attock's in 1606; of Surat's, Ahmadabad's, and Burhanpur's in 1623; and of Allahabad's, Patna's, and Dhaka's in 1624–5. And though sources are generally silent about the impact such events had on peasants or non-sedentary populations, we can guess at the immense fear and suffering Khusrau inflicted en route to Lahore. According to one source, scores of villages and their produce were burnt, likely to impede the progress of the pursuing imperial army.[48] Elsewhere, mention is made of

---

[44] The general account of Khusrau's rebellion uses the following sources: M. Khan, *Iqbalnamah-i Jahangiri*, pp. 10–11; Harvi, *Tarikh-i-Khan Jahani*, vol. 2, pp. 676–80; Nur al-Din Muhammad Jahangir, *Autobiographical Memoirs of the Emperor Jahangueir*, trans. D. Price (Calcutta, repr. 1972), pp. 80, 98; Shaikh Farid Bhakkari, *Dhakhirat al-Khawanin*, ed. S. Moinul Haq, vol. 1 (Karachi, 1961), p. 129; K. Husaini, *Ma'asir-i-Jahangiri*, pp. 78–83; Khafi Khan, *Muntakhab al-Labab*, ed. Kabir-ud-din Ahmad and Ghulam Qadir, vol. 1 (Calcutta, 1869), pp. 250–2.

[45] Jahangir, *Jahangirnama*, p. 43.

[46] Francisco Pelsaert, *A Dutch Chronicle of Mughal India*, trans. Brij Narain and S. R. Sharma (Lahore, repr. 1978), p. 54.

[47] Harvi, *Tarikh-i-Khan Jahani*, vol. 2, p. 689.

[48] K. Khan, *Muntakhab al-Labab*, vol. 1, p. 251.

Salim's army trampling crops and generally attacking and extorting as it marched from Agra to Allahabad. We also know that Prince Akbar's army stole camels, horses, and livestock as it prepared to do battle with Aurangzeb in 1681.

No princely rebellion, however, came close to Khurram's in the toll it exacted on the peasants of Bengal, Bihar, Awadh, and Allahabad. Khurram brutally extracted money to pay for field operations and reward followers. He placed great pressure on the landholding elites in the region and also on men such as Mirza Nathan – a long-serving imperial official in Bengal who was "conversant with the management of the affairs of Bengal and of the tax-collectors"[49] – to force the peasants to surrender ever larger sums of money. The prince also set up an extensive system of forced labor to build roads and move goods and supplies to the front lines around Allahabad. Following the collapse of Khurram's attempts to conquer eastern India in late 1624, the region was torn apart by another round of violence in *zamindar*-led revolts against the remnants of Mughal authority. This in turn led to the invasion of imperial forces to reassert the emperor's control. Such stories suggest that rural populations, like their urban counterparts, must have reacted with fear and panic upon hearing that a prince had launched a rebellion.

The imperial household, too, would enter a state of emergency. In the hours following Khusrau's escape from Agra, Jahangir called a meeting of his closest advisors in his inner chambers and demanded to know in which direction his son had headed. No one knew exactly. In some distress, Jahangir then asked: "What's to be done? ... Should I set out on horseback, or should I send Khurram?"[50]

One advisor suggested that a high-ranking nobleman should pursue Khusrau, but Jahangir vacillated. At first, he appointed his childhood friend and advisor Sharif Khan to the task; Jahangir then retracted the order and chose Shaikh Farid Bukhari instead. Confirmation then arrived that the prince was heading away from Agra toward the Punjab. Less fearful now, Jahangir resolved to march with a separate army behind Shaikh Farid Bukhari. Over the coming days, the emperor's confidence that he could overcome his son's challenge grew. By the time Jahangir learned that the imperial forces were locked in battle with Khusrau, his mood had shifted to downright reckless. Neglecting to eat, eschewing his

---

[49] Mirza Nathan, *Baharistan-i-Ghaybi*, trans. M. I. Borah, vol. 2 (Gauhati, 1936), pp. 741, 747.

[50] Jahangir, *Jahangirnama*, p. 31.

armor, and accompanied only by fifty horsemen, Jahangir sped ahead to the battlefield. Many years later, Jahangir's adrenaline still seemed to race at the memory: he noted with pride that his decision to go in immediate pursuit of Khusrau was one of the finest examples of his leadership.[51]

Like his grandfather at the onset of Khusrau's rebellion, Aurangzeb reacted with a combination of disbelief, anxiety, and fear when he first heard that his fourth son Akbar had turned against him. Akbar surprised him with an army numbering in the tens of thousands at a time when Aurangzeb had fewer than a thousand soldiers under his command. According to one near contemporary source, there was "great panic in the imperial camp and widespread confusion. ... No one," presumably including the emperor, "had any hope of escaping from this calamity."[52] Aurangzeb sent an immediate order to his oldest surviving son Mu'azzam – who was a week or more away – commanding him to come to the imperial camp at once. Mu'azzam arrived within a matter of days along with ten thousand horsemen. Even as he welcomed the prince's arrival, however, Aurangzeb had his artillery trained on Mu'azzam's army; he commanded Mu'azzam to come unaccompanied by any troops to their first meeting. Aurangzeb initially suspected that Mu'azzam might also take advantage of his vulnerability and betray him. It was only after he had been reassured of Mu'azzam's loyalty that Aurangzeb turned his attention back to dealing with Akbar, who, in the meantime, had been trying to shore up his own networks of political and military support.

Over the next week, despite being "extremely anxious (*mukaddar*) by the circulation of all kinds of news,"[53] Aurangzeb crafted a ruse to fool Akbar's Rajput allies into believing that the prince's "rebellion" was nothing more than a trap set by Aurangzeb and Akbar to massacre them on the day of the battle. Fearing for their lives and having become suspicious of Akbar's intentions, the Rajputs abandoned the prince's camp under cover of darkness on the eve of the battle against Aurangzeb. Left with no more than a few hundred supporters, Akbar was in turn forced to flee.[54] Thus ensued a five-year-long pursuit of Akbar by Aurangzeb's

---

[51] Ibid., p. 40.
[52] K. Khan, *Muntakhab al-Labab*, vol. 2, p. 266.
[53] Ibid., p. 267.
[54] Ibid., pp. 268–70.

forces; any attempts at negotiation were rejected. Akbar was finally left with no choice but to flee India for Safavid Iran where he died in 1704. In contrast to Jahangir's occasional murmurings of sadness and regret, Aurangzeb never showed any emotion when discussing Akbar's rebellion or even Muhammad Sultan's earlier one.

For the rebelling prince, the moment of breaking away seems to have been energizing and emboldened him to speak his mind. Khusrau, for instance, angrily denounced Jahangir's bad faith and broken promises. He also publicly decried Jahangir's poor judgment in surrounding himself with so many unscrupulous and self-serving advisors. Less than two decades later, Khurram publicly accused his stepmother Nur Jahan of being power hungry and condemned his father for allowing a woman to exercise so much authority. So also, in a stinging 1683 letter, Akbar hurled a long string of accusations at Aurangzeb for failing to be a good father; being fool hardy, power hungry, and a religious hypocrite; following doomed policies that undercut the empire's reputation for justice and wisdom; allowing atrocities to be committed in the Deccan; replacing the old nobility with inefficient ministers and untrustworthy nobles; and being a regicide and a fili-cide.[55] Akbar's bold tone shocked contemporary observers, and even Manucci commented that the prince was way out of line.[56] Manucci further remarked that Akbar's rebellion in the early 1680s had thrown the entire "kingdom into confusion."[57] Once the dust had settled, however, such rebellions injected fresh energy into the political system, thus renewing it.

A close look at the way Khurram's rebellion against Jahangir unfolded between the fall of 1623 and the winter of 1624 reveals how this might happen. This account also conveys the long, drawn-out character of some princely rebellions. These were not always single battles, over in days or weeks. Rather, after a clear statement of antag-onism, the rebellion of a prince might drag on for years. Its conclusion would necessitate either imprisonment of the emperor or, much more likely, capture of the prince himself and the subsequent punishment of his close supporters.

[55] B. N. Reu, "Letters Exchanged between Emperor Aurangzeb and His Son Prince Muhammad Akbar," *Procs. Ind. Hist. Cong.* 2 (1938): 356–60.
[56] Niccolao Manucci, *Mogul India*, vol. 2, p. 229.
[57] Ibid., p. 235.

### PRINCE KHURRAM'S STRUGGLES, 1623–4: A CASE STUDY

Khurram went into rebellion against Jahangir in the summer of 1622. After a series of military setbacks in Hindustan and the Deccan, Khurram was finally forced to take his rebellion to the eastern parts of the Mughal Empire – to Orissa, Bengal, and Bihar. Over almost a year, he fashioned a place for himself in the networks of this region. This would have appeared to him to be a necessary first step toward cultivating the kind of strong base for rebellion such as his father had built in Allahabad in the early 1600s. Here, he gained the support of groups either previously opposed to or only poorly integrated into the networks of imperial favor. His actions helped speed up processes whereby Mughal control over the region, fairly shallow prior to the 1620s, was deepened. Over subsequent decades, the Mughals built on these advances to successfully expand Bengal's frontiers to the east and also to transform Bengal into a partic-ularly wealthy province of the empire. Khurram's rebellion played a central, if rarely acknowledged, role in this longer story.

In the early 1620s, Jahangir's health had so deteriorated that he was often incapacitated for weeks if not months on end. In the withering heat of June 1622, when Khurram took to the field to oppose him, Jahangir complained, "Is it really necessary for me, with my illness and weakness, to get on a horse and gallop around in such hot weather, which is extremely disagreeable to me, running off after such an undu-tiful son?"[58]

But by November 1623, Khurram had been driven to the border between Orissa and Golkonda. At that point, the prince commanded a tired and worn-out force that ranged from four to six thousand cavalry and ten to twelve thousand infantry and camp followers. However, benefiting from the paralysis or indifference of the most senior Mughal generals who were supposed to have opposed him, Khurram established his authority over both Orissa and Bengal within a matter of months.

### Consolidating in the Eastern Regions

After defeating and killing the Mughal governor of Bengal, Khurram rewarded his loyalists by distributing much of the Rs. 3–4 million in captured war booty. He also began to award imperial titles, *mansab*s,

---

[58] Jahangir, *The Jahangirnama*, pp. 387; Jahangir, *Jahangirnama*, p. 403.

and administrative appointments to his primary supporters. Khurram's awards were a prelude to a wholesale assault on imperial prerogatives. Among them were the rights to hold elephant fights, to receive elephants as *peshkash* (tribute), to send *farman*s (orders emanating from an emperor), to have the *khutba* (public sermons) read in the name of the emperor, to undertake royal hunts, and to hold *jharoka*s (public viewings).[59] Although Khurram never openly proclaimed himself king (unlike Salim who did so during his rebellion), the prince played the part of a de facto emperor, thus contesting Jahangir's legitimacy.

Because Khurram needed revenues to flow uninterruptedly into the provincial coffers, he had to placate the local imperial officials. After placing his own loyalists within the provincial administration, Khurram proceeded to confirm most high-ranking imperial officials in their old posts. In the case of particularly valuable individuals, such as Mirza Nathan, who had greatly impressed the prince in his being "conversant with the management of the affairs of Bengal and of the tax-collectors and the *mutasaddi*s of the late Ibrahim Khan," Khurram offered enhanced *mansab*s and other rewards.[60]

Khurram's strategy for winning over a large and influential network of imperial administrators paid rich dividends, as we can judge by their role in the prince's invasion of Bihar, Awadh, and Allahabad. Aside from ensuring the smooth flow of Bengal's revenues to Khurram's front-line armies, these administrators also helped expedite the movement of huge stores of gunpowder, lead, iron, stone shot, and corn to the prince's base camp in Bihar.[61]

Not limited to such logistical aid, the support of Mughal officials was also essential in bolstering the prince's depleted forces as they advanced. Given Bengal's role as a frontier province that had seen little peace since the Mughals first invaded it in 1574, imperial officials such as Mirza Nathan tended to maintain larger personal contingents than were actually required by their *mansab* ranks. Thus Mirza Nathan's *mansab* rank demanded that he employ fewer than 100 cavalry, yet he maintained double that number of horsemen and 350 matchlock men.[62] Moreover, Mughal nobles such as the Mirza had networks that enabled them to mobilize large armies at short notice; sources speak of his rounding up 1,000 archers, horsemen, infantrymen, and musketeers from the region of Hajo and 4,000 Garuan

---

[59] Nathan, *Baharistan-i-Ghaybi*, vol. 2, pp. 712, 713, 714, 742, 773, 785.

[60] Ibid., pp. 728, 741, 747.

[61] Ibid., p. 740; B. P. Ambashthya, "Rebellions of Prince Salim and Prince Khurram in Bihar," *Journal of the Bihar and Orissa Research Society* 45 (1959): 337.

[62] Nathan, *Baharistan-i-Ghaybi*, vol. 1, p. 417.

tribesmen around Amjunga (Kamrup) on one occasion.[63] Over the course of his career in Bengal, Mirza Nathan also recruited large numbers of Usmani Afghans to fight in his various campaigns.[64] Muhammad Taqi/ Shah Quli Khan, Khurram's appointee to the governorship of Orissa, once asked Mirza Nathan to recruit and send 5,000 cavalry to Orissa. The Khan gave great latitude to Mirza Nathan, telling him he could "recommend whomsoever you consider fit for the imperial *mansab*. Please fix the salaries of those whom you consider fit for my service and pay them all their expenses. Please write about what is spent by you ... so that it may be paid off by a bill of exchange."[65]

Khurram also moved to establish strong ties to the *zamindari* elite of Bengal and Orissa, and he paid particular attention to those *zamindars* who already had ties to the Mughal administration. As local power holders and masters of their own troops and retainers, *zamindars* often were a crucial prop for the maintenance of Mughal authority in any province. This was especially true in Bengal, where Mughal personnel were not just thinly spread across the *suba*, but also heavily employed in more pressing military activities on the frontiers with Assam and Arakan. On his arrival in Khurda (Orissa), Khurram hosted Raja Purushottam, Raja Pancha, Raja Nilgiri, Bajadhar, Raja Narsingh Deva, and other *zamindars*. They "presented themselves and obtained the honor of kissing the ground."[66] Sensing an opportunity to reap monetary and political rewards, these men joined Khurram on his northward march against the forces of the then governor of Bengal, Ibrahim Khan Fath Jang. Once in Bengal, the prince recruited even more *zamindars* to join him in defeating the hapless governor. For Khurram recognized that any successful invasion of Bihar, Allahabad, and Awadh would depend on *zamindari* support, since they were the largest suppliers of naval vessels, indispensable to any military expedition in the eastern riverine regions of the empire.

Khurram thus advanced as far as the city of Allahabad. Following the prince's 1624 defeat at the Battle of Tons at the hands of Jahangir's forces, however, the prince lost the support of the Bengal *zamindars*, whose capacity to weaken the prince's hold over Bengal became immediately apparent as they rose in revolt against Khurram's *subahdar* in Bengal, Darab Khan, and besieged his residence in Dhaka. A similar revolt

[63] Ibid., vol. 2, pp. 528, 542.
[64] Ibid., p. 587.
[65] Ibid., p. 744.
[66] Ibid., p. 688; Charles Stewart, *History of Bengal* (Delhi, repr. 1971), p. 307.

followed shortly thereafter among Orissa's *zamindar*s – who now repledged their fealty to Jahangir's representatives.

In Bihar, too, Khurram had wooed prominent local *zamindar*s, among them Raja Narayan Mal Ujjainiya,[67] who was to prove a loyal ally even after members of his own family deserted to Jahangir's forces on the eve of the Battle of Tons.[68] Although the Raja was subsequently forced to submit to Jahangir, Khurram rewarded his loyalty after his accession to the Mughal throne by making him an imperial *mansabdar*.[69] Raja Narayan Mal's inclusion among the ranks of the Mughal nobility is an important reminder of the critical role princely rebellions played in accommodating otherwise obscure and local-level networks within the larger framework of Mughal power. Following Raja Narayan Mal's success in attaining an imperial *mansab*, the hitherto rebellious Ujjainiyas were to become an important and steady source of manpower for the Mughal army through the rest of the seventeenth century. In addition, they assisted Mughal efforts to reinforce imperial authority in the region around Rohtas and Shahabad.[70] Given their participation in a 1610 revolt against Jahangir – led by a pretender claiming to be Jahangir's son Khusrau – this is a remarkable turnabout.

## Roping in Religious Networks

While in the East, Khurram attempted to harness the support of local Muslim leaders. To this end, he undertook several *ziarat*s (pilgrimages) to important Muslim shrines. Shrines in Bengal had played an especially critical role in corralling the manpower necessary to clear the region's thick forests as well as facilitating trade and credit. As Richard Eaton has clearly shown, they served as focal points for shaping Bengali Muslim identity and as hinges between local and translocal articulations of Islam.[71] Khurram began his efforts to link

---

[67] Nathan, *Baharistan-i-Ghaybi*, vol. 2, pp. 726, 732.

[68] Ibid., p. 779. Bihar's *zamindar*s also largely turned on Khurram after Tons, killing the prince's loyalists when they had an opportunity. Thus, for example, Sayyid Mubarak Manikpuri was killed as he attempted to collect Rs. 200,000 from his *jagir*s in Sulaymanabad and Jahanabad before fleeing onward to Bengal. Nathan, *Baharistan-i-Ghaybi*, vol. 2, p. 782.

[69] On his death in 1637, Raja Narayan had reached the rank of 1500/1000. 'Abd al-Hamid Lahawri, *Padshahnamah*, ed. Kabir-ud-din Ahmad and Abdul Rahim, vol. 1 (Calcutta, 1867), pp. 22, 305.

[70] Ahmad Raza Khan, "Suba of Bihar under the Mughals, 1582–1707," unpublished Ph.D. dissertation, Aligarh Muslim University (1982), pp. 176–7.

[71] Richard M. Eaton, *The Rise of Islam and the Bengal Frontier, 1204–1760* (Delhi, repr. 1994), pp. 71–94, 207–19, 228–67.

these shrines to his emerging authority at the important shrine complex of
Shaikh Nur Qutb-i 'Alam in Pandua. Nur Qutb-i 'Alam (d. 1415) was known
as a miracle worker and widely considered the most important saint in the
*suba*. On arriving at the Shaikh's tomb, Khurram recited the *fatiha* (prayer for
the dead) and gave an offering of Rs. 4,000 to the shrine's custodians.[72] He
then traveled to Qadam Rasul in Rasulpur-Nabiganj, where he prayed at the
site of a footprint purported to be that of the Prophet Muhammad. Here, too,
Khurram distributed money to the guardians of the shrine.[73] During the
course of his stay in Bengal, Khurram also visited the shrine of Bahram Saqa
Burdwani in Burdwan, a minor saint whose significance lay in his close ties to
Khurram's great-grandfather Humayun; his shrine had continued to be
important to Nur Jahan and Jahangir.[74]

Following his arrival in Bihar, Khurram undertook another round of
pilgrimages. Among them was a *ziarat* to the tomb of thirteenth-century
mystic Shaikh Yahya Maneri. Shaikh Yahya's tomb stood at the center of a
series of important familial shrine complexes in Bihar (including those of
the Shaikh's father-in-law Shaikh Shihab-ud-Din in Jethuli and his sister-
in-law Bibi Kamalo in Gaya). Besides distributing a large amount of
money, Khurram also endowed a *degh* (food cauldron) for serving
travelers, pilgrims, and supplicants who visited the shrine. His patronage
won him popularity, as illustrated in the large number of soldiers who
flocked to his standard during the course of his two-day visit.[75]

Khurram cultivated relations with other religiously connected families
as well. Among them were the descendants of Shah Daula, one of the first
Sufis to venture to and settle in Bengal. In late 1623, Khurram took the
unusual step of visiting the Shah's family in their ancestral home in the
village of Bhaga, where members of Shah Daula's family held important
positions as religious figures and major landlords.[76] Khurram also visited
Shaikh Hameed Danishmand Mangalkot (d. 1659) in his hometown of
Mangalkot. (One of Shaikh Hameed's disciples, Mufti 'Abd-ul-Rahman
Kabuli, was a member of Khurram's retinue.) As the leading Naqshbandi
*pir* in Bengal and the person most responsible for introducing the *tariqa* in

---

[72] Nathan, *Baharistan-i-Ghaybi*, vol. 2, p. 707.

[73] Ibid., p. 710.

[74] Nur Jahan's first husband (Sher Afgan) and Jahangir's favorite foster brother (Qutbuddin
Khan Koka) were both buried within the confines of the shrine after they were killed in a
fracas that saw them on opposite sides. Ijaz-ul-Haq Quddusi, *Tazkira-i Sufiya-i Bangal*
(Lahore, 1965), pp. 97–8, 100, 102–4.

[75] Shaikh Kafeel Turabi, *Tazkira-i Marjan* (Patna, 1881), pp. 22–3.

[76] Quddusi, *Tazkira-i Sufiya-i Bangal*, pp. 359–60.

the *suba*, Shaikh Hameed was a well-known and popular figure. The Shaikh, however, was especially admired for maintaining a well-endowed *madrassa* that drew students from all over the eastern parts of the Mughal Empire.[77] Being a disciple of the famous Naqshbandi scholar Shaikh Ahmad Sirhindi, Shaikh Hameed enjoyed extensive contacts with Naqshbandis all across northern India.[78] On receiving the Shaikh's blessings for all his future endeavors, Khurram endowed Shaikh Hameed's family with a massive *madad-i ma'ash* grant of forty-two villages that he reconfirmed following his accession to the Mughal throne in 1628.[79]

Continuing with his patronage of the region's Islamic religious establishment, the prince confirmed an earlier *madad-i ma'ash* grant to the family of Makhdum Saiyid Hasan in 1624. They were members of an influential network of Zaidi Sayyids who had spread across the districts of Saran, Muzaffarpur, Patna, and Bhagalpur in Bihar.[80] The previous year, in 1623, Khurram awarded a *madad* grant in the village of Rampur (Bihar) to Shaikh 'Abdus Salam and Shaikh Muhammad, and another grant in the village of Chak Naseer (Bihar) to Maulana Zia.[81] When Khurram abstained from giving *madad* grants, he gave cash instead, as in the case of Shaikh 'Abdullah of Ghazipur (Bengal).[82] Although this Shaikh was a minor religious figure, his son, Miyan Saiyid Nizam-ud-Din of Maltipur, had a strong following especially among certain lower-ranking Mughal officials based in Bengal. (Among them was Mirza Nathan, who, after his decision to desert Khurram, went to the holy man for guidance.[83])

Khurram worked hard to project an image of personal piety and interest in the well-being of all Muslims. He described his rebellion as intended to protect Muslims and Muslim interests. At the same time, the prince strictly adhered to an orthopractic regime of Islamic ritual. Building on his 1621 decision to give up alcohol,[84] Khurram maintained all his Ramadan fasts during his stint in Bengal and Bihar. His decision drew an amazed reaction from Mirza Nathan, who noted that

---

[77] S. A. A. Rizvi, *A History of Sufism in India*, vol. 2 (Delhi, 1992), p. 231; Tapan Raychaudhuri, *Bengal under Akbar and Jahangir: An Introductory Study in Social History* (Delhi, 1969), p. 176.

[78] S. M. Ikram, *Rud-i Kausar* (Lahore, 1982), pp. 163–7, 510.

[79] Ibid., pp. 163–7, 510, 513.

[80] S. H. Askari, "Documents Relating to an Old Family of Sufi Saints in Bihar," *Procs. Ind. Hist. Rec. Com.* 26 (1949): 1.

[81] *Some Farmans, Sanads and Parwanas*, ed. K. K. Datta (Patna, 1962), pp. 10, 19.

[82] Nathan, *Baharistan-i-Ghaybi*, vol. 2, pp. 728–29.

[83] Ibid., 786.

[84] S. Lahori, *'Amal-i Salih*, vol. 1, p. 113.

[I]t was so extremely hot ... men and beasts suffered great hardship and very few men could keep fast. Though kings are not answerable for (nonobservance of) prayers and fasting and are responsible only for their dispensation of justice, yet His Royal Highness through his love of God and his desire for Divine favors, kept his fast in spite of this torture of heat.[85]

Mirza Nathan was not the only person who was impressed. Large numbers of Bengal-based Sufis and *'alims* considered the prince's piety sufficient reason to join his rebellion.[86]

### Befriending Afghans and Portuguese

In the 1620s, the Afghans were a powerful force in Bengal. Although the Mughals had been fairly successful in grinding down Afghan resistance to Mughal expansion in other parts of eastern India, this was not so in Bengal when Khurram arrived. A massive Afghan rebellion led by Musa Khan and Usman Khan had in fact rocked the province as recently as the early 1610s. This and other rebellions were especially threatening when the Afghans made common cause with the Portuguese or the Arakan-based Mags. Although Khurram undoubtedly viewed the Afghans as a threat, the prince also saw them as potential allies in his fight against Jahangir. As a result, shortly after crossing into Orissa from Golkonda, Khurram wrote to all important Afghan clan leaders soliciting their support. Many responded by sending contingents of troops to augment Khurram's weak forces. Shortly thereafter, Afghans played a key role in Khurram's efforts to defeat Ibrahim Khan, the governor of the province.[87]

Following the death of Ibrahim Khan, other prominent Afghans, including Haidar Khan, Masum Khan, Khwaja Daud, and Khwaja Ibrahim, joined Khurram's service.[88] Most important of all, however, was the allegiance of Pahar Khan and Adil Khan, who had earlier served as Ibrahim Khan's naval commanders.[89] Their willingness to serve Khurram helped

[85] Nathan, *Baharistan-i-Ghaybi*, vol. 2, p. 721.

[86] Ibid., p. 763.

[87] Stewart, *History of Bengal*, pp. 226, 228; Nathan, *Baharistan-i-Ghaybi*, vol. 2, pp. 689, 692.

[88] Nathan, *Baharistan-i-Ghaybi*, vol. 2, pp. 689, 692, 727. The confluence of interests between Khurram and long-standing Afghan opponents of Mughal rule in Bengal is perhaps best suggested by the lineage of Masum Khan and the two Khwajas. Masum Khan was son of Musa Khan and the two Khwajas were respectively the son and nephew of Usman Khan. Musa and Usman Khan had led the Afghan rebellion of the early 1610s. Ibid., pp. 689, 692.

[89] Ibid., pp. 710, 727.

alleviate the prince's otherwise complete dependence on Bengal's *zamindars* to provide naval support for his campaign.

Khurram appointed high-profile Afghans in his own princely entourage, including Darya Khan Rohilla, Bahadur Khan Rohilla, Babu Khan Barij, and 'Ali Khan Niyazi. Darya Khan Rohilla and Bahadur Khan Rohilla recruited Afghans almost exclusively in order to build their own military contingents.[90] Unfortunately, Darya Khan proved to be a hard taskmaster who eventually succeeded in alienating most of the Bengal-based Afghans who served under him. The Afghans deserted the Khan en masse after Khurram's defeat at the Battle of Tons. The collapse of the Khan's Afghan contingents coincided with the decision by most of Khurram's other Afghan allies to abandon his cause after it became clear that the prince had neither the resources nor the will to continue his rebellion in Bengal.

Khurram's association with Bengal's Afghan networks was short lived. Yet, it had a crucial long-term impact. Drawn as they were into Khurram's rebellion, many Afghans were exposed for the first time to the benefits of service under the Mughals. Once Jahangir's authority was reasserted in Bengal, many formerly recalcitrant Afghan chiefs signed up to serve under the emperor. In so doing, they parlayed the strength of their clan networks and entrenched political status in eastern Bihar and Bengal for access to the wealth and privileges that the Mughals afforded their supporters. From the mid-1620s onward, until the 1690s, large-scale Afghan rebellions became a thing of the past. In addition, the Afghans played a critical role in aiding the Mughals in ridding Bengal of the Portuguese and pushing the frontiers of the empire into present-day Assam and toward the city of Chittagong (along the Bay of Bengal). By the 1630s, an earlier antagonistic relationship between the Afghans and the Mughals evolved into a partnership. As in so many previous instances, a princely rebellion proved to be the catalyst that drew new networks into the framework of the empire and made possible a greater degree of Mughal control over formerly unsettled regions.

The other important group in Bengal was composed of the Portuguese and their Indian Christian allies. The Portuguese presence in the region dated back to 1514 when they first established settlements at Pipli (Orissa) and Hijli (Bengal). By the first decade of the seventeenth century, they were entrenched in Bengal's economy, with their superior naval technology

---

[90] Ibid., p. 734; Muzaffar Husain Khan Sulaimani, *Nama-i Muzaffari*, vol. 2 (Lucknow, 1917), p. 464.

ensuring a virtual monopoly over Bengal's export trade in cotton, textiles, silk, sugar, purified butter, rice, indigo, pepper, saltpeter, lac, wax, and slaves. The Portuguese successfully played Bengal's and Arakan's most powerful political groups against each other. Aside from having trading factories in the settlements of Chittagong, Satgaon, Hugli, Sripur, Dhaka, Chandikan, Katrabhu, Midnapur, and Jessore, Portuguese adventurers also managed to temporarily carve out an independent island kingdom on Sondip Island in the deltaic region of Bengal.[91]

Thanks to Portuguese control over Bengal's shipping lanes and internal waterways, various Mughal *subahdar*s were unable to subjugate them.[92] Just before Khurram's invasion of Bengal, Ibrahim Khan sought an accommodation with them. In return for Portuguese naval support, the Khan promised to protect their trading interests against the Dutch and English and also to safeguard their control over the river trade between Patna (Bihar) and Hugli (Bengal). Following Khurram's invasion of Bengal, the Portuguese betrayed Ibrahim Khan. Although Michael Rodriguez, the highest-ranking Portuguese official in the region, refused Khurram's request for cannon and Portuguese gunners, he did offer other assistance to Khurram in the pivotal battle against Ibrahim Khan.[93] Following the Khan's death, a number of Portuguese officers joined Khurram's service. They brought with them sizable contingents of Portuguese gunners and ships. Over the next few months, the Portuguese played a critical role in ferrying supplies for Khurram's troops as they advanced westward into Bihar and Allahabad.[94]

Just before the Battle of Tons, however, imperial forces lured the Portuguese with promises of money and goods, severely weakening Khurram and contributing to his defeat. To add to Khurram's woes, following their desertion, the Portuguese sailed down the Ganges attacking Mughal settlements and undermining Khurram's already tenuous political authority.[95] Although Khurram was absolutely powerless to punish the Portuguese for their betrayal, he did not forget, and, two years after his accession to the Mughal throne, he ordered the *subahdar* of Bengal, Qasim Khan, to attack the primary Portuguese settlement at Hugli. The capture of Hugli led to the destruction of Portuguese power, with important implications for the

[91] Raychaudhuri, *Bengal under Akbar and Jahangir*, pp. 94–6, 103, 244–5.
[92] Nathan, *Baharistan-i-Ghaybi*, vol. 1, p. 334; vol. 2, p. 635.
[93] Ibid., pp. 688–9, 693–4; Stewart, *History of Bengal*, p. 227; Jadunath Sarkar, *The History of Bengal*, vol. 2 (Calcutta, 1948), p. 308.
[94] Nathan, *Baharistan-i-Ghaybi*, vol. 2, pp. 734, 736, 745.
[95] Ibid., pp. 749–50, 752–3.

history of the entire region. Aside from paving the way for the uncontested assertion of Mughal control over Bengal, the conclusive removal of the Portuguese allowed the Mughals to focus their expansionist ambitions farther to the east.

Khurram's dreams of establishing himself in Orissa, Bengal, and Bihar crumbled with his defeat at the Battle of Tons in October 1624. Although the prince had extended his authority as far as Awadh and eastern Allahabad, his forces were tired and he was forced to retreat back to Bengal in the face of the advancing imperial army led by Mahabat Khan and Prince Parvez, Khurram's half brother. With the imperial forces in hot pursuit, Khurram was unable to regroup his forces, and he fled from Bengal to Orissa and onward to the Deccan. After Khurram's departure from Bengal at the end of 1624, Jahangir coerced and bribed in order to reassert his authority across the region, often building on the very foundations laid by Khurram over the previous year.

## THE GEOGRAPHY OF REBELLION

Jos Gommans's study of Mughal warfare throws an interesting light on the geography of princely rebellions. Gommans argues that the Mughal Empire had to contend with two types of frontiers (he acknowledges that these are not to be conceived as overly rigid) to establish its control over northern and central India – the first ecological and the second infrastructural. The first broadly separated arid northwestern and central India from humid eastern and northeastern India, divided by the monsoons.[96] The former was characterized by lower population density, "dry, savannah-like marchland intersected by cultivated zones," and the presence of significant nomadic communities that moved with their livestock. The latter, in contrast, received higher levels of year-round precipitation and was more densely populated, intensely cultivated, and largely inhospitable to nomadic pastoral production.

Gommans describes the second frontier as a function of India's network of long-distance communication routes. It was along these *limites* that India's financial and commercial resources as well as supplies of goods and people flowed. Control over these routes helped connect various administrative and commercial centers to one another and to their agrarian hinterlands. This, in turn, enabled the conversion of agricultural products into monetary wealth.[97]

---

[96] Jos Gommans, *Mughal Warfare* (New York, 2002), pp. 8–15.
[97] Ibid., pp. 15–22.

According to Gommans, these dual frontiers intersected to create five or six "nuclear zones or bases of political power" that featured agrarian surpluses, wide-ranging marchlands and long-distance commercial routes, sufficient fighting forces, and easy access to war animals and beasts of burden.[98] It was the Mughals' ability to extend their control over all four north Indian zones – broadly centered on Bengal, Agra-Rajasthan-Lahore, Malwa-Khandesh, and Kabul – by the end of Akbar's reign that effectively guaranteed their control over much of northern India through the seventeenth century. Importantly, princely rebellions invariably emerged from or were drawn to these nuclear zones thanks to their wealth in men, food, fodder, and money, as well as space to maneuver armies.

Locating the princely rebellions from the 1540s to 1681 within Gommans's cartography, it is clear that all of them sought to assert control over at least one of India's nuclear zones. In the case of Kamran, it was Kabul; the Mirzas, Delhi then Malwa; Salim, Ajmer then Agra; Khusrau, Lahore; Akbar, Rajasthan then Malwa-Khandesh. Khurram's five-year-long migratory rebellion in the 1620s was a little more complicated in its targets: Khandesh-Malwa, then Agra-Delhi, then Malwa-Khandesh, then Golkonda, then Bengal, then Khandesh-Malwa, and finally Ajmer. Failure to establish control over at least one region meant a swift end for a princely rebellion and the reassertion of imperial authority. With an eye to connecting Gommans's insights with the specificity of princely rebellions, two examples are examined next.

Our first example is Salim's 1599 rebellion. Salim launched this rebellion from Ajmer, a city smack in the center of the Mughal Empire and astride a number of militarily and economically important roads. Ajmer also enjoyed all the advantages of an arid, dry-land strongpoint. None was more important than its easy access to both seasonal military labor and the riches of a thriving pastoral economy, especially horses and camels. Salim went into rebellion in November 1599 to take full advantage of northern India's fighting season.

From Ajmer, Salim struck out – unsuccessfully as it happens – against Agra. That city's importance derived from the location of the Mughal treasury there and its position astride the commercial routes of both the Grand Trunk Road and the River Jamuna. Adding to Agra's value were the rich agricultural lands around it and also its proximity to the fighting landscapes of the arid zone (contemporary Rajashthan and Madhya Pradesh). Given the area's many advantages, Emperor Akbar, in turn, was determined

---

[98] Ibid., p. 22.

that Agra should not be surrendered without a fight. Strict instructions were sent to the imperial officers there to resist the prince. When Salim arrived outside Agra, he found the city in a defensive posture, its gates closed and soldiers manning its walls. Lacking the resources to undertake a lengthy siege, and fearing that a prolonged attack risked the possibility of full-scale conflict with Akbar, Salim instead settled on sacking the region around Agra and then decamping by boat to Allahabad.

Despite Allahabad's many strengths – including a relatively stable agrarian base and close proximity to dry-land spaces for fighting – the region did not offer Salim the long-term capacity to match Akbar's power, which was based on his undisputed control over what Gommans describes as north India's three major nuclear zones.

Rather than militarily confronting Salim, Akbar slowly sapped his son's rebellion. Containing the prince in Allahabad and gradually peeling away his supporters through financial and political inducements, Akbar forced the prince to maintain a standing and ruinously expensive army. Salim had once hoped to leverage his control over Allahabad into greater political authority under his father, but Akbar began to retract concessions as the prince's economic and military position faltered. By the summer of 1604, Salim was forced to surrender. He did so without a fight. Akbar's ability to grind down his son's rebellion depended on denying Salim access to key centers of power in northern India. Taking a page from Akbar's playbook, Salim/Jahangir did the same to his rebellious son Khurram between 1622 and 1627. Like Akbar before him, Jahangir was able to parry his own son's challenge.

Khurram's five-year-long rebellion was more complicated than Salim's. From his power base of Khandesh (which offered access to cheap and plentiful wheat and millet, rich pasturelands, wide marchlands, and great commercial wealth thanks to its control of three long-distance routes: northward to Agra and the Indo-Gangetic plain, southward to the heart of the Deccan plateau, and westward to Gujarat and northern Konkan), Khurram also made an unsuccessful bid to seize Agra in 1622. Military defeat forced him back to Khandesh, and then in retreat to Golkonda, which lay beyond the control of the Mughal Empire. The Golkonda ruler's refusal of refuge led to his flight in 1623 toward Bengal (detailed in the previous sections).

According to Gommans, Bengal is the only nuclear zone in what he characterizes as the humid/monsoon zone. Thanks to long rainy seasons, an abundance of rivers, and a dynamic environmental frontier, Bengal's agricultural (especially rice-growing) capacity was rapidly expanding throughout the medieval period. This, in turn, enabled an increasing population and a growing industrial sector. By the early 1600s, Bengal was a major region for the manufacture of cotton textiles and silk cloths. At the end of a long chain of rivers draining Hindustan, the Tibetan plateau, and northeastern India, Bengal was also a key region for the import and export of huge stores of goods.

In addition, Bengal had two military advantages relative to other parts of India. The first was access to large supplies of elephants. The second was the relative ineffectiveness of cavalry-based armies because of the dense networks of rivers and the humid climate, which were not welcoming to horses. After establishing himself in Bengal in early 1624, Khurram easily conquered adjoining Bihar. As he moved eastward into Awadh and Allahabad, however, he began to hit the limits of what a Bengal-based, humid-zone army could achieve. Lacking large numbers of horses and heavily dependent on ships provided by Bengal's *zamindars* and the Portuguese that were ill suited for navigating the mid-Gangetic region, Khurram's campaign faltered, culminating in his flight out of Bengal and return to Golkonda.

Over the next three years, Khurram bounced between or near various nuclear zones hoping to gain political traction. Ultimately, he found a safe base on the border between Ahmadnagar and Khandesh. There he slowly rebuilt his forces. When news of Jahangir's death arrived in October 1627, Khurram was ready to assert his right to the Mughal throne.

An examination of these events underscores the powerful geographical underpinning of princely rebellions. Princes clearly had no chance of political success without control over one or more of the nuclear zones of power; even control of one zone did not measurably better the odds of overthrowing a sitting emperor. Further, as the Mughal Empire grew and strengthened, bringing into its control more and more territory, and eventually all of India's major nuclear zones, the ability of a prince to mount and sustain a rebellion diminished. The ratio of power between emperors and challenger princes had conclusively shifted against the princes by the last decades of the seventeenth century.

Thus, Kamran's rebellion in the 1540s proved long and threatening precisely because Humayun initially had no substantial base of his own. In effect, Humayun was forced to engage in a war of attrition that entailed first taking Kabul, then slowly turning its resources against Kamran. This was a process that took time and was also prone to reversal. By contrast, Aurangzeb's undisputed control over the resources of Kabul, Agra-Delhi-Lahore, Bengal, and Malwa-Khandesh in the early 1680s made it impossible for Akbar to sustain a long-term rebellion. After 1687 and the conquest of

Golkonda – Gommans's fifth major zone of power – the odds of a Mughal Prince successfully taking on the emperor diminished even further. So much so that despite his age and serious questions about his political and military judgment, Aurangzeb did not face a rebellious son toward the end of his life. He was the first Mughal emperor since the 1550s to escape that fate.

How precisely Gommans's nuclear zones played into the sociopolitical machinations unfolding during a princely rebellion is a topic worthy of further study. Here, a prince might have been sent as governor to a particular province, one that precisely enclosed a nuclear zone. There, a prince may have established his stronghold on the basis of his existing ties to the region's leaders and groups, such that we would have to say that Gommans's zones were only a secondary factor or not a factor at all. For our purposes here, suffice it to say that princes brought Mughal state structures and a Mughal ethos to a region's inhabitants, wherever that region may be and whatever its resources.

We now turn to the ways in which imperial reactions to princely rebellions set in motion complementary processes that also resulted in embedding a state-centered Mughal political culture.

## THE EMPEROR STRIKES BACK

Historian Marcel Henaff argues that it is in the very nature of power to be public, to be performed and witnessed. Power therefore continuously "stages" and restages itself.[99] It is not so much an ineffable quality held by the emperor or the institution of the court as it is an essential quality variously made manifest. As James Scott suggests, in order to maintain their power, the powerful must constantly make their power visible, to demonstrate it to the powerless to keep them convinced and thus cowed.[100] A rebellion by a prince – its outbreak, the drama of its duration, and its aftermath – induced just such a restaging of imperial power. A challenge to the empire by one of its own afforded a particularly dramatic occasion for the emperor to reengage his power. The activation of social and political alliances whose management constituted imperial rule came front and center – calling in old obligations and debts; making overt assertions of the symbols of imperial power; and, when events had concluded, carrying out public retribution and the dishonoring of the prince and his supporters. This restaging of power in response to a princely

[99] Marcel Henaff, "The Stage of Power," *SubStance* 25, no. 2 (1996): 9.
[100] Scott, *Domination and the Arts of Resistance*.

rebellion strengthened the emperor's authority and ultimately consolidated imperial power.

To illustrate this point, we turn to Khusrau's failed 1606 rebellion during Emperor Jahangir's reign. Although this section is focused on Khusrau's rebellion, many of its generalizations about the embedding of imperial power and its legitimacy are applicable to other failed princely rebellions as well. The reasons and circumstances of Khusrau's rebellion are also briefly recounted here, returning to our earlier theme with the depiction of a particularly egregious example of imperial arrogance and princely affront. Emperor Jahangir turns out to have been as autocratic in his handling of his royal son's expectations as he was self-righteous in his reassertion of imperial power.

### Prince Khusrau Rebels

Upon Akbar's death in October 1605, Salim – now with the regnal name of Jahangir – ascended the imperial throne. Tension between him and his son Khusrau ran high; the young prince had powerful backers within the Mughal nobility who had hoped that he might succeed his grandfather Akbar, entirely sidestepping one generation. In the negotiations that accompanied Salim's peaceful accession, it was agreed that Khusrau should be given the governorship of Bengal. From Khusrau's perspective, this was an acceptable outcome. A contemporary eyewitness to these events, the chronicler Ni'matullah Khan Harvi, explains why:

> The prince desired to be sent far away from the court as a governor in order that he could rule as an independent king in the same way as his father Jahangir had done during his own princehood in Allahabad. There he [i.e., Salim] had spent his days in great ease and comfort and all the people acknowledged him as their king. Prince Khusrau fixed his sights on the same kind of "governorship."[101]

Over the next few months, however, Jahangir reneged on his promise to send Khusrau away. He had good reasons for doing so. Besides the fact that communication links with Bengal were poor, the province was also growing steadily wealthier. Then there was the issue of the province's relatively easy access to large pools of military manpower in eastern India. Jahangir seems to have rightly feared that Bengal would be transformed into a permanent appanage and a strong base of power from which

---

[101] Harvi, *Tarikh-i-Khan Jahani*, vol. 2, pp. 673–4. For a variant version, Ni'matullah Khan Harvi, *Tarikh-i Khan Jahani wa Makhzan-i Afghani*, trans. Muhammad Bashir Husain (Lahore, 1986), pp. 493–4.

Khusrau could continuously challenge him. The emperor was determined to prevent this from happening. Although he ultimately did permit Khusrau's *ataliq* (guardian) Raja Man Singh to travel to Bengal as Khusrau's *na'ib* (representative/deputy), he did not permit Khusrau to join him.

Jahangir used the excuse of "court intrigues," a minor rebellion in Awadh, and other dilatory tactics to postpone granting Khusrau permission to depart from the imperial court to Bengal. Simultaneously, the emperor appointed long-standing loyalists such as Wazir Khan Badauni and Lala Beg Baz Bahadur to independent and countervailing posts in Bengal and Bihar. Jahangir also maneuvered to pit his other sons against Khusrau. To that end, he awarded his second son Parvez adult status at age sixteen, temporarily proclaimed him heir, and appointed the young prince to lead an expedition of twenty thousand soldiers against the Rana of Mewar. Having asked a dozen or more high-ranking nobles to accompany his younger son's army, Jahangir set about weakening Khusrau's network of Rajput supporters by ordering important relatives of Raja Man Singh – Raja Jagannath (uncle), Madhu Singh (brother), and Maha Singh (grandson), among others – to join Parvez's expedition.[102] After Parvez's departure from the imperial court, Jahangir began to bestow favors on his third son Khurram, which must have added to Khusrau's growing fury.

Increasingly restricted to the grounds of his mansion and spied on by imperial informants who had penetrated his household, Khusrau became ever more hostile and disrespectful toward his father's closest advisors.[103] The final straw for Khusrau may very well have been receipt of information that Sharif Khan was lobbying Jahangir to consider blinding the prince.[104] Not only had he failed in his efforts to force Jahangir to allow him to take up his governorship, Khusrau had also come to fear for his life. Thus forced into rebellion, he slipped out of Agra one night in April 1606 with a small band of men and headed toward the Punjab, with a plan to use it as his base.

## Emperor Jahangir Fortifies

The very night Khusrau fled Agra, Jahangir took stock and renewed his ties with those areas through which Khusrau was suspected to have been

---

[102] K. Husaini, *Ma'asir-i-Jahangiri*, p. 71.
[103] Harvi, *Tarikh-i-Khan Jahani*, vol. 2, p. 674.
[104] Pelsaert, *A Dutch Chronicle*, p. 36.

fleeing. He called together his inner circle of advisors and ultimately appointed Shaikh Farid Bukhari to lead a pursuing army into the Punjab. The Shaikh knew the region well; he had in fact spent two years (1601–2) guarding the very highway between Agra and Lahore that Khusrau was now traveling. During his time in the Punjab, Shaikh Farid Bukhari seems to have attracted a number of locally based retainers. Among them was Daulat Khan Mayi, whose tribesmen, the Bhattis, were well known *zamindar*s in the region.[105] Another important servitor of the Shaikh was Sher Khan, an Afghan of the Tarin tribe, with strong ties in and around Lahore. Further, the Shaikh was a generous patron of the *'ulama'*, Sufi *khanaqah*s (hospices), saints, widows, and nobles across the region.[106] He is described in the sources as wont to feed five hundred people in a single sitting in addition to maintaining a diverse cavalry unit of at least three thousand men composed of Saiyids, Shaikhzadas, Chaghatais, and Afghans.[107] Many were drawn from the regions around Delhi and Lahore. Shaikh Farid Bukhari, this consummate networker, proved a savvy choice to lead the pursuit of Khusrau. His ties in the region served as a bulwark against Khusrau's efforts to cultivate support against his father.

It cannot be said that the court simply stood by and watched as Khusrau marched away. During the entire month of Khusrau's relatively short-lived rebellion, Jahangir undertook a flurry of initiatives. Pushing another nobleman to demonstrate his allegiance, the emperor sent Raja Basu, a prominent Pahari (mountain) Rajput, in pursuit of the prince. Jahangir himself followed in the footsteps of Shaikh Farid and Raja Basu, but the progress of the imperial army was slower, since the emperor saw fit to attend to his relationships with Sufi shrines along the way: he ordered Rs. 30,000 to be given to the custodians of the shrine of Shaikh Mu'in-ud-Din Chishti in Ajmer,[108] and he stopped to make large donations to the Delhi-based shrines of the Chishti luminaries Shaikh Nizam-ud-Din Auliya' and Shaikh Nasir-ud-Din Chiragh-i Dilli.[109] Indeed, it was likely a separate visit by Jahangir to the Delhi-based shrine of Naqshbandi saint Khwaja Baqi Billah (d. 1603) that prompted the famous Naqshbandi *pir* Khwaja Khawand Mahmud to later refuse to endorse Khusrau's rebellion. The main Naqshbandi following at this time

---

[105] Shah Nawaz Khan, *Maasiru-l-Umara*, ed. Abdur Rahim and Ashraf Ali, vol. 2 (Calcutta, 1890), pp. 24–30.

[106] Bhakkari, *Dhakhirat al-Khawanin*, vol. 1, pp. 138–9.

[107] Ibid., p. 141.

[108] Jahangir, *Jahangirnama*, p. 34.

[109] K. Husaini, *Ma'asir-i-Jahangiri*, p. 80.

came from various Central Asian immigrants, especially Uzbeks and Badakhshanis. Given that Badakhshanis were one of the main pillars of Khusrau's rebellion, Jahangir's efforts effectively split his son's support base. At the same time, Uzbek noblemen such as 'Abdi Khwaja and Abu'l Be Uzbek received imperial promotions (*mansabs*), and the latter was additionally gifted an unspecified sum of money and told to join Shaikh Farid Bukhari's expedition in the Punjab. Shaikh Farid Bukhari in turn received sums of money to entertain Abu'l Be Uzbek and his Uzbek followers. Jahangir justified such strategic largesse later in his memoirs. Referring to another sum of Rs. 900,000 given to Jamil Beg (a Badakhshani tribal chief and competitor of Khusrau's key supporter Hasan Beg Badakhshi), Jahangir explained that he made this gift to

encourage them [the Badakhshanis] ... with abundant hopes for the future; for these men were not yet quite at ease from their apprehensions, derived from recent refractory and rebellious proceedings [i.e., Khusrau's rebellion].[110]

He also ordered monies to be given to other prominent Badakhshanis "to distribute among their men and make them hopeful of my favor."[111]

Closer to home, Khusrau's rebellion prompted Jahangir to demand expressions of loyalty within the court itself. Jahangir gave his supporters images of himself and thereafter referred to them as his disciples. By doing so, he suggested that in serving him they were serving the Mughal Empire.[112]

On his way to the much-anticipated showdown with Khusrau, Jahangir visited the graves of emperors Akbar and Humayun, seeking the blessing of the Mughal lineage for his side in the battle. At the tombs, he publicly condemned Khusrau's rebellion, carefully distinguished it from his own earlier actions against Akbar, and also took the occasion to express contrition for his own earlier rebellion.[113] In the end, the contest between Khusrau and Jahangir was decided within a matter of hours at the Battle of Bhaironwal. Khusrau's force seems to have had little stomach for the fight thanks to a false rumor that the emperor himself had arrived to do battle. As his army collapsed around him, Khusrau heeded Hasan Beg

---

[110] Jahangir, *Autobiographical Memoirs*, p. 192. Jamil Beg later received an additional Rs. 7,000 for distribution among the Badakhshani cavalry. Jahangir, *Jahangirnama*, p. 36.

[111] Jahangir, *Jahangirnama*, p. 34.

[112] Ibid., p. 36. See also John F. Richards, "The Formulation of Imperial Authority under Akbar and Jahangir," in *Kingship and Authority in South Asia*, ed. John F. Richards (Madison, 1978), pp. 267–71.

[113] Jahangir, *Jahangirnama*, p. 38.

Badakhshi's call to withdraw from the field. Also on the advice of Hasan Beg, Khusrau fled in a northwesterly direction toward Rohtas and Kabul in the hope that he might be able to raise another army of ten to twelve thousand Badakhshanis. But this proved a fatal mistake. Unknown to Khusrau, Jahangir and Shaikh Farid Bukhari had already sent orders to the vast network of Mughal *jagirdars* and local *zamindars* across the Punjab to arrest Khusrau if he fled through their region. In the end, it was Qasim Khan Namakin (whose son had actually fought on Khusrau's side at Bhaironwal) who finally captured Khusrau, Hasan Beg Badakhshi, and a small clutch of princely loyalists and delivered them to the imperial court.

The entire court was invited to view Khusrau's surrender. Jahangir himself wrote an account:

On Thursday the third of Muharram 1015 [May 1], in Mirza Kamran's garden, Khusrau, hands bound and chains on his legs was brought in to me from the left [customarily the less honored side], in accordance with the custom and code of Genghis Khan. Husayn Beg [more commonly referred to as Hasan Beg] was made to stand on his right and Abdul Rahim on his left. Khusrau stood trembling and weeping between these two. Husayn Beg, thinking it might help him, began to speak wildly. When his object became apparent, he was not allowed to speak. I had Khusrau led away in chains, and I ordered the two miscreants put into an ox hide and a donkey skin, mounted backwards on an ass on a day of assembly, and paraded through the city. Since the ox hide dried more quickly than the donkey's skin, Husayn Beg stayed alive for four watches and died of suffocation. Abdul Rahim, who was in the donkey's skin, and who was given fluids from the outside, survived.[114]

The tone of this account suggests no regret on Jahangir's part. If anything, his words express satisfaction with the retribution visited upon those who had betrayed him. Following on this most public surrender and "to maintain order and discipline in the kingdom," Jahangir ordered hundreds of lower-ranking princely supporters to be publicly impaled or hanged. Their bodies were then lined up along one of the main highways leading into Lahore.[115] Khusrau's other non-noble supporters suffered jail terms, exile to Mecca, or execution. Contemporary observers and later Mughal historians defend Jahangir's brutality as necessary for reasons of "governance and warning/deterrence" (*siyasat wa 'ibrat*).[116]

---

[114] Jahangir, *The Jahangirnama*, pp. 57–8; Jahangir, *Jahangirnama*, p. 40.
[115] Jahangir, *Jahangirnama*, p. 40.
[116] M. Khan, *Iqbalnamah-i Jahangiri*, pp. 16–17. See also K. Husaini, *Ma'asir-i-Jahangiri*, p. 87; S. Lahori, *'Amal-i Salih*, vol. 1, pp. 34–5.

By all indications, however, Jahangir's retribution was highly selective. The Mughal nobility, for example, mostly escaped an imperial purge despite Hasan Beg Badakhshani's proclamation just before his death that Khusrau had widespread support among them. Jahangir did no more than make an example of two of the very highest rank, Mirza 'Aziz Koka and Raja Man Singh.[117]

Neither Raja Man Singh nor Mirza 'Aziz Koka played an active role in Khusrau's rebellion, but Jahangir strongly suspected them of being the prime movers behind it. Yet, lacking direct evidence, Jahangir was unwilling to kill them, perhaps for fear of creating martyrs.[118] Jahangir instead dug up a secret and treasonous letter Mirza 'Aziz Koka had written fourteen years before, in 1592, to Raja 'Ali Khan Faruqui, then ruler of Khandesh, expressing his disagreement with Akbar's Deccan policies. Using that letter, Jahangir disgraced him thus:

I summoned him [i.e., Mirza 'Aziz], placed the letter in his hand, and said, "Read it aloud to the people!" I suspected that when he saw it he might drop dead. . . . Every one of those present at court, both Akbari and Jahangiri servants who heard it, reviled and chided him.[119]

Citing Mirza 'Aziz's "treachery and defective loyalty," Jahangir confiscated all his lands, stripped him of his *mansab*, and imprisoned him. It was clear to everyone that the Mirza was paying the price for his support of Khusrau.[120] Although Mirza 'Aziz Koka was eventually restored to his former position, he never enjoyed the same respect from his fellow nobles. Furthermore, Jahangir's decision to elevate certain members of the Mirza's family (especially his estranged son Mirza Shamsi/Jahangir Quli Khan) while disregarding others effectively ensured that there would always be deep splits and a lack of cohesion within the larger Atga clan. As a result of Jahangir's maneuvers, the Atgas never regained their stature as one of the leading familial groups of the Mughal Empire.

Raja Man Singh proved a more formidable opponent for Jahangir, who had initially wanted to murder the Raja and his entire clan[121] but ultimately simply removed him from any positions of authority and declined to promote any of his clansmen within the Mughal hierarchy. Having lost

---

[117] Jahangir's anger toward Mirza 'Aziz Koka and Raja Man Singh is indicated by his characterization of the men as "hypocrites" (*munafiqan*) and "old wolves" (*kohnah-i gurgan*). See Jahangir, *Jahangirnama*, p. 79.

[118] S. Khan, *Maasir-ul-Umara*, vol. 1, pp. 686–7.

[119] Jahangir, *The Jahangirnama*, p. 63; Jahangir, *Jahangirnama*, p. 47.

[120] Harvi, *Tarikh-i-Khan Jahani*, vol. 2, p. 496.

[121] Ibid., pp. 497–8.

the governorship of Bengal and earning no other assignment, the Raja withdrew to his fortress stronghold of Rohtas in Bihar. In place of the Raja in Bengal, Jahangir appointed Qutb-ud-Din Khan, his own imperial foster brother (*koka*). Despite six or seven summons to the court over the next year or so, the Raja did not budge from Rohtas. Finally, in late 1607, Jahangir moved against the recalcitrant Raja by confiscating Rohtas and reassigning it to Qutb-ud-Din Khan Koka's son, Shaikh Ibrahim/Kishwar Khan. Raja Man Singh was now forced to appear at the Mughal court and submit to the authority of the emperor. After that, he had no choice but to accept Jahangir's bid to marry the Raja's widowed granddaughter. Raja Bhoj Singh Hada of Bundi – the woman's maternal grandfather and a close ally of Raja Man Singh – committed suicide to protest the emperor's demands and the accompanying loss of honor.[122]

Jahangir's assault on Raja Man Singh also resulted in the transfer of Maha Singh (Raja Man Singh's grandson and designated heir) to the northwestern and refractory region of Bangash in 1607. Without a doubt, Bangash was one of the least attractive assignments in the Mughal realm, given its poverty and rebellious population of Afghans, Uzbeks, and Hazaras. Adding salt to the Raja's wounds, Jahangir appointed Raja Ram Das Kachhwaha to be Maha Singh's *ataliq*. Although Raja Ram Das was a fellow Kachhwaha, he was from a lesser clan – namely the Sheikhawats as opposed to Raja Man Singh's Rajawats. Recommending Ram Das to Jahangir was his earlier refusal to support Raja Man Singh's efforts to back Khusrau following Akbar's death in 1605.[123] By promoting this nobleman to the position of *ataliq*, Jahangir signaled the end of uncontested Rajawat domination of the larger Kachhwaha clan. The emperor was also creating his own network of loyalists among the Kachhwahas. Mirroring tactics used to break Mirza 'Aziz Koka's authority over the Atga clan, Jahangir began promoting men like Raja Ram Das and Ra'i Sal Darbari (also a Sheikhawat) up the rungs of the Mughal hierarchy.

Jahangir's vengeance against Raja Man Singh eventually extended to the entire Rajawat clan. Total Rajawat *mansab* holdings fell from 24300 to 19500 between 1605 and 1612. They fell even more precipitously after the death of Raja Man Singh in 1614. The only Rajawat who continued

[122] S. Khan, *Maasiru-l-Umara*, vol. 2, p. 142; Muhammad Said Ahmad Maharvi, *Umara'-i Hunud* (Aligarh, 1910), p. 95.

[123] Kunwar Refaqat Ali Khan, *The Kachhwahas Under Akbar and Jahangir* (New Delhi, 1976), p. 174.

to receive promotions in the post-1606 period was Bhao Singh, one of Raja Man Singh's sons.[124] The secret to Bhao Singh's success, however, was his intense dislike of his father and his status as a trusted Jahangir loyalist from the emperor's days as a prince. Ultimately, Jahangir engineered Bhao Singh's accession to the throne of Amber following his father's death. By this, the emperor set aside the express desire of Raja Man Singh that his grandson Maha Singh succeed him. And so Jahangir finally succeeded in asserting his authority over the Rajawat–Kachhwaha clan.

The same methodical process of asserting his authority over recalcitrant nobles can be seen in Jahangir's handling of the Afghans. The emperor slowly promoted select loyalist Afghans up the rungs of the Mughal nobility to undermine the mass support Afghans had provided for Khusrau's rebellion. He chose such an approach over his advisor Sharif Khan's recommendation that he expel all Afghans from Hindustan. Jahangir feared an Afghan revolt if he did so.[125] Among those he incorporated or promoted in the Mughal hierarchy were Sher Khan Rukn-ud-Din Rohilla, Dilawar Khan Kakar, Pir Khan/Khan Jahan Lodi, Mubarak Khan Sarwani, Qiyam Khan, Sajawal Khan Niyazi, and 'Ali Khan Karora.[126] Among these men, Khan Jahan Lodi, who served as a bridge to various Afghan networks across Hindustan, played a key role in ensuring that Jahangir never faced an Afghan revolt (besides in Bengal) through the remaining years of his reign.

Jahangir's consolidation of his authority over recalcitrant ethnic and clan groups was matched by his moves to quell any remaining dissent in the Punjab and Kabul. In the Punjab, Jahangir awarded village headships and land grants to *chaudhuris* (semi-hereditary local officials) and *zamindars* "who had shown loyalty" during the crisis with Khusrau.[127] He gave large cash rewards to prominent loyalist Sufis such as the Naqshbandi *pir* Shaikh Husain Jami. Indigents, widows, and *faqirs* (Sufi mendicants) also received gifts in cash or kind as part of an effort to rebuild local-level support in the wake of the rebellion. His loyalist Shaikh Farid Bukhari received Bhaironwal, the site of the battle with Khusrau, as a land grant; likewise, other loyalists were awarded grants in Punjab and Kabul. Jahangir designated the high-ranking Turani nobleman and loyalist Shah

[124] M. Athar Ali, *The Apparatus of Empire* (Delhi, 1985), pp. 42, 48, 56.
[125] S. Khan, *Maasiru-l-Umara*, vol. 2, pp. 627–8.
[126] Ali, *Apparatus of Empire*, pp. 44–7.
[127] Jahangir, *Jahangirnama*, pp. 40–1.

Beg Khan-i Dauran as governor of *suba* Kabul. The Shah was to be assisted in his duties by Qazi 'Arif, a long-time Jahangiri supporter with strong family connections to Kabul, who had been appointed *qazi-ul-quzzat* (chief justice). Around the same time, Jahangir assigned Hasan Beg's former stronghold of Attock to Zafar Khan, a brother-in-law of the emperor, and Peshawar to a Salim-era princely loyalist and Afghan named Shaikh Rukn-ud-Din Rohilla/Sher Khan.

In the year following Khusrau's rebellion, the population of Kabul felt the generosity of Jahangir dramatically in their own lives. New *bulghar-khana*s (eating houses) were built throughout the city to provide free food to Kabul's residents. The emperor gave a further Rs. 10,000 to be distributed "amongst *faqir*s and the poor of Kabul" and commanded the distribution of Rs. 12,000 in cash every Thursday to the indigent.[128] The middle classes, too, benefited from Jahangir's largesse in this post-rebellion year. All urban dues were declared unnecessary forever. The city's students and literati received gifts; important men of Ghazni, the home region of Mirza 'Aziz Koka and the Atgas, received robes of honor; trees were planted to replace those cut down by Hasan Beg Badakhshi; and the emperor funded regular horse races to entertain the populace.

The discovery of a plot to assassinate Jahangir and elevate Khusrau in August 1607 provided the emperor with a final pretext to stamp out remaining opposition to his rule within the Mughal nobility. The plot's masterminds were mostly Khusrau's court-based partisans. Jahangir's reaction was swift and merciless. The main conspirators were executed, and individuals suspected of participation, among them Ghiyas Beg Tehrani Itimad-ud-Daula (Nur Jahan's father and so the emperor's future father-in-law), were placed under house arrest until they could clear their names.[129]

As for Khusrau, he had played his last move. Jahangir ordered that a hot spike be used to blind him.[130] Thus ended the war between father and son that had its roots in Akbar's efforts to counterbalance his troublesome son, Salim, with his grandson Khusrau. The tension between Jahangir and Khusrau goes to the heart of what made the Mughal system so dynamic, albeit in this instance also particularly brutal. Forced to confront Khusrau's challenge, Jahangir reinvigorated his ties to the Mughal nobility

[128] Ibid., p. 44.

[129] Ibid., p. 71; S. Khan, *Maasir-ul-Umara*, vol. 1, p. 129; Pelsaert, *A Dutch Chronicle*, p. 40.

[130] Harvi, *Tarikh-i-Khan Jahani*, vol. 1, p. 695; Pelsaert, *A Dutch Chronicle*, p. 40; Anon., "Intikhab-i Jahangir Shahi," trans. by H. Elliot and J. Dowson, in *The History of India as Told by its Own Historians*, vol. 6 (Delhi, repr. 1990), p. 448.

and to farther-flung political, social, and economic networks, impressing on his subjects his legitimacy to rule. Jahangir's efforts would take hold across the empire but were especially effective where he perceived his support to be weakest – Kabul, the Punjab, Delhi, and Bihar-Bengal.

By 1608, almost three years after his accession, Jahangir was finally firmly settled on the Mughal throne. Khusrau's 1606 rebellion, without a doubt, proved instrumental in consolidating his position as he went about rewarding those people who had been politically supportive and punishing those (including his own son) who had opposed his authority. Whereas Jahangir had not had to prove his mettle through a succession struggle against his brothers, by quashing his son's rebellion, he legitimized his right to rule.

And so it was with a number of other princely rebellions. Kamran's challenge forced Humayun to rebuild his authority and legitimacy to rule over the core parts of Babur's Kabul-based kingdom. The success of his efforts can be gauged by his ability to ultimately work from there toward a fresh invasion of India in 1555. So too the challenge of the Mirzas to Akbar in the mid-1560s not only brought about a new and assertive imperial presence across northern India, but also confirmed a growing perception that Akbar was the only true and legitimate heir to the Mughal throne.

Although Salim's rebellion did not generate the violence of other princely rebellions, it too influenced the running of the empire in beneficial ways. It led Akbar to back away from some of his more controversial religious initiatives. Salim's willingness to court Islamic religious opinion to the detriment of his father seems to have forced Akbar to reconsider the wisdom of policies that flew too forcefully in the face of the Muslim religious establishment.[131] This resulted in waning religious opposition to Akbar's rule during the last years of his reign. Mughal rule over northern India was stronger than ever on the eve of Akbar's death in 1605, and Salim's rebellion played a critical role in the process that led there.

## CONCLUSION

Princely disobedience and princely rebellions were endemic throughout the Mughal Empire. Every ruler – from Babur to Aurangzeb – had to deal with both. A study of princely misconduct across its entire range reveals at least five insights into the workings of the Mughal Empire. First, notwithstanding the power and importance of the emperor – demonstrated in elaborate

---

[131] Iqtidar Alam Khan, "Akbar's Personality Traits and World Outlook – A Critical Appraisal," in *Akbar and His India*, ed. Irfan Habib (Delhi, 1997), pp. 95–6.

rituals and a language of submission to him – the ever-present threat of princely disobedience if not actual violence reminded generations of emperors that the carefully constructed façade of their absolute power was not only brittle but demanded constant political vigilance. Emperors ignored princely threats at their peril. Humayun's inability or unwillingness to conclusively assert his authority through the 1530s thus came to be misinterpreted as a sign of political and military weakness. The upshot was ever more direct and violent princely challenges. Jumping ahead three generations, Shah Jahan's forced abdication by his son Aurangzeb curiously did not originate with his tolerance of dissent but rather because his draconian actions drove princely disobedience so far underground that he actually seems to have lost sight of it. In the interim, his younger three sons steadily chipped away at his political authority. Behind the façade of public unity and imperial glory was an emperor who was, unbeknownst to him, steadily losing his relevance in the eyes of his subjects. By contrast, Akbar's earlier success in counteracting the disobedience of both Murad and Salim reaffirmed his political legitimacy and right to the crown. Aurangzeb's continued ability to monitor and contain his princes' behavior to the end of his life offered the strongest possible proof that he remained a force to contend with.

A second point that emerges has to do with princely misconduct generating debate about the imperial project. Far from being merely signs of familial or imperial dysfunction, princely disobedience and rebellion offered crucial terrain across which the dynasty's elites deliberated about imperial policies. Cocooned at the imperial court, surrounded by complex forms of etiquette that demanded restraint and circumspection, emperors rarely heard direct criticism of their policies. Thus no matter how strongly Parvez may have opposed military expansionism in the Deccan in the 1610s, he likely never dared take his complaints directly to his father, Jahangir. And yet, successive generations of princes did manage to register opposition to Mughal policies. They mostly did so through lackadaisical military and administrative performances. In this regard, they rarely acted alone. They invariably reflected a well of discontent on the part of other powerful individuals representing important swathes within the Mughal nobility, and emperors eventually had to respond to these forms of indirect dissent. For example, Jahangir transferred Parvez out of the Deccan and replaced him with his half brother and rival Khurram, who favored an expansionist military policy in the south. Invariably, the removal of princes dovetailed with other personnel changes among Mughal officers serving in the provinces. Such responsiveness was absolutely crucial to the running of the empire. It forced an emperor to defend his policies, to find others who might push his vision forward, or to seek face-saving ways to reverse unpopular policies (for example, ending the pointless military campaigns carried out in Balkh and Badakhshan in the 1640s) before frustration flared into open rebellion.

The very persistence of contention from princes through the sixteenth and seventeenth centuries points to a third significant and defining feature of the Mughal system, namely, the diminished threat of noble-led rebellions during this same period. Indeed, although Akbar had faced two major rebellions (in the 1560s and 1580s), Jahangir and Shah Jahan had to deal with only one each (1626 and early 1630s), and Aurangzeb none. This decline suggests that expressions of noble disquiet toward an emperor were increasingly subsumed by or channeled through the drama and energies of princely disobedience and rebellion. What this points to is the remarkable success of the Mughals in effectively focusing large-scale, intra-elite bloodletting on two events: princely rebellions and wars of succession. Both necessarily involved princes, and neither threatened the fundamental legitimacy of the Mughal family to rule India – at least until after Aurangzeb's reign and the beginning of the end of the empire.

Fourth, princely rebellions gave the lie to Mughal claims that they had succeeded in imposing a pax-Mughalica across northern India. Although the Mughals were undoubtedly effective in eliminating large-scale and interregional conflicts after the 1580s, they were never able to fully control incidences of clan, family, or even anti-state violence at the local level. Such conflicts often intensified during princely rebellions. As some groups took advantage of a distracted imperial authority to settle scores, others threw their support behind one or another imperial party in an effort to leverage their own struggles. Like "specks of foam," to use Stuart Carroll's evocative descriptor of the ways elite violence tapped into the deep groundswell and never-ending cycles of non-elite violence in medieval France,[132] so too Mughal princely rebellions invariably found themselves riding waves of local conflict that the Mughals could never really rein in.

And finally, in the thrust and parry of Mughal familial politics, all the major contestants sought ties with any and every significant and influential individual and group. Besides renewing and deepening imperial ties to established elements within the empire, these efforts (whether by

---

[132] Stuart Carroll, *Blood and Violence in Early Modern France* (Oxford, 2006), p. 264.

prince or emperor) also reached out to groups that had previously been ignored or marginalized. Princely rebellions, and imperial responses in particular, engaged a powerful dynamic that abetted both social mobility and Mughal state formation between the sixteenth and seventeenth centuries. The negotiations, conflicts, rewards, and punishments that accompanied them were in fact crucial to driving home the weight of Mughal imperial authority in the most important parts of northern and central India.[133] Nor were princely rebellions the only violent process that served ultimately to embed Mughal power. As the next chapter will show, succession struggles proved another critical engine for the production and consolidation of Mughal imperial power.

---

[133] This dynamic remained relevant up to the last major princely rebellion of the seventeenth century, that of Prince Akbar against Aurangzeb (1681–7). As Aurangzeb went about the job of crushing Prince Akbar and defeating the Maratha leader Shambhaji, the prince's primary protector, the emperor reached out to various Ghat and Konkan-based Maratha opponents of Shambhaji, drawing them into closer relationships with the Mughals. In the process, Aurangzeb spawned a civil war among the various Maratha factions. Aurangzeb's successful efforts to assert his authority eventually culminated in Akbar's flight to the safety of Safavid Iran (1687) and Shambhaji's capture and execution by the Mughals (1689). That Aurangzeb's efforts failed to eventually yield long-term benefits for the Mughals was largely the result of a failure in imperial planning and vision.

# 6

## Wars of Succession

Sometime in the middle of 1595 news arrived at Emperor Akbar's court that Murad III, the ruler of the Ottoman Empire, had died and his oldest son, Mehmed, had ascended the imperial throne as Mehmed III. This was news enough, but the story surrounding the succession horrified the Mughal court. Mehmed III had nineteen brothers (most if not all of them minors), and, on becoming emperor, he had ordered their execution. News of this carnage shocked Akbar, who wondered how the Ottomans were able to sustain their imperial might following as they did such a barbaric practice. If Mehmed's reign is marked by "prosperity," Akbar exclaimed, then it must be a sign of divine retribution against humanity.[1] Akbar's comments offer us insight into Mughal thinking about succession practices at the end of the sixteenth century. It is notable that Akbar publicly signaled such a forceful rejection of the Ottoman system of succession secured by preemptively killing princes. Instead, Akbar's more temperate approach did no more than restrict potential heirs to his own direct line.

At no point between Babur's and Aurangzeb's reigns did the Mughals ever clearly articulate a system of imperial succession, and Mughal succession would remain relatively open ended. Unlike the Ottomans or the Safavids, who had begun to curtail political competition among princes by the end of the sixteenth century, the Mughals maintained a flexible system in which, after Akbar, only the lineal heirs of an emperor were offered any stake. Granted, in the often tense competition among brothers, the oldest tended to be the most privileged; nevertheless, in fact, a younger son could and usually did challenge the oldest brother's claim if and when

[1] Shaikh Abu'l Fazl, *Akbarnamah*, ed. Abdul Rahim, vol. 3 (Calcutta, 1886), p. 662.

opportunity arose. Once appanages had been phased out in the 1580s, brothers became more likely to come into conflict with one another because one's success necessarily meant death for the others.

This open-ended system has been widely considered a source of generalized instability and weakness since at least the mid-seventeenth century when François Bernier, a French traveler to Mughal India, pronounced it as such. This judgment held sway with the English historian Alexander Dow in the 1770s, a host of late nineteenth- and early twentieth-century colonial-era historians (James Mill, Hugh Murray, John Marshman, J. T. Wheeler, V. A. Smith, Pringle Kennedy, and B. P. Saxsena among others), and most recently with John Keay, Peter Robb, and Lisa Balabanlilar.[2] Such views are grounded in the perception that open-ended systems of succession promote factionalism, uncertainty, chaos, the waste of resources, and unnecessary bloodshed. Although none of these authors explicitly compares open-ended systems with their opposite number (namely designated systems of succession), the suggestion is always that the Mughals somehow missed an opportunity to strengthen their rule by not opting for a more orderly system.[3] As previous chapters have shown, however, the Mughal system of succession is precisely what led to determined efforts by princes, from early in their childhood, to build politically and militarily robust households as well as networks of friends and allies. These efforts were the backdrop against which they expressed defiance or launched outright rebellion. The dynasty's success in foregrounding a small group of direct royal heirs as the only legitimate aspirants to imperial power allowed the royal sons of the emperor to develop what this book argues is the unique institution of the Mughal Prince. Indeed, the princely institution's very vitality and its concentrated

---

[2] François Bernier, *Travels in the Mogul Empire*, trans. A. Constable (Delhi, repr. 1983), pp. 4, 14–15, 25; Alexander Dow, *History of Hindostan*, vol. 3 (Delhi, repr. 1973), p. 195; John Keay, *India: A History* (New York, 2000), p. 328; Peter Robb, *A History of India* (London, 2002), 95; Lisa Balabanlilar, "The Lords of the Auspicious Conjunction: Turco-Mongol Imperial Identity on the Subcontinent," *Journal of World History* 18, no. 1 (2007): 10.

[3] Unfavorable assessments of open-ended systems of succession have a long lineage within European historiography. One of the most significant critics was Max Weber. He argued that open-ended systems of succession promoted arbitrariness, uncertainty, and factionalism. In contrast, ordered systems of succession – most significantly primogeniture – enabled a rationalization of imperial power, promoted certainty, and helped prevent debilitating and expensive wars of succession. According to this line of reasoning, the decision by almost all early-modern European states to transition away from open-ended succession systems helped pave the way for all manner of crucial political and economic developments. None was more significant than the emergence of European capitalism, which led to the "rise of the West" and the "decline of the rest."

focus on direct heirs even created room for what we might call the figure of the Imperial Pretender, an individual who posed as one of the prominent sons or grandsons of an emperor in order to pursue his own political or pecuniary ambitions.[4]

This chapter explores key aspects of the succession struggle that marked every transition of Mughal power, looking at the ways an impending struggle impacted the lives of its participants as well as the dynasty as a whole. Inasmuch as the final struggle for the throne foregrounded bitter divisions and conflict, their aftermath provided an opportunity to forge a fresh political consensus. As expected, newly crowned emperors worked very hard to establish their legitimacy and assert their authority by claiming ex post facto the inevitability of their success and, especially in the seventeenth century, by making grand gestures of forgiveness and benevolence toward the supporters of a defeated princely opponent. With their newly ennobled supporters, typically drawn from the ranks of their princely retainers, the Mughal nobility was infused with fresh blood – an incorporative dynamism that, in good times, characterized the success of

---

[4] For more on the implications of "imposture" and its history in India and other parts of the world, see Jorge Flores and Sanjay Subrahmanyam, "The Legend of Sultan Bulaqi and the Estado da India, 1628–40," in Sanjay Subrahmanyam, *Explorations in Connected History* (New Delhi, 2005), pp. 104–42. It is worth briefly considering such pretenders for the light they shed on the aspirations surrounding the figure of the post-Akbar Mughal prince. The appearance of the first pretender coincided with the end of the appanage system. In 1610, four years after Jahangir turned down Khusrau's demand for Bengal, a man named Qutb appeared in Bihar claiming to be Khusrau. At one point, Qutb even managed to capture the important city of Patna after imperial officials refused to fight him for fear that he might be the real Khusrau, miraculously escaped from his father's clutches. Qutb was eventually captured and executed. Over the course of the seventeenth century, every emperor had to face challenges from one or more such pretenders. During Shah Jahan's reign, these included several individuals claiming to be Khusrau's oldest son Dawar Bakhsh and another posing as Danyal's third son Mirza Baysunghar. Over the course of Aurangzeb's reign, the empire contended with another wave of pretenders. They included individuals claiming to be Dara Shukoh (1663), Shuja' (1669), Shuja' (1674), Shuja''s son Zain-ul-'Abidin (1682–3), Aurangzeb's son Akbar (1694), a second (false) Akbar (1699), and finally Prince Akbar's son Buland Akhtar (1699). Most were captured and either imprisoned or killed. In 1670, Aurangzeb was alerted to the fact that in the city of Ayodhya, someone was selling jewelry once belonging to Aurangzeb's brother and rival Shuja', who had disappeared into Burma in 1660. Aurangzeb immediately ordered an investigation to find out who this person was and if he was putting out claims to be Shuja' (*Akhbarat-i Darbar-i Mu'alla*, National Library of India, Sarkar Collection 34, p. 316). Emperors took seriously any and every such threat. Significantly, most seventeenth-century pretenders emerged in areas that were marginal to imperial power – such as Kutch, Bangash, or eastern Bengal – or found political support among groups that felt marginalized by the Mughals – the Ujjainiyas, Afghans, Bhils, Kolis, and Jats. Even in these remote areas, people seemed to be well aware that only a Mughal prince could successfully aspire to imperial power in northern India.

the empire as a whole. At this juncture, at the start of a new reign, the stage was set for the empire to refocus its attention on the next generation of Mughal princes as they began the slow process of reconstituting princely power.

### COUNTDOWN TO THE WAR OF SUCCESSION

Princely maneuvering and jostling, as we have seen, were part and parcel of the Mughal political system. So too was the tension (sometimes minimal, other times extreme) among the contenders for the throne. All got sharper as emperors aged and princes anticipated their impending struggle. In addition to stepping up efforts to marshal money and military resources, princes took pains to strengthen their information networks and, in some cases, kill off rivals. Against this backdrop, fear and paranoia were rife among princes and their closest supporters. But they were not the only ones who lived in dread of the future. The rest of the imperial nobility were similarly on edge, and the buildup to a war of succession also touched the lives of vast swathes of the empire's population. Debilitating as this was, it had the crucial effect of focusing intense amounts of energy and attention on the dynasty itself. It was also an unavoidable reminder that the people were part of a community of imperial subjects. In the drama surrounding wars of succession, the broad consensus around the legitimacy of Mughal rule was revisited and renewed.

### The Importance of Revenues and Information

As indicated here and in previous chapters, Mughal princes anticipated the inevitable succession struggle by spending decades building resilient households and alliances. These efforts to gather money, men, and other resources for war increased when princes believed a conflagration was almost upon them. Consider Mu'azzam's example from the early 1700s.

In addition to tightening his control over the lucrative horse trade between Central Asia and the Mughal Empire, Mu'azzam began illegally tapping into various other revenue streams. We know this from a series of furious letters written by Aurangzeb condemning his son for sanctioning "unacceptable regulations" and seizing revenues to which he was not entitled.[5] Some part of this money seems to have been used for collecting

---

[5] Aurangzeb, *Kalimat-i Taiyabat*, Asiatic Society of Bengal, Ivanow 382, f. 37b; Aurangzeb, *Dastur-ul-'Amal-i Agahi*, National Library of India, Sarkar Collection 70, f. 27a.

camels and horses, sealing agreements of safe passage with Afghan tribes, and winning the support of the Punjab's *zamindars*. The bulk of it, however, was used to recruit battle-worthy soldiers – especially Afghans and Central Asian cavalrymen.[6] Again, these efforts did not escape Aurangzeb's attention. On one occasion, the emperor inquired sarcastically if his son was preparing to fight the Safavids.[7] Mu'azzam's response is not known.

In the run-up to the succession war, princes stepped up their intelligence gathering to keep a close watch on the actions of primary rivals, and also on the emperor. Early knowledge of failing health or death afforded a crucial head start over the other princes. Such news could come from any number of sources. Thus, in the fall of 1605, Salim received word from sympathizers among the nobility and the imperial harem that Akbar's health was deteriorating and that Khusrau's partisans were plotting to capture, imprison, and blind Salim after his audience with a dying Akbar.[8] In 1657, Aurangzeb's personal representative (*wakil*) at the Mughal court, 'Isa Beg, was a crucial source of information on both Dara Shukoh and Shah Jahan. In an apparent attempt to block the flow of news to Aurangzeb, Dara Shukoh temporarily imprisoned the Beg. Aurangzeb continued to receive invaluable intelligence from other sources, however. They may well have included his uncle (and former *ataliq*) Sha'ista Khan, his sister Roshan Ara, and such high-ranking members of the Mughal nobility as Mir Jumla, his son Muhammad Amin Khan, and Afzal Khan.

We know that Aurangzeb's sons and grandsons relied on many of the same types of sources as previous generations – related women, senior nobles, and personal representatives. Starting in the 1690s, however, there was a new conduit of crucial information about the health and actions of the emperor: imperial eunuchs. Eunuchs had played a role in all imperial courts, but no emperor had relied on them as heavily as did the aging Aurangzeb. At the center of a tightly knit group of eunuchs was Khwaja Talib/Khidmatgar Khan (d. 1704). Having served Aurangzeb since the 1630s, Khidmatgar Khan was one of the last surviving members of the

---

[6] Muhammad Qasim Lahori, '*Ibratnama*, ed. Zahur-ud-Din Ahmad (Lahore, 1977), p. 111. These efforts laid the groundwork for Mu'azzam and Mun'im Khan's rapid advance through the Punjab and onward to the rich prize of Delhi, as well as their success in raising large numbers of troops and materials of war on extremely short notice. Bhimsen Saxsena, *Nushka-i Dilkasha*, British Museum, Or. 23, f. 164b.

[7] Jadunath Sarkar, *Studies in Aurangzib's Reign* (Calcutta, repr. 1989), p. 41.

[8] Asad Beg Qazwini, *Waqa'i' Asad Beg*, Center for Advanced Study Library (Aligarh Muslim University), Rotograph 94, f. 29b.

emperor's generation. In a sign of Aurangzeb's complete trust in the Khan, the emperor appointed him one of Mu'azzam's primary caretakers during the prince's years under house arrest for treason. Judging by the Mughal news bulletins (*akhbarat*), Khidmatgar Khan had a large number of eunuch protégés who served other princes and princesses as well.

Khidmatgar Khan's growing importance as both a political force at the imperial court and a source of information about the emperor can be seen in the proliferation of efforts by Aurangzeb's sons and grandsons to woo him with gifts and audiences starting in the mid-1690s.[9] Following the transfer of most of Aurangzeb's sons and grandsons to other parts of the empire (a process completed by 1701–2), princely proxies such as A'zam's sister and partisan Zinat-un-Nisa and Kam Bakhsh's mother Udaipuri Mahal continued to cultivate ties to Khidmatgar Khan, his successor Khwaja Ambar (who was also titled Khidmatgar Khan after 1704), and other imperial eunuchs.[10] In 1707, a eunuch relayed the news of Aurangzeb's death to Zinat-un-Nisa first. She, in turn, sent an urgent communication telling A'zam to return to the court and establish himself as Aurangzeb's rightful successor.[11]

## The Option of Fratricide

To win their claim to the throne, Mughal princes were not above trying to kill one another even before a succession fight. The first example of attempted fratricide comes from 1539–40, on the eve of anticipated conflict among Babur's sons. Mirza Kamran, the prince holding Kabul, was the target of a poisoning plot, which he survived. There is no clear evidence pointing to his half brother Humayun's involvement, but Mirza Kamran believed he had instigated the attack through Babur's wives.[12] A generation later and likely sometime before the birth of his oldest son Salim in 1569, Akbar considered having his brother Mirza Hakim killed. In the end, Akbar decided against the scheme, largely because the Mirza was the only other candidate for the Mughal throne.[13] But Salim had no such compunctions when dealing with his only surviving brother Danyal.

Although no historical account directly implicates Salim in the death of Danyal in March 1605 – a mere seven months before Akbar's own

[9] *Akhbarat-i Darbar-i Mu'alla*, , vol. 17, nos. 37/9, 37/45, 37/48; vol. 19, pp. 174, 289.
[10] Ibid., vol. 29, p. 207; vol. 30, pp. 58, 85.
[11] Saxsena, *Nuskha-i Dilkasha*, f. 161b.
[12] Gulbadan Begum, *Ahwal-i Humayun Badshah*, British Library, Ms. Or. 166, f. 36b.
[13] Shaikh Abu'l Fazl, *Ain-i-Akbari*, ed. H. Blochmann, vol. 2 (Calcutta, 1877), pp. 230–1.

demise in October 1605 – circumstantial evidence suggests otherwise. Danyal was a long-standing alcoholic, and by late 1604 his alcoholism had gotten so bad that he was constantly ill and weak. In a desperate attempt to control his son's habit, Akbar had ordered Danyal to be placed under house arrest in the Deccan. Somehow, rust and lead-laden (in effect poisoned) alcohol was smuggled into the prince's quarters by a group of "wicked persons" who, according to the *Akbarnama*, "seeing their own good in his harm ... conspired to kill" the prince. Among those involved in the plot were a nephew of Khwaja Fathullah and a brother of Zamana Beg (later Mahabat Khan), both diehard supporters of Salim. Three days after Danyal's death and following a public trial, ten men were publicly beaten and stoned to death by Danyal's aggrieved supporters. This brutal form of capital punishment was most likely employed because of the conviction that the men had acted on Salim's orders.[14] With Danyal's death, Salim became Akbar's sole surviving son and de facto heir to the throne.

So too Khurram clearly hoped to thin the ranks of potential opponents when he ordered his half brother Khusrau's murder in early 1622 as he was about to go into rebellion against Jahangir. Given Jahangir's alienation from one son (Parvez) and the relative youth of the other (Shahryar), Khurram feared only the blinded but still popular Khusrau.[15]

Although the reigns of Shah Jahan and Aurangzeb do not offer any princely murders in the run-up to their wars of succession, it was not for want of trying. Shah Jahan's younger sons, for instance, were convinced that Dara Shukoh had stepped up his efforts to have them killed in the 1650s. The growing anxiety for their personal safety catalyzed their secret alliance against their oldest brother.[16] In Aurangzeb's reign, A'zam seems to have been at the forefront of a number of plots against

---

[14] Fazl, *Akbarnamah*, vol. 3, p. 838.

[15] Even in death, however, Khusrau maintained his popular appeal. One admittedly pro-Khurram chronicle, '*Amal-i Salih*, tells us that when news of the prince's demise (euphemistically referred to as that "painful incident") became known, people were speechless and grief struck. As long as Khusrau's body remained in Burhanpur, large numbers of people came every Friday night on pilgrimage (*ziarat*) to pay their respects. Later, when Khusrau's body was exhumed and shifted to its final burial place in the north Indian city of Allahabad, people lined the streets of every city, watching it pass. Makeshift shrines were set up. These too became sites of veneration and pilgrimage on Fridays. Salih Kambo Lahori, '*Amal-i Salih*, ed. Ghulam Yazdani, vol. 1 (Lahore, 1967), pp. 133–4.

[16] Aqil Khan Razi, *Waqi'at-i Alamgiri*, ed. Maulvi Zafar Hasan (Delhi, 1930), p. 15; Aurangzeb, *Anecdotes of Aurangzib*, trans. Jadunath Sarkar (Calcutta, repr. 1988), pp. 24–5.

his brothers Mu'azzam and Kam Bakhsh. One ostensibly involved A'zam paying Rs. 900,000 to one of Aurangzeb's spiritual preceptors for help in persuading the emperor that he had received visions from the Prophet Muhammad ordering Mu'azzam's execution. A skeptical Aurangzeb ordered that the preceptor be investigated. After proof was found of money changing hands, the man (but not A'zam) was severely punished.[17] Toward the end of Aurangzeb's life, A'zam repeatedly picked quarrels with Kam Bakhsh in the hope that his supporters might kill the prince in the ensuing melee. Reacting to the growing threat from A'zam, Aurangzeb ordered a sharp increase in Kam Bakhsh's bodyguards.[18] He also ordered the princes to attend separate imperial audiences, A'zam in the morning, Kam Bakhsh in the evening.[19] In the end, such measures were not sufficient to contain the threat of princely violence, and Aurangzeb finally decided to separate the two by transferring them to different parts of the empire. Given A'zam's known attempts to get rid of his brothers, it is not surprising that he too lived in fear for his life and is said to have worn a chain mail shirt under his clothes.[20]

With the threat of assassination always lurking, Mughal princes were perhaps understandably paranoid and fearful. We know that several princes resorted to alcoholism and drug abuse, and these in turn all too often became the cause of their premature death. Aurangzeb may in fact have been the only teetotaler prince in the first two hundred years of Mughal history.

### Anticipation at the Outbreak of War

When a war of succession ultimately commenced, it seemed to offer a release from years, perhaps decades, of pent up anticipation and tension. Consider the events 1657–9. In September 1657, Shah Jahan fell seriously ill. Along with a high fever, the emperor swelled up so much that he became unrecognizable; weak and yet proud, Shah Jahan withdrew completely from public life. Day-to-day management of the empire fell to Dara Shukoh. Rumors quickly spread that the emperor was dead and almost everyone, including Shah Jahan's younger sons, thought that all claims to

[17] S. A. A. Rizvi, *A History of Sufism in India*, vol. 2 (Delhi, 1983), pp. 370–1.
[18] Khafi Khan, *Muntakhab al-Labab*, ed. Kabir-ud-din Ahmad, vol. 2 (Calcutta, 1874), p. 547.
[19] *Akhbarat-i Darbar-i Mu'alla*, vol. 32, pp. 8, 9, 10, 17.
[20] K. Khan, *Muntakhab al-Labab*, vol. 2, p. 409.

the contrary were a mere ruse for Dara Shukoh to consolidate his power.[21] Consequently Shuja', Aurangzeb, and Murad mobilized their armies and began marching toward the court in Agra. Even once Shah Jahan had recovered sufficiently to reappear in public, his younger sons stuck to their belligerent agenda. Then, in the spring of 1658, Shah Jahan openly threw his support behind Dara Shukoh. With this roll of the dice, the emperor hoped to protect his throne and secure it for his beloved favorite son, but he failed on both counts. In the end, Aurangzeb was able to pick off his rivals to become the uncontested emperor by 1659.

A succession struggle was the moment of truth for a prince, when his mettle and his political, military, and personal preparation were put to one final test. Momentous as this event was for princes, it was no less so for the tens if not hundreds of thousands of princely retainers across the empire. If their master succeeded to the throne, their lives might be dramatically transformed. If their master failed, however, they would have to adjust to a new political dispensation that owed them nothing. Bhimsen Saxsena's *Tarikh-i Dilkasha* gives a rare feel for the anxiety felt by Aurangzeb's princely retainers during the 1657–9 contest.

The main character in this brief account is Muhammad Tahir Khurasani (d. 1675) – Aurangzeb's most senior officer in the Deccan and *ataliq* of his second son, Mu'azzam. Aurangzeb had left Muhammad Tahir behind in Burhanpur when he marched northward in the fall of 1657. On the eve of the Battle of Ujjain (May 1658), according to Bhimsen's account, Muhammad Tahir was "terribly perturbed at heart about the result." Desperate to glean any news about the battle's outcome, he asked the author's father, Raghunandan, to go to Burhanpur's bazaar. Raghunandan, also worried, went to the bazaar, purchased a quantity of sweets that he began handing out in the hope that he might hear something. Finally, someone told him that Aurangzeb had won. "On hearing these words," Bhimsen writes, "my father instantly returned to Muhammad Tahir and conveyed the news to him. After getting this information, Muhammad Tahir gained a little peace of mind." As news confirming Aurangzeb's victory trickled in, "Everyone, major or minor, big or small, received satisfaction."[22] Pent-up emotions gave way to wild celebrations.

---

[21] There was historical precedent for such a maneuver. When Humayun unexpectedly died in 1556 after falling down a staircase in Delhi, Akbar was in the Punjab. In an effort to secure Akbar's uncontested accession, Humayun's closest advisors decided to keep the emperor's death a secret. For the next seventeen days, a double named Mulla Bekasi took Humayun's place. Shaikh Abu'l Fazl, *Akbarnamah*, ed. Abdul Rahim, vol. 2 (Calcutta, 1879), p. 364.

[22] Bhimsen Saxsena, *Tarikh-i-Dilkasha*, trans. Jadunath Sarkar (Bombay, 1972), pp. 19–20.

Both Bhimsen's father and Muhammad Tahir Khurasani went on to successful careers in Aurangzeb's reign.

### The Dilemma of Choosing Sides

Among the nobility at court, a succession battle certainly caused its share of hand wringing, because everyone who mattered had to choose a side. As was the case during princely rebellions, neutrality was not an option, especially prior to 1707. For many nobles, loyalties had been long settled, so there was no difficult choice to be made on the cusp of a succession struggle. But what happened when a nobleman found himself in close physical proximity to a prince he did not support? Could he simply walk away? Join the other side? The simple answer was "no." He was expected to serve and fight under the nearest prince lest he later be accused of disloyalty.[23]

So the story went for Mukhtar Khan. Father-in-law of A'zam's son Bidar Bakht, he stood to profit immensely if A'zam ascended the throne. In 1707, the Khan was governor of Agra. According to one eighteenth-century historian, possession of Agra, with its strategic location and massive stores of treasure, increased by a scale of a hundred the chances of a successful accession.[24] In the race to get to Agra, however, a son of Mu'azzam (A'zam older brother and rival), 'Azim-ud-Din, beat out Bidar Bakht. Mukhtar Khan felt unable to stand up to 'Azim-ud-Din, and he surrendered the valuable city without a fight, tipping the balance of power toward Mu'azzam.[25] Mukhtar Khan's pusillanimity was fairly typical for a nobleman when openly confronted by a prince.[26] Mu'azzam best captured the prevailing sentiment when he remarked that even his

---

[23] This often led to situations where members of the same family fought on different sides during a war of succession, as seen in the case of the heirs of the famous Shah Jahan–era nobleman 'Ali Mardan Khan (d. 1657). Two sons, Ismail Beg and Ishaq Beg, died fighting for Dara Shukoh at the Battle of Samugarh in 1658. Another son, Ibrahim Khan, fought on the opposing side (for Prince Murad). In the meantime, a fourth son, Abdullah Beg, accompanied Dara Shukoh's son Sulaiman Shukoh in the fight against Prince Shuja' even as Hasan Beg (a son of Ishaq Beg) remained employed by Aurangzeb in the Deccan.

[24] Shah Nawaz Khan, *Maasiru-l-Umara*, ed. Ashraf Ali, vol. 3 (Calcutta, 1891), p. 658.

[25] Kamraj, *A'zam al-Harb*, British Museum, Or. 1899, ff. 226–7; Kamwar Khan, *Tazkirat us-Salatin Chaghta*, ed. Muzaffar Alam (Aligarh, 1980), p. 10; Mubarakullah Wazih, *Tarikh-i Iradat Khan*, ed. Ghulam Rasul Mehr (Lahore, 1971), p. 26.

[26] For instance, Mu'azzam's own representative (*wakil*) at Aurangzeb's court, Muhammad Ikhlas, felt obliged to serve under A'zam after the latter took control of the imperial court following his father's death. He was rewarded with a high *mansab* by A'zam. Kamraj, *A'zam al-Harb*, f. 115.

own sons would have been obligated to fight against him and for A'zam if they found themselves under their uncle's authority.[27]

Consider also the case of Najabat Khan. Once talked about as a possible marriage partner for Shah Jahan's daughter Jahan Ara, he was one of the most senior imperial nobles in 1656–7. Attached to Aurangzeb's expedition against the Sultanate of Bijapur in 1656, he ignored imperial orders to return to the court in Agra when Shah Jahan fell ill and elected instead to stay with Aurangzeb, not because he was a long-standing supporter of the prince. Rather, his support came late in the day, prompted it would seem by a newfound respect for the prince.[28]

In other cases, nobles agreed to fight for a prince despite severe misgivings. Such was certainly true of the many nobles who laid down their lives for A'zam at the Battle of Jaju in 1707. Although they found the prince insufferably arrogant and feared that he lacked the necessary temperament to succeed Aurangzeb, they believed that they owed him their loyalty given his proximity.[29]

Battle of Samugarh, ca. 1658 (Harvard Art Museums/Arthur M. Sackler Museum, Gift of Stuart Cary Welch, Jr., 1999.298)

[27] K. Khan, *Muntakhab al-Labab*, vol. 2, pp. 600–1.
[28] Aurangzeb, *Anecdotes*, p. 32.
[29] M. Lahori, *'Ibratnama*, pp. 107–8; Wazih, *Tarikh-i Iradat Khan*, p. 13.

Then there were those who, for reasons of physical proximity, feigned overt support to one prince while in fact secretly working on behalf of another. One such person, and likely the most important traitor in Mughal history, was Khalilullah Khan. The Khan was a distinguished noble at the court of Shah Jahan, and Dara Shukoh mistakenly gave him command of one of the wings of the imperial army at the Battle of Samugarh against his brothers Aurangzeb and Murad. Although the historian Jadunath Sarkar discounts the fantastic story that Khalilullah Khan prompted Dara Shukoh's disastrous decision to dismount from his elephant (thus depriving his army of a view of the prince),[30] the Khan did indeed keep his forces back during the battle because of a prior secret agreement with Aurangzeb.[31] His disloyalty sealed Dara Shukoh and Shah Jahan's military fate. Some weeks later, he again betrayed Shah Jahan when he warned Aurangzeb that a proposed parlay with the emperor was in fact a trap to capture and kill him. Such treasonous behavior was extremely risky, however. If caught, a nobleman could lose his life. Throughout Mughal history, there are many examples of nobles, such as Rustam Dil Khan or Ahsan Khan, who paid the ultimate price for betraying a prince. Kam Bakhsh executed both men in 1708 after he learned they were colluding with his half brother and rival Mu'azzam.[32]

The impossibility of a neutral position in a war of succession is perfectly exemplified in the extraordinary case of Shahnawaz Khan Safavi. He was the father-in-law of both Aurangzeb and Murad. Furthermore, one of his nieces had married Shuja'. By his own account, he had no connection with Dara Shukoh.[33] And yet, despite serving under Aurangzeb's direct command in the Deccan in 1657, he refused to join the fight against Dara Shukoh. Shahnawaz Khan claimed that his decision was taken out of respect for Shah Jahan, who was still alive. To allay Aurangzeb's fears, the Khan offered to resign his military commission, but this was not acceptable to the prince, who finally ordered that Shahnawaz Khan be arrested and imprisoned. Although Aurangzeb eventually released his father-in-law and even appointed him governor of Gujarat, relations between the two men had reached such a low point that Shahnawaz Khan eventually threw his support behind Dara Shukoh's last gasp effort

[30] Jadunath Sarkar, *History of Aurangzib*, vol. 2 (London, 1920), p. 57.
[31] Razi, *Waqiat-i-Alamgiri*, p. 62.
[32] Shah Nawaz Khan, *Maasir-ul-Umara*, ed. Abdur Rahim, vol. 1 (Calcutta, 1888), pp. 301–3.
[33] Aurangzeb, *Anecdotes*, p. 33.

to defeat Aurangzeb in 1659. The nobleman was killed fighting Aurangzeb's forces at the Battle of Deorai.

When Mughal nobles were called upon to join in a succession conflict, they were expected to do so. Refusal or even foot-dragging was treated as a sign of personal ambition, of putting one's own interests above those of the dynasty. Up until 1707, this was tantamount to treason. Against this backdrop, only great distance from a conflict zone or the need to maintain a powerful presence in a politically or administratively sensitive region was considered an acceptable excuse for nonparticipation. Even then, nobles had to play their cards very carefully.

For instance, in 1627–8, Khan Jahan Lodi irrevocably burnt his bridges with Khurram (soon to be Emperor Shah Jahan) when he chose to stay in Malwa rather than accompany the prince northward to Agra to claim the throne. Khurram never forgot the slight, especially since Khan Jahan Lodi was not bound by any obligations of loyalty to either princes Shahryar or Dawar Bakhsh. Within a year, the new emperor moved to punish the Khan, which in turn led Khan Jahan Lodi to revolt. Similar circumstances set Jujhar Singh Bundela on a collision course with Shah Jahan. Like Khan Jahan Lodi, Jujhar Singh Bundela tried to sit out the 1627–8 war of succession, having inherited a great deal of power and wealth from his father, the one-time rebel turned imperial nobleman Vir Singh Bundela.[34] Like Khan Jahan Lodi, Jujhar Singh was severely punished. Invariably, the Mughals coerced any and all powerful notables to invest themselves in the imperial political process.

## The General Population Gets Involved

If the immediate run-up to a succession struggle was a fearful time for princes, their retainers, their friends and allies, and the Mughal nobility in general, what of the general population of the empire? Did succession conflicts matter to the empire's mass subjects?

Following one of the central arguments of this book – that imperial, regional, and local-level politics were intimately linked and that dynastic politics played an important role in connecting them – it is clear that the Mughal public closely monitored princely succession struggles. Although there was not much fear of collateral fallout beyond the regions immediately involved, most people had good reason to dread the broader strife

[34] Shah Nawaz Khan, *Maasiru-l-Umara*, ed. Abdur Rahim and Ashraf Ali, vol. 2 (Calcutta, 1890), p. 198.

that might accompany a contested succession. Historical experience had taught them that even if their homes were not in the line of marching armies or caught amid battles, even if they managed to escape the concomitant displacement and destruction, the transition from one ruler to the next invariably resulted in a temporary slackening of imperial administrative and political controls, during which time all manner of actors tended to wreak havoc.

On the frontiers of the empire, the Safavids, the Uzbeks, the Deccan Sultanates, and the Rajas of Cooch Bihar and Assam each at various times exploited imperial succession struggles to attempt a land grab. The Rajas, for instance, made significant inroads into Eastern Bengal in 1658 because the province had been stripped of military resources by its then-governor Prince Shuja' as he pursued his claim to the Mughal throne.[35] The long-term threat this posed was considered so grave that after his accession, Aurangzeb ordered his prime minister, Mir Jumla, to lead a massive but ultimately unsuccessful expedition to conquer Cooch Bihar and Assam.

Within the empire itself, the Mughals faced all manner of potential challengers around times of succession-related strife. Some – such as the Portuguese in Bengal in 1627–8 – looked for any opportunity to assert their independence. Others – such as the Berads under Padiyah Nayaka, the Bundelas under Chatrasal Bundela, and the Razu *zamindar*s along the Andhra coast in 1707–8 – wanted to either renegotiate the terms of their relationship with the Mughals or be better incorporated into the rewards structure of the empire when they struck out in revolt. Then there were the individuals and groups that created disturbances as they sought profit in the absence of imperial order. The Italian adventurer/traveler/servitor Manucci offers a particularly harrowing eyewitness account of a 1658 attack on a convoy of travelers outside Delhi staged by "villagers and thieves," and from which he barely escaped with his life.[36] At times, a locality or region simply went up in flames as rival families, lineages, or other groups took advantage of a distracted imperial state to settle scores or gain power that they hoped would later be endorsed by the Mughals in order to restore normalcy and calm.

Even if local people were not directly impacted by violence, the threat of other tribulations always loomed. These might include looting, panic

---

[35] Shihab-din-Din Talish, *Fathiya-i 'Ibriya*, National Library of India, Sarkar Collection 77, f. 6.

[36] Niccolao Manucci, *Mogul India or Storio do Mongor*, trans. W. Irvine, vol. 1 (Delhi, repr. 1996), pp. 292–3.

buying, food shortages, price gouging by merchants, stalled economic activity, the threat of destitution, or the sudden arrival of large numbers of displaced people from other parts of the empire.

Given the potentially disruptive impact of an actual succession struggle, subjects of the empire were eager to find out all that could be known as the inevitable battle loomed. Accurate news, however, as one chronicler suggests, was hard to come by.[37] People had to rely on rumor and gossip – C. A. Bayly's "petty economy of information" – whose specifics we often find in Mughal and European sources from the period.[38] For instance, echoing widespread fears that Dara Shukoh and his brothers were gearing up for a succession fight, one 1652 East India Company communication breathlessly, if inaccurately, reports the rumor that Prince Shuja' tried to assassinate Dara Shukoh and seize Agra but was turned back outside the city and was being pursued by a royal army under Dara Shukoh's command.[39] Toward the end of Aurangzeb's reign, in 1693, a rumor that he had died not only led to panic among the Mughal forces besieging the fortress of Jinji, but also propelled his son Kam Bakhsh into an open confrontation with the emperor's representatives. Toward the end of Aurangzeb's life, "wild and heart-sickening rumors,"[40] "ominous rumor (s),"[41] and "terrifying rumors"[42] that the emperor was dead repeatedly swept through the empire. As well as reflecting the anxieties of the population, such rumors point to the public's intense interest and focus on the dynasty.

In modern democratic states, elections are held on pre-decided and fixed dates. The simple reason for this is to provide certainty and focus for voters and politicians alike. Neither accompanied changes in the leadership of the Mughal Empire. No one could guess when an emperor might die, so princes and their supporters always had to be ready to stake their claim to political power. Moreover, as emperors aged, the expectation that a succession struggle was imminent and unavoidable grew stronger. Princes responded by stepping up their preparations and some, as we have seen, even moved to kill off their rivals. A sense of anticipation mixed with fear descended on the empire. It enveloped everyone from princes and the

---

[37] Saxsena, *Tarikh-i-Dilkasha*, p. 256.
[38] C. A. Bayly, *Empire and Information: Intelligence Gathering and Social Communication in India, 1780–1870* (Cambridge, 1996), p. 18.
[39] W. Foster, *The English Factories in India, 1618–1669*, vol. 9 (Oxford, 1915), p. 132.
[40] Musta'idd Khan, *Maasir i Alamgiri*, ed. Agha Ahmad Ali (Calcutta, 1871), p. 509.
[41] K. Khan, *Muntakhab al-Labab*, vol. 2, p. 539.
[42] Saxsena, *Tarikh-i-Dilkasha*, p. 256.

Mughal nobility down to the empire's more humble subjects. In this process, the attention of all became focused on the dynasty and had the effect of legitimizing its authority to rule. Although relatively few players had any direct role in the choice of a new emperor, as the next section will show, all imperial subjects anticipated and expected that he would restore order and calm once the dust of battle had finally settled.

## THE AFTERMATH

Beyond all the years of planning discussed earlier and in preceding chapters, ultimate success on the day of actual battle required military skills (strategy, leadership, and so on) and, of course, always also a dose of good luck. Some fortuitous circumstance might favor a candidate even in the run-up to a contest. For instance, if Shah Jahan had followed his instincts and taken the field against Aurangzeb and Murad, it is unlikely that his sons would have prevailed at the pivotal Battle of Samugarh. Sometimes luck might be manifest in the course of a battle itself: Mu'azzam's forces benefited from the hot dusty winds blowing directly into the eyes of A'zam's forces during the Battle of Jaju, obscuring vision and limiting the range and effectiveness of his archers and musketeers, the sources tell us.

Rather than focusing on actual battlefield tactics and strategies, this section moves directly to the aftermath of a succession battle, to the processes set into play by the accession of a new emperor. By considering imperial recalibration following years of brutal political maneuvering and sometimes hard-fought succession battles, we can better appreciate the benefits that an open system of succession afforded the Mughal enterprise. The following discussion focuses on five topics: (i) the treatment of defeated princely rivals, (ii) the fate of a defeated prince's supporters, (iii) the fate of a triumphant prince's supporters, (iv) reactions to the rise of new imperial elites, and (v) the ways in which a new emperor might assert his imperial authority.

### How were Defeated Princely Rivals Treated?

I have tentatively posited a move from greater tolerance for princely rivals to harsh retribution against them over the course of the first hundred years of Mughal history. Contrast Humayun's behavior in 1530 to Khurram's in 1628. The former not only overlooked an accession-related challenge from Babur's brother-in-law Mahdi Khwaja, but four years on went so far as to contract his half brother Mirza Hindal's first marriage (with elaborate celebrations) to the Khwaja's sister. Humayun's patronage of Mahdi Khwaja continued in the years that followed.[43] Almost a century later, when Khurram had ascended the throne, his five princely rivals were shown no such equanimity; rather, they were murdered on his express orders in one fell swoop.

Historiographical treatments of imperial brutality toward princely rivals even prior to succession wars offer us another lens onto shifting attitudes at the official level. Here we might contrast Gulbadan Begum's account of Humayun's decision to blind Mirza Kamran in 1553 against later ones discussing Khurram's actions in 1628. Gulbadan Begum was Humayun's half sister and Akbar's aunt. In the late 1580s, on Akbar's specific request, she wrote what amounted to a semi-official history of the major events of the reigns of Babur and Humayun. In the section dealing with Mirza Kamran's blinding after years of obstinate opposition, Gulbadan Begum reflects a still-prevalent queasiness about mutilating, let alone killing, members of the royal family. She portrays Humayun as deeply conflicted about punishing his half brother. But the account also reveals a view among the nobles that an ideal ruler had to put aside personal feelings and act solely on the basis of imperial justice:

In the end, all the khans and sultans, noble and commoner, young and old, military and civilian who had suffered at the hands of Mirza Kamran gathered at an assembly and unanimously said to the emperor, "When one is an emperor and ruler, one cannot be a brother. If you want to give special treatment to your brother, you must abdicate; if you want to rule, you must forget about being a brother." ... In reply the emperor said, "Although I well comprehend what you say, I cannot bring myself to do it." All raised their voices and said, "What Your Majesty has been told is the only correct path to follow."[44]

Humayun eventually signed off on the decision to blind Mirza Kamran but only after getting an assembly of nobles to individually initial a document that stated that this was their express wish. According to Gulbadan Begum, "The emperor's hand was forced."

Gulbadan's depiction of an unsure and reluctant Humayun is echoed in a number of other sources from the late sixteenth century, including Shaikh Abu'l Fazl's *Akbarnama* and Bayazid Bayat's *Tarikh-i Humayun*. The idea of hurting or killing one's royal opponents remained a troubling

---

[43] Khwandamir, *Qanun-i-Humayuni*, ed. M. Hidayat Hosain (Calcutta, 1940), pp. 88–9; Begum, *Ahwal-i Humayun Badshah*, ff. 28b–29b.

[44] Begum, *Ahwal-i Humayun Badshah*, f. 82a.

part of what seemed to be required of a king and ruler. Contrast this, however, with later historiographical treatments of Khurram's decision.

Judging from a number of important contemporary sources produced during Khurram/Shah Jahan's reign – *Ma'asir-i Jahangiri, Iqbalnama-i Jahangiri, Padshahnama, 'Amal-i Salih, Zakhirat-ul-Khawanin*, and *Shahjahannama* – no effort is made to obfuscate the prince's involvement in the decision to kill his half brother, two first cousins, and two nephews. Unlike Humayun, Khurram is never shown to have any regrets, nor does he attempt to place the onus for the decision on anyone other than himself. Indeed, all these accounts implicitly laud Khurram's decisiveness and leadership. This hardening of imperial attitudes toward defeated rivals is especially striking in some of the accompanying commentary.

For instance, *Ma'asir-i Jahangiri* and *Iqbalnama-i Jahangiri* describe Khurram's actions as a "blessing" (*sawab*) because they rid the world of anxiety and rebelliousness.[45] *'Amal-i Salih* suggests that Khurram's actions were necessary to avoid future "contagion/corruption" (*fasad*).[46] *Zakhirat-ul-Khawanin* elliptically offers a saying ("The action of the wise is not without wisdom") and a verse ("One hundred thousand [Israelite] children were beheaded/before he [*kalimullah*, i.e., Moses] who conversed with God became master of insight") to indicate its approval.[47] Although generally echoing the necessity of Khurram's actions, the *Padshahnama* offers an almost gleeful account of the princes' swift dispatch to the "oasis of annihilation" (*wadi-yi fana*).[48] All these contrast sharply with the tone of reluctance and regret that hangs over Jauhar Aftabchi's eyewitness account of the blinding of Mirza Kamran in *Tazkirat-ul-Waqi'at*: "No one would draw the needle across Kamran Mirza's eyes."[49]

As imperial attitudes toward defeated princely rivals shifted in the seventeenth century, a new ideology of rule emerged, one in which kinship and brotherly love were conclusively trumped by the expectation that an emperor dispensed justice and order unflinchingly. Further evidence for this can be found in *Mau'izah-i Jahangiri*, a 1612 "mirror for princes" written by a high-ranking Mughal nobleman named Muhammad Baqir

[45] Kamgar Husaini, *Ma'asir-i-Jahangiri*, ed. Azra Alavi (Bombay, 1978), p. 491; Motamid Khan, *Iqbalnamah-i Jahangiri*, ed. Abdul Hai and Ahmad Ali (Calcutta, 1865), p. 303.

[46] S. Lahori, *'Amal-i Salih*, vol. 1, p. 182.

[47] Shaikh Farid Bhakkari, *Dhakhirat al-Khawanin*, ed. S. Moinul Haq, vol. 3 (Karachi, 1970), p. 53.

[48] 'Abd al-Hamid Lahawri, *Padshahnamah*, ed. Kabir-ud-din Ahmad and Abdul Rahim, vol. 1 (Calcutta, 1867), p. 79.

[49] Jauhar Aftabchi, *Tazkirat-ul-Waqi'at*, trans. S. Moinul Haq (Karachi, 1956), p. 105.

and dedicated to Emperor Jahangir. Comparing the quest for rulership to the drive for sexual conquest, he emphatically states:

Victorious emperors satisfy their driving passion for the virgin lady of sovereign rule only when the glare of their flaming sword has erased from life's tablet the name of their malicious enemy. Famous rulers raise the goblet of their desire to lips of repose only when they have shattered their enemy's cup of aspirations with the stone of victory.[50]

Just as Khurram/Shah Jahan showed no reluctance or remorse for killing his princely rivals, the same was true for his successor, Aurangzeb, when he turned down Dara Shukoh's request for clemency following his capture.[51] Aurangzeb also ordered the execution of his younger brother, Murad and Dara Shukoh's oldest son Sulaiman Shukoh. Lest there be any doubt, judging from Manucci's account, Dara Shukoh would have acted with the same dispatch had he ascended the throne. If this had come to pass, we are told, Dara Shukoh would have not only ordered Aurangzeb's decapitation but also commanded that parts of his body be hung on Delhi's four major gates for all to see.[52]

How do we explain this evolution of imperial attitudes? A central determinant seems to have been the move away from an appanage model to an imperial one that stressed the absolute indivisibility of the empire. In this scheme, the emperor was no longer a first-among-equals but rather the sole fount of all power and authority. As long as former rivals for political power remained alive, the emperor's position would be something less than cleanly singular. That this threat was not an idle one is evident in the bloody riots that broke out in Delhi following Dara Shukoh's capture and return to the city in 1659. Among the masterminds of the disturbances was one Haibat, who had been a trooper in the defeated prince's household.[53] Four years later, Aurangzeb had to quash a plot to spring Murad from his prison cell in Gwalior fort. That effort was led by a group of the prince's former household retainers who had been quietly camped at the fort waiting for an opportunity to free their master.[54] Both events led directly to Aurangzeb's decision to execute his brothers. There could be no second chances for defeated claimants to the throne.

---

[50] Muhammad Baqir, *Advice on the Art of Governance, Mau'izah-i Jahangiri of Muhammad Baqir Najm-i Sani*, trans. Sajida Alvi (Albany, 1989), p. 49.

[51] Aurangzeb, *Raqa'im-i Kara'im*, Asiatic Society of Bengal, Ivanow 383, ff. 205a-b.

[52] Manucci, *Mogul India*, vol. 1, p. 339.

[53] K. Khan, *Muntakhab al-Labab*, vol. 2, p. 86.

[54] Ibid., p. 155.

The lingering presence of princely contenders also posed a threat to the emperor's direct heirs, the next generation of princes. Were their descendants to vie for the Mughal throne, the sheer number of potential candidates would quickly negate any advantages an open-ended system of succession conferred. In this light, consider several succinct and often-quoted dictums of the time: "Ten poor men can sleep on one rug, but two kings cannot fit into one clime. /If a man of God eats half a loaf of bread, he gives the other half to the poor. /A king may take possession of an entire clime, but he will still hunger for another."[55] "As long as the head of a claimant to the throne is on his body/The body of the country is clothed in the garment of disturbance."[56] "As there is one God in Heaven, so there must be one King on earth."[57] "The art of reigning is so delicate that a King's jealousy might be awakened by his very shadow."[58] The Mughal Empire demonstrated an increasing conviction that no royal rival to the emperor (besides his own sons) could be spared his life.

## How were the Supporters of Defeated Princes Treated?

Whereas defeated princes faced a gory fate, the treatment of their supporters was quite a different story. In rare instances, particularly partisan or threatening supporters were executed. This happened to a group of Shuja"s servants after their capture by Dara Shukoh's forces in 1658.[59] Three decades earlier, the official responsible for Shahryar's household, Sharif-ul-Mulk, was also executed following Shah Jahan's accession to the throne. His case is somewhat unusual, though, because his partisanship was coupled with the crime of violating the imperial person: in 1626, he had ordered a cannonade on Prince Khurram's wife's tent outside the besieged city of Thatta. In all likelihood, it is the latter act that marked him as a dead man once Khurram ascended the throne. In general however – as Satish Chandra, M. Athar Ali, and Muzaffar Alam have

---

[55] Zahir-ud-Din Muhammad Babur, *The Baburnama: Memoirs of Babur, Prince and Emperor*, trans. W. M. Thackston (New York, 2002), p. 144. Two centuries later, the relevance of the verse in capturing the tenor of princely struggles had not diminished. See K. Khan, *Muntakhab al-Labab*, vol. 2, p. 37.

[56] K. Khan, *Muntakhab al-Labab*, vol. 2, p. 104.

[57] Cited in Shibli Nomani, *Alamgir*, trans. Saiyid Sabah-ud-din Abdur Rahman (Delhi, 1981), p. 76.

[58] According to François Bernier, in the wake of the imprisonment of Muhammad Sultan for rebellion, Aurangzeb warned his second son Mu'azzam to keep his own political ambitions in check by reciting this saying. *Travels in the Mogul Empire*, p. 84.

[59] K. Khan, *Muntakhab al-Labab*, vol. 2, p. 6.

previously observed – the Mughals mostly avoided killing a rival prince's supporters once a succession fight had concluded.[60] Indeed, a key feature of the Mughal system was the powerful impulse to reintegrate a rival prince's supporters into the imperial fold. In the end, despite an expectation of brutality toward defeated princely rivals, the same was rarely extended to a defeated opponent's supporters or the populace at large. This situation remained true until the war of succession of 1712–13.

The magnanimous approach to supporters of a defeated prince encompassed the powerful and inconsequential alike. Thus, on one end of the social spectrum, we can point to stories such as Jahan Ara's. Despite her history as a lifelong partisan of Dara Shukoh and her refusal to accept Aurangzeb's legitimacy until after the death of their father Shah Jahan in 1666, Aurangzeb eventually rehabilitated the princess by releasing her from house arrest in Agra, allowing her to return to Delhi, giving her a massive mansion in the city, making her the guardian of the deceased Dara Shukoh's daughter Jahanzeb Banu Begum, allowing her to officiate over the marriage of that daughter and his own son A'zam, and generally treating her with honor and respect until her death in 1681. So also, even though there was little love lost between Jahangir and Mirza 'Aziz Koka or Raja Man Singh, who had both supported his son Khusrau's rival claims to the throne and had questioned Salim/Jahangir's competence prior to Emperor Akbar's death, Jahangir eventually decided against casting them out of the Mughal nobility. And even though Raja Jaswant Singh repeatedly fought against and betrayed Aurangzeb (his desertion during the Battle of Khajwa against Shuja' almost cost Aurangzeb the throne), the emperor allowed him to remain one of the highest-ranking nobles in the empire until his death in 1678. Despite 'Abdullah Khan's unsavory reputation as a serial turncoat – first betraying Akbar in 1599, Salim in 1604, Jahangir in 1622, and finally Khurram in 1624 – he too never suffered any political consequences. These are just a few of the many striking examples of high-ranking individuals enjoying successful careers despite having chosen the losing side in a succession struggle.

The tendency to accommodate lower-ranking supporters of the losing side was equally strong. Despite a hard-fought war against Shuja' between 1658 and 1660, Aurangzeb eventually promoted Mirza Jani, the

---

[60] Satish Chandra, *Parties and Politics at the Mughal Court, 1707–1740* (Delhi, repr. 2002), p. 62; M. Athar Ali, "Toward an Interpretation of the Mughal Empire," in *Mughal India: Studies in Polity, Ideas, Society, and Culture* (Delhi, 2006), pp. 65–6; Muzaffar Alam, *Crisis of Empire in Mughal North India: Awadh & the Punjab 1707–1748* (Delhi, repr. 1997), pp. 43–4.

commander of Shuja''s artillery, to become commandant of Rajmahal (in Bengal). He also allowed Zia-ud-Din Muhammad Shah Shuja'i, another long-standing Shuja' servitor, to eventually become an important member of Prince Akbar's emerging princely household.[61] Following the 1659 Battle of Deorai (that ended any hopes of victory for Dara Shukoh), the defeated prince's supporters appealed to Aurangzeb for forgiveness, and it was readily granted. Such generosity of spirit drew the acerbic comment from Manucci that Aurangzeb's victory was largely accomplished by conferring "many distinctions and gifts on the men of Shahjahan, Dara, Murad Bakhsh, and Sulaiman Shukoh who came over to his side."[62]

Even those once part of a defeated prince's inner circle were not automatically denied access to imperial patronage. Thus, after a hiatus of a few years, Dara Shukoh's personal secretary, Chandar Bhan Brahmin, was granted the prestigious position of caretaker of Shah Jahan's tomb along with his son Tegh Bhan.[63] Shaikh Wajih-ud-Din, a tutor of Dara Shukoh and a princely appointee to the position of *sadr* in Allahabad, went on to become one of the compilers of the *Fatawa-yi 'Alamgiri*, an ambitious multivolume legal digest of Hanafi law sponsored by Aurangzeb. Even Khafi Khan's father Khwaja Mir – who was involved in the abortive effort to rescue Aurangzeb's imprisoned brother Murad – eventually found employment in the imperial service. Men whose loyalty had once been honored with the right to take on the appellation of their princely master ("Dara Shukohi," "Murad Bakhshi," "Shah Shuja'i," etc.), continued to publicly proclaim their former allegiance even after they had entered Aurangzeb's service, without concern for retribution. The Mughal newsletters from Aurangzeb's reign offer us striking examples of men such as Sundar Das Dara Shukohi, whose son received an imperial *mansab* in

---

[61] In 1687, following the failure of Akbar's rebellion against Aurangzeb, Zia-ud-Din Muhammad Shah Shuja'i would be counted among a small clutch of forty or fifty diehard princely supporters who chose a life of exile and possible hardship in Iran over submission to Aurangzeb. K. Khan, *Muntakhab al-Labab*, vol. 2, p. 285.

[62] Manucci, *Mogul India*, vol. 1, p. 292. Despite his own misgivings about Aurangzeb and his deep affection for Dara Shukoh, Manucci also eventually found his way into the service of the emperor's son Mu'azzam. His past association with Dara Shukoh never came up as a reason to disqualify him from imperial patronage. That forgiveness was central to Aurangzeb's efforts to co-opt and break his brothers' political support is evident from the way in which he wooed Murad's supporters following the prince's imprisonment in 1658. See Hatim Khan, *'Alamgirnama*, British Museum, Add. Or. 26233, f. 42a.

[63] *Akhbarat-i Darbar-i Mu'alla*, vol. 34, p. 221. Although the *Akhbarat* suggest Shah Jahan, other sources indicate that Chandar Bhan Brahmin ended up as the custodian of Jahangir's tomb.

1665; 'Ali Quli Beg Murad Bakhshi, an imperial superintendent (*muhtasib*) in the 1690s and early 1700s; and Khwaja 'Ishrat Shah Shuja'i, who served as imperial eunuch in the 1690s.[64]

Naturally not everyone was willing or even able to accommodate him- or herself to a new imperial dispensation. The refusal by Zinat-un-Nisa, Aurangzeb's daughter and a powerful political force in the last decade of his reign, to pay obeisance to Mu'azzam following her favorite brother A'zam's death at the Battle of Jaju in 1707 led to her confinement in the Red Fort in Delhi. After losing the 1627–8 war of succession with Khurram, Nur Jahan (d. 1645) lived the remainder of her life under strict house arrest as well. And in an early case from Akbar's reign, the nobleman Shah Abu'l Ma'ali's unjustified pretensions to being an equal of the then-teenaged emperor – Humayun had referred to Ma'ali as a son and granted him honors deserving of an imperial prince – led to his disgrace, rebellion, and eventual death.

The sources also point to sporadic instances of revenge by a new emperor against a loyalist of the defeated prince. Over the course of the seventeenth century, a small number of nobles were permanently removed from the imperial service. Thus, at the beginning of Aurangzeb's reign, Taqarrub Khan (Shah Jahan's personal physician), Sadiq Khan (the empire's chief chronicler), and the Qazi-ul-Quzzat (who refused to sanction the Friday sermon, a critical marker of kingly authority, in Aurangzeb's name as long as Shah Jahan was still alive) were part of a tiny group of high-ranking individuals who were prematurely cashiered. Yet, at the same time, even Dara Shukoh's close confidant and religious mentor Mulla Shah Badakhshi was allowed to live out his life in comfort after he humbled himself before Aurangzeb by constructing an auspicious chronogram ("the shadow of truth," *zill al-haq*) out of the year of the emperor's accession.[65]

We can speak of a sixteenth- and seventeenth-century Mughal custom of forgiveness, and a related cult of loyal nobles and households. An episode particularly revealing of this political culture took place in the aftermath of Mu'azzam's victory over A'zam in 1707. According to the contemporary chronicler Iradat Khan, a group of vengeful retainers from Mu'azzam's household urged the new emperor to punish certain Aurangzeb-era nobles who had supported his deceased brother

---

[64] *Akhbarat-i Darbar-i Mu'alla*, vol. 34, p. 217; vol. 19, pp. 95, 133, 146 160, 380; vol. 30, p. 51.

[65] M. Khan, *Maasir i Alamgiri*, p. 14.

A'zam. Mu'azzam (now crowned Bahadur Shah I) is said to have turned to his trusted chief counselor Mun'im Khan for advice. Acting as an intercessor for the old nobility, the Khan suggested that they be pardoned because they had done nothing beyond the pale of imperial experience in following a princely contender for the throne. On the contrary, Mun'im Khan went on, the very loyalty of these nobles to A'zam deserved to be commended. Characterizing the empire as a massive tent, he asserted that the nobility were the many "strong pillars" (*sutun-i 'umda*) and "powerful ropes" (*risman-i qawi*) needed to keep it standing. The nobility, he argued, encompassed generations of experience and expertise that were integral to the workings of the empire. The Khan advised against replacing Aurangzeb's nobility, warning that the new emperor risked losing a wealth of skills, relationships, and wisdom. Indeed, as we know, nobles were crucial to the networks and alliances on which the Mughal system so heavily depended. Mun'im Khan went on to advise that Bahadur Shah should win the old nobility to his side by rewarding each according to his talents and skills. In doing so, he would bring honor on himself. To the great annoyance of his critics, Bahadur Shah is said to have closely followed Mun'im Khan's counsel.[66]

An emperor's capacity for forgiveness had long been vaunted in medieval Indian culture. For example, the *Chachnama*, an early thirteenth-century account of the conquest of Sind by the Arabs, advocates, "Whenever kings and great men gain a victory, and chiefs and nobles of the party of the enemy fall into their hands, they should be pardoned."[67] Toward the end of the thirteenth century, Amir Khusrau, writing in *Qiran al-Sa'dain* (ca. 1289), approvingly quotes the ruler Bughra Khan telling his son that long-lasting political power depends on forgiving whenever possible and punishing only those who are really enemies.[68] In the *Akbarnama*, the official history of Akbar's reign, the emperor's willingness to forgive egregious offences is repeatedly highlighted as a mark of his greatness. On the day Aurangzeb released Mu'azzam from prison after almost eight years' incarceration, he advised his son "to stand midway between gentleness and severity." He recounted the story of their fifteenth-century Timurid forebear Sultan Ulugh Beg who was "fearless in shedding

[66] Wazih, *Tarikh-i Iradat Khan*, pp. 74, 75–6. See also Kamraj, *A'zam al-Harb*, ff. 419–20; Saxsena, *Nuskha-i Dilkasha*, ff. 167a–168a.
[67] André Wink, *Al-Hind: The Making of the Indo-Islamic World*, vol. 1 (Delhi, 1990), p. 154.
[68] Peter Hardy, *Historians of Medieval India: Studies in Indo-Muslim Historical Writing* (London, 1960), pp. 73–5.

blood" and was eventually overthrown by his own son. On the way to prison, according to Aurangzeb's recounting, Ulugh Beg asked a bystander what was the reason for his downfall. The man answered: "On account of your bloodshed ... men shrink from you."[69]

The link between forgiveness (*'afw*) and imperial greatness is repeatedly asserted in imperially sponsored chronicles such as the *Padshahnama* and the *'Alamgirnama*. It is also present in the *Ganj-i Sa'adat*, a didactic text written in 1663 by a Sufi Naqshbandi, Mu'in-ud-Din bin Siraj-ud-Din Khwand Mahmud and dedicated to the recently ascended Emperor Aurangzeb. To forgive, states the text emphatically, is "to abandon the banner of the sinner." To emphasize the significance of forgiving, a number of Prophetic sayings (*hadith*) are quoted. One states that forgiveness is both superior and more satisfying than one hundred acts of vengeance, another that the mark of a truly strong person is not one who is powerful, such as a king, but rather one who exercises self-control and mastery over his spirit in times of anger or hatred. The author reminds his reader that the Prophet himself forgave the Quraysh after his victory over Mecca and proceeds to list several other examples of forgiving leaders throughout history: the Caliph 'Ali, the Prophet's grandson Hussain, a number of the Prophet's Companions, the legendary Persian king Jamshid, the Sassanian king Khusrau I (Naushirvan), Mahmud of the Ghaznavid dynasty, and the Timurid prince Sultan Abu Sa'id.[70] Finally, the author tells of Sebuktigin of the Ghaznavid dynasty, who released a baby gazelle back to its distressed mother and was then visited in a dream by the Prophet Muhammad, who promised that he would become a king some day. If someone could be so magnanimous to an animal, the Prophet is reported to have said, then he more than deserved the right to rule over people.[71]

### What Happened to a Triumphant Prince's Supporters?

A new emperor was immediately concerned not only with matters of punishment and forgiveness, but also with the issue of reward. He had to figure out how best and how much to reward partisans within the imperial apparatus and also his own (once princely) supporters. Those already in the imperial service often received promotions in rank, title, and/or

---

[69] Aurangzeb, *Anecdotes*, p. 40.
[70] Mu'in-ud-Din bin Siraj-ud-Din Khwand Mahmud, *Ganj-i Sa'adat*, Asiatic Society of Bengal, Ivanow 1275, ff. 537a-545a.
[71] Ibid., f. 540b.

responsibility. In some instances, the rewards were particularly dramatic, as seen in the example of Asaf Khan, the father of Khurram/Shah Jahan's primary wife Mumtaz Mahal and a central player in Khurram's successful accession in 1627–8. In addition to receiving the highest *mansab* ever given to a nobleman up to that point in Mughal history, Asaf Khan also received the honorific "Yamin-ud-Daula" (Right Hand of the State), the position of *wakil* (honorary head of the nobility), the governorships of Lahore and Multan, and charge of a special imperial seal called the *azuk*.[72]

For former household retainers, years of service in a cause fraught with uncertainty and danger often culminated in massive rewards. Senior members of a princely household were usually inducted into the imperial nobility. For instance, large numbers of Salim/Jahangir's childhood companions and princely partisans ascended to the highest rungs of the imperial hierarchy.[73] A few (such as Vir Singh Bundela, who assassinated Akbar's advisor Shaikh Abu'l Fazl on Salim's behalf, and Salim's childhood friend Shaikh Hassu/Muqarrab Khan) even received special land grants called *al-tamgha jagir*s that gave them authority over the territory of their birthplaces. These particular rewards departed from earlier imperial policies that rotated provincial land assignments to prevent nobles from becoming entrenched in their homelands.

The new inductees into the imperial hierarchy were absolutely central to the consolidation of power by a new emperor, because they served as important political and military counterweights to nobles from previous reigns. So, when Jahangir ordered 'Abd-ul-Rahim Khan-i Khanan to bring Prince Danyal's family to the imperial court following his accession, he deputed his childhood friend and princely retainer Shaikh Hassu/Muqarrab Khan to make sure that the old Akbar-era nobleman fulfilled his command. When Aurangzeb appointed an imperial army to chase down Dara Shukoh in 1658, he deputed one Shah Jahan–era nobleman, Khalilullah Khan, together with a princely loyalist, Muhammad Tahir Khurasani (newly ennobled as Safshikan Khan), to the task. The equally important pursuit of Aurangzeb's other brother Shuja' was entrusted to Mir Jumla (Shah Jahan's last prime minister) along with Muhammad Beg/Zulfiqar Khan, who had long been Aurangzeb's chief attendant. When

---

[72] S. Khan, *Maasir-ul-Umara*, vol. 1, pp. 151–60.

[73] This list included Sharif Khan, Shaikh Hassu, Shaikh Khubu, Zamana Beg, Shaikh Shuja'at, Miran Sadr-i Jahan, Shaikh 'Ala-ud-Din, 'Ali Asghar Barha, Shaikh Bayazid, Khwaja Muhammad Muqim Harvi, Khan Beg, Lala Beg Kabuli, Vir Singh Bundela, Mir Zia-ud-Din Qazwini, Pukhta Khan Kabuli, Mirza Barkhurdar, Rukn-ud-Din Rohilla, Khwaja Fathullah, Khwaja Dost Muhammad, Raja Basu, and Amba Khan Kashmiri.

Bahadur Shah I wanted to break the hold of Aurangzeb's long-serving prime minister (*wazir*) Asad Khan and his son Zulfiqar Khan on the top positions of the empire, he appointed the head of his princely household, Mun'im Khan, to replace Asad Khan while confirming Zulfiqar Khan in his former position as *Mir Bakhshi* (paymaster general).

In addition to functioning as a powerful loyalist bloc within the Mughal nobility, princely inductees also extended the emperor's control over the administrative arms of the empire. Thus, in the shakeup that followed Shah Jahan's accession, of the nine governors who lost their positions in 1628–9, princely loyalists replaced six. Those newly promoted included Khwaja Baqi Khan (Sind), Khan 'Alam (Bihar), Lashkar Khan (Kabul), Wazir Khan (Agra), Jan Nisar Khan (Allahabad), and Qulij Khan (Delhi). The penetration of Shah Jahan's princely loyalists was even more profound if we note that the *suba*s of Lahore, Kashmir, Multan, and Ajmer were given over to men who either had long-standing familial and political ties to Shah Jahan or had joined his rebellion in its final year.

We see a similar pattern of princely loyalists being appointed to lower administrative positions. In the first decade of his reign, Aurangzeb sent many former princely *chela*s (disciples) into operation across the empire in subsidiary roles. Besides Kabul Beg Chela, the chief police officer (*kotwal*) of Agra in 1666, and Farhad Chela, who was appointed commandant of Sylhet in 1669, we encounter others such as Adam Chela, who was tasked with acquiring horses for the emperor. Then there were those who hunted with Aurangzeb, relayed special orders, served as local intelligence gatherers, or fulfilled special missions, such as Gada Beg Chela, who was ordered to destroy Hindu temples in Ujjain in retaliation for local resistance to new horse-branding regulations.[74] Thus the years of experience gained in a princely household, at all levels of its hierarchy, would be redeployed, on behalf of the new emperor, in the service of the empire as a whole.

The fortunes of long-standing supporters of the new emperor represent a sort of imperial meritocracy that rewarded service and capability over status or lineage. Akbar articulated just such a merit-based philosophy of leadership; he wrote the following to his son Danyal on the eve of the latter's first major administrative assignment as governor of Allahabad in 1597: "Consider nobility of caste and high birth as an outcome of a person's character, rather than goodness inherited from grandfathers or the greatness of the family. You can understand this truth by knowing that

---

[74] *Akhbarat-i Darbar-i Mu'alla*, vol. 34, pp. 236, 239, 241, 253, 329.

although smoke comes from fire it has no light."[75] Rather than relying on a fixed core of elite nobles who claimed the top positions by right of birth, the Mughals built a relatively fluid imperial system, one whose membership was regularly refreshed. Thus it is rare to find more than two generations of the same family reaching the highest pinnacles of power over successive reigns.

### Resistance to the New Nobles

The integration of large numbers of princely supporters into the nobility was never a seamless process, as Muzaffar Alam's work on relations in the post-1707 period between the *umara'-i jadid* (new nobles) and *khanazad*s (house-born) attests.[76] Even prior to the eighteenth century, a strong current of animosity existed among the older, more established elements of the nobility toward newly promoted outsiders. This manifested itself in snide asides such as that of a Mughal wit who remarked, "Khanship became cheap in Emperor Jahangir's reign."[77] Or in Mirza 'Aziz Koka's bitter complaints to Jahangir in 1612–13 that he had unjustly deviated from long-standing patterns of imperial patronage to the Chaghatais and Rajputs in favor of new groups such as the Shaikhzadas (who had ties to Jahangir dating back to his princely years). We might also read in the 1659 riots that occurred in Delhi following Dara Shukoh's forcible return an expression of the city's general distaste for the arriviste Afghans, Marathas, and Dakhanis who accompanied Aurangzeb up from the Deccan.

Elite anxieties about a changing social order were reflected in manuals – called *mirzanama*s – that detailed the proper conduct and etiquette of gentlemen. The best known was an anonymous work completed in the early 1660s. Although the author never directly refers to the recently concluded succession struggle between Aurangzeb and his brothers or the promotion of large numbers of Aurangzeb's princely retainers into the imperial nobility, it may be surmised that these developments played some role in inspiring its composition.

Rosalind O'Hanlon points to this *mirzanama* as articulating a shift away from an earlier vision of manliness realized largely through loyalty and

---

[75] Fazl, *Akbarnamah*, vol. 3, p. 722. For other discussions of the significance of merit to the Mughals, see Jos Gommans, *Mughal Warfare* (London, 2002), pp. 90–1, Harbans Mukhia, *The Mughals of India* (Malden, MA, 2004), pp. 59–60.

[76] Alam, *Crisis of Empire in Mughal North India*, pp. 20–31.

[77] S. Khan, *Maasiru-l-Umara*, vol. 3, p. 431.

service to the empire to a new and complex set of formulations that empha-size "man as sophisticated gentleman connoisseur, cosmopolitan in experi-ence, refined in literary and poetic sensibility, elegant in person, fastidious in dress, and intent on his own bodily cultivation with a greater degree of individual self-concern."[78] Aside from being defined "by his knowledge of manners, commodities and cultural repertoires," he is marked "by his ability to command, to savour, and consume them as connoisseur."[79] In this radically altered conception of courtly masculinity, imperial service not only became secondary to cultivating gentlemanly prestige but even repre-sented "risk, thankless trouble and distraction" and "degrading compro-mise of a dignified gentleman's independence."[80] Inasmuch as the exclusionary intent of the anonymous *Mirzanama* is clear – the manual offers itself as a guide to distinguishing between "true" and "false" *mirza*s as well *mirza*s and non-*mirza*s[81] – so too are its targets: imposters and the newly empowered non-*mirza*, whose access to imperial rank was achieved precisely through proven loyalty to their masters. Whereas the former are lambasted for their "cancerous temperament," the latter are derided as "mean and common."[82] Even if we have no evidence that the *Mirzanama* was ever widely read or that its injunctions had any currency within the ranks of the imperial nobility, the very fact of its appearance around a time of extraordinary social mobility and dislocation suggests a vain attempt by at least one person to hold the line against the rise of what were perceived by imperial insiders as parvenus and social upstarts.

In an episode from around 1667–8 involving Aurangzeb's foster brother Bahadur Khan Koka and Mahabat Khan, a holdover from Shah Jahan's reign, we see many of the social anxieties and tensions that informed the 1660 *Mirzanama* played out. Our source is once again the Italian Manucci. Setting the stage for an "amusing affair," Manucci tells us that following Aurangzeb's accession, Bahadur Khan Koka was "lifted from an obscure position to that of a general." His sudden rise, however, caused him to "become very high and mighty and vain-glorious." Furthermore, the Koka never ceased to draw attention to his close connection to Aurangzeb. Irritated by his pretensions to high status, Mahabat Khan "decided to teach him a lesson." He did so by arranging with his own foster brother that when

---

[78] Rosalind O'Hanlon, "Manliness and Imperial Service in Mughal North India," *Journal of the Economic and Social History of the Orient* 42, no. 1 (1999): 68.

[79] Ibid., 69.

[80] Ibid., 68.

[81] Anonymous, *Mirzanama*, Asiatic Society of Bengal, Ivanow 926, f. 131a.

[82] Ibid., ff. 131a-b.

Bahadur Khan was visiting Mahabat Khan in his tent, "he should, richly clad and with an aigrette of gold stuck into his turban, gallop past on a fine horse, acting the braggart, as if on his way to his own quarters." The foster brother did as told. As anticipated, Bahadur Khan turned to Mahabat Khan and asked after the identity of the "mighty warrior" who just rode by. Mahabat Khan replied: "foster-brothers are shameless creatures, and have no tact in what they do. They fancy that, being our brothers by milk, they are equal members of our house!"[83] Although Bahadur Khan Koka is said to have understood Mahabat Khan's message, according to Manucci he chose to ignore it.

Newly ascended emperors were not unaware of the tensions around the rise of their supporters, and they tried various stratagems to paper over such differences. These included pairing individuals of different backgrounds on important missions, as mentioned earlier, and fostering exchanges of gifts between new and old nobles. Most significantly, various emperors quietly encouraged marriages that tied new and old noble families to one another.[84] Such marriage ties helped redistribute power among imperial elites. Not atypical in this regard was the marriage of one of Sharif Khan's sons to a daughter of Ja'far Beg/Asaf Khan. Sharif Khan, a childhood friend and princely loyalist of Jahangir, who was promoted to the top ranks of the nobility in 1605–6, thus became linked to one of the highest-ranking nobleman from Akbar's reign.

One of the most consequential of such matchups, however, was the marriage in 1670 between the eldest son of 'Abid Khan, a recent Central Asian immigrant and supporter of Prince Aurangzeb, and a daughter of Sa'dullah Khan, Shah Jahan's prime minister. Although Sa'dullah Khan had passed away fourteen years before, his family continued to enjoy great imperial favor and prestige. A year after the marriage, the couple produced a boy, who is best known by his imperial title, Nizam-ul-Mulk. A favorite of Aurangzeb's as a young man and one of the leading imperial generals toward the end of his reign, the Nizam went on to become prime minister of the Mughal Empire and eventually founded Hyderabad in 1724, the largest and longest-lived Mughal successor state.[85]

[83] Manucci, *Mogul India*, vol. 2, pp. 113–14.

[84] In Mughal marriage practices, we find powerful corroboration of the insights of Claude Levi-Strauss that marriage is a powerful instrument for creating trust and reciprocal obligations between antagonistic families or groups. *Elementary Structures of Kinship*, trans. James Bell, John von Sturmer, and Rodney Needham (Boston, 1969), pp. 52–68.

[85] Munis D. Faruqui, "At Empire's End: The Nizam, Hyderabad, and 18th Century India," in *Expanding Frontiers in South Asian and World History: Essays in Honour of John F.*

## How did a New Emperor Assert his Authority?

No account of the aftermath of succession struggles would be complete without a discussion of how new emperors grappled with the legacy of their immediate predecessors (with whom they had often had strained relations). A Mughal emperor enjoyed a larger than life reputation, and, given the not-uncommon hostility between father and son, it was always a matter of great interest precisely how a new emperor would relate his own political persona, policies, personal habits, and hobbies to those of the previous emperor. In the rare case when a former emperor and his son had a good relationship, as between Humayun and Akbar, we see a whole-hearted embrace of a father's legacy. Akbar thus invoked the memory of his father to justify all manner of controversial policies in the 1560s, including bringing Rajputs into the nobility, moving the Mughal polity away from a Central Asian model of shared authority, and patronizing Indian-based Sufi orders rather than Central Asian ones such as the Naqshbandis. Akbar effectively wielded Humayun's legacy to position himself as less an innovator and more an implementer of his father's imperial vision. By so doing, he was not only able to dull some of Mirza Hakim's worst attacks on his legitimacy as a Mughal, but also to assuage the concerns of most imperial nobles about his radicalism.[86]

But what happened when a father-son relationship was more troubled? On one end of the spectrum are Humayun's attempts to largely ignore the figure of his father Babur. This is most evident in one of the earliest works from Humayun's reign, the *Qanun-i Humayuni*. Written four years after Humayun's accession at the emperor's specific request, the only substantive (if entirely bland) comment about the succession is that when Babur passed away, God anointed Humayun as his successor.[87] No mention is

---

Richards, ed. Richard M. Eaton, Munis D. Faruqui, David Gilmartin, and Sunil Kumar (New Delhi, forthcoming 2012)

[86] Munis D. Faruqui, "The Forgotten Prince: Mirza Hakim and the Formation of the Mughal Empire in India," *Journal of the Economic and Social History of the Orient* 48, no. 4 (2005): 487–523.

[87] Khwandamir, *Qanun-i-Humayuni*, p. 21. This silence is in stark contrast to the efforts that began in the 1580s under Akbar to concoct a deep and loving relationship between Babur and Humayun. At the heart of later accounts was Babur's supposed decision to sacrifice his own life in return for the life of his sick son Humayun. The trouble with this story is that one of our main sources for it – Humayun's half sister Gulbadan Begum – sows a discordant note when she quietly suggests that a dying Babur had also recalled Mirza Hindal to the imperial court and was desperately focused on news of his arrival. Mirza Hindal was Gulbadan Begum's full brother and a potential political competitor. Begum, *Ahwal-i Humayun Badshah*, ff. 16b-18a.

made of their troubled relations and of Babur's doubts about his son's capacity to rule. Perhaps, further, Humayun sought distance from Babur's warrior legacy. Babur, after all, actively portrayed himself as a descendent of the fourteenth-century conqueror and ancestor of the Mughals, Amir Timur, in India. Yet, as Irfan Habib has argued, although Timur is valorized in the Central Asian context, the memory of his massacres and brutality gave him a far more ambivalent reputation in India.[88] It is not inconceivable that Humayun sensed the limits of Babur's popularity, linked as it intimately was with his Central Asian and Timurid predecessor. Given Humayun's attempts to diversify the Mughal nobility as well as his efforts to shift the ideological foundations of the Mughal Empire away from its Central Asian and steppe roots in the 1530s, it is conceivable that Humayun viewed Babur's legacy as a hindrance to setting Mughal rule in India on a firmer foundation.

At the other end of the spectrum of troubled father-son relationships is Jahangir's complex engagement with the figure of his own illustrious and popular father, Akbar. Rather than ignoring his father as Humayun largely did, Jahangir managed to simultaneously and selectively embrace and distance himself from Akbar's imperial legacy – an approach that Jahangir shared with every emperor from Shah Jahan to Bahadur Shah I. Once Salim/Jahangir was ensconced on the imperial throne, he immediately set about publicly and extravagantly honoring his deceased father. This entailed crafting a stirring eulogy; maintaining a vigil for seven days at the site of Akbar's grave; ordering the construction of a magnificent mausoleum over his father's grave at Sikandra; commanding the distribution of large amounts of food and sweets to the poor in honor of his father's memory; and immediately dispatching his second son Parvez to fight the Rajput state of Mewar, which had consistently refused to acknowledge Akbar's authority. Loyalists began almost immediately asserting that Akbar had anointed Jahangir heir to the throne toward the very end of his life.

Although neither the official chronicle of Akbar's reign, the *Akbarnama*, nor Jahangir's autobiography the *Jahangirnama* indulges in this particular assertion of imperial legitimacy, the emerging contours of the argument (as well as its discrepancies) are apparent in other texts

---

[88] Irfan Habib, "Timur in the Political Tradition and Historiography of Mughal India," in *L'Heritage timouride Iran-Asie centrale-Inde XVe-XVIIIe siecles*, ed. Maria Szuppe (Aix-en-Provence, 1997), pp. 297–312.

written in the first years of Jahangir's reign. For instance, in Nur-ul-Haq Dehlawi's *Zubdat-ul-Tawarikh*, we are told that Salim

impelled by filial affection, and carried away with love, betook himself to His Majesty's sick-bed, and was privileged to have a sight of him. ... Tears came to His Majesty's [Akbar's] eyes, and he gave a sign from the head of the sandalwood couch that his own sword, representing the key to peace and order [sovereignty], be handed over to the Prince. Since the whole world had become powerless from the news of this heart-breaking event ... he [Salim] came out grieving and with heavy heart, and went to his palace.[89]

Asad Beg Qazwini offers an even more dramatic version in the *Waqa'i' Asad Beg*. According to the author, when Salim approached Akbar's deathbed, the emperor signaled to his attendants to invest Salim with his personal turban, robes, and dagger. After this transpired, they all prostrated themselves before Salim and paid him homage. "At that very moment His Majesty, whose sins are forgiven, bowed and then passed away."[90] Over the course of the next decade, these early accounts of investiture became the basis for even more elaborate renditions of the same story.[91]

Early in his reign, Jahangir consciously mimicked his father's hands-on style of management. To that end, shortly after his accession to the throne, he issued a *dastur-ul-'amal* (manual of guidance) that he expected to be circulated throughout the empire. The *dastur* contained twelve orders that covered such diverse topics as taxation; the building of infrastructural projects; the protection of trade; inheritance issues; the sale of intoxicants; the confiscation of property; torture; mistreatment of peasants; marriage by imperial officials; the slaughter of animals; and the salary scales of imperial officers, women of the harem, and religious figures.[92] In this way, Jahangir sought to promote an image – not unlike that of his father – of a sovereign involved in the minutiae of his subjects' everyday life. Similar considerations seem to have informed his decision to install a

---

[89] Shireen Moosvi, *Episodes in the Life of Akbar* (New Delhi, 1994), p. 114.
[90] Qazwini, *Waqa'i' Asad Beg*, f. 30a.
[91] Even if Ni'matullah Khan Harvi's *Tarikh-i Khan Jahan wa Makhzan-i Afghani* (written in the mid-1610s) cannot top the drama of *Waqa'i' Asad Beg*, it more than makes up for it by offering fresh details of the "event." Thus we now learn that the sword gifted by Akbar to Salim belonged to Babur, who passed it down to Akbar's father Humayun just prior to his own death. As well as his sword, Akbar also gave Salim his personal rosary and good luck amulets as well as a warm hug and kiss. See Ni'matullah Khan Harvi, *Tarikh-i-Khan Jahani wa Makhzan-i-Afghani*, ed. S. M. Imam-ud-Din, vol. 2 (Dhaka, 1962), pp. 660–1.
[92] Nur-ud-Din Muhammad Jahangir, *Jahangirnama*, ed. Muhammad Hashim (Tehran, 1980), pp. 6–7.

"chain of justice" outside his royal quarters in the Agra fort. In Jahangir's own words, the chain's purpose was to afford "the oppressed" a chance to "attract the attention (of the emperor),"[93] thereby demonstrating his interest in issues of daily governance.

Elsewhere, Jahangir continued Akbar's efforts to project Mughal imperial authority as a blessing from God (*wahbi*).[94] This *wahbi* was manifest in the body of the emperor as divine light. Jahangir, exactly like Akbar before him, employed several metaphors for light and illumination in his rituals of kingship. Jahangir's "chain of justice," for example, was gold, and thus illuminated. He continued the imperial *jharoka* ceremony, in which the emperor presented himself to public view to bestow blessings upon his subjects and give them the chance to view the divine light radiating from his person. Jahangir assumed the name Nur-ud-Din, meaning "Light of Religion." His newly minted gold coins had names such as "Nur-i Shahi" (Light of Kingship), "Nur-i Sultani" (Light of Sovereignty), "Nur-i Daulat" (Light of the Realm), "Nur-i Karam" (Light of Mercy), "Nur-i Jahan" (Light of the World), "Nur-i Mehr" (Light of Compassion), and "Nurani (Luminous)."[95] Likewise, newly minted silver coins received such names as: "Kaukab-i Ta'alli'" (Star of Eminence), "Kaukab-i Iqbal" (Star of Good Fortune), "Kaukab-i Murad" (Star of Desire), and "Kaukab-i Bakht" (Star of Luck).[96]

Yet, Jahangir – whose strategic leadership skills have been underrated by historians until fairly recently – also deliberately distinguished himself from his father. Whereas Akbar mostly eschewed the support of the Islamic religious establishment ('*ulama*') after the early 1580s, Jahangir made efforts to improve his relations with it as well as harness it in support of his imperial authority, as he had done as prince. His efforts to placate the '*ulama*' after he became emperor were especially broad ranging. He recognized the holders of *a'imma*s (charitable land grants in the form of *madad-i ma'ash* grants) as an "army of prayer" and proceeded "with one stroke of the pen" to confirm all the *madad-i ma'ash* grants issued during Akbar's reign.[97] Religious elites and *madad-i ma'ash* holders naturally welcomed such imperial generosity. There had been great fear shortly

---

[93] Ibid., 5; Husaini, *Ma'asir-i-Jahangiri*, p. 61.

[94] For a detailed discussion, see John F. Richards, "The Formulation of Imperial Ideology under Akbar and Jahangir," in *Kingship and Authority in South Asia*, ed. John F. Richards (Madison, 1978), pp. 252–85.

[95] Husaini, *Ma'asir-i-Jahangiri*, pp. 64–5.

[96] Ibid.

[97] Jahangir, *Jahangirnama*, p. 7.

after Jahangir's accession that each claim would be subject to fresh imperial investigations, and this resulted in financial uncertainty as well as
worries about corruption charges and possible confiscation. Jahangir
also ordered deserving Muslim religious scholars to be brought before
him on a daily basis for bestowal of new *madad* grants. Over the course
of his first few years, Jahangir gave out so many new *madad* grants that
one of his nobles, Ja'far Beg/Asaf Khan, complained openly and bitterly of
Jahangir's generosity. According to this nobleman, the number of *madad*
issued in Jahangir's first five years equaled the number awarded by Akbar
over the course of his entire forty-nine-year reign.[98] Jahangir appears to
have been unperturbed by such criticism, however, and continued to issue
large numbers of these grants through the remainder of his reign.

Other clearly Islamic gestures followed. Shortly after ascending the
throne, Jahangir gave Rs. 20,000 to Mirza Muhammad Reza Sabzwari
to divide among *faqirs* and other needy peoples of Delhi. This act was
followed by an imperial decision to give tens of thousands of rupees to
Dost Muhammad, Jamal-ud-Din Inju, and Miran Sadr-i Jahan (all former
princely loyalists) to spend in alms and charity across the empire.
Furthermore, Jahangir set aside Friday evenings for exclusive meetings
with religious scholars and learned Sufis. He also commissioned a highly
remunerated panel of Muslim religious experts to collect all the appella-
tions of God for inscription on the emperor's personal rosary.

Finally, Jahangir decided to confirm Miran Sadr-i Jahan, who enjoyed
strong ties with conservative elements within the *'ulama'*, as his *sadr-us-
sudur* (chief justice). This appointment underscored the seriousness of the
new emperor's desire to improve relations with the religious establishment
and their support networks where these had been soured during the
previous reign. Sure enough, sources report widespread appreciation of
Jahangir's having allowed the "desolate garden" of Islam to bloom again
after the thirty years of Akbar's reign.[99]

There are strong suggestions that the political threat posed by his own
son Khusrau and his powerful backers among the Mughal nobility was a
crucial factor shaping Jahangir's engagement with Akbar's legacy. After
all, Khusrau repeatedly used Jahangir's past disloyalty to Akbar as

---

[98] S. Khan, *Maasiru-l-Umara*, vol. 3, p. 350; Saiyid Sabah-ud-Din Abdur Rahman, *Bazm-i
Timuriya*, vol. 2 (Azamgarh, 1972), p. 148; Ghulam Ali Azad Bilgrami, *Ma'asir-ul-Kiram*,
ed. Abdullah Khan, vol. 2 (Hyderabad, 1913), p. 193.

[99] See Harvi, *Tarikh-i-Khan Jahani*, vol. 2, p. 668. In focusing on the last three decades of
Akbar's reign, the author is pointing to the onset of Akbar's first public moves away from
simply being a traditional Muslim sovereign.

grounds to question his right to the throne. This situation lasted right up to Khusrau's princely rebellion in 1606. By co-opting parts of Akbar's legacy, Jahangir seems to have hoped to downplay his past misbehavior toward his father and undermine any aspirations Khusrau may have harbored to claim his grandfather Akbar's legacy.

Significantly, Jahangir's selective distancing from Akbar also seems to have been driven by his determination to outmaneuver Khusrau. Thus, in his furious moves to placate the *'ulama'* after his accession, he mimicked Khusrau's own cultivation (also in opposite to Akbar) of religious figures such as Shaikh Nizam-ud-Din Thanesari (d. 1626), one of the most power-ful Chishti *pirs* in the Punjab in the final years of Akbar's reign.[100] The last thing Jahangir likely wanted was a reprise of the situation of 1580–1, when several Islamic-oriented networks had declared Akbar a *kafir* (infidel), encouraged a massive rebellion against his authority, and thrown their weight behind Mirza Hakim. The success of Jahangir's efforts can be gauged by the fact that barring a few individuals (Thanesari among them), the emperor retained the support of much of the religious establish-ment during and despite Khusrau's rebellion.

Jahangir's cautious and tempered engagement with Akbar's legacy undoubtedly helped him consolidate authority early in his reign and turn aside Khusrau's political challenge. As his reign progressed, his early use of the light metaphor was extended to all manner of persons and things, from his consort to elephants, gardens, streams, and houses – all these came to be associated with the prefix *nur* (light).[101] Judging by his autobiography, the *Jahangirnama*, Jahangir never ceased to emphasize both a literary and physical connection to Akbar, continuing his praise of the "divine aura" and wisdom of the "exalted" Akbar, and also making occasional imperial visits to Akbar's tomb.[102] Talking about one such visit in 1608, Jahangir states that although he walked the roughly five and a half miles from Agra to Sikandra, he wished he could show his devotion to his father's memory

---

[100] The sources of his authority included his intellectual heft, access to wealth (he was reputed to have unlocked the secret of alchemy's holy grail – namely, turning coarse metals into gold), and intimate social connections to the Punjab's *madad-i ma'ash* holders (thanks in large part to his father-in-law's earlier defense of their entitlements against Akbar's efforts to reorganize the Mughal land revenue system). Rahman Ali, *Tazkira-i 'Ulama'-i Hind* (Lucknow, 1914), p. 525; Ghulam Sarwar, *Khazinat-ul-Asfiya*, vol. 1 (Lucknow, 1894), pp. 463–4.

[101] Corinne Lefèvre, "Recovering a Missing Voice from Mughal India: The Imperial Discourse of Jahangir (r. 1605–1627)," *Journal of the Economic and Social History of the Orient* 50, no. 4 (2007): 463–4.

[102] Jahangir, *Jahangirnama*, pp. 16, 20.

by walking upside down![103] The long-term efficacy of Jahangir's tight embrace of Akbar's legacy can be seen in his success in ultimately denying his other son Khurram any opportunity to leverage his own admittedly close ties to his grandfather (who raised him in the first thirteen years of his life) against his father.

A new Mughal emperor attended with great care to the questions of how best to tackle his princely opponents and their supporters, where within the new imperial dispensation to place his own supporters, and how to honor (or not) the previous emperor whose place he was assuming. Even as the empire replenished its ranks by accommodating waves of talented, bright, ambitious, and resourceful princely outsiders, it retained the wisdom and skill of those who had actual experience in running a successful imperial enterprise.

## CONCLUSION

Between the 1550s and the late 1710s, the Mughals never wavered in their broad commitment to an open-ended system of succession. The attempt by Shah Jahan to try and rig the succession process in favor of his oldest son ended in disaster for both of them. Yet, although certain customs were maintained over the two centuries covered by this book – among them the tendencies to favor the oldest son and to refrain from punishing the supporters of princely rivals post-succession – Mughal succession practices were also marked by powerful discontinuities. Among the most important were (i) the determination to deny princes from collateral lines a place on the imperial stage, (ii) the move to wars of succession as the primary means for determining the next emperor, and (iii) the decision to execute defeated princely rivals in order to prevent reprises of concluded succession struggles and maintain the empire's focus on the next rising generation of princes.

Clearly, changes in Mughal succession practices were tied up with larger and broader transformations, most notably the move away from a corporate model of leadership (best epitomized by the presence of princely appanages) to a truly imperial model that privileged the notion of an indivisible and unitary empire ruled by a single dominant emperor. For princes, the impact of this change was stupendous: political success now demanded that all princes become imperial actors. The stakes were higher, and so were the risks. Each prince had to first galvanize support and then

---

[103] Ibid., p. 79.

fight for the privilege to become the next emperor, since failure would mean death.

A Jaunpur-based Jain merchant named Banarasi captures the general stress in the lead up to a war of succession in a wonderfully evocative account. Recalling events around the time of Akbar's death in October 1605, he tells us

> The whole town was in a tremor. Everyone closed the doors of his house in panic; shopkeepers shut down their shops. Feverishly, the rich hid their jewels and costly attire underground; many of them quickly dumped their wealth and their ready capital on carriages and rushed to safe, secluded places. Every householder began stocking his home with weapons and arms. Rich men took to wearing thick, rough clothes such as are worn by the poor in order to conceal their status and walked the streets covered in harsh woolen blankets or coarse cotton wrappers. Women shunned finery, dressing in shabby, lustreless clothes. None could tell the status of a man from his dress and it became impossible to distinguish the rich from the poor. There were manifest signs of panic everywhere although there was no reason for it since there were really no thieves or robbers about.[104]

At the end of an emperor's life, the entire empire was united in a community of fear, but also in the shared and renewed acknowledgment of the Mughal dynasty's centrality to order in everyday life and thence its authority to rule. Banarasi tells us that on receipt of the news that Jahangir had ascended the Mughal throne and that "his power reigned supreme and unchallenged," there was "great relief and people heartily hailed the new king."[105] And so it was that the place of the emperor and the dynasty at the heart of the natural order of things was reaffirmed.

A new reign signaled the emergence of a new order marked by the wholesale elevation of former princely retainers to the highest rungs of power. Considering that the length of the average Mughal reign between 1526 and 1712 was roughly twenty-five years, this meant the fairly steady circulation of imperial elites. There is little doubt that this turnover of elites and the broad cross-section of society that they represented provided the Mughal Empire the special dynamism and vitality that was evident throughout the sixteenth and seventeenth centuries.

As argued earlier, the task of each new emperor to reckon with his predecessor's legacy is of special import for our understanding of imperial reigns post-Akbar. We examined the consequences of Jahangir's complex interactions with Akbar's legacy. In a similar vein, Aurangzeb's reign

---

[104] Banarasidas, *Ardhakathanaka*, trans. Mukund Lath (Jaipur, 1981), p. 38.
[105] Ibid., p. 40.

offers a fascinating example. In 1658, justifying his decision to overthrow Shah Jahan, Aurangzeb declared that his predecessor's failure to protect Islam against heresy had led to a loss of God's favor. This early effort to set himself apart from his father arguably committed Aurangzeb, over the course of the next forty-nine years, to uphold the centrality of Islam in the political life of the empire or risk his political legitimacy. Although I do not believe that Aurangzeb's religious policies were the primary cause for the collapse of the empire, they did create a dissonant strain that added to the mounting political, military, and economic difficulties that confronted his successors. These challenges and the concomitant collapse of the princely institution set the stage for the rapid unraveling of Mughal rule. In the following chapter, we consider how the various processes that constituted the princely institution came apart after the 1680s and through the last years of Aurangzeb's reign.

# 7

# The Prince Shackled, 1680s–1707

In 1681, Akbar, the fourth son of Aurangzeb, allied with Rajputs in rebellion against his father. They came remarkably close to overthrowing the emperor. In retrospect, the period around Akbar's rebellion was the high-water mark of Mughal princely power. With seemingly unfettered access to the wealth of the empire, Aurangzeb's four surviving sons (Mu'azzam, A'zam, Akbar, and Kam Bakhsh) maintained powerful, cohesive, and far-reaching princely households. As with previous generations of imperial princes, they had little difficulty forging diverse and expansive alliances. Inasmuch as Akbar's rebellion attests to princely confidence in challenging the emperor, Mu'azzam's audacious and repeated challenges to Aurangzeb's policies in the Deccan offer additional evidence that the princes continued to assume a robust place in the political life of the empire through the early to mid-1680s.

Beginning in the late 1680s, however, in a process that would intensify over the rest of Aurangzeb's reign, the power of the princes was slowly degraded. This development was manifested most visibly in weakening households. Princely households – like the empire – seem to have been victims of their own success. Between the sixteenth century and the end of the seventeenth, as their size swelled, they became less intimate and more institutional. Maintaining them required ever more access to sources of wealth. This, however, was no longer easy to manage in the face of collapsing law and order across Mughal India because of powerful Jat, Bundela, Sikh, Berad, Rajput, and Maratha insurgencies and a concomitant and growing inability to extract local resources after the 1680s. Princes responded in a number of ways – by trying to retrench, by not paying salaries, and by borrowing officers and other personnel from the emperor to help manage their own households. Such measures, however, ended up undermining the ties that bound the successful princely household.

Aurangzeb on a palki, ca. 1690 (© Victoria and Albert Museum, London, 2006AM7227–01)

The eclipsing of the princely household foreshadowed other problems as well. None was more significant than the increased difficulty princes had building alliances with the most powerful members of the imperial nobility. Whereas nobles had previously felt obliged to subsume their own political and military ambitions in the face of greater princely claims to authority, after the 1680s, the most powerful nobles gradually came to view their own long-term interests as distinct from those of their princely masters. Aurangzeb's decision to turn to competent nonroyal military commanders for his campaigns in the Deccan and his increasing disaffection with his own heirs both reflected and furthered the chasm between princes and nobles over the last decade of his reign.

Even as princely capacities to build muscular households and alliances faded, the strain of intra-familial competition between different generations of princes also took its toll. Aurangzeb was the longest-lived Mughal ruler (he died at the age of eighty-nine in 1707), and his sons increasingly faced competition from not only their own generation but the following one as well. The proliferation of royal contenders ultimately boded poorly for the princely institution as a whole. Nowhere is the recession of princely power better attested to than in the fact that Aurangzeb suffered no rebellions after Prince Akbar's abortive attempt in 1681. And this was despite extreme old age and military failure. This chapter examines the factors that helped undermine the princely institution and with it its hitherto pivotal role in Mughal state formation.

### THE PRINCELY HOUSEHOLD UNDERMINED

The princely household of the first half of the sixteenth century was a relatively simple affair, but it was transformed with increased imperial wealth over the course of the seventeenth century. Reflecting increased resources as well as administrative capabilities and demands, the princely household became more bureaucratized. Ultimately, the institution became too big for the resources available to support it and thus began to falter. The difficulties, which began to manifest after the 1680s, were mostly a consequence of diminishing *jagir* income linked to (i) spreading political turmoil associated with various anti-Mughal rebellions as well as the destabilizing effects of the Mughal-Maratha conflict in the Deccan and (ii) increasingly obstreperous local elites who, witnessing a distracted imperial authority faced with conflicts on multiple fronts, resisted efforts to funnel local wealth upward and outward. A key consequence for princes was an ever-greater susceptibility to imperial oversight and control as Aurangzeb willingly stepped in not only to help make up revenue shortfalls but also to offer personnel. Having little choice but to accept the emperor's help, princes signed away some of their independence.

The early, pre-1580s princely household was compact, but we know very little about its specific structure. A 1554 list produced by a retainer, Bayazid Bayat, does offer some insight into the relatively simple princely establishment that accompanied Akbar as he marched into India to help his father Humayun reconquer Delhi. Among the functionaries mentioned are paymasters (*bakhshis*) and administrative heads (*diwans*), a chief officer for transportation and luggage (*mir-i saman*), superintendent of the library (*darogha-i kitabkhana*), librarian (*kitabdar*), chief judge (*qazi*), secretary/scribe of the office of justice (*munshi-i dar-ul-'adalat*), scribes (*munshi*s), a secretary for writing royal orders (*parwanachi*), overseer of the kitchens (*mushrif-i bawarchikhana*), overseer for supplies (*baqawal*), a treasurer/bookkeeper (*khazanchi*), minder of the royal camp (*urdubegi*), superintendent of the royal wardrobe (*tushak-chi*), butler and stirrup holders (*rikabdar*s), superintendent of the stables (*akhtabegi*), and a keeper of official records (*daftardar*).[1]

Almost 150 years later, in the early 1700s – the last years of Aurangzeb's reign – the news bulletins (*akhbarat*s) issued from A'zam's princely household in Gujarat mention countless more titles.[2] The *akhbarat* variously refer to a general officer for transportation and luggage (*mir-i saman*); chief overseer of the prince's stirrup (*diwan-i rikab*); general for the transportation and luggage of the prince's entourage (*mir-i saman-i rikab*); general of artillery (*mir-i atash*); quartermaster general (*mir-i manzil*) superintendent of justice (*darogha-i 'adalat*); first, second, and third paymasters (*bakhshi-i awwal, dowom and siwom*); minister of overseers (*diwan-i mushrif*); general of the hunt (*mir-i shikar*); superintendent of the trackers (*darogha-i qara-walan*); superintendent of the hunters (*darogha-i shikaran*); minister of the scribes (*diwan-i munshi*); chief of endowments and religious grants (*sadr*); superintendent of the stables (*darogha-i istabal*); superintendent of the workshops (*darogha-i karkhanajat*); superintendent of the princely body-guards (*darogha-i surkhposhan*); superintendent of the guard (*darogha-i chauki*); superintendent of the library (*darogha-i kutbkhana*); superintendent of the weapons (*darogha-i silah*); superintendent of the armory (*darogha-i qurkhana*); inspector for branding and verification (*mutassadi-i dagh wa tashiha*); superintendent of the matchlockmen (*darogha-i barqan-dazan*); superintendent of the elephant stables (*darogha-i filkhana*); super-intendent of the camel stables (*darogha-i shutrkhana*); superintendent of the bullocks (*darogha-i gau*); superintendent of the eunuchs (*darogha-i khwa-san*); superintendent of the artillery (*darogha-i topkhana*); assistant in the artillery unit (*peshkar-i topkhana*), overseer of carpets and cushions (*mushrif-i farashkhana*), superintendent of the march (*darogha-i kuch*); superintendent of plates and vessels (*darogha-i zarufkhana*); superintendent of the charitable kitchen (*darogha-i langarkhana*); superintendent of the cloakroom (*darogha-i khil'atkhana*); superintendent of the military camp's bazaar (*darogha-i ganj-i bazaar-i urdui*); superintendent of the housing of the single horsemen (*darogha-i 'amarat-i ahadis*); superintendent of the post

---

[1] Bayazid Bayat, *Tadhkira-i-Humayun wa Akbar*, ed. M. Hidayat Hosain (Calcutta, 1941), pp. 176–85.

[2] *Akhbarat-i Darbar-i Mu'alla*, National Library of India, Sarkar Collection 41, pp. 1–230.

(*darogha-i dak*); superintendent of the runners (*darogha-i harkaran*); super-intendent of the music chamber (*darogha-i nuqqarkhana*); superintendent of the princely apartment (*darogha-i shabkhana*); and superintendent of drinking water (*darogha-i abdar*). And this list is by no means a complete one.

Elaboration of administration necessarily gave rise to stricter and more formal hierarchies, and there is no doubt that late-seventeenth-century princely households were much larger than their pre-1580s counterparts. The later households also played a changed role in a very different political landscape. Although more hierarchical and bureaucratic, the ethnic makeup of the later household had also grown much less homogenous as princely establishments became hubs of networks and alliances that reached to almost every nook and corner – barring the extreme southern parts – of the subcontinent. It is fascinating to imagine exactly what went on in the rooms, court-yards, field outings, and campaigns of the prince's household where all these different categories of people, from different linguistic, regional, or religious backgrounds, interacted.

Crucial to operations and personnel alike was the plentiful inflow and outflow of cash and goods. Toward the end of the 1600s, however, this flow became seriously compromised. As a prince, Aurangzeb had complained at length about funding problems in his correspondence during the mid-seventeenth century, but those problems were of a political rather than a systemic nature, since Shah Jahan appears to have deliberately starved the prince of funds. Before Aurangzeb's predicament in the 1650s, the sources do not indicate widespread concern about raising money or balancing income and expenditures. Ultimately, even Prince Aurangzeb managed to raise the funds he needed by other means, not the least of which were trading ventures and his military campaigns against the Sultanates of Bijapur and Golkonda.

Before the 1680s, Aurangzeb appears to have been benevolent and gener-ous with his own sons and grandsons. Following his accession in 1658, at royal birthday celebrations, weddings, and anniversaries or after successful military campaigns, Aurangzeb gifted them with massive sums. But after the 1680s, we see the onset of a financial crunch.

### The Post-1680s Financial Crisis

Although contemporary Mughal historians have long agreed that expan-sion into the Deccan in the 1680s played an important role in precipitating a crisis in the imperial *jagirdari* system – a crisis that meant the dynasty could no longer disburse funds to nobles and run its own households – the scholarship has debated endlessly how and why that Deccan expansion proved such a problem. One school of thought, most cogently represented by Irfan Habib, Athar Ali, and Satish Chandra among others, asserts that imperial expansion into the Deccan opened the floodgates to all manner of new claimants for imperial *jagir*s as Aurangzeb sought to co-opt local power elites to the Mughal side. The surfeit of these claimants and the insufficiency of land for disbursement resulted in long waits – sometimes four or five years – to get *jagir* assignments. One important result was increased factionalism as claimants looked to a higher patron to enable them to get a *jagir* from which to pay the salaries of their own retainers. Furthermore, nobles desperately squeezed as much money as they could out of their *jagir*s before they were reclaimed by the imperial state and given to someone else, and the peasants responded by resisting – fleeing or fighting – noble extortion. This level of exploitation and instability meant the breakdown of the *jagirdari* system, the growing incapacity of nobles to fulfill obligations imposed on them by the dynasty, and a loss of faith in the Mughal Empire itself at all levels of society.[3]

Among those who have most forcefully argued against the foregoing proposition is John F. Richards, who insists that the failure of the *jagirdari* system cannot be blamed on the number of claimants for *jagir*s exceeding the amount of productive land held in reserve (*paibaqi* ) by the empire.[4] Rather, the problem lay with Aurangzeb's attempts to expand the amount of productive (and usually conflict-free) land under the direct administration of the state (*khalisa sharifa*) to support his campaigns in the Deccan. This expansion of total state holdings in effect starved the *mansabdar*s. They now either were given lands from which they could derive no revenue because of conflict or had to wait years before being assigned productive *jagir*s. During the lean years, they had to live by their wits or at the sufferance of creditors. Not surprisingly, once individuals got their hands on productive lands, they were loath to see them transferred. Those with the means to embed their authority over a lucrative region were encouraged to dig in their heels and obstruct any efforts to transfer their assignment. This process produced an ever-growing population of disgruntled and demoralized imperial officials, with ruinous effects for the empire.

---

[3] M. Athar Ali, *The Mughal Nobility under Aurangzeb* (Delhi, repr. 1997), pp. 92–4; Irfan Habib, *The Agrarian System of Mughal India, 1556–1707* (Delhi, repr. 1999), pp. 312–13; Satish Chandra, *Parties and Politics at the Mughal Court, 1707–1740* (Delhi, repr. 2002), pp. 29–33.

[4] John F. Richards, *Mughal Administration in Golconda* (Oxford, 1975), pp. 157–62, 308–9.

The debate over what caused the "*jagirdari* crisis" does not seem easily resolvable. Judging from *akhbarat* from the last decades of Aurangzeb's reign, however, this much is clear: a broad cross-section of the imperial nobility had begun to suffer terrible financial hardship on one of two counts. On the one hand, they were simply unable to get a *jagir*. Again and again, we come across examples of individuals plaintively and unsuccessfully petitioning the emperor for a *jagir* assignment. On the other hand, even if they had a *jagir*, many were drawing insufficient resources from it to meet their imperial obligations. In the face of an inability to raise sufficient funds from their *jagirs*, some nobles took to begging for cash grants.[5] Others allowed the salaries of their retainers to fall into arrears.[6] In some cases, according to the contemporary observer Niccolao Manucci, this could amount to two or even three years of back pay.[7] Not surprisingly, tensions mounted and occasionally even boiled over into murderous attacks on nobles by their own servitors.[8]

Muzaffar Alam, Jos Gommans, Richard Barnett, Chetan Singh, and others have suggested that exacerbating these difficulties was increasing resistance from intermediate landholding groups (*zamindars*) that were unwilling to surrender local revenues to weakened imperial representatives. These *zamindars*, often in contrast to imperial *mansabdars*, were embedded in kin ties within the regions of their influence. The Mughal nobility had become stuck in a vicious cycle: reduced access to cash forced a scaling back of military contingents, which undermined their authority over the intermediary *zamindars*, which, in turn, led to the extraction of even fewer financial resources. Ultimately, the nobles' only recourse was to move their financial expectations from a mobile and transferable imperial *mansabdar* to a stationary, locally based *zamindar*, preferably with the imprimatur of the Mughal state. Toward the end of Aurangzeb's reign, only those nobles who were assigned *jagirs* in their own homelands (*watan jagirs*) managed to come anywhere near maintaining their prescribed military contingents. Those itinerant Mughal nobles who relied on *jagirs* away from home, serving the crucial function of sustaining the empire's hold on territories near and far, saw their prospects dwindle and fade away. Under the strain of nonstop warfare in the Deccan, Aurangzeb had every incentive to allow the emergence of semipermanent holdings,

---

[5] *Akhbarat-i Darbar-i Mu'alla* , vol. 19, p. 255; vol. 25, pp. 138, 214.

[6] Ibid., vol. 23, pp. 137, 221, 230, 240.

[7] Niccolao Manucci, *Mogul India or Storio do Mongor* , trans. W. Irvine, vol. 2 (Delhi, repr. 1996), pp. 354–5.

[8] *Akhbarat-i Darbar-i Mu'alla* , vol. 23, p. 82.

but this was to the detriment of the trans-local imperial nobility. If the lot of the nobles became marked by precariousness in this increasingly desperate environment, how did Mughal princes fare?

Though *jagir*s were increasingly hard for noblemen to get, there is no evidence that imperial princes suffered from this problem. In general, the turnaround between assignments seems to have been a relatively rapid six months. Thus, when a bundle of *jagir* holdings was transferred out of Kam Bakhsh's possession in July 1694, he was compensated for their loss by new assignments that December.[9] Other evidence points to similarly short waits for both Mu'azzam in 1694 and A'zam in 1700.[10]

For princes then, the problem was not the unavailability of *jagir*s but rather their diminishing financial returns. Here again, the evidence is incontrovertible: after the 1680s, princes faced real difficulties in collecting the money promised to them by their *mansab* ranks. The effects of the financial crisis can be seen in Kam Bakhsh's desperate appeal in 1700 to his father for a cash grant to pay the salaries of three thousand cavalrymen in his personal contingent.[11] In that same year, his older brother Mu'azzam requested a cash grant to make up income that could not be extracted from his *jagir*s.[12] A number of other examples point to the increasingly challenging financial environment for princes over the last decades of Aurangzeb's reign.[13]

At the heart of the prince's difficulties was the devastating breakdown in law and order across large swathes of territory; near constant unrest and outright attacks were launched by various groups including Marathas, Kolis, Jats, Sikhs, Bundelas, Rajputs, and Berads, among others. The inability of the Mughals to tackle these threats in turn undermined local *zamindari* willingness to comply with imperial rule, and these local leaders (often connected to the very groups in rebellion) became less and less willing to surrender tax money and other funds. Records from the 1690s and early 1700s clearly point to these cascading effects.

## The Squeeze on Princely Households

Even though a deteriorating social order made it more difficult for princes to collect funds, this was by no means the only financial problem they

---

[9] Ibid., vol. 19, pp. 110, 329, 330.
[10] Ibid., p. 328; vol. 23, p. 339.
[11] Ibid., vol. 23, p. 225.
[12] Ibid., p. 9.
[13] Ibid., vol. 17, nos. 36/1, 36/24, 37/4; vol. 19, p. 182.

faced. Cash-strapped nobles began to illegally seize the revenue of princely *jagirs*,[14] princely employees became increasingly corruptible,[15] and merchants now demanded to be paid in cash and refused to extend credit.[16]

In response, princes appear to have tried to curtail mismanagement in their households and streamline operations. In the early 1690s, A'zam turned to the guidance of a long-standing Afghan retainer, Mustafa Khan Kashi, to trim the number of men in his employment because he could no longer meet their salaries. On Kashi's advice, A'zam capped the number of standing cavalry at six thousand. He also kept a waiting list of four to six thousand horsemen who might be inducted should there be vacancies in the core group or if there was a sudden military need.[17] The sources suggest a subsequent drop in complaints about late salary payments, and in due course other princes imitated A'zam's reforms.[18] Although Khafi Khan suggests that A'zam's older brother and primary political rival Mu'azzam was initially an exception to this rule, it is clear that by the early 1700s, he too had come around to the view that a large but poorly paid and discontented household was a political liability. Under the oversight of Mun'im Khan, Mu'azzam's head of household after 1703, management was tightened, outlays trimmed, and the number of princely soldiers – many of whom bordered on mutinous – culled. The prince worked to ensure that those who remained on his rolls were paid on a more regular basis and that ability and service were more properly rewarded.[19]

Emperor Aurangzeb was not pleased about such troop reduction ploys, however. He seems to have viewed them as an excuse to get out of military and service obligations rather than an attempt to economize and stave off a household's collapse. In one episode, Aurangzeb chastised his grandson Bidar Bakht for not maintaining adequate troops and weapons despite all the resources supposedly at his disposal. Look at Ghazi-ud-Din Khan (one of his favorite nobleman and the father of Nizam-ul-Mulk, founder of Hyderabad), he approvingly tells his grandson; he maintains more forces

---

[14] Ibid., vol. 19, p. 460.

[15] Musta'idd Khan, *Ma'asir-i 'Alamgiri*, ed. Agha Ahmad Ali (Calcutta, 1871), p. 403.

[16] Aurangzeb, *Anecdotes of Aurangzib*, trans. Jadunath Sarkar (Calcutta, repr. 1988), p. 48.

[17] Khafi Khan, *Muntakhab al-Lubab*, ed. Kabir-ud-Din Ahmad, vol. 2 (Calcutta, 1874), p. 440.

[18] Ibid.

[19] Mubarakullah Wazih, *Tarikh-i Iradat Khan*, ed. Ghulam Rasul Mehr (Lahore, 1971), p. 66.

than he is required to.[20] But princes throughout the empire were cutting corners to sustain their cash reserves and other resources.[21]

Even as princes tried to deal with a severe resource crunch by economizing, they also stepped up efforts to raise money by any means available. This was clearly what drove Mun'im Khan's attempts to improve *jagir* income collection from Mu'azzam's holdings in the Punjab and tighten controls over the lucrative horse trade between Kabul (the seat of Mu'azzam's governorship in the early 1700s) and India. Meanwhile, on the other side of the empire, Mu'azzam's son 'Azim-ud-Din, who was governor of Bengal in the last decade of Aurangzeb's life, struggled (albeit unsuccessfully) to assert his control over that province's revenue ministry (*diwani*) and finances.

Prince A'zam led successive military campaigns not so much to win territory and control but rather to parley for money. He thus agreed to lift the siege at the fort of Wakhinkheda (in southern India), which belonged to the Berad chief Pidiyah Nayak, in 1692 in exchange for a cash payment of Rs. 200,000.[22] Such behavior so frustrated Aurangzeb that by 1701–2, A'zam and the other imperial princes operating in the Deccan had all been transferred out.

Even after he had been removed from the Deccan, A'zam continued his revenue-raising efforts, many of which stung his father the emperor. In 1703, he sold the revenue rights to one of his *jagirs* (Sorath) in Gujarat to Muhammad Beg Khan, the *faujdar* (military commandant) of that region. That contract remained in place for more than a year until Aurangzeb ordered Muhammad Beg Khan's removal in 1704 with a severe reprimand to A'zam for breaking the law by, in effect, giving one of his own *jagirs* as an *ijara* (revenue-farm).[23] Aurangzeb also chastised A'zam around this time for the tyranny exercised by his soldiers over the *jagirs* under his control, and for generally allowing mercenary interests to overwhelm all concern for royal custom, propriety, law, and noble etiquette.[24] In another

---

[20] Aurangzeb, *Dastur-ul-'Amal-i Agahi*, National Library of India, Sarkar Collection 70, f. 27b. See also Aurangzeb, *Ruq'at-i 'Alamgiri*, pp. 31–2.

[21] It is curious that barring 'Azim-ud-Din, Mughal princes of this era – and unlike their counterparts in the earlier half of the seventeenth century – did not involve themselves in trade as a source of revenue. Why this was the case is unclear and deserves further research.

[22] John F. Richards, "The Imperial Crisis in the Mughal Deccan," *Journal of Asian Studies* 35 (1976): 247.

[23] Ali, *The Mughal Nobility under Aurangzeb*, p. xxiiv; *Akhbarat-i Darbar-i Mu'alla*, vol. 29, p. 54; Aurangzeb, *Raqa'im-i Kara'im*, Asiatic Society of Bengal, Ivanow 383, f. 201b.

[24] Aurangzeb, *Dastur-ul-'Amal-i Agahi*, ff. 11b–12a. See also ff. 19a–b.

extraordinary episode, we learn of A'zam appropriating the pay of lower-ranking *mansabdars*.[25]

## Aurangzeb's Help: A Mixed Blessing

Of all the Mughal elites during this period, only Aurangzeb himself maintained access to huge amounts of money, whether in the form of *khalisa* revenues or steady revenue streams from relatively undisturbed regions such as Bengal. Aurangzeb, it is clear, was not entirely unsympathetic to the growing financial difficulties experienced by his heirs. The sources reveal him repeatedly offering temporary cash grants to sons and grandsons in a crunch.

In 1692, for example, A'zam, Bidar Bakht, and Kam Bakhsh were all supported with cash salaries from the emperor. We know this because in October of that year, Aurangzeb ordered that this practice be discontinued and the princes reassigned *jagirs*.[26] At other junctures, Aurangzeb offered temporary cash assistance when the income from a particular princely *jagir* had been disrupted. He seems to have been especially generous toward princes including Mu'izz-ud-Din (later Emperor Jahandar Shah, r. 1712–13) who continued to maintain active political or military profiles despite all sorts of financial difficulties.[27] After Mu'azzam was released from prison in 1695 for having schemed with the Sultanate of Golkonda in 1687, Aurangzeb offered Rs. 500,000 in cash to help him reconstitute his household.[28] A year later, in May 1696, he sent additional cash payments to help Mu'azzam pay the salaries of men serving in his army.[29]

Aurangzeb's help took other forms as well. When told about economically underperforming princely *jagirs*, Aurangzeb was not averse to taking them back and assigning more productive ones instead.[30] He would supply *jagirs* or horses to individuals serving under a prince.[31] Most importantly, he loaned large numbers of imperial officers to help the princes (despite their adulthood) run their households, thus drawing on imperial *jagirs* to subsidize the princes, who then did not have to pay salaries out of their

[25] Aurangzeb, *Kalimat-i Taiyibat*, ed. S. M. Azizuddin Husain (Delhi, 1982), p. 13.
[26] *Akhbarat-i Darbar-i Mu'alla*, vol. 17, no. 36/1.
[27] Ibid., vol. 23, pp. 121, 223, 224; vol. 25, p. 211.
[28] Ibid., vol. 19, p. 328.
[29] Ibid., vol. 21, nos. 40/27, 40/32.
[30] Aurangzeb, *Dastur-ul-'Amal-i Agahi*, f. 21a.
[31] *Akhbarat-i Darbar-i Mu'alla*, vol. 17, no. 37/14.

own personal resources. This was distinct from another long-standing imperial practice, in which the emperor rewarded princely retainers with imperial *mansabs* and *jagirs* but allowed them to continue to serve within princely households.

Judging by the examples of Salim, Khurram, Aurangzeb, and Dara Shukoh, adult princes worked fairly hard to insulate the daily management of their households from individuals directly appointed by the emperor. However, financial duress toward the end of the seventeenth century opened the doors for imperial access deep into the heart of princely households. It is clear that Aurangzeb used imperial appointees to assert more forceful control over these households. Consider the case of Aurangzeb's oldest surviving son, Mu'azzam, as an example.

In 1687, Mu'azzam was caught colluding with the Sultanate of Golkonda to oppose Mughal war aims in the Deccan. The prince was imprisoned, his harem shipped off to faraway Delhi, and his household reduced, in the words of one imperial historian, to "a drop in the ocean."[32] Twenty-five years of princely efforts aimed at building a powerful household were negated in one fell swoop. Some of Mu'azzam's "best servants" (*naukaran-i 'umda*) were absorbed into the imperial service;[33] the remainder drifted to imperial nobles or left Mughal service entirely.

It was not until 1694 that Aurangzeb began to rehabilitate Mu'azzam and permit him to rebuild his household. In December of that year, Mu'azzam's former *mutasaddis* (officials/superintendents/administrators) were allowed to reenlist with the prince. Some did. Many presumably did not because we see Aurangzeb appointing imperial *mutasaddis* to help Mu'azzam manage his reemerging household.[34] Around the same time, many other key imperial appointments were made at the highest levels of Mu'azzam's household.[35] To help his son collect his *jagir* income, Aurangzeb also sent imperial officers to the prince's *jagir* holdings in such diverse places as Bijapur, Gulbarga, and

[32] M. Khan, *Maasir i Alamgiri*, p. 295.

[33] Bindraban Das Ra'i, *Lubb-ut-Tawarikh*, Asiatic Society of Bengal, Ivanow 161, f. 157b; *Akhbarat-i Darbar-i Mu'alla*, vol. 17, no. 36/24.

[34] *Akhbarat-i Darbar-i Mu'alla*, vol. 19, p. 319.

[35] They included the prince's *diwan, mir tuzuk, darogha-i kutcheri, darogha-i topkhana, bakhshi-i tan, mir bakhshi, akhtabegi, mir saman, bayutat-i sarkar, qurbegi, bakawali, qushbegi, tirawalbegi, darogha-i dagh wa tashiha, waqa'i'-navis, nazir-i diwan-i shikar, darogha-i khwassan, darogha-i jawaharkhana, darogha-i kilid-i jawaharkhana, amin-i dagh wa tashiha, bakhshi-i sarkar, nazir-i deorhi mahal*, and *sadr-i sarkar*. *Akhbarat-i Darbar-i Mu'alla*, vol. 18, p. 204; vol. 19, pp. 304–5, 307, 312, 318, 319, 321, 326, 331, 338, 339, 347, 354, 359, 364, 365, 366, 379.

Gooty in Central India and Delhi in the North.[36] Everyone understood that if Mu'azzam was to have a political future, he had to first establish some sort of revenue stream; here Aurangzeb's help was vital.

The evidentiary record is clear: the degree of imperial control exercised over Mu'azzam's household was not unusual for this period. Even in the case of sons and grandsons who did not spend long stints in prison, the number of imperial assignees within their households increased markedly between the 1690s and early 1700s. Although necessary, such reliance came at a high price. Again, Mu'azzam's example is instructive.

Aurangzeb's involvement in staffing Mu'azzam's household waned somewhat over the remaining years of his life, but he never fully relinquished the hold he had established in the mid-1690s. Thus, even as he continued to appoint men to the prince's household,[37] the emperor also forged a deep network of informers in Mu'azzam's harem,[38] forbade certain former princely loyalists from entering Mu'azzam's employment,[39] chose his son's representatives (*wakils*) at the imperial court,[40] moved against princely retainers in financially lucrative assignments,[41] and kept a close watch on the *jagir* assignments of men working with the prince.[42] The active comings and goings of imperial officials – many of who held dual appointments in the prince's household and in the imperial administration of Kabul – attest to the watchful eye Aurangzeb kept on Mu'azzam and his establishment.

We see the emperor repeatedly meddling with the internal workings of other princely establishments as well. This included poaching on princely troops for imperial needs;[43] micromanaging staffing decisions;[44] ordering rival princes to share important employees;[45] shunting individuals between

---

[36]  Ibid., vol. 19, p. 318.

[37]  Ibid., vol. 23, p. 323.

[38]  Jadunath Sarkar, *Studies in Aurangzib's Reign* (Calcutta, repr. 1989), p. 41.

[39]  *Akhbarat-i Darbar-i Mu'alla*, vol. 21, no. 40/10.

[40]  Ibid., vol. 25, p. 110.

[41]  Ibid., vol. 29, p. 58.

[42]  Ibid., vol. 18, p. 216.

[43]  Ibid., vol. 19, pp. 33, 38, 44, 83, 105; vol. 25, p. 7.

[44]  For instance, forbidding princes from having one person hold multiple appointments or suggesting a preference for Muslims for certain kinds of jobs. Aurangzeb, *Dastur-ul-'Amal-i Agahi*, f. 28a; *Akhbarat-i Darbar-i Mu'alla*, vol. 19, p. 142. For other examples of close imperial oversight, see *Akhbarat-i Darbar-i Mu'alla*, vol. 16, pp. 130, 138; vol. 17, no. 36/7; vol. 32, pp. 14, 20, 24, 25, 26, 28, 29; vol. 23, p. 383.

[45]  From 1701–2 onward and likely up until Aurangzeb's death in 1707, A'zam and Bidar Bakht shared a common *wakil* (representative) at the imperial court. His name was Sultan Nazr. *Akhbarat-i Darbar-i Mu'alla*, vol. 15, p. 9; vol. 23, p. 223; vol. 25, pp. 87, 89, 115, 177, 214, 231, 250; vol. 30, p. 104; vol. 32, pp. 37, 43.

princely households;[46] forcing individuals serving princes to consistently report to the imperial court for audiences;[47] and, most damaging of all, ordering the dismissal of key princely retainers when he believed they threatened his political or financial interests. Although such activities were not unheard of prior to the 1680s, the extent of these practices under Aurangzeb and the relative weakness and desperation of the princes clearly distinguish this particular situation from the earlier period. A particularly good example is that of Aurangzeb's interference in relations between A'zam and his retainer Mustafa Khan Kashi. By the mid-1690s, according to historian Khafi Khan, A'zam had handed over the administration of his household to the Khan and consulted him on every political matter, big and small.[48] When Aurangzeb realized that the Khan was fuelling A'zam's political ambitions, causing him to challenge the emperor's power, he ordered him dismissed, and there was not a thing A'zam could do to reinstate this extremely valued employee.[49]

### Trouble in the Princely Households

Although it is an overstatement to suggest that the princes lost control of their households in the last decades of Aurangzeb's reign, it is clear that they no longer enjoyed the same autonomy as previous generations of Mughal princes. Cohesive princely households also increasingly gave way to fractured and undisciplined ones. In one incident in November 1694, two senior retainers of A'zam's Deccan-based household got into a fight after leaving the prince's quarters. The conflict quickly escalated as each called in reinforcements. Dozens were injured or killed in the ensuing skirmishes, parts of A'zam's camp were destroyed, and hostilities spread to other camps as well. Even canons were deployed before the fighting was brought under control by imperial troops, called out to quell the disturbance. A furious Aurangzeb dismissed a large number of A'zam retainers, thus shaming and weakening the prince.[50]

One month later, Mu'azzam's oldest son Mu'izz-ud-Din complained to the emperor that many of his servants (*naukaran*) had deserted his service,

[46] Ibid., vol. 19, pp. 273, 275, 279, 370, 394; vol. 25, p. 18; vol. 17, no. 37/69; vol. 32, p. 28.

[47] Ibid., vol. 23, pp. 50, 153; vol. 25, pp. 378, 380; vol. 30, p. 120; vol. 29, p. 29.

[48] K. Khan, *Muntakhab al-Labab*, vol. 2, p. 440.

[49] Ibid, p. 443. Despite the expulsion of Mustafa Khan Kashi, members of his family continued to serve in A'zam's household until the 1707 Battle of Jaju in which A'zam died fighting for the Mughal throne. Kamraj, *A'zam al-Harb*, British Museum, Or. 1899, f. 199.

[50] *Akhbarat-i Darbar-i Mu'alla*, vol. 19, pp. 232–3, 245.

leaving him "without hope." Aurangzeb was moved to issue orders for Mu'izz-ud-Din's men to be rounded up by imperial officers. When imperial officials finally caught up with the deserters, another bloody fight ensued. Like the previous one, this battle also involved use of artillery. In the end, reinforcements from Mu'azzam's camp and contingents of Dakhani troops had to be called in to help reassert imperial authority.[51] Although such incidents stand out for the ferocity of the fighting, we encounter a number of other episodes from this period in which princely retainers openly battled one another, resulting in stern reprimands and even punishment from Aurangzeb.[52] This kind of public fractiousness was a new development for princely households.

Princes clearly worried about the lack of discipline afflicting their households. They seem to have placed a large share of the blame on the imperial assignees serving them. In A'zam's case we see bitter complaints to the emperor about the poor behavior of imperial appointees in his service, their lack of respect for his authority, and their willingness to desert.[53] In some cases, this led to public tension between imperial and non-imperial princely servitors. One such incident involved an assassination attempt by Kam Bakhsh's *koka*, Hiddu, against the imperial eunuch Khwaja Yaqut/Mahram Khan. In 1698, the latter was serving as the appointed superintendent (*nazir*) of Kam Bakhsh's harem. He had often been at loggerheads with the prince on account of his fastidiousness in carrying out imperial directives. The Khwaja's abrasive manner toward the prince bespoke his sense that he was responsible and loyal only to Aurangzeb. Kam Bakhsh's involvement in the failed plot became apparent when he refused to surrender his *koka* for imperial punishment. Ultimately, Hiddu had to be forcibly separated from Kam Bakhsh's protective embrace during an open-court session. Determined to make an example of the prince's misbehavior, Aurangzeb ordered him placed under temporary house arrest.[54] In this, Aurangzeb had once again demonstrated that he, not his sons, was the ultimate arbiter of the fate of their households.

Not surprisingly, with the defanging of princely households, Aurangzeb was the first emperor in three generations to not face a rebellion in his old

[51] Ibid., vol. 19, pp. 345, 350, 352–3.

[52] Ibid., vol. 17, no. 37/14.

[53] Aurangzeb, *Dastur-ul-'Amal-i Agahi*, ff. 8a, 17a, 20a-b; *Akhbarat-i Darbar-i Mu'alla*, vol. 25, p. 60; vol. 29, p. 72; vol. 30, p. 122.

[54] M. Khan, *Maasir i 'Alamgiri*, pp. 397–400; K. Khan, *Muntakhab al-Labab*, vol. 2, pp. 435–7; Aurangzeb, *Raqa'im-i Kara'im*, f. 199b; Sarkar, *Studies in Aurangzeb's Reign*, p. 86.

age. Even the great Emperor Akbar had not evaded this ignoble fate. Such success, however, came at a steep price.

With the fading of the princely institution, it is no surprise that the empire suffered in its relations with the diverse groups over whom it sought to maintain dominion. Remarkably, the *akhbarat* for the last decades of Aurangzeb's reign reveal hardly any Berads, Telegus, Tamils, Marathas, and Kannadas serving in the upper echelons of princely households, although the princes operated for long stretches in regions dominated by these groups. This topic is considered more fully in the next two sections in which I explore the increasing difficulties faced by Mughal princes in corralling the most powerful political and military networks behind them.

### PRINCELY ALLIANCE BUILDING UNDERMINED

During Aurangzeb's reign, the empire had become massive, thanks in no small part to his own militaristic endeavors. Against this backdrop, the role of the princes – both sons and grandsons – in projecting Mughal authority across vast stretches of the Indian subcontinent had become more crucial than ever. Although Aurangzeb's heirs were not entirely unsuccessful in forging ties with Afghans, Marathas, Bundelas, Jats, Siddis, and Rajputs on behalf of the empire and their own ambitions, the relative ease with which previous generations of princes had built and sustained powerful networks of political and military support had evaporated. We get some sense of the mounting difficulties through an examination of Prince A'zam's experience in Gujarat in 1702–3.

### An Increasingly Shackled Prince A'zam

From the news bulletins (*akhbarat*) generated from A'zam's princely court in Gujarat for the Raja of Amber, we get a picture of A'zam working incessantly to mobilize the support of local leaders and inveigling his way into local networks of influence. The newsletters also reveal the challenges he faced as he tried to conciliate different constituencies, make friends while not alienating their enemies, and assert Mughal power in the face of increasingly violent conflicts across the province.

Aurangzeb moved A'zam from the governorship of Malwa to Gujarat when the incumbent governor of Gujarat died suddenly in 1701. A'zam was at first reluctant, but Aurangzeb pointed out that Gujarat was at "the center of the empire" and thus strategically a good base for the prince.[55] Ultimately, A'zam remained in Gujarat until 1705.

The surviving *akhbarat* for A'zam's stint in Gujarat begin in July 1702 when monsoon floods dominated the news. We learn that the prince's camp was inundated, merchants had suffered huge financial losses, large numbers of peasants had drowned, and crops across the region had been severely damaged.[56] We hear again of peasant woes in an angry complaint submitted to A'zam about the crop damage inflicted by hunting expeditions. A'zam's immediate response was to order a two-month halt, until the end of the rainy season, to all large-scale hunts.[57] The moment the two months were up, however, A'zam immediately resumed his hunting expeditions and carried on with them over the rest of the eleven-month period covered by the news briefs.

The hunts (see Chapter 3) were important occasions for alliance building and adjudication. A'zam displayed not only his military and physical prowess, but also his skills as a leader and law enforcer. He is often described as granting forgiveness. For example, perhaps questionably, he forgave *mansabdars* who had unjustly killed seven people in Patan.[58] When complaints reached his court that Aghur Khan, the chief customs officer in Surat, had extorted Rs. 10,000, A'zam ordered the petitioners to approach the imperial court since the Khan was an imperial appointee.[59] Although irritated by the refusal of a group of Muslims to serve under a Hindu commander (Gulab Ra'i) on account of his religion, A'zam decided to let the matter pass, against the advice of Mir Ahmad Khan, the provincial paymaster of the imperial forces, who urged the prince to punish such "ignorant" and "petty" officers.[60]

A'zam's desire to endear himself to Gujarat's provincial officers was such that he overlooked complaints of unfair or bad leadership. Consider Mustafa Quli Beg, who was serving as the chief revenue official and military commandant of Pethlad in July 1702. Shaikh Ghulam Muhammad, the chief judicial constable at A'zam's princely court, lodged a complaint on behalf of Pethlad's peasants accusing the Beg of mistreating them and charging illegal taxes. A few days later,

---

[55] Aurangzeb, *Ruqa't-i 'Alamgiri*, pp. 24, 25; Ibid., *Kalimat-i Taiyabat*, National Library of India, Sarkar Collection 111, f. 25; Ibid., *Raqa'im-i-Kara'im*, f. 204b.

[56] *Akhbarat-i Darbar-i Mu'alla*, vol. 41, pp. 1, 16.

[57] Ibid., p. 2.

[58] Ibid., p. 44.

[59] Ibid., p. 75.

[60] Ibid., pp. 117–18.

عاشم شاه خلف جهانگیر پادشاه عظیم اباد اوکرده و سابق بنه نام بود ۳

Azzum Shaw the Son of King Allum Ghcer

Azam Shah, 18th century (The Bodleian Library, University of Oxford, MS. Douce Or. a.3 fol. 3r)

Mustafa Quli Beg arrived at A'zam's court to answer the charges. The prince granted him an audience, and we learn that the Beg made him a gift of a diamond worth a startling Rs. 7,000 (slightly more than $100,000 in 2009 dollars). We also learn that A'zam was impressed with Mustafa Quli's willingness – as well as that of his sons Akbar Quli and Murshid Quli – to maintain larger contingents than their ranks demanded. A'zam was also pleased to learn that these men had effectively deployed their forces to suppress violent uprisings. As a result, no reprimand followed. To the contrary, A'zam recommended the Beg and one of his sons for increased military ranks and allowed them to return to Pethlad. Although additional complaints against Mustafa Quli continued to be lodged over the next few months, court officials do not seem to have gone beyond the promise to investigate.[61]

We also learn how A'zam reached out to religious leaders and groups. Several requests were made by local elites to convert to Islam; all were granted.[62] Sometimes the prince even awarded converts with personal congratulations and gifts.[63] He regularly gave gifts to individuals connected with Sufi shrine complexes as well as with non-Sufi religious establishments such as *madrassas* (Islamic religious schools).[64] He routinely visited Sufi shrines and invited important religious figures to accompany him on his hunts or tours around the province.[65] Projecting a pious leaning, A'zam ordered Muslim officials to tie their turbans in the proper canonical manner and asked that they attend Friday prayers regularly.[66] He also forbade Hindus from burning their dead on the banks of the River Sabarmati in response to Muslim complaints of half-burnt bodies floating in the river.[67]

Even though the cumulative effect of these measures translated into strong support for the prince among certain Muslim communities, a tide of discontent with Mughal rule nonetheless swelled across Gujarat. The *akhbarat* speak of A'zam's faltering efforts to win over disgruntled merchants and local landed elites (*zamindars*). Between peasant unrest and powerful Maratha incursions and raids from the south, the towns and rural areas of Gujarat suffered upheavals and regular outbreaks of violence. Merchants appealed to A'zam for help, complaining of extortion by imperial provincial officials and thefts in their homes and businesses (often by robbers on the payroll of officials). They complained of demands for money by Mughal officials, made when Marathas attacked the cities of Surat, Dohad, and Jhabwa. A'zam's attempts to intervene were ineffective, however. He was not only unwilling to come down too harshly on imperial officials, but was also unable to get defaulters among the ranks of the provincial nobility to repay their loans. On one occasion, merchants went on strike in protest, closing their shops in Ahmadabad – an important portent of the eventual loss of merchant confidence in the Mughals' capacity to govern. Over the decades that followed, disillusioned

[61] Ibid., pp. 3, 4–5, 6–7, 15, 36.
[62] Ibid., pp. 36, 64.
[63] Ibid., p. 66.
[64] Ibid., pp. 80, 107, 129, 172, 173, 206–7, 209.
[65] Ibid., pp. 90, 93, 96, 108–9.
[66] Ibid., pp. 2, 63.
[67] Ibid., p. 140.

merchants gradually moved their support to local and regional elites who increasingly were Mughal supporters in name only.

As with the merchants, the *akhbarat* also highlight growing disillusionment among *zamindars* with A'zam and the Mughal court. No doubt some still fought alongside the Mughals and died resisting the Marathas.[68] For example, we see certain Koli *zamindars* willing to stand up to other Koli *zamindars* when the latter rose in rebellion around Surat and Cambay.[69] Generally though, *zamindars* across Gujarat were increasingly emboldened to resist A'zam's efforts to force them to kneel in the face of the growing crisis brought on by devastating Maratha attacks. Some turned down repeated demands to appear at the prince's court for an audience. In one instance, A'zam went so far as to send a gift horse to entice a landlord to come and see him, princely fiat being insufficient.[70] In another example, even after a *zamindar* of Nagarpur had killed two *mansabdars* who tried to collect tribute (*peshkash*), A'zam offered him another chance to avoid being branded a rebel.[71] Judging from the *akhbarat* for A'zam's stint in Gujarat, it seems clear that the balance of power was slowly but inexorably shifting against the Mughals. Imperial princes such as A'zam were among the primary victims of this transforming political landscape.

### Father-Son Rivalry among Aurangzeb's Heirs: A'zam Versus Bidar Bakht

Yet for all the problems A'zam faced in Gujarat, his greater challenge remained the inevitable war of succession in which he faced the possibility of countless rivals, including his oldest son Bidar Bakht. By the early 1700s, Aurangzeb had lost confidence in A'zam and his two surviving brothers, Mu'azzam and Kam Bakhsh. This is apparent in his willingness to pit his sons against his adult grandsons, of which there were nine. In 1700, the oldest, Mu'izz-ud-Din, was thirty-nine years old, roughly the same age as Aurangzeb had been when he dethroned Shah Jahan. Among his grandsons Aurangzeb especially favored three, among them were two sons of Mu'azzam – Mu'izz-ud-Din and 'Azim-ud-Din (b. 1664). The other was A'zam's son Bidar Bakht (b. 1670). Records show how A'zam

---

[68] Ibid., p. 176.
[69] Ibid., pp. 120, 142.
[70] Ibid., p. 157.
[71] Ibid., p. 204.

and Bidar Bakht clashed and competed for friends among the imperial nobility as well as regional elites in the provinces.

Aurangzeb came to admire Bidar Bakht early in the prince's life. When he was only eighteen years old, Aurangzeb praised him in open court. Such public praise from this emperor was almost unprecedented, and it helped stoke increasing tensions between Bidar Bakht and his father.[72] Adding fuel to the fire, over the years that followed, Aurangzeb repeatedly chastised A'zam for neglecting Bidar Bakht. The emperor upbraided A'zam, saying it was his duty as a father to train and groom his own son, and that the task should not be laid at the feet of his grandfather.[73] To Bidar Bakht, he often complained about A'zam, saying he was arrogant (*mustaghani*) and that "his actions have a rotten smell" (*az waqa'i' u bu-yi bad amad*).[74] We learn of one incident in which Aurangzeb transferred an official from Bidar Bakht to A'zam's army midway through a campaign. When the officer in question refused to go out of loyalty to Bidar Bakht, Aurangzeb unexpectedly pardoned him rather than punishing him for his blatant disobedience.[75] Although we know very little about A'zam's popularity among the men who served under him, one 1702 source highlights great affection for Bidar Bakht. The sources also provide a glimmer of why Bidar Bakht enjoyed such popularity: he is notably solicitous of the opinions of his generals; he can also be seen inquiring about the heat, inspecting trenches, paying close attention to the disposition of his cannon, rewarding good service, consoling wounded soldiers, and sometimes endangering himself by his close supervision of assaults on the fort of Khelna.[76]

The hostility between father and son was manifest in their rival Rajput allies. Bidar Bakht befriended the twelve-year-old Jai Singh Kachhwaha and successfully lobbied for him to succeed his father Raja Bishan Singh, who died in 1699, as the ruler of Amber. At the time, Jai Singh was serving under Bidar Bakht's command, and their friendship intensified over the next several years. During the 1702 siege of Khelna, the two met on an almost daily basis, sharing confidences.[77] In 1703, when Bidar Bakht was appointed governor of Malwa, Jai Singh became one of his primary deputies. Ultimately Jai Singh's hostility toward Durga Das

---

[72] Ibid., vol. 16, p. 56.

[73] Aurangzeb, *Ruqa't-i 'Alamgiri*, pp. 5–6; Ibid., *Anecdotes*, p. 56.

[74] Aurangzeb, *Dastur-ul-'Amal-i Agahi*, f. 30b.

[75] *Akhbarat-i Darbar-i Mu'alla*, vol. 19, p. 394.

[76] *'Ara'iz-o-Faramin*, National Library of India, Sarkar Collection 46, pp. 9–13, 15, 19, 23, 27, 29–30, 31–2, 35, 39–40 50, 57, 83, 93–5, 131.

[77] Ibid., pp. 27, 83, 101.

Rathor – who was in turn a close ally of Prince A'zam and a protector of the interests of the rival Rajput kingdom of Marwar – led Bidar Bakht to try and undermine any settlement of long-standing political differences between Durga Das Rathor and Aurangzeb.[78] So too, even as A'zam sought to cultivate the Rana of Mewar and the Jat leader Churaman, Jai Singh and Bidar Bakht worked to undermine both in the interest of advancing Jai Singh's ambition to expand his realm in eastern Rajasthan and Malwa.

By 1707, the rift between A'zam and Bidar Bakht ran so deep that the former stalled his son's advance into Malwa and onward to Agra during the war of succession. Bidar Bakht, for his part, refused to hire additional soldiers in the run-up to the decisive Battle of Jaju for fear of exciting his father's suspicions that he had his own designs on the imperial throne.[79] These actions cost A'zam the chance to become the next Mughal emperor and cost both princes their lives. This is hinted at by none other than Kamraj, an A'zam partisan and author of an extremely detailed history of the 1707 war of succession.[80]

There is no doubt that by the end of Aurangzeb's reign, the task of building networks of friends and allies had become much harder for the older generation of princes as a result of bitter and long-lasting competition from their offspring. Although A'zam's conflict with Bidar Bakht was the most ferocious example of father-son rivalry among Aurangzeb's heirs, Mu'azzam too faced repeated challenges from 'Azim-ud-Din (the powerful governor of Bihar and Bengal for almost ten years, until 1706). Yet even as princes struggled and fought among themselves, the gravest challenge to the princely institution came not from rivalry within the royal family but from a new breed of independent-minded Mughal nobleman who evinced few ties of loyalty to any of Aurangzeb's heirs.

---

[78] It should be said that Bidar Bakht's task was never particularly difficult since Durga Das Rathor had a long history of opposition to Aurangzeb. It began in 1678–9 when Durga Das Rathor opposed Aurangzeb's efforts to control the succession to the throne of Marwar following the death of Raja Jaswant Singh. Over the next few years, Durga Das Rathor was both at the forefront of a Rajput rebellion against Aurangzeb as well as efforts to encourage Prince Akbar to rebel against his father. When Akbar's rebellion failed in 1681, Durga Das Rathor offered his protection to the fleeing prince, eventually conveying him to the Maratha chief Shambhaji and safety in the Deccan. Robert Hallisey, *The Rajput Rebellion against Aurangzeb: A Study of the Mughal Empire in Seventeenth-Century India* (Columbia, MO, 1977).

[79] Wazih, *Tarikh-i Iradat Khan*, p. 26.

[80] Kamraj, *A'zam al-Harb*, ff. 133–5, 143–4.

THE NOBLE THREAT TO PRINCELY ALLIANCE BUILDING

In this later Mughal period, a small cluster of extremely powerful nobles came into prominence. Although these nobles were not immune to the resource crunch related to falling *jagir* revenues, they nonetheless managed to transcend these difficulties by drawing heavily on alternative sources of income, especially tribute payments and cash exactions from the populations of peninsular India. Aiding these efforts was the fact that starting in the 1690s, Aurangzeb increasingly came to rely on this group of nonroyal generals (as opposed to his fractious sons and grandsons) to lead his armies and spearhead military forays in the south, now the primary theater of military and financial opportunities.

Aurangzeb himself never gave up on the conceit of the all-powerful prince. Nowhere is this more apparent than in his use of the names of his sons and grandsons to impress Mughal power across the imperial landscape. Thus, in the latter half of his reign, he renamed several towns and cities after his heirs. Gorakhpur became Mu'azzamabad; Dhankot became Mu'azzamnagar; Satara became A'zamtara; and Pune, Belgaon, Ausa, and Balungarh became, respectively, A'zamgarh, A'zamnagar, A'zamgir, and 'Azimgarh. He also took pains to uphold princely prerogatives. In 1685, for example, when a high-ranking nobleman (Ruhullah Khan) was ordered to deliver an imperial order to Mu'azzam, Aurangzeb gave the Khan strict instructions to treat his son with utmost dignity and respect.[81] (At the time, Aurangzeb and Mu'azzam were locked in severe disagreements over imperial plans to conquer the Deccan kingdoms of Bijapur and Golkonda.) The emperor rarely tolerated rudeness of speech or manner toward a prince.[82] Other forms of misconduct – such as leaving a prince's service without prior permission, desertion during a military campaign, or theft of *jagir* revenues – were likewise punished.[83] As Aurangzeb explained in a letter to one of his grandsons, punishment was necessary to avoid future infractions.[84] Despite such solicitousness toward his heirs, Aurangzeb nonetheless reached past his sons and grandsons for dependable warrior-statesmen to help him pursue his overall political and military goals.

The initial entry of the nobleman into the imperial fray occurred in the 1680s as the royal sons and grandsons became individually suspect or

---

[81] *Akhbarat-i Darbar-i Mu'alla*, vol. 16, pp. B1, D2.
[82] Ibid., vol. 25, p. 35; Aurangzeb, *Ruqa't-i 'Alamgiri*, pp. 40, 59.
[83] *Akhbarat-i Darbar-i Mu'alla*, vol. 17, no. 36/28; vol. 18, pp. 62, 67, 80; vol. 19, p. 460; vol. 25, p. 60; vol. 29, p. 72.
[84] Aurangzeb, *Ruqa't-i 'Alamgiri*, p. 38.

otherwise unreliable. In 1687, Aurangzeb ordered the arrest of his oldest living son Mu'azzam and his four sons for treason after discovering their collusion with the Sultanate of Golkonda to prevent its conquest. With the death of Aurangzeb's oldest son, Muhammad Sultan, in 1676, the escape of another (Akbar) to Iran a decade later, and the relative youth of the younger generation of Mughal princes, by the late 1680s Aurangzeb was left with only two possible successors: his sons Kam Bakhsh and A'zam. But because of Kam Bakhsh's perceived instability and Aurangzeb's long-standing decision to deprive him of any military or gubernatorial experience, in effect, Aurangzeb only had one feasible successor, A'zam. Meanwhile, the emperor remained engaged in territorial expansion; in fact, his reign was in almost permanent campaign mode, with multiple armies in the battlefield at any given time. Having no princely candidate other than A'zam to help him with this project of expanding the empire, Aurangzeb was forced to turn to key individuals in the Mughal nobility.

From the late 1680s onward, two dominant groups of nobles stepped forward to work with Aurangzeb. In an outcome no one could have predicted, it would be these men who helped the emperor achieve his most important military objectives over the next twenty years. Ghazi-ud-Din Khan Feroz Jang (b. 1649) and his son Chin Qilich Khan (b. 1671) led the first group. Aurangzeb's long-standing chief minister Asad Khan (b. 1626) and his son Zulfiqar Khan (b. 1649) led the other.[85] These two camps controlled noble-led politics by the end of Aurangzeb's reign. And herein lay the problem for Aurangzeb's heirs: although these two noble camps were extremely hostile toward each other, their dislike for Aurangzeb's sons and grandsons was almost as intense. Their loyalty to the emperor was such that it consistently stood in the way of their ability or willingness to ally with any one prince. Consider Ghazi-ud-Din Khan and his family.

Aurangzeb had carefully nurtured Ghazi-ud-Din Khan and Chin Qilich Khan for decades. Following Ghazi-ud-Din Khan's arrival in India in the late 1660s, Aurangzeb honored him with a favorable marriage to the daughter of Shah Jahan's great chief minister Sa'dullah Khan (d. 1656). This honor came on top of others awarded to Ghazi-ud-Din Khan's father, Abid Khan, one of Aurangzeb's favorite nobles as well as his minister for religious endowments (*sadr-us-sudur*). Following the birth of Ghazi-ud-Din Khan's first son, the emperor gave the boy his name, Mir

---

[85] For more biographical information, Chandra, *Parties and Politics at the Mughal Court*, pp. 40–9.

Qamar-ud-Din (he was later ennobled with the title Chin Qilich Khan).
Over the ensuing years, Aurangzeb took a deep interest in the boy's
development. Besides granting him a nominal imperial rank at the unusu-
ally early age of six (a privilege hitherto reserved for princes of the blood),
the emperor requested that Ghazi-ud-Din Khan leave his son under his care
for one day a week so that he might personally play a part in training him.

Such kindnesses to Ghazi-ud-Din Khan's family, on top of their close
personal contacts, bred deep loyalty to Aurangzeb. Thus, in 1681, Ghazi-
ud-Din Khan distinguished himself during Prince Akbar's rebellion by
volunteering to lead a dangerous weeklong reconnoitering mission that
no other noble was willing to undertake. Some years later, in 1685, when
an army led by A'zam was trapped outside the walls of Bijapur and starved
for supplies, Ghazi-ud-Din Khan led the difficult relief expedition, thus in
turn earning the exalted honorific of "distinguished son" (*farzand-i arjomand*) following the successful completion of this mission. In 1687, it was
Ghazi-ud-Din Khan who brought Mu'azzam's secret collusion with
Golkonda to Aurangzeb's attention. He also played a key role in the
subsequent arrest of the then nominal heir as well as his four sons.
Protected by the emperor's affection and confident in their growing
strength, Ghazi-ud-Din Khan and, to a lesser degree, Chin Qilich Khan
felt free to dismiss the princes.

Asad Khan and Zulfiqar Khan also had long-standing and powerful
connections to the emperor. Asad Khan was appointed Aurangzeb's chief
minister in 1676, a post he retained until the emperor's death thirty-one
years later. In the final five years of Aurangzeb's reign, Asad Khan's son
ascended to the position of paymaster general (*mir bakhshi*). Zulfiqar
Khan thus became one of the highest-ranked imperial ministers after his
father. Although the historical record shows that Asad Khan and Zulfiqar
Khan had strong private misgivings about many of Aurangzeb's policies,
they never aired their views in public. Loyalty to the emperor demanded as
much. Such loyalty also frequently placed them on a collision course with
Aurangzeb's sons and grandsons. No clash is more shocking than what
transpired with Kam Bakhsh in 1693.

After Mughal forces had encircled the Maratha stronghold of Jinji,
Aurangzeb decided to appoint Kam Bakhsh (for the first and last time) to
be supreme military commander. Asad Khan and Zulfiqar Khan, seasoned
warriors both, accompanied the prince. Unfortunately, the siege proved a
difficult one, with endless fighting, food shortages, and little progress
toward taking the fort. By the spring of 1693, Kam Bakhsh had reached
the end of his tether. Against Aurangzeb's explicit orders, he opened secret

negotiations with the besieged Maratha ruler Rajaram to try and work out a settlement that might afford the Mughals a face-saving withdrawal. When Asad Khan and Zulfiqar Khan discovered Kam Bakhsh's plan, they immediately, even gleefully, arrested the prince. In addition to ordering the execution of several of the prince's intimates, Asad Khan, in an unprecedented act by a nobleman, abused Kam Bakhsh to his face.[86] Then the prince was loaded onto an elephant and dragged back to the imperial court to face his father's judgment. In response to bitter complaints by Kam Bakhsh about his mistreatment and in an apparent effort to prevent his son from being further dishonored, Aurangzeb threatened to remove Asad Khan from the post of *wazir*. There was no follow-through, however. On the contrary, Aurangzeb warned Kam Bakhsh: "Whoever speaks badly of him [Zulfiqar Khan] is himself a bad man."[87] And that was the end of the matter. Over the remainder of Aurangzeb's life, Asad Khan and Zulfiqar Khan had other run-ins with Kam Bakhsh, as well as with A'zam and Bidar Bakht.[88] But they rarely faced any serious repercussions thanks to Aurangzeb's protection. This, in turn, engendered more loyalty to the emperor and also worsening relations with the various princes.

Between 1687 and the end of his reign, Aurangzeb's reliance on men such as Ghazi-ud-Din Khan, Zulfiqar Khan, and, starting in the late 1690s, Chin Qilich Khan to run the all-consuming Deccan campaigns only increased. As a result, these men had plenty of opportunity to deepen their acquaintance with and involvement in the region.

By contrast, Aurangzeb appears to have slowly moved to freeze his sons and grandsons out of a permanent role in the Deccan, at best cycling them in and out of campaigns there. Thus, following his disastrous Jinji venture in 1692–3, Kam Bakhsh never held another military command. Although Mu'azzam was finally released from prison in 1695, he was immediately removed from the Deccan with an appointment in northern India. He did not return to the Deccan until after Aurangzeb's death. None of Mu'azzam's sons, with the exception of Mu'izz-ud-Din, served in the Deccan either. In Mu'izz-ud-Din's case, after three years of campaigning, he too was permanently removed to northern India along with his father and brothers. A'zam undertook various assignments in the 1690s, but these were invariably matched by long stints of inactivity. Between 1693 and 1694, illness kept him largely out of action, and then for three years,

---

[86] K. Khan, *Muntakhab al-Labab*, vol. 2, pp. 419–20; Manucci, *Mogul India*, vol. 2, p. 296.
[87] Aurangzeb, *Anecdotes*, p. 55.
[88] *Akhbarat-i Darbar-i Mu'alla*, vol. 30, p. 43; Aurangzeb, *Ruqa't-i 'Alamgiri*, p. 62.

beginning in 1695, he was permanently stationed in command of a reserve army in the town of Pedgaon, around ninety miles from the imperial base camp at Islampuri. He saw little action during this time. Finally in 1699–1700, despite a successful major campaign against the forts of Satara and Parli, A'zam was removed from the Deccan. The prince was clearly angered by the move, especially since Aurangzeb never articulated a reason for his decision. In the end, however, he had to comply with his father's orders.[89] Over the next six years, he served as a reluctant governor, first of Malwa, and then of Gujarat.

In the case of Bidar Bakht, after his recall from Malwa in 1693, he spent nearly nine years in the Deccan. Like his father A'zam, though, Bidar Bakht was transferred out of the region following his greatest military triumph there, the taking of the fort of Khelna in 1702. For the next four years, even as fighting raged with unrelenting ferocity, no imperial prince led any of the Mughal armies in the Deccan.

The irrelevance of the princes must have been more than apparent to Zulfiqar Khan in 1702 as he marched more than six thousand miles and fought almost twenty major battles without any princely input or oversight. He sent all requests to the imperial court through his father, Asad Khan, and even directly to the emperor. Indeed, the story of Zulfiqar Khan is very much that of a nobleman who both accumulated the privileges and emulated the general life story of a prince. Like princes before him, Zulfiqar Khan used his time and military campaigns in the Deccan to build alliances, accumulate wealth, and fortify his power, acting almost as a ruler in his own right.

What emerges from the sources is the picture of a nobleman in a nearly unstoppable search for material resources and power. Thus, starting in 1690–1, Zulfiqar Khan masterminded and led a series of raids and tribute-levying expeditions against the southern Indian kingdoms of Tanjore and Trichinopoly. Some part of the money raised was passed on to the imperial court, but a substantial amount seems to have been retained by the Khan to fund his military and personal expenses. In 1694, Zulfiqar Khan again raided Tanjore and forced its ruler to disgorge an annual tribute of three million rupees and part with valuable revenue-yielding lands.[90]

Zulfiqar Khan, perhaps not unlike the Mughal princes from time to time, appears in the sources as not merely ambitious, but downright greedy and cunning in his pursuit of resources. For instance, during the siege of Jinji, he

[89] *Akhbarat-i Darbar-i Mu'alla*, vol. 23, p. 191; K. Khan, *Muntakhab al-Labab*, vol. 2, p. 474.
[90] Jadunath Sarkar, *History of Aurangzib*, vol. 5 (Calcutta, repr. 1952), p. 81.

was widely accused of accepting secret payments from the Marathas to forestall the fort's capture. Following Kam Bakhsh's arrest in 1693, Zulfiqar Khan and his father are said to have confiscated around Rs. 450,000 in money and military equipment from the prince's establishment, in the process draining it of resources.[91] Kam Bakhsh's household never recovered from this loss. In 1694, after Aurangzeb ordered Zulfiqar Khan to execute Yachapa Nayak (one of the most powerful landholders in the Vellore region and an erstwhile ally of the Khan), the nobleman pocketed huge amounts of the Nayak's money. Through the 1690s, Zulfiqar Khan also developed substantial commercial interests in the vibrant cloth trade along the Coromandel Coast. Supplementing these sources of income was Zulfiqar Khan's appointment in 1702 to the highly lucrative post of paymaster general of the imperial armies (*mir bakhshi*). Later, in 1705, he was suspected by Aurangzeb of taking bribes from Pidia Nayak – the perennial Berad rebel – to enable his escape from the besieged fort of Wakhinkheda.[92]

Thanks to the *akhbarat* and other contemporary records, we know the names of some of the people who served under Zulfiqar Khan. One is struck by their diversity. As well as Hindus and Muslims, his topmost commanders included two Dakhani-Afghans (Daud Khan Panni and his brother Sulaiman), a Bundela (Dalpat Singh Bundela), and a Rajput (Ram Singh Hada). Just below the top tier were Rao Khandoji (a Maratha), Rashid Oghlal (a Turk), Rustam Beg Mingbashi (a Turk), and Bharat Chand and Prithvi Chand (Kayasths both). Prior to his execution in 1694, the Telegu *zamindar* Yachapa Nayak had also been recommended by Zulfiqar Khan for a high imperial *mansab* and thus was roped into serving him. Moving down the ranks to middling commanders and officers in Zulfiqar Khan's forces, we encounter the names of Iranians, Turks, Indian Muslims, Rajputs, Buksariyas, Khatris, Kayasths, and Bundelas as well as Dakhanis, Marathas, Afghans, Berads, Nawaits, and Telegus.

Although the contingents of some of Zulfiqar Khan's top officers, including those of Dalpat Rao Bundela and Ram Singh Hada, were fairly homogenous (drawing as they did on either Bundelas or Rajputs), Daud Khan Panni's divisions clearly reflected the diversity of the Deccan. Beyond a core group of Afghans, Daud Khan Panni recruited heavily among the Marathas as well as other Deccan-based groups.[93] By 1700, Zulfiqar Khan's networks of friends and allies in the Deccan far outstripped those of any Mughal Prince.

[91]  *Akhbarat-i Darbar-i Mu'alla*, vol. 18, pp. 24, 83.
[92]  Bhimsen Saxsena, *Tarikh-i-Dilkasha*, trans. Jadunath Sarkar (Bombay, 1972), p. 249.
[93]  *Akhbarat-i Darbar-i Mu'alla*, vol. 29, pp. 66, 78.

No doubt Zulfiqar Khan, Ghazi-ud-Din Khan, and Chin Qilich Bahadur participated in a long tradition of extremely rich, well-connected, and powerful Mughal nobles. During Akbar's reign, they had included 'Abd-ul-Rahim Khan-i Khanan, Raja Man Singh and Mirza 'Aziz Koka; in Jahangir's, Asaf Khan, Mahabat Khan, and Khan Jahan Lodi; and in Shah Jahan's, Raja Jai Singh, Sa'dullah Khan, 'Ali Mardan Khan, Mir Jumla, and Raja Jaswant Singh. Two features, however, distinguish the highest-ranking nobles of Aurangzeb's last years from their forerunners. The first was their ability to accrue wealth, power, and networks of support with little or no reliance on imperial princes. Consequently, at best they felt only a tenuous connection to Aurangzeb's sons and grandsons; at worst they viewed them as direct competitors. Thus, in addition to sabotaging Kam Bakhsh outside Jinji in 1693, Zulfiqar Khan undermined the same prince's efforts to reach political or military pacts on other occasions too: with Shahu in 1703 and Pidia Nayak in 1705. The Khan seems to have been angling to take over both initiatives. This brings up the second point of difference with previous generations of Mughal nobles.

Emboldened by their own power and success, Aurangzeb's nobles avoided being closely embraced by any of the imperial heirs. Their ability to maintain a distance from all imperial contenders was something to which previous generations of Mughal nobles neither aspired to nor achieved. And this development held great danger for the princes and the dynasty. Deprived of opportunities to build their own networks of friends and allies in the most important military arena of the empire, the princes now also struggled to maintain their political relevance with a critical constituency in the evolving Mughal power structure. Loyalties that were once automatically owed by nobles to the princes were now being held back. As power and authority slowly drained out of the princely institution, its vital role as an interface between the most powerful nodes in Indian society and the dynasty also weakened. Zulfiqar Khan's dreams in the 1690s of eventually declaring his independence in the Deccan attest to the rough waters that lay ahead for princes and the Mughal Empire.[94] Aurangzeb's pernicious role in these momentous changes is undeniable, although many other factors also came into play. Old and physically infirm, his anxiety that someone within his own family might be tempted to overthrow him if given the resources to do so appears to have made way for a fundamental shift in the balance of power between the dynasty and its most powerful servitors.

[94] Chandra, *Parties and Politics at the Mughal Court*, p. 43.

But Aurangzeb had good reason to fear challenges from within his own family. After all, his reign began with a rebellion by his oldest son Muhammad Sultan. Then, in 1681, just when he thought he had contained a troublesome rebellion in the autonomous Rajput kingdom of Marwar, another son, Akbar, made common cause with his Rajput enemies. Furthermore, this occurred against the backdrop of long-standing and continuing tensions with his second son Mu'azzam. It is to this contentious relationship between Aurangzeb and Mu'azzam that we now turn. The drama of this relationship throws light on how Aurangzeb sought to balance, on the one hand, his desire to afford his sons some political leeway – the better, it seems, to avoid the kind of violent eruption that led to Shah Jahan's overthrow in 1658 – and, on the other, his determination nonetheless to keep their political ambitions in check.

## AURANGZEB VERSUS THE MUGHAL PRINCE: THE CASE OF PRINCE MU'AZZAM

Aurangzeb's treatment of his heirs marked a determined break from Shah Jahan's policies vis-à-vis his sons (see Chapter 5). Whereas Shah Jahan had been intolerant of dissent, Aurangzeb began his reign by allowing his sons greater leeway. As long as a prince did not openly rebel, Aurangzeb allowed him to stake out positions, even when they were at odds with his own policies. However, starting in the mid-1680s, as he grew older and as warfare in the Deccan intensified, Aurangzeb appears to have tightened the reins. We see this evolution of the emperor's attitude in the worsening relations with his son Mu'azzam. In this father-son relationship, we see an emperor straining to control a recalcitrant prince without forcing him into rebellion. On Mu'azzam's part, we see concerted efforts to distinguish his public image from that of his father and also from that of his primary princely competitor, Prince A'zam.

### Aurangzeb Parries Mu'azzam's Defiance

Mu'azzam was born in 1643 to Aurangzeb and Nawab Ba'i, a Hindu Pahari Rajput princess. At the age of twenty, following his father's accession to the throne, Mu'azzam was sent to the Deccan as its governor (1663). His main objective was to deal with the growing threat posed by the Marathas under the leadership of Shivaji. But Mu'azzam appears to have been already

Bahadur Shah I (formerly Prince Mu'azzam), ca. 1710 (© Victoria and Albert Museum, London, 2006BF5086–01)

convinced that the Marathas were militarily undefeatable.[95] The prince thus sought to conciliate and co-opt the Marathas rather than pursue his father's preferred military solution. Aurangzeb sent various Mughal nobles to force Mu'azzam to forsake his alternate approach. By 1669, the Mughal high command was deeply fractured between those supporting these different positions; civil war within the Mughal camp seemed a distinct likelihood. Aurangzeb now moved to reassert his authority over Mu'azzam by sending his foster brother and close confidant Bahadur Khan Koka to take charge of the faltering campaign.

[95] Saxsena, *Tarikh-i-Dilkasha*, p. 41.

Hemmed in and insulted, Mu'azzam was close to rebellion in 1670. But Aurangzeb discovered the plot. He responded swiftly, not by severely punishing his son – as Jahangir or Shah Jahan would have done – but rather by sending the prince's mother, Nawab Ba'i, to dissuade him, which she did successfully.[96] Mu'azzam was eventually recalled to the Mughal court and spent the next seven years under Aurangzeb's watchful eye.

In 1680, Mu'azzam came close to rebelling again, in disagreement this time over Aurangzeb's decision to employ scorched-earth tactics against his Rajput opponents. As in 1670, Aurangzeb was well informed about his son's discontent. For the second time, he dispatched Mu'azzam's mother to reason with him. As one contemporary chronicler put it, his mother "offered her advice and dissuaded the prince from helping the Rajputs or interceding on their behalf."[97] The chronicler goes on to state that Mu'azzam was never punished, but Aurangzeb once again intensified his vigilance.[98]

### As Father-Son Tensions Rise, Mu'azzam Shapes a Distinct Political Identity

Over the next six years, between 1681 and 1687, Mu'azzam was at best a grudgingly obedient son. Aurangzeb's grievances against him piled up. Mu'azzam was deputed to prevent his younger brother Akbar (following his 1681 rebellion) from fleeing to the Deccan, but he failed (by all accounts deliberately) in that mission.[99] Next, when Aurangzeb ordered Mu'azzam to invade the Konkan region along India's western seaboard in 1683 (to cut off Akbar's escape and Maratha supply routes to the sea), again the prince led a half-hearted, stumbling mission that failed miserably. Two years later, as Mughal forces attacked the Deccan Sultanate of Golkonda, Aurangzeb learned that Mu'azzam was going behind his back and engaging in secret negotiations aimed at forestalling its conquest. Although Aurangzeb ultimately agreed to the very settlement Mu'azzam had negotiated (which included a massive indemnity and a change in the kingdom's top leadership), he nonetheless accused the prince of treason and temporarily barred him from the Mughal court. Here, judging by Aurangzeb's actions, he continued to assume that such an imperfect

---

[96] *Akhbarat-i Darbar-i Mualla*, vol. 34, pp. 330, 334, 348; Saxsena, *Tarikh-i-Dilkasha*, p. 60.
[97] K. Khan, *Muntakhab al-Labab*, vol. 2, p. 264.
[98] Ibid., pp. 265, 266–7.
[99] Manucci, *Mogul India*, vol. 2, p. 235.

relationship with his son could continue and did not require any more heavy-handed treatment.

Less than a year later, in 1685–6, Aurangzeb found himself again obstructed by Mu'azzam's preference for a negotiated settlement to a military campaign – this time against Bijapur (the other important Muslim kingdom in the Deccan). Although the emperor ultimately commanded the prince to fall in line behind his aim to conquer the state, Aurangzeb suspected continued "mischief and disloyalty."[100] What followed was another imperial reprimand: this time, a number of Mu'azzam's senior advisors were expelled from the imperial camp.

This pattern of a barely compliant prince and an emperor responding with mild shows of authority finally ended during a renewed campaign against the Sultanate of Golkonda that followed the conquest of Bijapur. Mu'azzam viewed Aurangzeb's determination to conquer Golkonda as a direct affront. After all, it was he who had personally assured the ruler of Golkonda safety from Mughal attack if he remained in compliance with Mughal demands. Manucci – the Italian adventurer in Mu'azzam's service in the years leading up to the events outside Golkonda – describes his master's annoyance with the emperor:

[Mu'azzam] said the world would wonder that so great a king should pay no heed to the promises made by his son and heir. He therefore entreated [Aurangzeb] to abandon this intention of his, for the King of Gulkandah was quite helpless, and could not impede His Majesty's projects against Sambha Ji.[101]

What followed in 1686–7 was a massive conspiracy – involving Mu'azzam, his sons, his most senior wife, her father, and large numbers of princely retainers – aimed at thwarting Mughal policy against Golkonda. Besides sharing Mughal military dispositions and tactics with the Golkondans, Mu'azzam also allowed food to be carried into the besieged citadel. It did not take long for Aurangzeb to learn about his son's treasonous activities. With his own prestige as well as his capacity to enforce discipline over Mughal forces in the Deccan so directly confronted, he finally resorted to punitive measures.

The punishment was swift and dramatic. Aurangzeb broke up Mu'azzam's household, executed a number of his closest followers, confiscated all the prince's belongings, and ordered the prince's harem – including his mother Nawab Ba'i – to leave in disgrace for Delhi. He

---

[100] M. Khan, *Maasir i Alamgiri*, p. 293.
[101] Manucci, *Mogul India*, vol. 2, p. 283.

ordered Mu'azzam and his sons imprisoned in the harshest possible circumstances. He barred Mu'azzam from cutting his hair or nails for almost six months and ordered that the prince be denied comfortable clothes, good food, or cool water. The prince was also deprived of contact with anyone other than his immediate captors.[102] Yet of note is that although indeed harsh, these deprivations do not compare with Khusrau's earlier blinding by his father, Emperor Jahangir.

Although the harshest aspects of Mu'azzam's imprisonment were eased after six months, he remained in prison or under house arrest for another seven years until 1695. In a historical account, *Lubb-ul-Tawarikh*, written in the mid-1690s by one of Mu'azzam's supporters, Bindraban Das Ra'i, we read a sort of princely apology. Rather than justifying the prince's actions against his father, Ra'i alludes to a "sickness" (*bimari*) that had afflicted Mu'azzam, resulting in "exhaustion" (*khaste*). Ra'i reasons that Mu'azzam had never really departed from the path of obedience and wisdom and that he had always maintained great affection and love for his father.[103] To make sure, however, that Mu'azzam would never have another opportunity to stir up mischief in the Deccan, Aurangzeb permanently transferred him to northern India following his release. Over the coming years, Mu'azzam's four sons would also be transferred out of the Deccan. None of them was ever allowed to return to the Mughal court or lead an imperial army in the Deccan for the duration of Aurangzeb's life.

By extending his patronage and authority beyond his uncooperative heirs to nobles such as Ghazi-ud-Din Khan, Chin Qilich Khan, and Zulfiqar Khan and using various means to monitor their activities and forestall their ambitions, Aurangzeb sought to undo any threat his heirs might pose to his occupancy of the Mughal throne. In the end, despite Shah Jahan's angry prediction in 1658 that Aurangzeb would be dethroned by one of his sons, Aurangzeb died quietly in his sleep on March 2, 1707.

## CONCLUSION

In early 1707, sensing he was at death's doorstep, Aurangzeb ordered A'zam (who had returned from Gujarat the previous year) and Kam Bakhsh to leave on fresh provincial assignments far removed from the imperial court.

---

[102] *Akhbarat-i Darbar-i Mualla*, vol. 16, p. 42; K. Khan, *Muntakhab al-Labab*, vol. 2, pp. 330–5; Ishwar Das Nagar, *Futuhat-i-'Alamgiri*, ed. Raghubir Singh and Qazi Karamatullah (Vadodara, 1995), pp. 265–7; M. Khan, *Maasir i Alamgiri*, pp. 293–5.
[103] Ra'i, *Lubb-ut-Tawarikh*, ff. 156b-157b.

He hoped to preempt the possibility of a civil war breaking out in the imperial camp, a war that might necessitate a son killing him. A'zam – determined to lay claim to the treasure and human and military resources at the court in the event of his father's death – used various ploys to postpone his departure. When these failed, he sought unsuccessfully to leave portions of his princely household at the court. Even after he had finally been forced to vacate the court, he marched with deliberate delay. Although barely lucid by this point in time, Aurangzeb continued to receive daily reports of his son's actions. In response, he sent out letters demanding that A'zam remove his household and move away more quickly. He also recalled to his side powerful military loyalists, including Zulfiqar Khan, in an attempt to protect the court should A'zam turn belligerent.[104]

Aurangzeb's forcefulness in the last decades of his life ensured that no serious challenge would come from within his family after Prince Akbar's revolt in the early 1680s. By contrast, all three previous rulers – Akbar, Jahangir, and Shah Jahan – experienced violent princely struggles in the last years of their reigns. Although we might describe Aurangzeb as successfully reining in his heirs, the story is markedly different when viewed in terms of the health of the empire at large. Aurangzeb's actions had terrible, if unintended, consequences not only for the princely institution but also for the dynasty. In the next and concluding chapter, we consider what transpired in the years following Aurangzeb's death in 1707 and the final decision to move away from an open-ended succession in 1719.

[104] *Akhbarat-i Darbar-i Mualla*, vol. 32, pp. 6–43.

# Conclusion

Aurangzeb died in early 1707. For his three surviving sons – Mu'azzam, A'zam, and Kam Bakhsh – the news of their father's death prompted each to immediately stake his claim to be the next Mughal emperor. Each sought anew to raise monies, recruit soldiers, and dispatch spies for the latest intelligence. Their renewed efforts included special attention to wooing powerful imperial nobles. Mu'azzam, based in the northwestern territories of the Mughal Empire, successfully rallied most of the northern nobles to his cause. By contrast, A'zam and Kam Bakhsh had a much harder time winning support among the nobility based at and beyond the imperial court in the Deccan. Kam Bakhsh was simply abandoned by the general Chin Qilich Khan and the latter's relative, Muhammad Amin Khan, en route to the stronghold of Bijapur. Nor did the prince dare give chase to the Khans' battle-hardened contingents as they made their way back, presumably, to ally with A'zam. In A'zam's case, although long-drawn negotiations with Zulfiqar Khan finally won the latter's grudging support, the prince had no luck with Ghazi-ud-Din Khan, the governor of Berar (in the Deccan) and father of Chin Qilich Khan. A'zam sent repeated requests to Ghazi-ud-Din Khan to join his expedition in its impending confrontation with Mu'azzam, but the noble snubbed him. More ominously, Chin Qilich Khan and Muhammad Amin Khan both deserted A'zam as he marched out of the Deccan despite first promising him support; as they abandoned the prince's army, they plundered its baggage train. Like Kam Bakhsh, A'zam could do little but swallow these insults, since he was in no position to arrest or punish the nobles.

The decisions by Ghazi-ud-Din Khan, Chin Qilich Khan, and Muhammad Amin Khan to sit out the 1707 war of succession, and the timid princely responses to these affronts, presented a state of affairs entirely without precedent in Mughal history. During the 1657–9 war of succession, when Shahnawaz Khan Safavi had tried to stay neutral, Prince Aurangzeb arrested and confined him forthwith before setting out to battle Dara Shukoh and Shah Jahan. Similarly, 'Abdur Rahim Khan-i Khanan and his son Darab Khan were placed under arrest by Khurram when they offered less than enthusiastic support for his rebellion in 1622–3.

The audacity of the dissenting nobles of 1707 speaks to the degree to which princes' authority and the princely institution itself had become compromised – especially in relation to the most powerful nobles. The undermining of the Mughal Prince, a process that had begun in the last decades of Aurangzeb's rule, would continue and intensify through the brief reign of Mu'azzam/Bahadur Shah I between 1707 and 1712.

Following Bahadur Shah's death in 1712, the former Aurangzeb favorite Zulfiqar Khan – described in one source as "of imposing stature, noble-minded, good-natured and of universal generosity" and in another as neither fearing God's final judgment or retribution[1] – emerged as the first noble kingmaker in the empire's history. The Khan single-handedly engineered the military defeat of the strongest of Bahadur Shah's four sons, 'Azim-ud-Din/ 'Azim-ush-Shan, and the accession of the weakest, Mu'izz-ud-Din/Jahandar Shah. Without a strong personal household or alliances of his own, Jahandar Shah was completely dependent on Zulfiqar Khan's support. In 1713, Farrukh Siyar, the twenty-nine-year-old son of Jahandar Shah's deceased brother 'Azim-ush-Shan, overthrew his uncle, marking a first break from Akbar's move to restrict heirs to the direct line of the reigning emperor. Like his predecessor, Farrukh Siyar suffered from a weak princely household and tepid political support across the empire. His accession owed everything to the backing of the next major set of king-makers in Mughal history, 'Abdullah Khan and Hussain 'Ali Khan, often referred to as the Saiyid brothers.

Eventually, in 1719, the Saiyid brothers themselves overthrew Farrukh Siyar and handpicked his successor from among a crowded field of princes confined in the imperial harem. Their decision to seek a prince from a collateral line was necessitated by the fact that Farrukh Siyar did not have a brother or male heir to succeed him. In this event – in the selection of an emperor by noblemen and in the choice of a sheltered prince lacking any

---

[1] Burhan ibn Hasan, *Tuzuk-e-Walajahi*, ed. T. Chandrasekharan (Madras, 1957), pp. 69–70; Shah Nawaz Khan, *Maasiru-l-Umara*, ed. Abdur Rahim and Ashraf Ali, vol. 2 (Calcutta, 1890), p. 105.

military or political training – the Mughals' open-ended system of succession came to a final and conclusive end, also spelling the final demise of the princely institution and the destruction of the Mughal dynasty as an effective political force.

This concluding chapter, then, examines the period between the accession of Bahadur Shah I and the murder of Farrukh Siyar. It explores how the unfolding phenomena outlined in the previous chapter – weakened princely households and the inability of princes to form profitable alliances with the most powerful players across the empire – gained momentum in the decade after Aurangzeb's death. In the vacuum left by the demise of the once redoubtable Mughal Prince, groups across the empire abandoned their allegiance to the dynasty and instead gravitated toward newly rising regional elites, thus setting the stage for the emergence and consolidation of post-Mughal successor states. Here we consider especially the example of the nobleman Murshid Quli Khan, founder of the semi-independent state of Bengal. In tracing the establishment and rise of this post-Mughal successor state, we see the developments that coincided with and spelled the end of the Mughal princely institution.

## THE PRINCELY INSTITUTION ATROPHIES UNDER BAHADUR SHAH I, 1707–1712

Mu'azzam defeated his brother and main rival A'zam at the Battle of Jaju in June 1707 to become Bahadur Shah I. In many ways, his path to the imperial throne was typical of the post-1580s Mughal Prince. And although Kam Bakhsh managed to hold on to parts of the Deccan until January 1709, most observers assumed that it was only a matter of time before he too would be defeated and killed.

Mu'azzam's princely household spearheaded the actual fighting at the Battle of Jaju. Contemporary accounts (including Ni'mat Khan's *Jangnama* and *Badshahnama*, Kamwar Khan's *Tazkirat-us-Salatin Chaghta*, Kamraj's *A'zam al-Harb*, and Bhimsen Saxsena's *Tarikh-i Dilkasha*) all concur in their admiration for his fighting troops. We learn also that as the prince marched out of the northwestern territories, where he had been based since the late-1690s, to take Lahore and proceeded onward to Delhi and Agra, he marshaled support from the *zamindar*s and Sikhs of the Punjab; Delhi's Chishtis; disgruntled Kacchwaha and Hada Rajputs; Jats led by Churaman; and important clusters of imperial noblemen serving in Kabul, Sindh, the Punjab, and Hindustan. Even prominent supporters of A'zam such as Muhammad Yar Khan and Mukhtar Khan (the governors of Delhi and Agra, respectively) and Baqir Khan (the commandant of Agra fort) felt compelled to support Mu'azzam once within his physical proximity. In his skill at garnering support from diverse constituencies and in demanding their loyalty and respect, Mu'azzam was like previous successful Mughal princes. Few doubted that with his years of service in the Deccan between the 1660s and the 1680s and more recently in northern India, he was eminently qualified to run the empire.

However, Mu'azzam/Bahadur Shah was unlike the majority of his predecessors in three critical and, for him and the dynasty, unfortunate ways. He was already old when he mounted the throne; he failed or chose not to dispatch any of his adult princes on long-term military or administrative assignments; and he had only lukewarm support from the court-based imperial nobility.

Bahadur Shah was sixty-four years old in 1707. By contrast, Aurangzeb was forty on his accession in 1658; Shah Jahan and Jahangir were both thirty-six on theirs in 1628 and 1605, respectively; Akbar was thirteen in 1556, Humayun twenty-two in 1530, and Babur twenty-one when he captured Kabul in 1504. To his sons and other imperial onlookers, Bahadur Shah was widely perceived as a temporary, stopgap emperor with only a few years of rule left in him when he ascended the throne. As such, his four adult sons – Jahandar Shah (b. 1661), 'Azim-ush-Shan (b. 1664), Rafi'-ush-Shan (b. 1671), and Jahan Shah (b. 1674) – were reluctant to accept gubernatorial or extended military assignments outside the imperial court. As senior princes, none of them wanted to be away from the seat of imperial power when their father died. They were the first generation of post-Akbar princes to be permanently based at court while their father was on the throne. And other than 'Azim-ush-Shan's second son, Farrukh Siyar, who served as his father's deputy in Bengal, Bahadur Shah's grandsons were similarly clustered at the imperial court.

Bahadur Shah likely acquiesced to this unusual ingathering of the Mughal family at the imperial court in hopes of keeping an eye on his restive sons (whose average age in 1707 was just shy of forty) and discouraging princely rebellions in his remaining years on the throne. In hindsight, however, this arrangement came at a steep price. All the dynamics at play in the lives of prior Mughal princes were slowly shut down.

As long as they remained at the imperial court, princes could not optimize their capacity to build independent alliances and bases of power. Nor could they tap into additional revenue streams such as those derived from military campaigns or by presiding over a provincial court. Along with *jagir* income, campaigns and court fees had been central to the financial resilience of every major prince from Salim to Mu'azzam. After 1707, however, difficulties in accessing income from their *jagir*s or other sources made princes almost entirely dependent on cash handouts from the emperor.

The princes' reliance on the emperor only strengthened their commitment to remain at the imperial court. Doing so, however, meant that they could maintain only the tiniest princely households. Long gone was the mid-seventeenth-century household whose tens of thousands swore primary allegiance to a prince. No longer was the household itself self-contained and mobile, a symbol of Mughal power and authority, nor were princely establishments anymore a powerful draw for individuals and groups across the empire looking for ways to enter into the imperial system. On the eve of Bahadur Shah's death in 1712, his oldest son, Jahandar Shah, is said to have had no more than one hundred horsemen and no cash to spare.[2] The same was true for Bahadur Shah's youngest sons, Rafi'-ush-Shan and Jahan Shah. Commanding little muscle, the imperial princes had no choice but to turn to the empire's most powerful nobleman, Zulfiqar Khan, in the hope of fulfilling their ambition to become the next emperor.

Despite his ability to marshal support as he marched to secure the throne, Mu'azzam/Bahadur Shah himself enjoyed only weak backing within the imperial court. There were many reasons for this. For one, he had suffered incarceration there at Aurangzeb's hands between 1687 and 1695, after which he had been sent away to northern India. Moreover, Mu'azzam's half-sister Zinat-un-Nisa, herself a force to reckon with in the empire toward the end of Aurangzeb's reign, had favored her full brother, A'zam, to be Aurangzeb's heir. Neither of the two commanding noble factions led by Asad Khan/Zulfiqar Khan and Ghazi-ud-Din Khan/Chin Qilich Khan were warmly disposed toward Mu'azzam/Bahadur Shah either. The former – given their control over the first and third most powerful ministries – simply feared losing their power and privilege in the new dispensation. The latter, who had earlier reported Mu'azzam's collusion with Golkonda in 1687 and played a hand in his subsequent arrest and imprisonment, feared the emperor's revenge. Indeed, it might safely be said that no emperor since Humayun had come to the throne with less support among the highest rungs of the Mughal imperial establishment than Bahadur Shah in 1707. It should come as no surprise then that, like Humayun, Bahadur Shah was forced to engage in debilitating political compromises.

---

[2] William Irvine, *Later Mughals* (Delhi, repr. 1996), p. 160.

Following his success at Jaju, Bahadur Shah forgave all of his opponents and worked to reincorporate them into the imperial fold. Such gestures fit within long-standing Mughal practice, but Bahadur Shah's political frailty was on clear display during the subsequent bitter struggle over the office of the *wazir* (prime minister).

Bahadur Shah wanted to give the position of *wazir* to his long-standing confidant Mu'nim Khan. But he faced implacable opposition from Asad Khan, who had held the position since 1676, his son Zulfiqar Khan, and their powerful backers, including the princess Zinat-un-Nisa, within the imperial establishment. Each of these individuals had favored A'zam in the recently concluded conflict. Although in the end, Bahadur Shah did install Mu'nim Khan as *wazir*, his victory was pyrrhic, involving huge concessions to the father-son duo, Asad Khan and Zulfiqar Khan. For example, he was forced to permit them to oversee when and how Mu'nim Khan could deploy the *wazir*'s seal. He also had to appoint Zulfiqar Khan as first *bakhshi* (paymaster general) of the empire as well as governor of the entire Deccan.[3] These were mighty concessions, enabling Zulfiqar Khan such great opportunities to amass wealth and distribute patronage, that an astonished author of the mid-eighteenth-century *Ma'asir-ul-Umara* versified:

Oh God, Oh God! What grace and kindness is this!
His benevolence makes criminals (*mujriman*) courtiers (*muhtaram*).[4]

Bahadur Shah's capitulation bewildered contemporary and later observers, all of whom agreed that in the case of Zulfiqar Khan, the emperor had taken (or been forced to take) imperial mercy to the point of his own undoing.

Sure enough, in May 1710, Zulfiqar Khan accomplished something remarkable. He blocked Bahadur Shah's authority to induct new Mughal nobles. Henceforth, all *mansab* grants to new nobles required the countersignature of an imperial *bakhshi* (most of whom owed their office to Zulfiqar Khan's influence) alongside the emperor's signature.[5] A long-standing prerogative of emperors to personally and rapidly select and augment the ranks of their supporters now lay strangled.

But Zulfiqar Khan did not rest at this. He weakened and isolated Mu'nim Khan, who was nonetheless permitted to remain *wazir* until his death in 1711. The Khan then blocked all attempts by Bahadur Shah to fill the

---

[3] Satish Chandra, *Parties and Politics at the Mughal Court, 1707–1740* (Delhi, repr. 2002), pp. 82–4.

[4] Shah Nawaz Khan, *Maasiru-l-Umara*, vol. 2, p. 98.

[5] Muzaffar Alam, *The Crisis of Empire in Mughal North India: Awadh & the Punjab 1707–1748* (Delhi, repr. 1997), p. 29.

*wazir*'s position through the remainder of his reign. Zulfiqar Khan also undermined Chin Qilich Khan, a potential rival within the nobility, pushing him to finally resign all his commissions toward the end of 1710, albeit on the plaint that the emperor had failed to recognize his service and standing.

After Mu'nim Khan's death in 1711, the emperor's political strength vis-à-vis Zulfiqar Khan continued to deteriorate. Bahadur Shah's fortunes were especially hurt by his failure to quell a persistent rebellion in the Punjab. And certainly if, as Muzaffar Alam observes, a Mughal emperor's power derived from balancing different noble factions, cultivating people's awe for his office and person, and continuing to push territorial expansion, then Bahadur Shah's reign fell short on all counts.[6]

Against the backdrop of Zulfiqar Khan's rising power, Bahadur Shah's four sons variously sought to reach some sort of political agreement with the Khan prior to the inevitable war of succession. As Zulfiqar Khan bargained with each of them, it became clear that 'Azim-ush-Shan, being the strongest Mughal Prince of his generation and an emerging favorite of his father, was the least amenable to the noble's political ambitions.

Born in 1664 to a daughter of the Rajput ruler Rup Singh Rathor (who died fighting for Dara Shukoh at the Battle of Samugarh), 'Azim-ush-Shan's early career was closely connected with his father's. When Mu'azzam was imprisoned in 1687, 'Azim-ush-Shan was imprisoned with him. Following his father's release and departure for Hindustan in 1695, 'Azim-ush-Shan was appointed to the governorship of the financially thriving eastern provinces of Bengal (1697–8) and Bihar (1702–3). Like previous successful princely governors, 'Azim-ush-Shan took an active interest in his provinces' political, socioeconomic, and cultural life. Among other things, this meant wooing powerful *zamindar*s and religious networks, maneuvering supporters into key administrative positions, crushing Afghan and *zamindari* opponents of Mughal rule, and making an extensive effort to rebuild the city of Patna (which was renamed 'Azimabad in his honor). Most significantly, however, it entailed attempts

---

[6] Ibid., pp. 19–20, 30–1. Arguably Bahadur Shah sensed his own weakness. Might we not read this from his erratic, controversial, and much derided attempt to base his imperial authority in the claim to be the supreme *mujtahid* (interpreter of Islamic law and theology) for the Mughal Empire? Was this effort – echoing Leslie Peirce's insights with regard to the Ottoman Empire in the seventeenth century – part of an abortive attempt to anchor imperial legitimacy in a new religious unifying framework in the wake of political and military failure? Leslie Peirce, *The Imperial Harem: Women and Sovereignty in the Ottoman Empire* (New York, 1993).

to assert his control over Bengal's growing agricultural and trade income.[7] The prince's financial ambitions often collided with Aurangzeb's dependence on Bengal's revenues to sustain his Deccan campaigns.[8] Tiring of 'Azim-ush-Shan's shenanigans, Aurangzeb finally decided to shift the prince out of Bengal and Bihar in 1706. 'Azim-ush-Shan did not leave empty handed, however. As he marched out of the province, he took with him between Rs. 90 and 110 million in cash (an extraordinary $1.3–1.6 billion in 2009 dollars). Although a large percentage of this amount was intended for Aurangzeb's military expenses, the emperor's death in March 1707 allowed 'Azim-ush-Shan to use the money to both fund his father's succession struggle and enrich himself.

Following Bahadur Shah's accession, 'Azim-ush-Shan moved swiftly to reassert his control over Bengal and Bihar. Although he never visited the provinces again, the presence of his second son, Farrukh Siyar, and an alliance of convenience with the long-standing *diwan* (chief finance and revenue officer) of the province, Kartalab Khan/Murshid Quli Khan, allowed him to maintain his political authority and financial interests across the region.[9] Among the key signs of 'Azim-ush-Shan's rising political star were his ability to get imperial forgiveness for former rebels such as Jai Singh Kachhwaha of Amber and Ajit Singh Rathor of Marwar in 1708,[10] and his tightening grip over key administrative appointments across a number of imperial provinces, especially the Punjab.[11] Along with his ally Hidayatullah Khan, the prince also increasingly muscled in on the *wazir*'s responsibilities following Mu'nim Khan's death in 1711.[12] Recognizing the

---

[7] Ghulam Husain Salim, *Riyazu-s-Salatin*, ed. Abdul Hak Abid (Calcutta, 1890), pp. 243–4.

[8] Aurangzeb, *Dastur-ul-'Amal-i Agahi*, National Library of India, Sarkar Collection 70, f. 27a.

[9] The two men were at loggerheads for most of the last decade of Aurangzeb's reign. 'Azim-ush-Shan even tried to have Kartalab Khan assassinated in 1703. When the prince was moved out of the region in 1706, Kartalab Khan (now renamed Murshid Quli Khan) seemed to have won the struggle. The victory of Mu'azzam/Bahadur Shah the following year, however, led to Murshid Quli Khan's transfer to the Deccan. In 1710, putting their differences aside, 'Azim-ush-Shan engineered the Khan's return as the deputy governor and *diwan* of Bengal. 'Azim-ush-Shan had come to the realization that Murshid Quli Khan was the only man who could keep order in Bengal and ensure continued Mughal and princely access to its wealth. Upon Bahadur Shah's death, Murshid Quli Khan pledged his loyalty to 'Azim-ush-Shan but adopted a neutral position after that prince's death. See Abdul Karim, *Murshid Quli Khan and His Times* (Dacca, 1963), pp. 18–44.

[10] Mubarakullah Wazih, *Tarikh-i Iradat Khan*, ed. Ghulam Rasul Mehr (Lahore, 1971), pp. 99–100.

[11] Chandra, *Parties and Politics*, pp. 74–5; Alam, *Crisis of Empire*, p. 77.

[12] Chandra, *Parties and Politics*, p. 93.

prince's power, a visiting Dutch delegation singled him out for extra gifts in January 1712, one month before Bahadur Shah's death.[13]

In an earlier generation, if there were to be any contenders against 'Azim-ush-Shan's claim, they would have been his brothers. Testifying to the changed times as much as the growing vulnerability of the princely institution, however, it was the nobleman Zulfiqar Khan and his followers who most openly challenged the prince's political ambitions. In one striking episode toward the end of Bahadur Shah's reign, Zulfiqar Khan's protégé 'Abd-us-Samad Khan was bold enough to engage in an unprecedented public altercation with the prince in the imperial court.[14] At the same time, Zulfiqar Khan was forging an anti–'Azim-ush-Shan alliance among Bahadur Shah's other sons. By the time Bahadur Shah died at the end of February 1712 and another war of succession was upon the empire, 'Azim-ush-Shan was on the defensive.

Foolishly perhaps, 'Azim-ush-Shan decided against engaging Zulfiqar Khan and his brothers in open battle. Instead, adopting a defensive posture, he barricaded himself behind earthen walls. Within a matter of days, however, his brothers and their noble benefactor had overwhelmed him. Following 'Azim-ush-Shan's defeat and death, Zulfiqar Khan's support enabled Jahandar Shah to overcome his other brothers, Rafi'-ush-Shan and Jahan Shah, as well. In 1712, then, the most powerful nobleman in the Mughal Empire overwhelmed its most powerful prince and placed his handpicked candidate on the throne. The decades-long hemorrhaging of the princely institution and the shift of power from princes to nobles was fast approaching its denouement.

As went the princely institution, so too did the authority of the emperor and the dynasty. Although historians have typically explained the short duration of Jahandar Shah's reign in terms of his personal shortcomings – especially his love of the good things in life (drink, late night entertainments) and his willingness to indulge every whim of his wife Lal Kanwar and her family – I would argue that the seeds of his destruction predated his accession. The same was true for Farrukh Siyar, 'Azim-ush-Shan's son and the last effective ruler of the Mughal Empire.

---

[13] Irvine, *Later Mughals*, p. 152.
[14] Ibid., p. 189.

## JAHANDAR SHAH, FARRUKH SIYAR, AND THE END
## OF THE PRINCELY INSTITUTION

Jahandar Shah enjoyed little support at the imperial court and even less in the provinces of the empire. Consequently, his reign carried a heavy taint of illegitimacy. Playing defense, Jahandar Shah moved swiftly to bolster his authority. Some steps, such as rewarding household followers and other supporters by offering them exalted positions within the imperial hierarchy, were typical of newly crowned Mughal emperors. Others, however, marked a clear and important break with earlier customs.

First was his decision to allow the bodies of his brothers and a nephew to rot under the open sun for a number of days before ordering their interment. Even Aurangzeb, filled as he was with hatred for Dara Shukoh, insisted that his older brother receive a fitting burial in Humayun's tomb in Delhi after his execution. Jahandar Shah also displayed extreme vindictiveness toward his defeated brothers' supporters. A small number of high-ranking nobles were executed, and others suffered imprisonment and the confiscation of their property. To make matters worse, the new emperor pointedly refused to incorporate troops formerly connected with his brothers into the imperial army. He rejected outright the Mughal model of forgiving opponents and buying their support through generous patronage, so much so that one contemporary historian declared that the destruction of the Mughal dynasty was a consequence of Jahandar Shah's lack of compassion.[15]

Jahandar Shah's poor judgment soon resulted in groups of imperial nobles, former partisans of 'Azim-ush-Shan, and thousands of demobilized troops fleeing eastward to Bihar and Bengal, areas under Farrukh Siyar's nominal control. Rather than helping consolidate his rule after a disruptive war of succession, Jahandar Shah's actions paved the way for another wrenching conflict. Although this book has repeatedly argued that intra-Mughal conflict and strife were central and ultimately positive features in Mughal state formation, succession struggles or rebellions had to be adequately spaced to give the empire time to recuperate from their short-term destruction and upheaval. Without this recovery time, an open-ended system of succession was no longer a source of political dynamism but rather dynastic suicide.

In January 1713, after less than a year on the throne, Jahandar Shah was overthrown and executed by Farrukh Siyar. Unfortunately for the

---

[15] Wazih, *Tarikh-i Iradat Khan*, pp. 132–7.

new emperor, his grip on power proved almost as tenuous and compromised as his predecessor's.

Like Jahandar Shah, Farrukh Siyar's weakness as emperor is traceable
to his princely years. Thus, although he served as 'Azim-ush-Shan's representative in Bengal, the real power in the province did not reside with him
but rather with the deputy governor and treasurer Murshid Quli Khan.
Every substantial financial and political lever was concentrated in the
latter's hands. By all accounts, Farrukh Siyar's household was small, and
his networks of political and military support inconsequential. Two episodes from the buildup to Farrukh Siyar's bid for succession perfectly
highlight the extent to which the princely institution in the early 1710s
was a mere shadow of what it had been even toward the end of
Aurangzeb's rule.

The first opens with Farrukh Siyar approaching the most powerful
allies of his father in Bengal and Bihar for their support after receiving
news that Jahandar Shah had succeeded to the Mughal throne. Despite
having lived in the eastern provinces since the late-1690s and acting as his
father's deputy since 1707, Farrukh Siyar could find no important backers. His disappointment and desperation were so intense that he is said to
have contemplated suicide. He knew that he was in no position to mount
a political challenge against Jahandar Shah and Zulfiqar Khan. After all,
he had only four hundred household followers under his command in the
spring of 1712.[16] The tide began to turn in Farrukh Siyar's favor only
after Jahandar Shah overreached politically by trying to remove two
former partisans of 'Azim-ush-Shan, the brothers Husain 'Ali Khan and
'Abdullah Khan, from their respective positions as deputy governors
of Bihar and Allahabad. Within a month of defecting to Farrukh Siyar,
the Saiyid brothers mobilized their connections among Afghans,
Shaikhzadas, Buksariyyas, and Ujjainiyas, as well as Mughal regional
administrators, to swell the prince's army to around twenty-five thousand men.[17] Farrukh Siyar's eventual success in defeating Jahandar Shah
owed everything to the financial, political, and military backing of the
Saiyid brothers and almost nothing to his own princely resources. Salim,
Khurram, and Aurangzeb may have also looked to powerful noble allies
for assistance in their struggles to attain the Mughal throne, but they
never depended on the support of one backer, nor were they themselves
devoid of independent resources.

[16] Irvine, *Later Mughals*, p. 199.
[17] Ibid., p. 212.

A second instance highlighting Farrukh Siyar's singular weakness was his failure to impose his authority over Murshid Quli Khan, the *diwan* of Bengal. After announcing his bid for the throne in the city of 'Azimabad/Patna (Bihar), Farrukh Siyar demanded that the Khan remit the revenues of Bengal and Orissa to him. Confident in his power to resist the prince (whom he had known since Farrukh Siyar was a thirteen-year-old youth), Murshid Quli Khan refused his ostensible superior's request. Between June and November 1712, Farrukh Siyar sent three expeditions to dislodge the Khan. All failed spectacularly. Ultimately, the prince was forced to accept Murshid Quli Khan's power over Bengal, a situation that did not change with his accession to the imperial throne.

As had been the case with Jahandar Shah, Farrukh Siyar's reign opened with a disquieting spate of executions. Most shocking was Farrukh Siyar's decision to put Zulfiqar Khan to death, after initially and dishonestly granting him clemency. Others similarly paid with their lives for supporting the previous regime. As with Jahandar Shah, Farrukh Siyar's actions seem to have been driven by his sense of political weakness as well as a determination to stamp his authority on the empire. In the end, Farrukh Siyar's attempts to strengthen his position foundered in the face of the Saiyid brothers' control over the most important positions in the empire – that of the *wazir* and first *bakhshi*. Even as the empire experienced droughts, famines, general scarcity, *zamindar* revolts, collapsing imperial machinery, and a rapidly depleting imperial treasury, the Saiyid brothers thrived.

As Muzaffar Alam puts it, "In contrast to the general plight of the *mansabdars* and the crisis of the imperial treasury," some of the nobles' fortunes grew. He singles out the wealth of those in the service of Husain 'Ali Khan, the *mir bakhshi*, as an example, stating that such noblemen as a cohort had succeeded in eclipsing the power of the emperor: "The factions of the nobles like Husain Ali Khan had large followings among the state functionaries, at times even larger than the emperor could singly muster up on his own."[18] Farrukh Siyar was not indifferent to this turn of events, and, after an initial period of cooperation, he turned against the Saiyid brothers. What followed was a long and torturous political struggle that ended only when the Saiyid brothers overthrew, blinded, and executed Farrukh Siyar in the spring of 1719.

Because Farrukh Siyar had no surviving sons and there was no precedent of an emperor dying without direct heirs, the Saiyid brothers took the opportunity to raise their own candidate from among the large number of

[18] Alam, *Crisis of Empire*, p. 38.

princes contained – or we might say imprisoned – in the imperial harem. Their choice was the youngest son of Rafi'-ush-Shan (d. 1712) and a first cousin of Farrukh Siyar. He was a twenty-year-old, tuberculosis-ridden prince named Rafi'-ul-Darjat. Just over three months later, he was dead, killed by the disease. Four months after that, his successor and older brother Rafi'-ul-Daulah, another Saiyid nominee, had also died from the same disease. By this point, the Mughal system of contested successions and the institution of the Mughal Prince had been definitively exhausted. The year 1719 marked the final collapse of the Mughals as an effective ruling dynasty as well.

Ultimately, any story about the gradual demise of the Mughal princely institution and its effect on the empire is incomplete without a brief look at who filled the resulting political vacuum and how. This account may be best told through the extraordinary career of someone we have occasionally encountered in this book: Murshid Quli Khan, the founder of a semi-independent successor state in Bengal.

Likely born into a southern Indian Hindu family, Murshid Quli Khan was bought as a child by an Iranian trader/Mughal administrator who named him Muhammad Hadi and raised him as a son. Following the death of his master/patron/father, Muhammad Hadi himself drifted into Mughal service in the early 1690s. He developed a reputation for honesty combined with financial acumen, eventually coming to the attention of Aurangzeb, who granted him various assignments and ultimately promoted him to the post of *diwan* of Bengal. One of his first acts as *diwan* was to impose direct control over the revenue-collecting apparatus of the province. His next major move was to transfer a large number of *jagir* assignments out of the increasingly wealthy province and convert them into crown territories. Such consolidating moves enabled Murshid Quli Khan to "tighten his control over the countryside"[19] and also to remit Rs. 10 million to Aurangzeb in the Deccan in his first year on the job. This nobleman's actions, however, attracted the ire of the then-governor of Bengal, 'Azim-ush-Shan, who saw a direct threat to his own financial and political interests. Aurangzeb nonetheless moved to minimize princely interference in the Khan's work. Thus, in one letter the emperor warned his grandson: "[Murshid Quli] Khan is a servant (*naukar*) of the

---

[19] Muzaffar Alam and Sanjay Subrahmanyam, "Introduction," in *The Mughal State, 1526–1750*, ed. Muzaffar Alam and Sanjay Subrahmanyam (Delhi, 1998), p. 48. See also John R. McLane, *Land and Local Kingship in Eighteenth-Century Bengal* (Cambridge, 1993), pp. 34–8; Kumkum Chatterjee, *Merchants, Politics & Society in Early Modern India, Bihar: 1733–1820* (Leiden, 1996), pp. 31–6.

emperor; if any injury happens to his person or property, revenge will be taken on you, my boy."[20] Shortly thereafter, in 1703, 'Azim-ush-Shan was ordered to leave Bengal and base himself at some remove in Bihar.[21]

Over the last years of Aurangzeb's reign, Murshid Quli Khan was allowed to further entrench his power. In addition to holding the governorship of Orissa, the *diwani* of three provinces (Bengal, Bihar, and Orissa), and the position of *faujdar* (military commandant) of five major districts,[22] Murshid Quli Khan increasingly controlled the process of administrative appointments to the region. His Iranian family – the relatives of his deceased master/patron/father – was a significant and early beneficiary of his largesse.[23]

Barring one brief stint in the Deccan in the early 1710s, Murshid Quli Khan spent the remainder of his life, until his death in 1727, in Bengal. His general policy was to accommodate himself to whoever occupied the Mughal throne. He rarely had any difficulty in winning imperial favor thanks to his willingness to continue remitting substantial amounts of Bengal's revenue to the imperial court in Delhi. In return, however, he expected no imperial interference in the affairs of regions under his control.

And so, replicating the manner in which earlier generations of Mughal princes had gathered the most important political, economic, or social actors and resources under their banner, the Khan did the same. In the process, the recalcitrant were crushed and the obedient rewarded.[24] Attaching their fortunes to the Khan or to a member of his immediate family became the only route by which ambitious and upwardly mobile provincials might now attain power and prestige.[25] Nowhere is this better attested than in connections forged between Murshid Quli Khan's provincial court in Murshidabad and emerging Hindu and Jain banking networks and Bengal's *zamindar*s.

---

[20] Salim, *Riyazu-s-Salatin*, pp. 249–50.
[21] Aurangzeb, *Kalimat-i Taiyabat*, Asiatic Society of Bengal, Ivanow 382, ff. 34a-b, 69b-70a.
[22] Karim, *Murshid Quli Khan*, p. 24.
[23] Ibid., pp. 24–5.
[24] See Alam and Subrahmanyam, "Introduction," pp. 46–55.
[25] The life story of Mirza Muhammad 'Ali/'Alivardi Khan points to the extraordinary success that might flow from attaching oneself to one of the post-Mughal regional rulers. 'Alivardi Khan came from a family with deep associations to Prince A'zam's household. 'Alivardi Khan himself grew up in the prince's household, in time becoming a trusted retainer. Following A'zam's death in 1707, he drifted into the service of Shuja'-ud-Din Muhammad Khan (son-in-law of Murshid Quli Khan). By 1740, he was so empowered that he overthrew Shuja'-ud-Din's son (Murshid Quli Khan's grandson) to become the ruler of Bengal. Yusuf Ali Khan, *Tarikh-i-Bangala-i-Mahabatjangi*, ed. Abdus Subhan (Calcutta, 1969), pp. 1–6.

Distinct from Mughal princes, who always thought in imperial terms and never looked to threaten overall dynastic control, Murshid Quli Khan was distinguished by a narrow provincial focus and efforts to render imperial Mughal authority nominal. The differences in the Khan's intentions come into especially sharp focus when compared to those of an earlier and similarly long-standing governor of Bengal, the Emperor Shah Jahan's son Shuja' (d. 1660). Despite spending almost two decades in Bengal, the prince never lost his ambition to fulfill his destiny as a Mughal emperor striding across the imperial stage. The story of Murshid Quli Khan represents the rise of new regionally based and regionally focused elites and polities after 1719, and the conclusive disappearance of effective Mughal princes and an expansive Mughal dynasty.

The Mughal emperors of the seventeenth century ascended the throne backed by mighty households, expansive networks of supporters, and multifold experiences across the empire as administrators and generals. The sons and grandsons of Aurangzeb, however, gradually surrendered these strengths. In their imperial lives and careers, we see the consequences of the death of the Mughal princely institution.

How does this account of the princes of the Mughal Empire fill out and deepen our knowledge of the Mughal state; its eventual decline; and, more broadly, the political workings of Indian society during this period?

Discussions of the Mughal state are well illuminated by the work of sociologist Karen Barkey, who studies the contemporary Ottoman state. Barkey has persuasively argued that the Ottoman Empire was different from its Western European counterparts. Drawing on the writings of Charles Tilly, Michael Mann, Perry Anderson, and others,[26] she states that the Western European states' power "developed throughout the seventeenth and eighteenth centuries at the expense of established local forces and institutions, provoking various movements of opposition."[27] Although acknowledging variation among different states in Western Europe, Barkey highlights how international war making, state-led

---

[26] See Charles Tilly, "War Making and State Making as Organized Crime," in *Bringing the State Back In*, ed. Peter Evans et al. (Cambridge, 1985); Charles Tilly, *Coercion, Capital, and European States, AD 990–1990* (Oxford, 1990); Michael Mann, *The Sources of Social Power, Vol. 1: A History of Power from the Beginning to A.D. 1760* (Cambridge, 1986); Perry Anderson, *Lineages of the Absolutist State* (London, 1979); Theda Skocpol, *States and Social Revolutions: A Comparative Analysis of France, Russia, and China* (Cambridge, 1979).

[27] Karen Barkey, *Bandits and Bureaucrats: The Ottoman Route to State Centralization* (Ithaca, 1994), p. 1.

expansion, and consolidation of territory had cascading results in the Western European context: to build armies, state makers needed to extract more resources from their subjects; exactions and a gradual diminution of local autonomy, however, led to revolts and rebellions against the state; in response, certain Western European states resorted to ever more intense and creative forms of coercion and control; in time, the state, juggernaut-like, crushed all opposition to itself and came to establish a virtual monopoly over violence, thus giving rise to the modern state. Yet Barkey asks: "Does this experience provide an exhaustive theory of a uniform global process?"[28] In other words, is this story of the rise of the centralizing modern state in Western Europe also the story of the state in other parts of the world during the seventeenth century or in the early modern period more generally? Barkey says no.

Drawing on the Ottoman example, Barkey offers an alternative model of early-modern state formation. Although not entirely discounting the use of military force as an instrument in the growth of Ottoman state power in the seventeenth century, she argues that here a far more significant process was the state's willingness to engage in "'public' cooptation, incorporation, and bargaining" as a way to "buy off or channel newly emerging opposition."[29] Military force was not the first but rather only the final resort. Thus, she suggests, against the Western European example in which "challengers were broken," in the Ottoman case "challengers were first 'house-broken.'"[30]

Historians working on Ming and Qing China or Tokugawa Japan have variously marshaled similar kinds of arguments pointing to a preference for negotiated versus military outcomes as part of state or dynastic expansion and consolidation.[31] For the Indian and Islamic contexts, André Wink offers a forceful articulation of the same idea: "Unlike state expansion in modern Europe," state formation or annexation was "not primarily determined by the use of military power." Rather, Wink notes, it included "conciliation, gift-giving, sowing dissension among and 'winning over'

---

[28] Ibid.
[29] Ibid., pp. 2, 8.
[30] Ibid., p. 2.
[31] David Robinson, *Bandits, Eunuchs and the Son of Heaven: Rebellion and the Economy of Violence in Mid-Ming China* (Honolulu, 2001); Peter Perdue, *China Marches West* (Cambridge, MA, 2005); Jane Kate Leonard and Robert Anthony, *Dragons, Tigers, and Dogs: Qing Crisis Management and the Boundaries of State Power* (Ithaca, 2002); Eiko Ikegami, *Bonds of Civility: Aesthetic Networks and the Political Origins of Japanese Culture* (Cambridge, 2005); Mark Ravina, *Land and Lordship in Early Modern Japan* (Palo Alto, 1999).

of an enemy's local supporters, and involving the use of force only secondarily . . .. In India, as in all Islamic states, sovereignty was primarily a matter of allegiances."[32]

As the reader of this book will recognize, the Mughal story supports the views of Karen Barkey and these historians of different parts of Asia. As they argue, so also this book demonstrates that the Mughal Empire worked primarily on the basis of alliance building and negotiation to co-opt local power brokers and other groups. Like its Islamic or East Asian contemporaries, it tended to resort to military solutions only after all avenues for negotiation, patronage, and co-optation had been exhausted.

What this book has contributed in particular to the scholarship on Mughal state formation is its account of the very special place of the Mughal Prince in facilitating the drawing in of individuals or groups to the state. They accomplished this in their different capacities as provincial governors, military commanders, imperial representatives, rebels, and warring claimants for the throne. This book has argued that as long as Mughal princes were the ones doing the negotiating, cajoling, and enticing, more and more groups were drawn into acknowledging Mughal legitimacy and authority. Starting in the late seventeenth century, however, as the primacy of the emperor's heirs was increasingly called into question and their prior role as pivots between India's diverse populations and the dynasty devolved to (or was forcibly filled by) other actors – notably powerful Mughal nobles or rising groups such as the Marathas, Jats or Sikhs – the Mughal dynasty lost a crucial pillar in its edifice of effective rule. It was now only a matter of time before these new groups, and not imperial princes, came to be seen as the key interface with a world of power, wealth, and other privileges.

The Mughals were ultimately rendered little more than gatekeepers to the symbolic resources of a once-flourishing imperial authority. They no longer had armies to command or tax revenues to enrich their coffers, nor were their edicts heeded. No doubt emperors could still entice the region's most famous writers and poets to their court; they also continued to hand out titles and credentials to entities such as the English East India Company; yet theirs was a weakening hand and the long twilight of the Mughal dynasty proved irreversible.

---

[32] André Wink, *Land and Sovereignty: Agrarian Society and Politics under the Eighteenth-Century Maratha Svarajya* (Cambridge, 1986), pp. 26–7.

# Bibliography

## Primary Sources

'Abd al-Baqi Nihawandi, *Ma'asir-i Rahimi*, Asiatic Society of Bengal, Ivanow 140.

*Ma'asir-i-Rahimi*, ed. M. Hidayet Hosain, vols. 1–3 (Calcutta, 1931).

'Abd al-Hamid Lahawri, *Padshahnamah*, ed. Kabir-ud-Din and Abdul Rahim, vol. 1 (Calcutta, 1867).

*Padshahnamah*, ed. Abdul Rahim, vol. 2 (Calcutta, 1872).

'Abd al-Qadir Badauni, *Muntakhab al-Tawarikh*, ed. W. N. Lees and Ahmad Ali, vol. 2 (Calcutta, 1865).

*Muntakhab al-Tawarikh*, ed. Ahmad Ali, vol. 1 (Calcutta, 1868).

*Muntakhab al-Tawarikh*, ed. Ahmad Ali, vol. 3 (Calcutta, 1869).

*Muntakhab-ut-Tawarikh*, trans. George Ranking, W. H. Lowe, and Sir Wolseley Haig, vols. 1–3 (Karachi, repr. 1976).

Ahmad Yadgar, *Tarikh-i Shahi*, trans. Saiyid Nazir Niyazi (Lahore, 1985).

Ali Muhammad Khan, *Mirat-i-Ahmadi*, ed. Syed Nawab Ali, vols. 1–2 (Baroda, 1927–1928).

*Mirat-i-Ahmadi*, trans. M. F. Lokhandwala, vols. 1–2 (Baroda, 1965).

'Alvi, *Iftitah-i Sultani*, National Library of India, Buhar Collection 394.

Anon., *Akhbarat-i Darbar-i Mu'alla*, National Library of India, Sarkar Collection 14–41.

*Akhlaq-i Padshahan*, Asiatic Society of Bengal, Ivanow 1391.

'Ara'iz-o-Faramin*, National Library of India, Sarkar Collection 46.

*A Descriptive List of Farmans, Manshurs and Nishans: Addressed by the Imperial Mughals to the Princes of Rajasthan*, ed. N. R. Khadgawat (Bikaner, 1962).

*A Calendar of Documents on Indo-Persian Relations*, vols. 1–2 (Karachi, 1979).

*The English Factories in India, 1618–1669*, ed. W. Foster, vols. 1–9 (Oxford, 1906–1927).

*Faramin-i Salatin*, ed. Bashiruddin Ahmad (Delhi, 1926).

*Imperial Farmans (AD 1577 to AD 1805). Granted to the Ancestors of His Holiness the Tikayal Maharaj*, ed. K. M. Jhaveri (Bombay, 1928).

"Intikhab-i Jahangir Shahi," in *The History of India as Told by its Own Historians*, trans. H. Elliot and J. Dowson, vol. 6 (Delhi, repr. 1990).

*Lata'if-ul-Akhbar*, Center of Advanced Study Library (Aligarh Muslim University), Persian Ms. 15.

*Mirzanama*, Asiatic Society of Bengal, Ivanow 926.

*Mughal Archives: A Descriptive Catalogue of the Documents Pertaining to the Reign of Shah Jahan*, vol. 1, ed. Mohd. Ziauddin Ahmed (Hyderabad, 1977).

*Mughal Documents (A.D. 1526–1627)*, ed. S. A. I. Tirmizi, vol. I (Delhi, 1989).

*Mughal Documents (A.D. 1628–1659)*, ed. S. A. I. Tirmizi, vol. II (Delhi, 1995).

*Mughal Farmans*, ed. K. P. Srivastava (Lucknow, 1974).

*Selected Documents of Shahjahan's Reign*, ed. Yusuf Husain Khan (Hyderabad, 1950).

*Some Farmans, Sanads and Parwanas*, ed. K. K. Datta (Patna, 1962).

'Aqil Khan Razi, *Waqiat-i 'Alamgiri*, ed. Maulvi Zafar Hasan, (Delhi, 1930).

'Arif Qandahari, *Tarikh-i-Akbari*, ed. Imtiaz Ali Arshi (Rampur, 1962).

Asad Beg Qazwini, *Waqa'i' Asad Beg*, Center for Advanced Study Library (Aligarh Muslim University), Rotograph 94.

Aurangzeb, *Anecdotes of Aurangzib*, trans. Jadunath Sarkar (Calcutta, repr. 1988).

*Adab-i 'Alamgiri*, ed. Abdul Ghafur Chaudhuri, vols. 1–2 (Lahore, 1971).

*Dastur-ul-'Amal-i Agahi*, National Library of India, Sarkar Collection 70.

*Kalimat-i Taiyabat*, Asiatic Society of Bengal, Ivanow 382.

*Kalimat-i Taiyabat*, National Library of India, Sarkar Collection 111.

*Kalimat-i Taiyibat (Collection of Aurangzeb's Orders)*, ed. S. M. Azizuddin Husain (Delhi, 1982).

*Muqaddama-i Ruq'at-i 'Alamgiri*, ed. Saiyid Najib Ashraf Nadvi, vol. 1 (Azamgarh, 1930).

*Ruq'at-i Alamgiri*, ed. Saiyid Muhammad Abdul Majeed (Kanpur, 1916).

*Raqa'im-i Kara'im*, Asiatic Society of Bengal, Ivanow 383.

*Raqaim-i-Karaim (Epistles of Aurangzeb)*, ed. S. M. Azizuddin Husain (Delhi, 1990).

Bakhtawar Khan, *Mir'at al-'Alam*, ed. Sajida Alvi, vols. 1–2 (Lahore, 1979).

Banarasidas, *Ardhakathanaka*, trans. Mukund Lath (Jaipur, 1981).

Bayazid Bayat, *Tadhkira-i-Humayun wa Akbar*, ed. M. Hidayat Hosain (Calcutta, 1941).

"Tarikh-i Humayun," in *Three Memoirs of Humayun*, ed. and trans. W. M. Thackston (Costa Mesa, 2009).

Bhimsen Saxsena, *Nuskha-i Dilkasha*, British Museum, Or. 23.

*Tarikh-i-Dilkasha, trans.* Jadunath Sarkar (Bombay, 1972).

Bindraban Das Khushgu, *Safina-i-Khushgu*, ed. S. S. M. Ataur Rahman (Patna, 1959).

Bindraban Das Ra'i, *Lubb-ut-Tawarikh*, Asiatic Society of Bengal, Ivanow 161.

Burhan ibn Hasan, *Tuzuk-e-Walajahi*, ed. T. Chandrasekharan (Madras, 1957).

Chandar Bhan Brahman, *Char Chaman*, British Library, Add. 16863.

*Chahar Chaman*, trans. Muhammad Murtaza Qadiri (Hyderabad, 1992).

Dara Shukoh, *Majma' al-Bahrayn*, British Library, Ashburner Coll. 127.
*Majma'-ul-Bahrain*, ed. and trans. M. Mahfuz-ul-Haq (Calcutta, 1929).
*Risala-i Haqnuma*, National Library of India, Zakariya Collection 177.
*Safinat al-Auliya'*, British Library, Ethe 647.
*Sakinat-ul-Auliya'*, ed. Tara Chand and Reza Jalali Naini (Tehran, 1965).
*Sirr-i Akbar*, British Library, Ethe 1980.
*Sirr-i Akbar*, ed. Tara Chand and Sayyid Muhammad Reza Jalali Naini (Tehran, repr. 1989).
Francisco Pelsaert, *A Dutch Chronicle of Mughal India*, trans. B. Narain and S. R. Sharma (Lahore, repr. 1978).
François Bernier, *Travels in the Mogul Empire, AD 1656–1668*, trans. A. Constable (Delhi, repr. 1997).
Ghulam Ali Azad Bilgrami, *Ma'asir-ul-Kiram*, ed. Abdullah Khan, vol. 2 (Hyderabad, 1913).
Ghulam Hasan Siddiqui, *Sharaif-i 'Usmani*, Asiatic Society of Bengal, Ivanow 277.
Ghulam Husain Salim, *Riyazu-s-Salatin*, ed. Abdul Hak Abid (Calcutta, 1890).
Gulbadan Begum, *Ahwal-i Humayun Badshah*, British Library, Ms. Or. 166.
*The History of Humayun: Humayun-Nama*, trans. Annette S. Beveridge (New Delhi, 1983).
"Humayunnama," in *Three Memoirs of Humayun*, ed. and trans. W. M. Thackston (Costa Mesa, 2009).
Hasan 'Ali ibn Ashraf al-Munshi, *Akhlaq-i Hakimi*, British Library, Ethe 2203.
Hatim Khan, *Alamgirnama, British Museum*, Add. Or. 26233.
'Inayat Khan, *'Inayatnama*, British Library, Ethe 411.
*Shahjahannama*, trans. A. R. Fuller (Delhi, 1990).
Ishwar Das Nagar, *Futuhat-i-Alamgiri*, ed. and trans. Raghubir Singh and Qazi Karamatullah (Vadodara, 1995).
Jahan Ara Begum, "Mu'nis-ul-Arwah," in *Princess Jahan Ara Begum, Her Life and Works*, Qamar Jahan Begum (Karachi, 1992).
"Risala-i Sahibiya," ed. Muhammad Aslam, *Journal of the Research Society of Pakistan* 16, no. 4 (1979): 77–110.
Jalaluddin Tabatabai, "Shash Fath-i Kangra," in *The History of India as Told by its own Historians*, trans. by H. Elliot and J. Dowson, vol. 6 (Delhi, repr. 1990).
Jauhar Aftabchi, *Tazkirat-ul-Waqi'at*, trans. S. Moinul Haq (Karachi, 1956), p. 105.
"Tadhkiratu'l-waqiat," in *Three Memoirs of Humayun*, ed. and trans. W. M. Thackston (Costa Mesa, 2009).
Kaksar Sabzwari, *Sawanih*, Asiatic Society of Bengal, Ivanow 285.
Kamgar Husaini, *Ma'asir-i-Jahangiri*, ed. Azra Alavi (Bombay, 1978).
Kamraj, *A'zam al-Harb, British Museum*, Ms. Or. 1899.
Kamwar Khan, *Tazkirat us-Salatin Chaghta*, ed. Muzaffar Alam (Aligarh, 1980).
Khafi Khan, *Muntakhab al-Labab*, ed. Kabir-ud-Din Ahmad and Ghulam Qadir, vol. 1 (Calcutta, 1869).
*Muntakhab al-Labab*, ed. Kabir-ud-Din Ahmad, vol. 2 (Calcutta, 1874).
*Khafi Khan's History of 'Alamgir*, trans. S. Moinul Haq (Karachi, 1975).
Khwaja Nizamuddin Ahmad, *The Tabaqat-i-Akbari*, trans. Brajendranath De, vols. 1–3 (Calcutta, repr. 1996).

Khwandamir, *Qanun-i-Humayuni*, ed. M. Hidayat Hosain (Calcutta, 1940).
    *Qanun-i-Humayuni* (also known as Humayun nama), trans. Baini Prashad (Calcutta, 1940).
Mirza Haydar Dughlat, *Tarikh-i-Rashidi*, ed. W. M. Thackston, vol. 1 (Cambridge, MA, 1996).
Mirza Nathan, *Baharistan-i-Ghaybi*, trans. M. I. Borah, vols. 1–2 (Gauhati, 1936).
Monserrate, Fr., *The Commentary of Father Monserrate, S.J., On His Journey to the Court of Akbar*, trans. J. S. Hoyland (Oxford, 1922).
Mubarakullah Wazih, *Tarikh-i Iradat Khan*, ed. Ghulam Rasul Mehr (Lahore, 1971).
Muhammad Baqir, *Advice on the Art of Governance, Mau'izah-i Jahangiri of Muhammad Baqir Najm-i Sani*, trans. Sajida Alvi (Albany, 1989).
Muhammad Kazim, *Alamgirnamah*, ed. Khadim Husain and Abdul Hai, vols. 1–2 (Calcutta, 1868).
Muhammad Masum, *Tarikh-i Shah Shuja'i*, Maulana Azad Library (Aligarh Muslim University), University Farsia Akhbar Collection, 69/2.
Muhammad Qasim Lahori, *'Ibratnama*, ed. Zahur-ud-Din Ahmad (Lahore, 1977).
Muhammad Sadiq Hamadani, *Tabaqat-i Shah Jahani*, Maulana Azad Library (Aligarh Muslim University), Habibgang Collection, 22/46.
Muhammad Sadiq Isfahani, *Shahid-i Sadiq*, Asiatic Society of Bengal, Ivanow 1365.
Mulla Kami Shirazi, *Fathnama-i Nur Jahan Begum*, Center of Advanced Study Library (Aligarh Muslim University), Rotograph 10.
Mu'in al-Din bin Siraj al-Din Khawand Mahmud, *Ganj-i Sa'adat*, Asiatic Society of Bengal, Ivanow Coll. 1275.
Musta'idd Khan, *Maasir i Alamgiri*, ed. Agha Ahmad Ali (Calcutta, 1871).
    *Maasir-i-'Alamgiri*, trans. Jadunath Sarkar (Calcutta, repr. 1990).
Mu'tamid Khan, *Ahwal-i Shahzadegi*, National Library of India, Buhar Collection 74.
    *Iqbalnamah-i Jahangiri*, ed. Abdul Hai and Ahmad Ali (Calcutta, 1865).
Niccolao Manucci, *Mogul India or Storio do Mogor*, trans. William Irvine, vols. 1–4 (New Delhi, repr. 1996).
Ni'mat Khan, *Badshahnama*, British Museum, Or. 24.
    *Waqa'i' Nimat Khan-i 'Ali* (Lucknow, 1873).
    *Jangnama*, ed. Khwaja Muhammad Isa (Kanpur, 1884).
Ni'matullah Khan Harvi, *Tarikh-i Khan Jahani wa Makhzan-i Afghani*, Asiatic Society of Bengal, Ivanow 100.
    *Tarikh-i-Khan Jahani wa Makhzan-i-Afghani*, ed. S. M. Imam-ud-Din, vols. 1–2 (Dhaka, 1960–1962).
    *Tarikh-i Khan Jahani wa Makhzan-i Afghani*, trans. Muhammad Bashir Husain (Lahore, 1986).
Nur-ud-Din Muhammad Jahangir, *Autobiographical Memoirs of the Emperor Jahangueir*, trans. D. Price (Calcutta, repr. 1972).
    *The Jahangirnama: Memoirs of Jahangir, Emperor of India*, trans. W. M. Thackston (New York, 1999).
    *Jahangirnama*, ed. Muhammad Hashim (Tehran, 1980).
Sa'dullah Khan, *Maktubat-i Sa'dullah Khan*, ed. N. H. Zaidi (Lahore, 1968).
Sadiq Khan, *Tarikh-i Shah Jahan wa Aurangzeb*, British Museum, Or. 1899.
Salih Kambo Lahori, *'Amal-i Salih*, ed. Ghulam Yazdani, vols. 1–2 (Lahore, 1967).

Shah Nawaz Khan, *Maasir-ul-Umara*, ed. Abdur Rahim, vol. 1 (Calcutta, 1888).
*Maasiru-l-Umara*, ed. Abdur Rahim and Ashraf Ali, vol. 2 (Calcutta, 1890).
*Maasir-l-Umara*, ed. Ashraf Ali, vol. 3 (Calcutta, 1891).
The *Maathir-ul-Umara*, trans. H. Beveridge and Baini Prashad, vols. 1–2 (New Delhi, repr. 1979).
Shaikh Abu'l Fazl, *Akbarnamah*, ed. Abdul Rahim, vols. 1–3 (Calcutta, 1878–1886).
The *Akbarnama of Abu-l-Fazl*, trans. H. Beveridge, vols. 1–3 (New Delhi, 1998).
*Ain-i-Akbari*, ed. H. Blochmann, vols. 1–2 (Calcutta, 1872–1877).
The *A'in-i Akbari*, trans. H. Blochmann, D. C. Phllott, and Jadunath Sarkar (New Delhi, 1978).
Shaikh Farid Bhakkari, *Dhakhirat al-Khawanin*, ed. S. Moinul Haq, vols. 1–3 (Karachi, 1961–1974).
Shihab al-Din Talish, *Fathiya-i 'Ibriya*, National Library of India, Sarkar Collection 77.
Sujan Ra'i Bhandari, *Khulasat-ul-Tawarikh*, ed. Maulvi Zafar Hasan (Delhi, 1918).
Thomas Roe, *The Embassy of Sir Thomas Roe to India, 1615–1619*, ed. W. Foster (Delhi, repr. 1990).
Yusuf Ali Khan, *Tarikh-i Bangala-i-Mahabatjangi*, ed. Abdus Subhan (Calcutta, 1969).
Zahir-ud-Din Muhammad Babur, *The Baburnama: Memoirs of Babur, Prince and Emperor*, trans. W. M. Thackston (New York, 2002).
Zain Khan, *Tabaqat-i-Baburi*, trans. S. H. Askari (Delhi, 1982).
Zulfiqar Ardistani, *The Religion of the Sufis: From the Dabistan of Mohsin Fani*, trans. David Shea and Anthony Troyer (London, repr. 1979).

## Secondary Sources

Abdul Ghani, *Persian Language and Literature at the Mughal Court*, vol. 3 (Westmead, repr. 1972).
Abdul Karim, *Murshid Quli Khan and His Times* (Dacca, 1963).
Abul Hasnat Nadvi, *Hindustan Ki Qadim Islami Darsgahain* (Azamgarh, 1936).
Afzal Husain, *The Nobility under Akbar and Jahangir: A Study of Family Groups* (New Delhi, 1999).
Agha Mehdi, *Tarikh-i Lucknow* (Lucknow, 1976).
Ahmad Raza Khan, "Suba of Bihar under the Mughals, 1582–1707," unpub. Ph.D. dissertation, Aligarh Muslim University (1982).
Alexander Dow, *History of Hindostan*, vol. 3 (Delhi, repr. 1973).
Ali Anooshahr, "The King who would be Man: The Gender Roles of the Warrior King in Early Mughal History," *Journal of the Royal Asiatic Society* 18, no. 3 (2008): 327–40.
Allison Busch, "Hidden in Plain View: Brajbhasha Poets at the Mughal Court," *Modern Asian Studies* 44, no. 2 (2010): 267–309.
Andre Gunder Frank, *ReOrient: Global Economy in the Asian Age* (Berkeley, 1998).

André Wink, *Akbar* (Oxford, 2009).
"India: Muslim Period and Mughal Empire," *Oxford Encyclopedia of Economic History*, ed. Joel Mokyr (Oxford, 2003).
*Al-Hind: The Making of the Indo-Islamic World*, vol. 1 (Delhi, 1990).
"A Rejoinder to Irfan Habib," *Indian Economic and Social History Review* 26, no. 3 (1989), 363–7.
*Land and Sovereignty in India: Agrarian Society and Politics under the Eighteenth Century Maratha Svarajya* (Cambridge, 1986).
Andrea Hintze, *The Mughal Empire and Its Decline: An Interpretation of the Sources of Social Power* (Aldershot, UK, 1997).
Andrew Newman, *Safavid Iran: Rebirth of a Persian Empire* (London, 2006).
Annemarie Schimmel, "Khankhanan Abdur Rahim and the Sufis," in *Intellectual Studies in Islam*, ed. Michel Mazzaoui and Vera Moreen (Salt Lake City, 1991).
Arshad Karim, "Muslim Nationalism: Conflicting Ideologies of Dara Shikoh and Aurangzeb," *Journal of the Pakistan Historical Society* 33, no. 4 (1985): 288–96.
Ashin Das Gupta, *Indian Merchants and the Decline of Surat, c. 1700–1750* (Wiesbaden, 1979).
Asok Das, *Mughal Painting during Jahangir's Time* (Calcutta, 1978).
B. B. L. Srivastava, "The Fate of Khusrau," *Journal of Indian History* 42, no. 2 (1964): 479–92.
B. J. Hasrat, *Dara Shikuh: Life and Works* (Delhi, repr. 1982).
B. N. Reu, "Letters Exchanged between Emperor Aurangzeb and His Son Prince Muhammad Akbar," *Procs. Ind. Hist. Cong.* 2 (1938): 356–60.
B. P. Ambashthya, "Rebellions of Prince Salim and Prince Khurram in Bihar," *Journal of the Bihar and Orissa Research Society* 45 (1959): 326–41.
B. P. Saxsena, *History of Shahjahan of Dihli* (Delhi, repr. 1962).
Beatrice Manz, "Tamerlane's Career and Its Uses," *Journal of World History* 13, no. 1 (2002): 1–25.
*The Rise and Rule of Tamerlane* (Cambridge, 1989).
Beni Prasad, *History of Jahangir* (Oxford, 1922).
Bonnie Wade, *Imaging Sound: An Ethnomusicological Study of Music, Art, and Culture in Mughal India* (Chicago, 1998).
Brij Bhukan Lal, *Tarikh-i Daryabad* (Daryabad, 1924).
Bruce B. Lawrence, "Veiled Opposition to Sufis in Muslim South Asia." In *Islamic Mysticism Contested*, ed. Frederick de Jong and Bernd Radtke (Leiden, 1999).
"Biography and the 17th Century Qadiriya of North India," in *Islam and Indian Regions*, ed. A. L. Dallapiccola and S. Zingel-Ave Lallemant (Stuttgart, 1993).
C. A. Bayly, *Empire and Information: Intelligence Gathering and Social Communication in India, 1780–1870* (Cambridge, 1996).
*The Imperial Meridian: The British Empire and the World* (Cambridge, 1989).
C. R. Naik, '*Abdur-Rahim Khan-i-Khanan and His Literary Circle* (Ahmedabad, 1966).
Carl Ernst, "Muslim Studies of Hinduism? A Reconsideration of Arabic and Persian Translations from Indian Languages," *Iranian Studies* 36, no. 2 (2003): 173–95.

Catherine Asher, "A Ray from the Sun: Mughal Ideology and the Visual Construction of the Divine," in *The Presence of Light: Divine Radiance and Religious Experience*, ed. Matthew Kapstein (Chicago, 2004).

 *The Architecture of Mughal India* (Cambridge, 1992).

Catherine Asher, and Cynthia Talbot, *India before Europe* (Cambridge, 2006).

Charles Stewart, *History of Bengal* (Delhi, repr. 1971).

Charles Tilly, *Coercion, Capital, and European States, AD 990–1990* (Oxford, 1990).

 "War Making and State Making as Organized Crime," in *Bringing the State Back In*, ed. Peter Evans et al. (Cambridge, 1985).

Chetan Singh, *Region and Empire, Panjab in the Seventeenth Century* (Delhi, 1991).

Cl. Huart and Louis Massignon, "Dara Shikoh's Interview with Baba La'l Das at Lahore," in *On Becoming an Indian Muslim*, ed. and trans. M. Waseem (Delhi, repr. 2003).

Claude Levi Strauss, *Elementary Structures of Kinship*, trans. James Bell, John von Sturmer, and Rodney Needham (Boston, 1969).

Claude Markovits, *The Global World of Indian Merchants 1750–1947* (Cambridge, 2000).

Colin Imber, *The Ottoman Empire, 1300–1650* (New York, 2002).

Corinne Lefèvre, "Recovering a Missing Voice from Mughal India: The Imperial Discourse of Jahangir (r. 1605–1627)," *Journal of the Economic and Social History of the Orient* 50, no. 4 (2007): 452–89.

David Robinson, *Bandits, Eunuchs and the Son of Heaven: Rebellion and the Economy of Violence in Mid-Ming China* (Honolulu, 2001).

Douglas Streusand, *Formation of the Mughal Empire* (Delhi, 1989).

E. D. Maclagan, "Jesuit Missions to the Emperor Akbar," *Journal of the Asiatic Society of Bengal* 65 (1896): 38–112.

E. P. Thompson, "The Moral Economy of the English Crowd in the Eighteenth Century," *Past and Present* 50, no. 1 (1971): 76–136.

Eiko Ikegami, *Bonds of Civility: Aesthetic Networks and the Political Origins of Japanese Culture* (Cambridge, 2005).

Ellison B. Findly, *Nur Jahan: Empress of Mughal India* (Oxford, 1993).

 "Jahangir's Vow of Non-Violence," *Journal of the American Oriental Society*, 107, no. 2 (1987): 245–56.

Eva Orthmann, "Sonne, Mond und Sterne: Kosmologie und Astrologie in der Inszenierung von Herrschaft unter Humayun," in *Die Grenzen der Welt, Arabica et Iranica ad honorem Heinz Gaube*, ed. L. Korn, E. Orthmann, and F. Schwarz (Wiesbaden, 2008).

 "'Abd or-Rahim Khan-e Khanan: Staatsmann und Mäzen," unpub. M.A. thesis, University of Tubingen (1995).

F. Steingass, *Comprehensive Persian-English Dictionary* (New Delhi, repr. 1981).

F. W. Buckler, *Legitimacy and Symbols: The South Asian writings of F. W. Buckler* (Ann Arbor, 1985).

Farhat Hasan, *State and Locality in Mughal India: Power Relations in Western India, c. 1572–1730* (Cambridge, 2004).

"*Mughal Records on the English East India Company: A Calendar to 1740,*" unpub. M.A. thesis, Aligarh Muslim University (1987).

G. T. Kulkarni, *The Mughal-Maratha Relations: Twenty Five Fateful Years (1682–1707)* (Pune, 1983).

Ghulam Sarwar, *Khazinat al-Asfiya*, vol. 1 (Lucknow, 1894).

Gijs Kruijtzer, *Xenophobia in Seventeenth-Century India* (Leiden, 2009).

Halil Inalcik, *The Ottoman Empire: The Classical Age 1300–1600* (New York, 1973).

Hamid Algar, "The Naqshbandi Order: A Preliminary Survey of Its History and Significance," *Studia Islamica* 44 (1976): 123–52.

Harbans Mukhia, *The Mughals of India* (London, 2004).

Henry Beveridge, "Sultan Khusrau," *Journal of the Royal Asiatic Society* 39 (1907): 599–601.

Hermann Kulke, *The State in India: 1000–1700* (Delhi, 1995).

Hidayat Husain, "The Mirza Nama (The Book of the Perfect Gentleman) of Mirza Kamran," *Journal of the Asiatic Society of Bengal* 9, no. 1 (1913): 1–13.

Ibn Hasan, *The Central Structure of the Mughal Empire* (New Delhi, repr. 1980).

Iftikhar Ghauri, *War of Succession between the Sons of Shah Jahan, 1657–1658* (Lahore, 1964).

Ijaz-ul-Haq Quddusi, *Tazkira-i Sufiya-i Bangal* (Lahore, 1965).

*Tazkira-i Sufiya-i Sind* (Karachi, 1959).

Iqtidar Alam Khan, *Gunpowder and Firearms: Warfare in Medieval India* (Delhi, 2004).

"State in Mughal India: Re-examining the Myths of a Counter-vision," *Social Scientist* 30, no. 1–2 (2001): 16–45.

"Akbar's Personality Traits and World Outlook – A Critical Appraisal," in *Akbar and His India*, ed. Irfan Habib (Delhi, 1997).

"The Turco-Mongol Theory of Kingship," in *Medieval India – A Miscellany*, vol. 2 (Bombay, 1972).

"The Nobility under Akbar and the Development of His Religious Policy, 1560–1580," *Journal of the Royal Asiatic Society* 1–2 (1968): 29–36.

*Mirza Kamran* (Bombay, 1964).

Irfan Habib, "Timur in the Political Tradition and Historiography of Mughal India," in *L'Heritage timouride Iran-Asie centrale-Inde XVe-XVIIIe siecles*, ed. Maria Szuppe (Aix-en-Provence, 1997).

"A Reply to André Wink," *Indian Economic and Social History Review* 26, no. 3 (1989): 368–72.

"Review of *Land and Sovereignty in India: Agrarian Society and Politics under the Eighteenth Century Maratha Svarajya*," *Indian Economic and Social History Review* 25, no. 4 (1988): 527–31.

*Atlas of the Mughal Empire* (New Delhi, 1982).

"The family of Nur Jahan during Jahangir's Reign: A Political Study," in *Medieval India: A Miscellany*, vol. 1 (Bombay, 1969).

"Mansab System, 1595–1637," *Proceedings of the Indian History Congress* 29 (1967): 221–42.

*The Agrarian System of Mughal India* (Bombay, repr. 1999).

Ishwari Prasad, *The Life and Times of Humayun* (Calcutta, 1956).

J. M. Rogers, *Mughal Miniatures* (London, 1993).

Jack Goody, *Succession to High Office* (Cambridge, 1966).

Jadunath Sarkar, *Studies in Aurangzib's Reign* (Calcutta, repr. 1989).

    *The History of Bengal*, vol. 2 (Calcutta, 1948).

    *History of Aurangzib*, vols. 1–5 (Calcutta, 1924–1930).

Jalaluddin, "Sultan Salim (Jahangir) as a Rebel King," *Islamic Culture* 47 (1973): 121–5.

James Scott, *Domination and the Arts of Resistance: Hidden Transcripts* (New Haven, 1990).

Jane Bestor, "Bastardy and Legitimacy in the Formation of a Regional State in Italy: The Estense Succession," *Comparative Studies in Society and History* 38 (1996): 549–85.

Jane Hathaway, *The Politics of Households in Ottoman Egypt: The Rise of the Qazdaglis* (Cambridge, 1997).

Jane K. Leonard and Robert Anthony, *Dragons, Tigers, and Dogs: Qing Crisis Management and the Boundaries of State Power* (Ithaca, 2002).

John F. Richards, "The Mughal Empire," in *The Magnificent Mughals*, ed. Zeenut Ziad (Karachi, 2002).

    "Early Modern India and World History," *Journal of World History* 8, no. 2 (1997): 197–209.

    *The Mughal Empire* (Cambridge, 1993).

    "The Seventeenth Century Crisis in South Asia," *Modern Asian Studies* 24, no. 4 (1990): 625–39.

    "Norms of Comportment among Imperial Mughal Officers," in *Moral Conduct and Authority: The Place of Adab in South Asian Islam*, ed. Barbara D. Metcalf (Berkeley, 1984).

    "Mughal State Finance and the Premodern World Economy," *Comparative Studies in Society and History* 23 (1981): 285–308.

    "The Formation of Imperial Authority under Akbar and Jahangir," in *Kingship and Authority in South Asia*, ed. John F. Richards (Madison, 1978).

    "The Imperial Crisis in the Mughal Deccan, *Journal of Asian Studies* 35 (1976): 237–56.

    *Mughal Administration in Golconda* (Oxford, 1975), 157–62, 308–9.

John Keay, *India: A History* (New York, 2000).

John R. McLane, *Land and Local Kingship in Eighteenth-Century Bengal* (Cambridge, 1993).

Jorge Flores and Sanjay Subrahmanyam, "The Legend of Sultan Bulaqi and the Estado da India, 1628–1640." In Sanjay Subrahmanyam, *Explorations in Connected History* (New Delhi, 2005).

Jos Gommans, *Mughal Warfare: Indian Frontiers and Highroads to Empire, 1500–1700* (London, 2002).

Jurgen Habermas, *Structural Transformation of the Public Sphere* (Cambridge, 1989).

K. A. Nizami, *Akbar and Religion* (Delhi, 1989).

    "Naqshbandi Influence on Mughal Rulers and Politics," *Islamic Culture* 39 (1965): 41–52.

Karen Barkey, *Bandits and Bureaucrats: The Ottoman Route to State Centralization* (Ithaca, 1994).

Karen Leonard, "The 'Great Firm' Theory of the Decline of the Mughal Empire," *Comparative Studies in Society and History* 21, no. 2 (1979): 151–67.

Kathryn Babayan, *Mystics, Monarchs and Messiahs: Cultural Landscapes of Early Modern Iran* (Cambridge, MA, 2002).

Khalid Abou el Fadl, *Rebellion and Violence in Islamic Law* (Cambridge, 2001).

Kumkum Chatterjee, *Merchants, Politics and Society in Early Modern India* (Leiden, 1996).

Kunwar Refaqat Ali Khan, *The Kachhwahas Under Akbar and Jahangir* (New Delhi, 1976).

L. Binyon et al, *Persian Miniature Painting* (Oxford, 1933).

Lachman Singh, *Tarikh-i Zila'-i Bulandshahr* (Bulandshahr, 1874).

Leslie Peirce, *The Imperial Harem: Women and Sovereignty in the Ottoman Empire* (New York, 1993).

Lisa Balabanlilar, "The Lords of the Auspicious Conjunction: Turco-Mongol Imperial Identity on the Subcontinent," *Journal of World History* 18, no. 1 (2007): 1–39.

Louise Marlow, "Advice and advice literature," *Encyclopaedia of Islam III*, Brill Online.

M. Athar Ali, "The Religious Issue in the War of Succession, 1658–1659," in *Mughal India: Studies in Polity, Ideas, Society, and Culture* (Delhi, 2006).

"Towards an Interpretation of the Mughal Empire," in *Mughal India: Studies in Polity, Ideas, Society, and Culture* (Delhi, 2006).

"Sulh-i Kul and the Religious Ideas of Akbar," in *Mughal India: Studies in Polity, Ideas, Society, and Culture* (Delhi, 2006).

*The Mughal Nobility under Aurangzeb* (Delhi, repr. 1997).

"The Perception of India in Akbar and Abu'l Fazl," in *Akbar and His India*, ed. Irfan Habib (Delhi, 1997).

"The Mughal Polity: A Critique of 'Revisionist' Approaches," *Modern Asian Studies* 27, no. 4 (1993): 699–710.

*The Apparatus of Empire: Awards of Ranks, Offices and Titles to the Mughal Nobility, 1574–1658* (Delhi, 1985).

"Towards an Interpretation of the Mughal Empire," *Journal of the Asiatic Society of Great Britain and Ireland* 1 (1978): 38–49.

"The Passing of Empire: The Mughal Case," *Modern Asian Studies* 9, no. 1 (1975): 185–96.

M. M. U. Bilgrami, *Tarikh-i Khat-i Pak-i Bilgram* (Aligarh, 1958).

Marcel Henaff, "The Stage of Power," *SubStance* 25, no. 2 (1996): 7–29.

Maria E. Subtelny, "Babur's Rival Relations: A Study of Kinship and Conflict in 15th–16th Century Central Asia," *Islam* 66, no. 1 (1989): 101–18.

Mark Ravina, *Land and Lordship in Early Modern Japan* (Palo Alto, 1999).

Michael Mann, *The Sources of Social Power, Vol. 1: A History of Power from the Beginning to A.D. 1760* (Cambridge, 1986).

Michael N. Pearson, "Premodern Muslim Political Systems," *Journal of the American Oriental Society* 102, no. 1 (1982): 47–58.

"Shivaji and the Decline of the Mughal Empire," *Journal of Asian Studies* 35 (1976): 221–35.

*Merchants and Rulers in Gujarat: The Response to the Portuguese in the Sixteenth Century* (New Delhi, repr. 1976).

Milo C. Beach, *Mughal and Rajput Painting* (Cambridge, 1992).

Muhammad Ismail, *"Sufi Literature in India during the 17th Century,"* unpub. M. Phil. thesis, Aligarh Muslim University (1986).

Muhammad Quamruddin, *Life and Times of Prince Murad Bakhsh 1624–1661* (Calcutta, 1974).

Muhammad Said Ahmad Maharvi, *Umara'-i Hunud* (Aligarh, 1910).

Mulla Khairullah, *Tarikh-i Khandan-i Rashidi*, KU Mss. 15/2.

Munis D. Faruqui, "Of Hidden Books Uncovered: Dara Shukoh, Vedanta, and Imperial Succession in Mughal India," in *Religious Interactions in Mughal India*, ed. Vasudha Dalmia and Munis D. Faruqui (New Delhi, forthcoming 2012).

"Awrangzib," *Encyclopaedia of Islam* III, Brill Online.

"At Empire's End: The Nizam, Hyderabad, and 18th Century India," in *Expanding Frontiers in South Asian and World History: Essays in Honour of John F. Richards*, ed. Richard M. Eaton, Munis D. Faruqui, David Gilmartin, and Sunil Kumar (New Delhi, forthcoming 2012).

"The Forgotten Prince: Mirza Hakim and the Formation of the Mughal Empire," *Journal of the Economic and Social History of the Orient*, 48, no. 4, (2005): 487–523.

Muzaffar Alam, *The Languages of Political Islam in India, c. 1200–1800* (Chicago, 2004).

"Witnessing Transition: Views on the end of Akbari Dispensation," in *The Making of History: Essays Presented to Irfan Habib*, ed. K. N. Pannikar, T. J. Byres, and U. Patnaik (New Delhi, 2000).

*The Crisis of Empire in Mughal North India: Awadh and the Punjab 1707–1748* (Delhi, 1986, repr. 1997).

Muzaffar Alam and Sanjay Subrahmanyam, *The Mughal State, 1526–1750* (Delhi, 1998).

Muzaffar Husain Khan Sulaimani, *Nama-i Muzaffari*, vols. 1–2 (Lucknow, 1917).

Nabi Hadi, *Dictionary of Indo-Persian Literature* (New Delhi, 1995).

Nancy Kollmann, *Kinship and Politics: The Making of the Muscovite Political System, 1345–1547* (Palo Alto, 1987).

Nicholas Henshall, "The Myth of Absolutism," *History Today* 42, no. 6 (1992): 40–7.

Om Prakash, *The Dutch East India Company and the Economy of Bengal 1630–1720* (Princeton, 1985).

P. Calkins, "The Formation of a Regionally Oriented Ruling Group in Bengal, 1700–1740," *Journal of Asian Studies* 29, no. 4 (1970): 799–806.

Perry Anderson, *Lineages of the Absolutist State* (London, 1979).

Peter Hardy, "Abul Fazl's Portrait of the Perfect Padishah," in *Islam in India: Studies and Commentaries*, ed. Christian Troll (Delhi, 1985).

*Historians of Medieval India: Studies in Indo-Muslim Historical Writing* (London, 1960).

Peter Perdue, *China Marches West* (Cambridge, MA, 2005).

Peter Robb, *A History of India* (London, 2002).

R. Shyam, "Mirza Hindal," *Islamic Culture* 45 (1971): 115–36.

R. J. Barendse, *The Arabian Seas, 1640–1700* (Leiden, 1998).

R. K. Das, "The End of Prince Shuja," *Procs. Ind. Hist. Cong.* 28 (1966): 165–8.

R. R. Diwakar, *Bihar through the Ages* (Patna, 1958).

Rahman Ali, *Tazkira-i 'Ulama'-i Hind* (Lucknow, 1914).

Ram Sharma, "Aurangzib's Rebellion against Shah Jahan," *Journal of Indian History* 44, no. 1 (1966): 109–24.

Richard Barnett, *North India between Empires, Awadh, the Mughals, and the British, 1720–1801* (Berkeley, 1980).

Richard Eaton, *A Social History of the Deccan, 1300–1761: Eight Lives* (Cambridge, 2005).

*Rise of Islam and the Bengal Frontier* (Berkeley, 1993).

Robert Hallisey, *The Rajput Rebellion against Aurangzeb: A Study of the Mughal Empire in Seventeenth-Century India* (Columbia, MO, 1977).

Roger Savory, *Iran under the Safavids* (Cambridge, 1980).

Rosalind O'Hanlon, "Kingdom, Household and Body: History, Gender and Imperial Service under Akbar," *Modern Asian Studies* 41, no. 5 (2007): 889–923.

"Cultural Pluralism, Empire and the State in Early Modern South Asia – A Review Essay," *Indian Economic and Social History Review* 44, no. 3 (2007): 363–81.

"Manliness and Imperial Service in Mughal North India," *Journal of the Economic and Social History of the Orient* 42, no. 1 (1999): 47–93.

Ruby Lal, *Domesticity and Power in the Early Mughal World* (Cambridge, 2005).

S. Arasaratnam, *Merchants, Companies and Commerce on the Coromandel Coast 1650–1740* (Delhi, 1986).

S. Arasaratnam and A. Ray, *Masulipatnam and Cambay: A History of Two Port Towns, 1500–1800* (New Delhi, 1994).

S. Inayat Khan, "The Rajput Chiefs and Prince Shah Jahan's Revolt: Consequences," *Islamic Culture* 61, no. 4 (1987), 63–93.

S. A. A. Rizvi, *A History of Sufism in India*, vol. 2 (Delhi, 1983, repr. 1992).

S. H. Askari, "Documents Relating to an Old Family of Sufi Saints in Bihar," *Proceedings of the Indian Historical Records Commission* 26 (1949).

S. I. A. Jaunpuri, *Tarikh-i Salatin-i Sharqi aur Sufiya-yi Jaunpur* (Jaunpur, 1988).

S. M. Burke, *Akbar the Greatest Mogul* (Delhi, 1989).

S. M. Ikram, *Rud-i Kausar* (Lahore, 1982).

S. M. Azizuddin Husain, *The Structure of Politics under Aurangzeb 1658–1707* (Delhi, 2002).

"Aurangzeb ki takht nashini," *Islam aur asr-i jadid* (April 1994): 44–73.

S. Moinul Haq, *Prince Awrangzib: A Study* (Karachi, 1962).

S. Nurul Hasan, "The Theory of the Nur Jahan 'Junta' – a Critical Examination," *Proceedings of the Indian History Congress* 21 (1958): 324–35.

S. P. Verma, *Mughal Painters and Their Works: A Biographical Survey and Comprehensive Catalogue* (Delhi, 1994).

Saiyid Roshan Ali, *Saiyid al-Tawarikh* (Delhi, 1864).

Saiyid Sabah-ud-Din Abdur Rahman, *Bazm-i Timuriya*, vol. 2 (Azamgarh, 1972).

Sajida Alvi, "Religion and State during the Reign of the Mughal Emperor Jahangir (1605–1627)," *Studia Islamica* 69 (1989): 95–119.

Sanjay Subrahmanyam, *Explorations in Connected History*, vols. 1–2 (Delhi, 2005).

"Reflections on State-Making and History-Making in South Asia, 1500–1800," *Journal of the Economic and Social History of the Orient* 41 (1998): 382–416.

"The Mughal State – Structure or Process? Reflections on Recent Western Historiography," *Indian Economic and Social History Review* 29, no. 3 (1992): 291–321.

Satish Chandra, *Parties and Politics at the Mughal Court* (Aligarh, 1959, repr. 2002).

Scott Levi, *The Indian Diaspora in Central Asia and Its Trade, 1550–1900* (Leiden, 2002).

Shaikh Ali Mushtaqi, *Gulistan-i Kairana* (Amroha, 1888).

Shaikh Kafeel Turabi, *Tazkira-i Marjan* (Patna, 1881).

Shams-ud-Din Belgaumi, *Tarikh-i Mukhtasar-i Dakhan* (Belgaum, 1944).

Shibli Nomani, *Aurangzeb 'Alamgir par ek nazar* (Karachi, repr. 1960).

*Alamgir*, trans. Saiyid Sabah-ud-din Abdur Rahman (Delhi, 1981).

Shireen Moosvi, "The Pre-Colonial State," *Social Scientist* 33, no. 3–4 (2005): 40–53.

*Episodes in the Life of Akbar* (New Delhi, 1994).

*The Economy of the Mughal Empire c. 1595: A Statistical Study* (New Delhi, 1987).

"Evolution of *Mansab* System under Akbar until 1596–1597," *Journal of the Royal Asiatic Society* 2 (1981): 175–83.

Stephen Blake, "Nau Ruz in Mughal India," in *Rethinking a Millennium: Perspectives on Indian History from the Eighth to the Eighteenth Century. Essays for Harbans Mukhia*, ed. Rajat Datta (Delhi, 2008).

*Shahjahanabad: The Sovereign City in Mughal India, 1639–1739* (Cambridge, 1991).

"The Patrimonial-Bureaucratic Empire of the Mughals," *Journal of Asian Studies* 39, no. 1 (1979): 77–94.

Stephen Dale, *The Muslim Empires of the Ottomans, Safavids, and Mughals* (Cambridge, 2010).

*The Garden of Eight Paradises: Babur and the Culture of Empire in Central Asia, Afghanistan and India (1483–1530)* (Leiden, 2004).

*Indian Merchants and Eurasian Trade, 1600–1750* (Cambridge, 1994).

Stephen Dale, and Alam Payind, "The Ahrari *waqf* in Kabul and the Mughul Naqshbandiyya," *Journal of the American Oriental Society* 119, no. 2 (1999): 218–33.

Stewart Gordon, *The Marathas 1600–1818* (Cambridge, 1993).

Stuart Carroll, *Blood and Violence in Early Modern France* (Oxford, 2006).

Sumathi Ramaswamy, "Conceit of the Globe in Mughal Visual Practice," *Comparative Studies in Society and History* 49, no. 4 (2007): 751–82.

Sushil Chaudhuri, *Trade and Commercial Organization in Bengal 1600–1720* (Calcutta, 1975).

Tapan Raychaudhuri, *Bengal under Akbar and Jahangir: An Introductory Study in Social History* (Delhi, 1969).

*The Army of the Indian Moghuls* (Delhi, repr. 1994).

Tapan Raychaudhuri and Irfan Habib, ed., *The Cambridge Economic History of India*, vol. 1, c. 1200–1750 (Cambridge, 1982).

Theda Skocpol, *States and Social Revolutions: A Comparative Analysis of France, Russia, and China* (Cambridge, 1979).

Toby Falk, "The written record," in *Humayun's Garden Party-Princes of the House of Timur, and Early Mughal Painting*, ed. Sheila Canby (Bombay, 1994).

William Irvine, *Later Mughals* (Delhi, repr. 1996).

Yuri Bregel, "Atalik," *Encyclopaedia of Islam* II, Brill Online.

Yusuf Abbas Hashmi, "The War of Succession among the Sons of Shah Jahan and the Stand of Aurangzeb," *Proceedings of the All Pakistan History Conference* 1 (1951): 247–70.

Z. A. Desai, "The Major Dargahs of Ahmadabad," in *Muslim Shrines in India*, ed. Christian Troll (Delhi, 1992).

Zahiruddin Faruki, *Aurangzeb and His Times* (Delhi, repr. 1972).

Zahiruddin Malik, "The Core and the Periphery: A Contribution to the Debate on the Eighteenth Century," *Social Scientist* 18, no. 11–12 (1990): 3–35.

# Index

*Index*